Register Now

to Yc

Your print purchase of *Social, Economic, and Environmental Justice* **includes online access to the contents of your book**—increasing accessibility, portability, and searchability!

Access today at:
http://connect.springerpub.com/content/book/978-0-8261-3539-1
or scan the QR code at the right with your smartphone. Log in or register, then click "Redeem a voucher" and use the code below.

D2CA2HW4

Scan here for quick access.

Having trouble redeeming a voucher code?
Go to https://connect.springerpub.com/redeeming-voucher-code

If you are experiencing problems accessing the digital component of this product, please contact our customer service department at cs@springerpub.com

The online access with your print purchase is available at the publisher's discretion and may be removed at any time without notice.

Publisher's Note: New and used products purchased from third-party sellers are not guaranteed for quality, authenticity, or access to any included digital components.

SOCIAL, ECONOMIC, AND ENVIRONMENTAL JUSTICE

Kalea Benner, PhD, MSW, LCSW, is an associate professor with the College of Social Work at the University of Kentucky. Dr. Benner's practice experience has focused on the intersection of child welfare and mental health, working with youth and their families as well as within the school setting. After a decade in social work practice, she returned to complete her doctoral degree in social work at the University of Missouri, receiving her PhD in 2009. Dr. Benner's research interests include developing social work practitioners who are prepared for the complexity of substance abuse disorder prevention, intervention, and recovery. Additionally, Dr. Benner's research interests include student engagement and influences on academic success. Her work emphasizes interprofessional education and program efficacy, particularly as they relate to student learning, reflecting her value of multidisciplinary perspectives on student success. Dr. Benner enjoys mentoring students in research and working with students to disseminate their work through publications and presentations.

Diane N. Loeffler, PhD, MSW, is a senior lecturer in the University of Kentucky's College of Social Work, a member of the Lewis Honors College Faculty, and a faculty affiliate of the Appalachian Center and Appalachian Studies Program. Dr. Loeffler earned her BA from the University of Iowa and her MSW and PhD from the University of Kentucky (UK). Dr. Loeffler teaches widely across the BASW and MSW programs at UK with an emphasis on policy, macro practice, and social justice. Dr. Loeffler has published and presented on a variety of topics including social work education and social justice, community development, and rural development.

Natalie D. Pope, PhD, MSW, LCSW, is an associate professor and director of doctoral programs in the College of Social Work at the University of Kentucky. She earned her MSW and PhD from the University of Georgia and was born and raised in Atlanta, Georgia. Prior to receiving her PhD, Dr. Pope worked as a case manager and clinical social worker. As a practitioner, she worked primarily in mental health services for young children and parents, child protective services, and psychosocial support for family caregivers. As a practitioner and a researcher, Dr. Pope has always been drawn to understanding people's lived experiences and the meaning people attribute to their experiences. During her PhD program, this interest grew as she engaged in specialized training in qualitative research methods, obtaining an Interdisciplinary Qualitative Studies Graduate Certificate. Dr. Pope's passion for qualitative inquiry informs her scholarship and teaching in ways that include focusing on the emic perspective in her research, teaching and mentoring students in qualitative methods, and collaborating with colleagues on qualitative and mixed methods projects. Dr. Pope has published numerous journal articles and has also delivered many national conference presentations on research in the areas of family caregiving across the life span, behavioral health of community-dwelling older adults, and planning for future care in aging families. Finally, an important aspect of Dr. Pope's work includes service to her institution, the community, and the profession. For 4 years she has worked on behalf of inclusion and diversity efforts at the University of Kentucky as the College of Social Work's Diversity and Inclusion officer. Dr. Pope serves on the editorial board for the Journal of Women and Aging and is an active member of the Fayette County Senior Services Commission in Lexington, Kentucky, where she resides with her husband and son.

SOCIAL, ECONOMIC, AND ENVIRONMENTAL JUSTICE
Building Social Work Practice Skills

Kalea Benner, PhD, MSW, LCSW
Diane N. Loeffler, PhD, MSW
Natalie D. Pope, PhD, MSW, LCSW

Copyright © 2022 Springer Publishing Company, LLC
All rights reserved.

No part of this publication may be reproduced, stored in a retrieval system, or transmitted in any form or by any means, electronic, mechanical, photocopying, recording, or otherwise, without the prior permission of Springer Publishing Company, LLC, or authorization through payment of the appropriate fees to the Copyright Clearance Center, Inc., 222 Rosewood Drive, Danvers, MA 01923, 978-750-8400, fax 978-646-8600, info@copyright.com or on the Web at www.copyright.com.

Springer Publishing Company, LLC
11 West 42nd Street, New York, NY 10036
www.springerpub.com
connect.springerpub.com/

Acquisitions Editor: Kate Dimock
Compositor: S4Carlisle Publishing Services

ISBN: 978-0-8261-3538-4
ebook ISBN: 978-0-8261-3539-1
DOI: 10.1891/9780826135391

Instructor Materials:
Qualified instructors may request supplements by emailing textbook@springerpub.com

Instructor's Manual ISBN: 978-0-8261-3645-9
Instructor's PowerPoints ISBN: 978-0-8261-3646-6
Instructor's Test Bank ISBN: 978-0-8261-3648-0
Instructor's Syllabus ISBN: 978-0-8261-3647-3

21 22 23 24 25 / 5 4 3 2 1

The author and the publisher of this Work have made every effort to use sources believed to be reliable to provide information that is accurate and compatible with the standards generally accepted at the time of publication. The author and publisher shall not be liable for any special, consequential, or exemplary damages resulting, in whole or in part, from the readers' use of, or reliance on, the information contained in this book. The publisher has no responsibility for the persistence or accuracy of URLs for external or third-party Internet websites referred to in this publication and does not guarantee that any content on such websites is, or will remain, accurate or appropriate.

Library of Congress Cataloging-in-Publication Data

Names: Benner, Kalea, author. | Loeffler, Diane N., author. | Pope, Natalie D., author.
Title: Social, economic, and environmental justice : building social work practice skills / Kalea Benner, PhD, MSW, LCSW, Diane N. Loeffler, PhD, MSW, Natalie D. Pope, PhD, LCSW (GA)
Description: New York, NY : Springer Publishing Company, LLC, [2022] | Includes bibliographical references and index.
Identifiers: LCCN 2021014753 (print) | LCCN 2021014754 (ebook) | ISBN 9780826135384 (cloth) | ISBN 9780826135391 (ebook)
Subjects: LCSH: Social service--Moral and ethical aspects. | Social justice. | Environmental justice.
Classification: LCC HV10.5 .B3546 2022 (print) | LCC HV10.5 (ebook) | DDC 361.3/2--dc23
LC record available at https://lccn.loc.gov/2021014753
LC ebook record available at https://lccn.loc.gov/2021014754

Kalea Benner: https://orcid.org/0000-0003-2872-9218
Diane N. Loeffler: https://orcid.org/0000-0002-5945-2146
Natalie D. Pope: https://orcid.org/0000-0002-4423-8278

Contact sales@springerpub.com to receive discount rates on bulk purchases.

Publisher's Note: **New and used products purchased from third-party sellers are not guaranteed for quality, authenticity, or access to any included digital components.**

Printed in the United States of America.

CONTENTS

Contributors   xiii
Preface   xv
Acknowledgments   xix

1. **Setting the Stage for Justice-Driven Social Work Practice   1**
   Kalea Benner, Natalie D. Pope, and Elaine C. Strawn

   Introduction   1
   Justice-Informed Social Work Practice   2
   Social Justice   3
   Economic Justice   5
   Environmental Justice   6
   Interdependence of Social, Economic, and Environmental Justice   7
   The Outcome Goal: Equality Versus Equity   8
   Threats to Justice—Paternalism, Power, and Authority   9
   Justice in Macro Social Work Practice   9
   Intersectionality, Social Determinants, and Interdependence of Injustice   10
   Achieving Justice in Social Work Practice   11
   The Social Work Mission   13
   Conclusion: Our Call to Action   13

2. **Theoretical and Conceptual Underpinnings of Justice-Driven Practice   17**
   Diane N. Loeffler, Natalie D. Pope, Kalea Benner, and Lenzi G. Dodgen

   Introduction   17
   Context for Justice-Informed Social Work Practice   18
   Bending the Arc   19
   Oppression   20
   Addressing Oppression in Social Work Practice   22
   Intersectionality   22
   Understanding and Mitigating Bias   23
   Bias   23
   Trauma-Informed Practice   23
   Person in Environment Explored   26
   Examining Theories as Just Practice   27
   Conclusion   30

3. **Framing Social Work Practice in the Human Rights Context**   33
Emily Bergeron

Introduction   33
Case—A Global Pandemic Illustrates the Need to Protect Human Rights   33
Human Rights as a Foundation to Understand the Impact of The Pandemic   34
Healthcare as a Human Right Impacted by COVID-19   35
Housing as a Human Right Impacted by COVID-19   36
A Human Rights Approach to Addressing a Global Pandemic   36
Overview of Human Rights   37
What Are Human Rights?   37
History of Human Rights   38
United Nations's Universal Declaration of Human Rights   39
What Constitutes a Human Right?   40
Housing as a Culmination of Human Rights   40
Environmental Justice as a Culminating Example of Human Rights   42
Human Rights in the United States   43
Human Rights as Justice-Informed Social Work Practice   44
Conclusion   45

4. **Poverty as the Great Oppressor**   47
Shiyou Wu

Introduction   47
Definitions of Poverty   47
Measures of Poverty   48
Populations and the Context of Power, Oppression, and Privilege   51
Magnitude and Scope of Poverty   55
Role of Social Work to Identify Unmet Systemic Needs   60
Strategies for Engaging in "Just" Poverty Practice   63
Conclusion   67

5. **Social and Economic Disparities Within the Educational System**   69
Shantel D. Crosby, Kristian Jones, and Angelique G. Day

Introduction   69
History of Educational Disparity   69
History of Primary Education in the United States   70
Contemporary Education in the United States   71
Populations and Context of Power, Oppression, and Privilege   72
Social Class in School Settings   72
Youth of Color in School Settings   73
Immigrant Youth in School Settings   74
Sexual Minority and Gender-Expansive Youth in School Settings   75
Homeless and System-Involved Youth in School Settings   75
Intersectionality in School Settings   77
Magnitude and Scope of Educational Disparity   77
Achievement Gap Differences   78

Role of Social Work to Identify Unmet Systemic Needs   78
  Strategies for Engaging in Justice-Informed Social Work Practice in Schools   81
  Conclusion   84

6. **Justice-Informed Social Work Practice Within the Criminal Justice System**   87
  Karen M. Kolivoski

  Introduction   87
  Overview of the Criminal Justice System in the United States   88
  Overview of the Criminal Justice System and Social Work   92
  Pervasive and Structural Barriers   97
  Strategies to Effect Change   100
  Crossover Youth   101
  Conclusion   102

7. **Health Disparities and Social Justice**   105
  Kathryn M. Cardarelli, Rafael E. Perez-Figueroa, and Brendan Mathews

  Introduction   105
  Overview of Health Disparities in the United States   105
  Theoretical Frameworks for the Study of Health Disparities   106
  Health Disparities in Unique Populations   108
  Structural Factors and Health Disparities   110
  Health Disparities and Social Work Practice   112
  Strategies to Address Health Disparities   113
  Key Elements for Success   115
  Conclusion   117

8. **Disparities in Mental Health Services: A Matter of Justice in the Clinical Setting**   119
  Martha J. Markward and Kalea Benner

  Introduction   119
  Meaning of Mental Health   119
  History of Mental Health Service Provision   120
  Social Justice and Mental Health Service   122
  Impact of Untreated Mental Illness   123
  Disparities in Mental Health Services and Social Justice   123
  Social Justice Concerns and Disparities in Mental Health Services   127
  Addressing Social Justice Concerns in Mental Health Services   129
  Implications for Social Work Practice   132
  Conclusion   135

9. **Environmental Justice and Disasters: Social Workers' Role in Combating Structural Inequalities**   137
  Allison Gibson

  Introduction   137
  Environmental Justice and the Environmental Movement   137
  Climate Change and Disasters   139

Disasters in the Context of Power, Oppression, and Privilege 139
Pervasive and Structural Barriers in Disasters 140
Role of Social Workers to Address Unmet Systemic Needs 145
Engaging in Environmental Justice-Oriented Social Work Practice 145
Conclusion 153

10. **Food Justice** 155
    Michelle L. Kaiser, Erica K. Pence, Kathryn Burleson, Michelle D. Hand, Whitney Gherman, Nicholas A. Stanich, Mara Sydnor, and Jennifer K. Weeber

    Introduction 155
    Food Security 156
    Food Security Measurement at the Individual, Household, and Community Levels 158
    What's in a Label? Hunger Versus Food Insecurity 160
    Prevalence of Food Insecurity in the United States 163
    Factors Contributing to Household and Community Food Insecurity 166
    Consequences of Food Insecurity 168
    Strategies to Address Food Insecurity for Households and Communities 169
    College Food Insecurity 181
    Conclusion 183

11. **Utilizing Policy to Address Unaffordable and Unavailable Housing** 185
    Terri Lewinson

    Introduction 185
    Unaffordable and Unavailable Housing as a Challenge to Justice 185
    Understanding Affordable Housing 186
    Overview of Housing Policy 187
    Public Housing 190
    Mixed-Income Development 191
    Rental Market Affordability 196
    Strategies for Ensuring Affordability 199
    Homelessness 202
    So, Why Is Housing Still Unaffordable? 204
    Affordable Housing Interventions 206
    Conclusion 210

12. **Financial Justice and Social Work Practice** 213
    Diane N. Loeffler, Jennifer K. Weeber, Chloe McKenzie, Mae Humiston, and R. Scott McReynolds

    Introduction 213
    Financial Literacy 214
    Financial Literacy and Social Work Practice 218
    Financial Capability 220
    Financial Capability and Social Work Practice 220

Financial Inclusion and Access   222
Unbanked and Underbanked   222
Who Is Unbanked? Underbanked?   223
Access to the "American Dream"   225
Homeownership Today   227
Accessing Credit and Debt   228
Where Do We Go From Here?   233
Conclusion   233

13. **The Pervasive Influence of Economic Inequality and Income Disparity   235**
    Keith M. Kilty

    Introduction   235
    Economic Inequality   236
    Defining Economic Inequality   236
    Less Extreme Inequality   237
    Income Inequality   240
    Wealth Inequality   241
    Inequality, Social Justice, and Social Work   242
    Earning a Living in America   244
    Consequences of Economic Inequality   246
    Solutions to Economic Inequality   251
    Conclusion   254

14. **Implementing Justice-Driven Social Work Practice   257**
    Kalea Benner, Natalie D. Pope, Diane N. Loeffler, and Elaine C. Strawn

    Introduction   257
    Justice-Informed Social Work Practice   257
    Overlapping Justice Needs   259
    Integrating Justice Strategies in Social Work Practice   262
    Strategies to Support Clients   270
    Conclusion   272

15. **A Call to Action: Justice-Informed Social Work Practice   275**
    Laura E. Escobar-Ratliff

    Introduction   275
    Need for Social Workers   275
    Social Workers Are (Not) Superheroes   276
    Expertise in Change, Not Individuals   277
    Cultural Humility   278
    Building Upon Resilience   279
    Kaizen Method   280
    Sustainable Practice   281
    Conclusion   282

Index   285

CONTRIBUTORS

Kalea Benner, PhD, MSW, LCSW   Associate Professor, Associate Dean and MSW Program Director, University of Kentucky, Lexington, Kentucky

Emily Bergeron, PhD, JD   Assistant Professor, Department of Historic Preservation, University of Kentucky, Lexington, Kentucky

Kathryn Burleson, PhD   Program Director, Conscious Alliance, Boulder, Colorado

Kathryn M. Cardarelli, PhD, MPH   Associate Professor, Department of Health, Behavior, & Society, University of Kentucky, Lexington, Kentucky

Shantel D. Crosby, PhD, MSW   Assistant Professor, Kent School of Social Work, University of Louisville, Louisville, Kentucky

Angelique G. Day, PhD, MSW   Associate Professor, School of Social Work, University of Washington, Seattle, Washington

Lenzi G. Dodgen, BASW   Survivor Advocate, Violence Intervention & Prevention Center, University of Kentucky, Lexington, Kentucky

Laura E. Escobar-Ratliff, DSW   Clinical Assistant Professor, College of Social Work, University of Kentucky, Lexington, Kentucky

Whitney Gherman, MSW   Extension Educator, Family and Consumer Sciences, SNAP-ED, Ohio State University-Marion County Office, Marion, Ohio

Allison Gibson, PhD, MSW   Assistant Professor, College of Social Work, University of Kentucky, Lexington, Kentucky

Michelle D. Hand, PhD, MSW   Assistant Professor, School of Social Work, West Virginia University, Morgantown, West Virginia

Mae Humiston, BA   Independent Consultant and Grant Writer

Kristian Jones, MEd   Doctoral Student, School of Social Work, University of Texas at Austin, Austin, Texas

Michelle L. Kaiser, PhD, MSW, MPH   Associate Professor, College of Social Work, Ohio State University, Columbus, Ohio

Keith M. Kilty, PhD Professor Emeritus, College of Social Work, Ohio State University, Columbus, Ohio

Karen M. Kolivoski, PhD, MSW Assistant Professor, School of Social Work, Howard University, Washington, District of Columbia

Terri Lewinson, PhD, MSW Associate Professor, School of Social Work, Andrew Young School of Policy Studies, Georgia State University, Atlanta, Georgia

Diane N. Loeffler, PhD, MSW BASW Program Director, College of Social Work, University of Kentucky, Lexington, Kentucky

Martha J. Markward PhD, MSW Contributing Faculty Member, Walden University, Minneapolis, Minnesota

Brendan Mathews, MPH Student, Department of Health, Behavior, & Society, University of Kentucky, Lexington, Kentucky

Chloe McKenzie, MPA PhD Student, College of Social Work, University of Kentucky, Lexington, Kentucky

R. Scott McReynolds, MDiv Executive Director, Housing Development Alliance, Inc., Hazard, Kentucky

Erica K. Pence, MSW PhD Student, College of Social Work, Ohio State University, Columbus, Ohio

Rafael E. Perez-Figueroa, MD, MPH Assistant Professor, Department of Health, Behavior, & Society, University of Kentucky, Lexington, Kentucky

Natalie D. Pope, PhD, MSW, LCSW Associate Professor and Doctoral Program Director, College of Social Work, University of Kentucky, Lexington, Kentucky

Nicholas A. Stanich, MS Former Executive Director, Franklinton Farms, Columbus, Ohio

Elaine C. Strawn, MA, BS First-Grade Teacher, Columbia Public Schools, Columbia, Missouri

Mara Sydnor, MSW, LSW House Director and Co-Adviser, Tri Delta, Ohio State University, Columbus, Ohio

Jennifer K. Weeber, MSW Northfork Local Food Coordinator, Community Farm Alliance, Berea, Kentucky

Shiyou Wu, PhD, MSW Assistant Professor, School of Social Work, Arizona State University, Phoenix, Arizona

PREFACE

The chapters in this book represent an effort to create a foundational textbook for social workers that introduces the student to justice-informed social work practice and is an initial step—a starting point—for considering how to center oneself in justice-oriented practice across systems and structures. Within the social work profession, justice is conceptualized as a constellation of social, economic, and environmental justice. We view these as interrelated and recognize that individuals and groups impacted by any one injustice are likely impacted by all three.

We view this text as an *initial* step—a starting point for demonstrating how social workers can assert themselves into justice work. You will hear from a multitude of practitioners on why justice work is needed as well as how it can be employed with our clients. Implementing justice-informed practice ensures social workers hear all voices, an important component of starting where the client is. Ultimately, attending to all voices also reflects the social work commitment to see clients in the context of their lives, as they are at present, but also as they hope to be.

The justice orientation within social work requires we see the client within the context of their unique situation and that we acknowledge the structural oppression that shapes how that client interacts with the world and accesses resources, services, and opportunities. We must ensure our work examines the social welfare systems in which our clients engage because structural oppression is cross-cutting and impacts all marginalized groups, albeit differently. Structural discrimination within our multiple social welfare systems places those who engage in these systems in a position of relying upon an unfair system to achieve a just result. That is unacceptable.

Although population-based books are common in social work scholarship, we have intentionally opted for a different approach. In this text, we focus on structural oppression and inequities connected to our clients' engagement in systems and structures that, although often purported to support them, frequently are broken and inflict harm. The text starts with an overview of key concepts and theoretical underpinnings that provide foundational knowledge and then moves into chapters that focus on human rights, and varying systems related to education, criminal justice, housing, the environment, poverty, finances and wealth, and food insecurity.

In the chapters that follow, you will learn about the ways that injustice presents itself in the various systems in which social workers practice. Structural discrimination has systemic implications and systemic consequences as well. These book contributors have lived the work upon which you are embarking; most are social work practitioners and researchers who continue to seek justice-informed practice.

In this text we do not claim to have been exhaustive in terms of identifying and describing the multiple domains of social work practice. Nor can we enumerate every injustice experienced or speak to that injustice within every marginalized group. But, it is truly our hope that this book and the chapters within it serve to *start* the conversation. While social justice is a guiding, orienting value to social work, justice-informed practice can oftentimes feel abstract and impractical. By situating universal aspects of social work practice (e.g., engagement, assessment, intervention) within the context of various practice arenas (e.g., educational, legal, health, housing), we hope to bring to life what it means to engage in just practice. We will hear from social workers with boots-on-the-ground who share with much vulnerability, how they conceptualize a justice-informed framework for practice. This text offers you foundational knowledge and tangible recommendations that you can apply and transfer to best fit the work you are doing in the multiplicity of practice settings, and with the diverse client populations with and in which you work. This book should also leave you with more questions than when you began reading and we hope will solidify your commitment to your life-long education, unlearning, and discovery around just practice.

Our desire is that this brief overview of the challenging systems and structures our clients face can present a foundation for lifelong learning, for understanding the nature of structural oppression, and for your role as a practitioner in disrupting and creating systemic change. We must recognize there is no simple answer to the complexities of social work practice but that our mission remains to ensure every voice is present in finding solutions to the identified needs. We advocate for those whose voices are hard to hear because of the oppression that silences our clients.

Understanding how people are still impacted by the remnants of historic barriers and privileges in education, land ownership, healthcare, and other systems enables us to approach our work with our clients and our communities more holistically. Good intentions can have poor outcomes. We need to utilize the knowledge, values, and skills of the social work profession to be able to empower our clients to become their best advocates.

We expect that some of these areas of practice may be unfamiliar—like the role of social workers in supporting communities after a natural disaster or promoting financial justice among young people. Some are more familiar—housing, food insecurity, and education. Within each chapter, context for understanding oppression and injustice today is interwoven with an understanding of how policies and programs, over time, have created and perpetuated inequity. Themes of structural racism thread through the book as a powerful example of the intergenerational harm and trauma that systemic oppression creates.

To be clear, we recognize that this book does not include every aspect of justice nor everything to know about it; it truly is only a starting point for social work students to examine inequity. Additionally, we humbly recognize there is considerable content we did not include that impacts our clients daily and that our voices and those of the chapter authors are not representative of all of the clients with whom we work. But our commitment is unwavering, our mission is true, and our aspiration is intentional that this text allow for conversations and learning about structural inequality and injustice that significantly impact our clients daily.

As social workers, we are trained to identify the myriad of factors which brings our clients to our services. While a client may seek our services to obtain housing or help transition after their divorce, that is not the only factor impacting their current situation. Through an assessment process we gain a deeper and broader understanding of the factors which brought our clients to this point in their lives. In recognizing the trauma, the physical and mental health issues, the transportation difficulties, the lost educational opportunities, and other concerns, we can more effectively and appropriately assist our clients. The same holds true for the environment in which our clients live. There is a myriad of systemic factors which have also impacted and brought our clients to us. Within this assessment process, being justice-driven means that we recognize and commit to dismantling barriers that are structural and systemic and that our practice focuses on creating pathways for achieving true capability.

In writing this text, we wrestled with language and its ever evolving nature. In this volume each chapter is authored by different scholars and practitioners, whose choices in language are their own. As editors, we have sought some uniformity and in keeping with the current recommendations in style from the American Psychological Association we capitalize Black and other constructs of race throughout the manuscript. Our orientation to justice demands that we continue to evolve in our own thoughtfulness and use around language. Any errors are our own and we hope to grow from those.

We are continually growing and deepening our understanding of and commitment to the eradication of injustices around us. Thank you for joining with us in this journey and for sharing in the work that we are called to do as social work professionals.

Kalea Benner
Diane N. Loeffler
Natalie D. Pope

ACKNOWLEDGMENTS

We gratefully acknowledge the clients who have guided and shaped our social work practice and profession. We hope this book provides a starting point for true reflection and deep learning about the inequities that exist in the world around us and about how social work practitioners must rise in response to these inequities. In our work as practitioners, educators, and researchers, we have been in the privileged place of learning from so many who have courageously shared their own experiences with systems of oppression and injustice and from those who have made the decision to spend their careers working to confront these systems. It is with humble gratitude to each client, student, colleague, and mentor that we share this volume of work with you.

SETTING THE STAGE FOR JUSTICE-DRIVEN SOCIAL WORK PRACTICE

Kalea Benner | Natalie D. Pope | Elaine C. Strawn

LEARNING OBJECTIVES

Students will be able to:

- Describe the difference between equity and equality and articulate the limitations of an equality-based approach to just practice.
- Define social, economic, and environmental justice and articulate the importance of framing justice as a collective, and not individual, endeavor.
- Ascertain the differing aspects of justice (social, economic, and environmental) and articulate the role of social work in each of these types of justice work.
- Identify ways in which justice-informed practice aligns with the mission and vision of the social work profession.

INTRODUCTION

No matter what policies are in place, and what our Constitution so eloquently states, all people living in the United States do not have equal access to opportunities. Although our country has an abundance of resources, the reality is that those are not shared equally, nor equitably, across our population. This distribution discrepancy between what is available and what is accessible provides the catalyst for just and antioppressive social work practice in the 21st century.

The social work profession has historically been grounded in justice. The justice lens of social work dates back to the profession's origins and the work of Jane Addams and others. The settlement housing efforts of Jane Addams were certainly conceptualized through a justice lens in that they sought to alleviate poverty in communities by intentionally integrating those with both higher and impoverished economic statuses in neighborhood housing and providing resources such as education and childcare to the residents. This holistic perspective in identifying and meeting needs has been the hallmark of the social work profession, looking beyond the individual to encompass social and environmental solutions as well.

This holistic perspective also allows social workers to view clients within the context of the environmental, situational, and structural settings that create, as well as obstruct, availability and access to resources. It is incumbent upon us, as social workers, to practice such that each client is viewed as having inherent and unique value and worth. As change agents, empowering clients, from individuals to communities, to transform lives, social work is inherently responsive to assessing, identifying, and advocating for justice-oriented change. As such, social workers must have the associated values, knowledge, and skills essential to implementing justice-informed practice.

JUSTICE-INFORMED SOCIAL WORK PRACTICE

Justice-informed practice is a mandated educational standard for every social work program. The accreditation body of social work education, the Council on Social Work Education ([CSWE], 2015), requires that all social work curricula educate social workers to advance human rights and social, economic, and environmental justice. Programs are evaluated upon their ability to meet this accreditation standard as all social workers must be prepared for justice-informed practice.

However, that same justice lens was not professionally formalized by the National Association of Social Workers (NASW) until 1996 when social justice was added as one of six core professional values in the Code of Ethics. Although not directly named, justice was a theme throughout prior versions of the Code, captured by terms such as "fairness." Additionally, the professional value that social workers respect the dignity and worth of the individual (NASW, 2017) effectively represents justice, as dignity is inextricably entwined with justice. Without question, justice is dignity.

CASE STUDY 1.1—THE IMPACT OF JUSTICE IN PRACTICE

Latonya is a Black woman, married, and a 37-year-old mother of two who is employed on the assembly line at a local Toyota plant. In the past 5 years, Latonya has experienced two episodes of major depressive disorder, which has had a significant impact on her family and her job. She feels that another episode is looming, is experiencing insomnia but struggling to get out of bed, has not made a family dinner in over a week due largely to a lack of appetite, has been late to work twice in that same amount of time, and so forth. Latonya scheduled an appointment with a social worker but had to wait 3 weeks to be able to have an appointment after her work hours. She uses public transportation and the bus took over an hour to get there, requiring two bus changes. Upon her arrival, right at the appointed time, the receptionist jokingly told her that she was lucky to get an evening appointment. The receptionist gave her paperwork to complete while stating that the appointment could not start until the paperwork was completed but that her appointment would not be extended for the time the paperwork took.

The social worker noted that Latonya was reserved and seemed hesitant to engage, which the social worker identified as reluctance. When the social worker inquired about the possibility of medication, Latonya said she was hoping to avoid taking medication because she experienced considerable side effects in prior instances (weight gain, no libido, and dry mouth, which made her think everyone knew she was taking antidepressants because she drank frequently) and wanted to start with therapy instead. When the social worker sought to establish buy-in, and have Latonya agree to return, Latonya was cautious and asked if it would take another 3 weeks to get in. The social worker assured her that she had appointments available the following week and she could schedule one with the receptionist on the way out. When Latonya scheduled the appointment, the next one available outside of her working hours was 2 weeks away. The social worker was not surprised when Latonya failed to show for that appointment.

(continued)

> ### CASE STUDY 1.1—THE IMPACT OF JUSTICE IN PRACTICE (*continued*)
>
> Latonya's example demonstrates the importance of examining a client's holistic needs and ensuring social, economic, and environmental justice. In this case, there are many factors influencing the client's willingness and ability to engage in services, all of which contribute to the inability to engage in treatment and result in a lack of justice for Latonya. Much of the effect on Latonya's participation was not due specifically to the engagement with the social worker, but was impacted more by her social, economic, and environmental influences. Justice-informed social work practice must include not just the intervention with and advocacy on behalf of the client, but also must ensure that the services are available in a manner that supports access and utilization. The time of the appointment and ensuing lack of immediate availability, the travel involved, the casual inference by the receptionist that Latonya was "lucky" to have spent the last 3 weeks waiting for an appointment, the last hour on a bus, and finally, the social worker's failure to recognize the social, economic, and environmental effects that ultimately culminated in what the social worker identified as "hesitancy" and "reluctance." Social workers must cultivate awareness of these influencing factors as all can be addressed and subsequently result in better outcomes for the client by increasing access and utilization of services.

Latonya's example highlights the various and often subtle ways in which social, economic, and environmental aspects influence someone's ability to engage in change. Latonya actively sought help, but there were multiple barriers that resulted in her failure to return, which ultimately were an unjust outcome for her. Merced et al. (2020) found that the social worker plays a significant role in determining utilization of services and that a perceived lack of inclusivity, biased messaging (unintentional or otherwise), and other factors such as locale can all contribute to whether a client engages in services. Social work practice must be able to identify these systemic influences to best position our clients for success. In order to identify strategies of change, we must first understand social, economic, and environmental justice and how those connect with social work practice.

SOCIAL JUSTICE

Despite the moral and professional imperative for social workers to promote justice for all people, there is no universally accepted definition of social justice for social work practitioners or otherwise. Social justice in the United States is sometimes equated with racial justice because so much of social injustice impacts people and communities of color. Certainly, much of the current social justice movement reflects racial justice efforts, with advocacy frequently focused on addressing racial disparities. The former National Basketball Association Most Valuable Player (NBA MVP) and All-Star, Kareem Abdul-Jabbar (2020), likened racism to dust, omnipresent but rarely noticed until a light is shown, subsequently proving racism is inescapably everywhere. Social workers should take note of this analogy, which may be helpful when considering a justice approach as well. Injustice is everywhere but unless a justice-oriented approach is used, the lack of visibility makes it seem nonexistent.

While social justice is sometimes equated with racial justice, the term encompasses inequalities beyond those based on race or ethnicity. Additionally, social justice is a universal concern and is certainly not unique to the United States. The United Nations (UN) describes social justice as understood only within the context of an individual nation, grounded on a framework that comprises the sociological, political, and cultural aspects of a specific locale. Thus, social justice can be addressed only when understood in the context in which the injustice occurs.

The NASW (n.d.) adds economic implications to how social justice is conceptualized, stating social justice encompasses "economic, political and social rights" (para. 2), and that everyone is deserving of opportunities to access these rights. The focus on opportunities is challenging because not all opportunities are equal or equitable. For instance, one might argue that anyone can go to college, but affordability and preparedness for college are not the same across all groups in society. Similarly, one might suggest that everyone has access to employment and the ability to "climb a career ladder," yet this does not take into account the differential experiences of people. For some, transportation or childcare is a barrier to employment. For others, racist and sexist policies and people within the workplace create barriers to climbing the proverbial career ladder.

The NASW's definition of social justice emphasizes individual rights and opportunities, but simply giving access to opportunities is not sufficient when people may not have had the preparation to be able to take advantage of those opportunities. As a result, others, such as theorists like Rawls (1999), suggest justice is akin to fairness. The notion of fairness is understood by all of us yet is extremely difficult to conceptualize and apply across all groups. The concept of fairness views social justice from a more macro perspective in which fairness is seen as a form of social obligation.

The advocacy group Children's Rights Education (n.d.) explores social justice as a form of mutual social obligation, with shared responsibility for the success of all, that requires "equal chances to succeed in life" (para. 7). By emphasizing mutual obligation, this fairness approach takes the onus off those who are vulnerable and places responsibility for achieving justice on all of society. This distinction between individual and communal responsibility is an important one and is a point of contention for many with respect to addressing injustice. And although social justice as defined by the NASW and advocacy groups emphasizes equality, the goal of "equality" becomes ephemeral, impossible to achieve, making it difficult to actualize.

In contrast, the Center for Economic and Social Justice (CESJ, n.d.) extends the concept of social justice by providing a more holistic perspective through incorporation of macro aspects, identifying social justice as a guiding virtue in establishing social institutions. Those justice-organized and justice-oriented social institutions provide "access" to what is needed, "as tools for personal and social development" (para. 7). Again, the CESJ emphasizes access, circling back to the NASW framework of social justice.

The CESJ explicitly frames social justice as a function of human institutions. The lack of justice in these institutions, whether educational, legal, medical, and so forth, has culminated in a perspective that most institutions are far from tools of "development" or justice oriented. The CESJ approach contrasts with experiences that explicitly situate injustice in the context of structural racism and discrimination that is embedded in the history of the United States, where policies are implemented to normalize privilege with certain identities (being White, male, heterosexual, able-bodied, etc.) and serves to maintain the marginalization of other populations. This concept is important for all social workers as much of our work is done within the context of structures and systems, so we must be aware of the distrust in these systems to achieve a just result. The CESJ's definition of social justice seeks to address that structural discrimination by identifying systems and structures as part of the solution in addressing social injustice.

In many ways, conceptualizing social justice as virtuous conveys it is idealistic, a goal or belief, not a behavior or an action. Social workers must embrace social justice as an action, something we do as a result of what we believe; otherwise social justice becomes what we espouse but not something for which we strive, and ultimately impacts the lives of our clients by failing to address their needs. Social workers must attend to, and understand, the context to be able to address aspects of injustice within it. Creating justice requires addressing injustice in the person's environment, not merely focusing on the person experiencing it.

ECONOMIC JUSTICE

Social injustice is just one form of injustice faced by our clients; economic injustice represents an equally visible and damaging form of disparity that social workers must address. In 2006, the UN likened the social justice movement of the recent decades to efforts aimed at securing distributive justice. Those efforts recognize the gap in wealth equality, where a small percentage of the population holds the majority of wealth and its associated power. Distributive justice seeks to effectively disperse wealth across the population and close the exceedingly disparate wealth-equality gap. This form of social justice, what the UN terms as "distributive justice," is also known as "economic justice."

In many ways, economic justice is the most visible aspect of justice work, and therefore it has become a focus for many justice efforts. Many aspects of social justice cannot be regulated by law because of the associated ephemeral qualities of values, virtues, access, and opportunities. However, economic justice as an element of social justice can be regulated, through ensuring minimal standards of income, healthcare, housing, and food security. Thus, economic justice is integral to social justice but is fairly distinct in specificity.

The UN (2006) describes economic justice as opportunities for "meaningful" employment and the compensation of "fair rewards" (p. 14). Thus, economic justice entails access to job opportunities that provide an adequate and appropriate income for an expected standard of living. While understanding the intent behind identifying employment as "meaningful" may vary by individual, presumably "meaningful" should at a minimum include standards of living associated with well-being.

In contrast to the UN's focus on employment, the Southern Poverty Law Center (n.d.) emphasizes that economic justice goes well beyond employment opportunities and specifically addresses structural discrimination that allows those who are poor to be targeted by countless explicit and implicit acts, from predatory lending practices to legal systems whose fines, fees, and bail are particularly punitive toward the poor.

This broader view of economic justice addresses those policies and practices that disproportionately impact the poor, not just regarding income but also those related to availability of resources. Many social workers engage in efforts to support and create income and resources for clients. For generations, a welfare state has been utilized to provide a minimal standard of living that provides a safety net and allows individuals with children to have a monthly income (and other resources) if other sources do not exist or are insufficient. That safety net no longer exists in the most recent iteration of Temporary Assistance for Needy Families (TANF) as use is limited to a maximum of 5 years, in comparison to prior versions that had no time limits.

The focus of our government and our policies, indeed even of social workers, on meeting basic needs through policies and practices that focus solely on minimal income and maintenance has largely failed. We continue to have significant disparities in income and in wealth. Our focus should broaden to include financial justice and those policies and practices that create opportunities for low-income households to accumulate wealth and/or asset holdings (Sherraden, 1991). We should also ensure that efforts address financial literacy and capability to build knowledge and opportunities to build assets. For example, addressing money management access to banking institutions and identifying housing as a related wealth asset are essential aspects of financial and economic justice.

As income disparities become more pronounced, varying policies from minimum wage to subsidizing housing have been implemented, providing resources to supplement disparate, inadequate income. Because the minimum wage is not a sustainable income to meet a minimal standard of living (known as a "living wage"), we subsidize minimum wage with resources such as healthcare, childcare, housing, and a food allowance to compensate for a lack of income. These resources and policies are developed in response to economic injustice and have assumed the role of an arbiter to try to remedy the extreme wealth gap in the United States. However, even with these resources, families continue to live in poverty.

One criticism of economic-justice endeavors is that many of our efforts seek to support the income of those who are poor through supplementing resources to which those with higher incomes tend to have ready access, such as affordable healthcare, stable housing, and food security. However, by supplementing income, rather than focusing on the UN's emphasis on "fair" compensation, which would be more reflective of a living wage, we are effectively subsidizing the minimum wage to ensure a marginal standard of living that the minimum wage alone cannot provide. Simply put, even when subsidized with a variety of resources, our minimum wage does not provide a minimal standard of living.

Finally, economic justice also encompasses gaps in assets, not just wealth. While current policies fail to establish an adequate standard of living, they are also increasing the wealth gap through intentionally providing resources to those who are not impoverished. An example of policies favoring individuals in higher income brackets is using the mortgage interests as tax deductions, which lowers the amount of taxes owed. Of course owning a home and having a mortgage are more likely to occur in higher income families than renting, which is more common among those in lower income brackets. Therefore, economic justice encompasses not just earnings but also income related to owning assets, which favors those with higher income.

Much as social justice requires an understanding of the structures and systems contained within the individual's context, economic justice requires an understanding of the policies that impact the person's access to income, wealth, assets, and ability to sustain an appropriate standard of living.

ENVIRONMENTAL JUSTICE

In addition to social and economic justice, environmental justice has emerged as a cross-cutting issue that disproportionately impacts individuals, typically based upon wealth, income, and location (Skelton & Miller, 2016). Those same environmental impact factors are likely to influence us by the place and the community in which we live: impoverished settings are more likely to have schools and students with poorer educational outcomes (Taylor, 2017), reduced health outcomes, and higher mortality (Mode et al., 2016), all of which reflect poorer well-being and quality of life.

Beyond the influence of the community as our environment, the lens of environmental justice has been focused on industrial impact and natural disasters. In the 2015 Educational Policy and Accreditation Standards (EPAS) from the CSWE, environmental justice was added as an essential component of the justice lens for social work practitioners, complementing social and economic justice that had been identified in the prior EPAS. Environmental justice addresses aspects that impact individuals but are well beyond their control.

The Environmental Protection Agency (EPA, n.d.) describes environmental justice as ensuring that laws impacting the environment are "developed, implemented and enforced" (para. 1) in a fair manner without disproportionate impact or consequences on any particular group. Much like social and economic justice, environmental justice is a human rights issue. Much of why environmental justice has come to the forefront of the justice movement is that environmental degradation, pollution, and other negative impacts of industry and society do typically impact in a disproportionate manner. In the United States, and around the globe, those most impacted by the environmental effects of industry, and subsequently those who live in our most polluted environments, are most commonly communities of color and/or the poor (Skelton & Miller, 2016).

However, there are many more facets of environmental justice that extend well beyond the impact of industry. Natural disasters disproportionately affect impoverished communities who do not have the financial resources or assets to aid in recovery. Recovery efforts through employment opportunities in impoverished communities are also limited when natural disasters occur.

Climate change considerations that exacerbate natural disasters are also emerging as an integral component of environmental justice. Recovery from these natural disasters is always hardest on the impoverished and further exacerbated as those who are poor are more likely to rent and less likely to have insurance sufficient to replace belongings and provide alternate housing while repairs are being made. This disparity was made startlingly apparent in some locales, such as New Orleans, after Hurricane Katrina, as housing that was affordable prior to Hurricane Katrina was no longer affordable once rebuilt. When given the opportunity to start from scratch, builders and developers opted to construct housing that was too expensive for the average New Orleans resident. This continues with each major national disaster and is a justice issue as marginalized populations are disproportionately impacted.

Other aspects of the environment that disproportionately impact certain populations are the community resources that are unequally available to support the citizens. In this way, environmental justice is an important component of social justice. Some communities have food deserts, where access to healthy and/or affordable food is negligible. Other communities from Martin County, Kentucky—in Central Appalachia—to Flint, Michigan, fail to provide safe drinking water to their citizens. Environmental justice reflects aspects of living most often seen as universal human rights that can be compromised in areas where there is limited access to adequate healthcare, affordable housing, or secure, safe environments.

INTERDEPENDENCE OF SOCIAL, ECONOMIC, AND ENVIRONMENTAL JUSTICE

Social work practice encompasses all of these facets of justice: social, economic, and environmental. Certainly, these are inextricably linked so that any client impacted by social injustice is likely to also experience economic or environmental injustice. Our practice efforts must start with a fundamental orientation to understanding the client's context of injustices and all change efforts should work to address those injustices.

CASE STUDY 1.2—COMPOUNDING INJUSTICES

Child welfare encompasses all of the services that are provided to help improve children's quality of life. Often these services are provided directly to children, as in the free breakfast and lunch programs, or may target the entire family, such as TANF, because improving the quality of life for the family subsequently should improve well-being for the child. Those services that are specifically designed to protect and ensure the child's well-being are known as "public child welfare."

The public child welfare system is tasked with ensuring children are safe in the home or finding alternatives if not. While the ultimate goal is to keep children with their families, in

(continued)

CASE STUDY 1.2—COMPOUNDING INJUSTICES (*continued*)

some situations, when safety is not assured, children may be placed in foster care. The majority of children placed in foster care are placed into the state's custody due primarily to some form of abuse or, most commonly, neglect. Foster care is designed to provide a temporary, safe, appropriate home for children whose families are unable to adequately or appropriately care for them.

While public child welfare is necessary to ensure child safety, children of color are overrepresented in the foster care system, particularly Black and Indigenous children. Notably, all children in foster care have experienced loss and concomitant trauma, which subsequently impacts health. Additionally, children in foster care often have dismal educational outcomes. While education can be a protective factor, foster youth are at greatest risk for diminished educational achievement (Kirk et al., 2012). Children in foster care are less likely to graduate from high school and subsequently less likely to enroll in college, and even if enrolled, less than 10% eventually attain a bachelor's degree (Legal Center for Foster Care and Education, 2018). For the more than 400,000 children in foster care, diminished educational attainment impacts economic opportunities and leads to diminished income as well, thus reflecting the interconnectivity of social and economic injustices.

This example highlights much of the incongruity that occurs when social workers seek to achieve just results within systems that may not be just. As a system grounded in protecting children from harm, public child welfare and the foster care system reflect the challenges associated with justice-informed social work practice. A system designed to effect change and create a more just environment for the child can also contribute to disparate results for participants, from the manner in which children enter the system to the reduced opportunities upon exiting.

As social workers try to navigate systems designed to promote justice for clients, we must be continuously aware that those same systems may subsequently and simultaneously promote injustice as well.

THE OUTCOME GOAL: EQUALITY VERSUS EQUITY

In seeking to meet our clients' needs, understanding the difference between equality and equity is vital to implementing justice-informed social work practice. The lack of a universally accepted understanding of what justice consists of, or even means, makes it challenging to concretely implement justice in social work practice. Much of the early justice efforts focused on equality, providing resources uniformly across populations. But those efforts were challenged based on the idea that resources should be individualized to needs rather than uniformly dispensed. A central criticism of providing equal resources is the lack of effective distribution of resources. An example is that, as part of the coronavirus disease 2019 (COVID-19) pandemic response, the government provided an initial $1,200 economic impact payment for those taxpayers who made under $100,000. Via this policy, all taxpayers who made less than $100,000 were treated equally, when the reality is that individuals and families in this income bracket represent a wide range of income and support needs. Some taxpayers most certainly were in more significant need than others.

More recent social justice efforts have focused on equity, which seeks to provide what is needed (which can certainly be controversial to differentiate need versus want—does everyone need Wi-Fi access? a cell phone? transportation?); therefore, it varies across individuals and populations. Equity can be seen as reflecting Rawls's vision of fairness in terms of providing what is needed, while equality can be seen as fairness in terms of having the same resources regardless of need. Equity is individually based, while equality is focused on the group. Equity is the focus of social work practice, which is predicated upon effective engagement and assessment of clients, both of which should always be conducted in the context of justice and are essential in determining client needs and how best to meet those needs. In this manner, social work strives for equity. Equity is seen as relying on a fairness principle because equity requires use of only those resources that are needed.

THREATS TO JUSTICE—PATERNALISM, POWER, AND AUTHORITY

While all social workers seek to deliver justice-informed practice, there are multiple threats that social workers should be aware of. One of the chief threats to justice-informed practice is paternalism, interpreting client needs from the social worker's own perspective. Paternalism occurs when someone makes decisions based upon what they think is best rather than what the other person wants or believes they need.

Not only does paternalism get in the way of just practice, but it also impedes client self-determination, a core ethical principle of the social work profession. An example of this is the social worker who insists a partner not return to a violent relationship out of concern for the partner's safety. Ultimately, clients have the right to self-determination even if that means returning to relationships that have been unsafe in the past. While the social worker can express concerns and can problem-solve to develop a safety plan for that client, ultimately the decision to return is the client's. Any manipulation of that decision-making process, based upon what the social worker perceives is best, is paternalism and does not represent just practice. Impeding our clients' self-determination must be avoided because it threatens the client's right to justice-informed practice.

Power and authority are additional threats to justice-informed social work practice. Social workers are in a position of authority with their clients, which can impact relationships and work processes. Additionally, authority can sometimes be seen as synonymous with power, which is the antithesis of self-determination. Authority is seen as a legitimate influence, sanctioned by education and employment, whereas power is manipulating or assuming control that coerces or violates autonomy. While every social worker has some element of authority, it can still be seen as a threat to the client who needs to maintain a sense of autonomy and self-determination. Social workers should be careful to ensure that the client is engaged as a change agent, acting as a partner in the change process. Ultimately, any threat that impedes justice-informed practice is a disservice to our clients.

JUSTICE IN MACRO SOCIAL WORK PRACTICE

Understanding the influence of social, economic, and environmental justice (and injustice) is also relevant in social work practice with communities, organizations, and policies, commonly referred to as "macro practice." While the impact of injustice can be clearly identified in individual situations, communities are impacted by injustice as well, further compounding the effect on individuals and families. Communities experience a lack of opportunities and resources just as individuals do, yet are not as frequently targeted for intervention in social work practice. Micro social work practice, which focuses on change efforts primarily at the individual level, requires a justice lens, but also has to be conducted within a larger macro framework, examining justice in communities, organizations, and the policies that implement our social services. Inequities that affect individuals are further compounded by the inequities that occur at the larger, community level.

As an example, many communities are funded by taxes paid as a percent of property owned by residents in those communities. This type of funding causes communities with properties of lower value to have fewer resources to offer residents, while those areas with residents who are already well sourced have significantly more assets available to support members. Thus, social workers must be attentive to community resources and the frequent disparate allocation of those resources to meet needs within the community.

Finally, much of macro work involves advocacy on our clients' behalf as well as for just policies that provide the context for social work practice. Policies for the social services safety net determine benefits, funding, eligibility, and so forth. But policies also influence educational outcomes, mandatory sentencing in the criminal justice system, or lack of regulation of predatory lending practices. Policies, and ensuring they have just and equitable outcomes, are an important aspect of macro practice for social workers.

INTERSECTIONALITY, SOCIAL DETERMINANTS, AND INTERDEPENDENCE OF INJUSTICE

Just practice also speaks to the intersectionality of marginalized identities and interdependence of justice efforts. Intersectionality commonly references aspects of identity related to race and ethnicity, gender, sexual orientation, and so forth, that result in marginalization based upon status associated with those identities. Additionally, social determinants have significant impact, particularly related to health. Social determinants reflect living conditions such as socioeconomic status, neighborhood or community resources, education, and employment. Those social determinants can also magnify the impact of intersectionality.

Much as social determinants and intersectionality of identities are related, interdependence may also be used to conceptualize justice efforts by understanding the interconnectivity of differing aspects of justice. Notably, a client experiencing one form of injustice often experiences multiple injustices. Largely, this can be due to structural discrimination, the sanctioned policies and practices that serve to implement dissimilar opportunities across populations, impacting justice by limiting opportunities. An example is that children who grow up in impoverished circumstances will still have increased risk for diabetes and cardiovascular disease, even when they have higher socioeconomic status as adults.

Much as social, economic, and environmental injustices overlap, efforts aimed at increasing justice must target multiple aspects as well. For instance, economic policies affect income, resulting in increased social equity and subsequently impacting environmental resources such as housing and access to sufficient food. Social workers should be aware of this interdependence as any efforts aimed at change cannot be done in isolation and must account for the multifaceted complexity of justice-oriented practice.

FROM THE FIELD 1.1

JUSTICE MEANS NEEDS MUST BE HOLISTICALLY MET
by Elaine Strawn

A Title 1 school means the school receives federal funds specifically to assist students from low-income families in meeting their educational goals. In my school, learners bring a variety of experiences and knowledge to the classroom with them, requiring the teacher to assess and decide who needs what to succeed. For some learners, the priority is making sure basic needs such as food, shelter, sleep, and feeling safe and loved are being met. For others, it may be more academically oriented support due to a lack of experience with books, being read to, and intentional conversations for learning. As more and more children come to school unable to focus, self-regulate, and have appropriate social skills, teachers, social workers, and administrators are emphasizing the importance of building community and focusing on the whole child before learning can occur. Schools are seeing more children in crisis as their families face one or more challenges of housing instability, food insecurity, English as a second language, an incarcerated parent, substance abuse, or violence in their homes. When children are so deeply impacted by family traumas, learning is compromised; thus, addressing a child's holistic needs is a critical foundation for academic success.

Addressing needs holistically is integral to our practice. There are many individual influences in each person's context that we must understand and utilize in social work practice. This is possible only when we understand clients' intersectionality and interdependence of justice needs.

ACHIEVING JUSTICE IN SOCIAL WORK PRACTICE

Social workers have a professional and moral mandate to integrate justice in practice, yet the variety of ways in which injustice impacts people poses challenges in best determining how justice can be implemented. Achieving justice requires change. Notably, change, particularly justice-oriented change, can cause uncertainty and discomfort. The seemingly ambiguous nature of justice can also make it hard for us to sometimes see a clear path forward. Social workers must occasionally live in this space of experiencing ambiguity and discomfort in order to best meet our clients' needs.

Not only must social workers cultivate the ability to work effectively in uncertain circumstances but also must be able to effectively assess our clients' needs, always within the pragmatic context of understanding existing resources. Social workers are adept at conceptualizing, developing, and implementing programs to address unmitigated needs, which position us well to engage in just practice. Social workers must be creative in identifying what *should* be, not just living in the space of what is.

With social, economic, and environmental justice as our charge, there are overarching commonalities in understanding justice that we must subsequently implement in our social work practice:

- Social responsibility
- Opportunity
- Culturally informed practice

Social responsibility—First and foremost, in all that we do, social workers must view justice from a social responsibility perspective, in contrast to that of personal or individual responsibility. Working from this paradigm helps create empathy for our clients and mitigates blaming the individual for unfortunate circumstances through an empowerment, strengths-based orientation. Social responsibility dictates that the success of others is something for which we are all mutually responsible; success is ensured only when *all* succeed. By assuming the social responsibility position, we are able to emphasize mutual, shared goals in justice-oriented social work practice. A social responsibility perspective also requires that we look beyond the person, guaranteeing that any identified challenges are seen as structural or systemic, rather than individual. Many of the challenges that society attributes to the individual are actually attributable to the systems in which people are engaged.

Opportunity—Social workers are committed to ensuring opportunities, not just services, exist for clients. The UN states each person should have the opportunity to earn the resources to have their needs met. Often that requires social work advocacy at the macro level, working with communities and legislators to educate, problem-solve, and effect change.

Not only are opportunities essential to justice, but access to those opportunities must exist as well. While we are taught that people are considered equal, we know that, in reality, opportunities are often not distributed equitably, nor is access equitable either. As a result, we must seek to dismantle barriers that prevent utilization of resources or result in disparate outcomes for our clients. Without this awareness, we are likely to accept the status quo and not seek to create change.

Culturally informed practice—Social workers must intentionally utilize culturally informed practice, knowing that culture can simultaneously exist both as a strength and as a source of stigma or even oppression. Culture can create privilege or promote exclusion. Culture informs all that we do, and we must be aware of the impact of these dynamics as we seek to empower our clients.

Much of our work related to implementing culturally informed practice requires a willingness to examine power structures including those that benefit us, as well as the power dynamics that are always relevant in social work practice. The social worker holds inherent power in the client relationship, especially with involuntary clients who are typically involved in the legal or educational systems and may not feel autonomy in the decision to work with the social worker. Regardless if voluntary or not, though, the social worker has authority and implicit power as dictated by the position of influence with the client. We must be willing to own this power and ensure it does not influence client decisions or our own facilitation efforts with clients.

Another aspect of culturally informed practice required of each of us as social workers is to center our work with an understanding of how our own histories, biases, and so forth impact what we do and how we do it. As Satell (2017) so aptly stated, we must transform ourselves first, by recognizing the role we play in maintaining what is, and move from our comfort zone to a place of growth, toward what should be.

Additionally, there is inherent power and privilege that might stem from our personhood (race, gender, sexual orientation) as well as our role as social workers. This willingness to examine the role of self emerges from the construct of cultural humility, where we must have sufficient self-awareness to understand our perspectives so that they do not influence our relationships with clients or our work to help clients meet their needs (Foronda et al., 2016). We cannot make assumptions as to what is best for clients and we must allow clients to be the experts on their lives; thus they have the right to autonomy in their decision-making. This willingness helps to avoid paternalism and ensures the right to self-determination. This commitment is to understanding the client's holistic aspects and perspectives rather than our own that inform our social work practice.

THE SOCIAL WORK MISSION

We hope that this text will help you understand not only justice-informed social work practice as a concept but also what justice looks like in practice. Implementing justice in social work practice is tangible and meaningful, allowing social workers to be change agents for individuals, families, organizations, and communities. As social workers, we have a profoundly simple mission that is disturbingly complex to implement: we must empower clients to effectively create change in their lives. We must acknowledge that this is hard work, mainly because of stigmas and barriers associated with access and utilization of services and because of the uncertainty associated with how best to position clients to achieve change. Because of the motivations that call us to this profession, no one is better suited for the work of justice-oriented practice than social workers.

Another aspect that makes implementing justice challenging is fear. Oftentimes, because justice-informed practice requires asking questions and assessing aspects of discrimination, oppression, or marginalization, fear of offending, or getting it wrong, impacts our ability to get it right and sometimes even whether we do anything at all. We should always be respectful in our interactions and be aware of our language, but even so, there will be times when we do not get it right. For example, one of my clients, "Josiah," was a 12-year-old who had been hit by a car and experienced a traumatic brain injury. He wanted to "play" cars and set up an elaborate track for us, describing community points of interest along the track. Josiah asked me to start and insisted that I go first when I tried to defer to him. So I started my car and made what I thought was appropriate "vrooming" noises but noticed him shaking his head. When it was his turn, and Josiah started his car, he made music thumping noises, which reflected his experiences with how to play cars, and what was important to him about cars—the music. It was a good lesson for me. We can never assume even basic knowledge about life experiences and cannot let fear stop us from finding out what those might be.

Justice-informed social work practice is not for the faint of heart; it is a lifelong pursuit with no end in sight. We must live with the ambiguity of starting over with each client; what was right for one may not be right for another. How to best meet client needs within that framework of justice-informed practice is messy and becomes a challenge. Certainly, we have not always gotten it right, both as a profession and as a society, but we must continue to develop our skills while ensuring that our motivation to be successful is grounded in what is just and equitable for our clients. In this way, we will continue to recognize the dignity of our clients. Justice is always grounded in the dignity of the individual.

CONCLUSION: OUR CALL TO ACTION

Social workers have an innate sense of justice, a clarion call to ensure fairness that extends beyond ourselves to encompass the welfare and well-being of others. Social workers are willing to step into the figurative ring, whether it is the courtroom, the legislative session, or the community seeking reform. While we must have the ability to advocate with stakeholders who shape policy, we must also cultivate the requisite skills to grieve with the mother who lost custody of her daughter because she was incapacitated by drug use, or stand eye to eye with someone who perpetrated sexual assault and know there is value in respecting that individual's rights and in repairing the trauma that occurred.

Social workers are willing, and able, to stand up and confront these behaviors because we respect all people and value the inherent right to dignity that each of us possesses. We fiercely advocate for all marginalized and oppressed populations while realizing our role is that of a facilitator, empowering clients to make change rather than determining what is best for those clients. Thus, we serve. And in all ways, our service must be justice oriented, determining not what is right for others but ensuring others have the right to determine what is best for them. In this, you and I stand together. Let us make the most of what lies ahead; let us take a stand; let us draw a line; and let us make sure we back it up. As a social worker, you will cheer, you will celebrate, and you will mourn. That is the true measure of our humanity: to know our successes and our failures are not tied to any single thing but instead to *every* single thing. Only when we are able to position others in a way to create meaningful change can we truly say success is achieved.

DISCUSSION QUESTIONS

1. Consider what a just world would look like.
    a. Give an example of a client impacted by injustice. What would change for this client if justice were achieved?
2. In what ways are social, economic, and environmental justice interdependent?
3. Explain the statement that many of the challenges that people experience are attributed to the systems in which people are engaged rather than the person.
4. Think about you personally engaging clients in justice-informed social work.
    a. If you assume most clients experience some form of injustice, how would you go about exploring this?
    b. How would you address resistance from a client who states, "Life's not fair, the sooner I accept that, the better off I'll be?"
    c. What will your biggest challenges be in exploring injustice with a client?

REFERENCES

Only key references appear in the print edition. The full reference list appears in the digital product on Springer Publishing Connect: connect.springerpub.com/content/book/978-0-8261-3539-1/chapter/ch01

Center for Economic and Social Justice. (n.d.). *Defining economic justice and social justice.* http://www.cesj.org/learn/definitions/defining-economic-justice-and-social-justice

Council on Social Work Education. (2015). *Educational policy and accreditation standards for baccalaureate and master's social work programs.* Commission on Educational Policy. https://www.cswe.org/Accreditation/Standards-and-Policies/2015-EPAS

Environmental Protection Agency. (n.d.). Learn about environmental justice. https://www.epa.gov/environmentaljustice/learn-about-environmental-justice

Legal Center for Foster Care and Education. (2018). *National fact sheet on the educational outcomes of children in foster care.* https://fosteringchamps.org/national-fact-sheet-on-the-educational-outcomes-of-children-in-foster-care

Merced, K., Imel, Z. E., Baldwin, S. A., Fischer, H., Yoon, T., Stewart, C., Simon, G., Ahmedani, B., Beck, A., Daida, Y., Hubley, S., Rossom, R., Waitzfelder, B., Zeber, J. E., Coleman, K. J., & Coleman, K. J.

(2020). Provider contributions to disparities in mental health care. *Psychiatric Services, 71*(8), 765–771. https://doi.org/10.1176/appi.ps.201800500

National Association of Social Workers. (2017). *Code of Ethics of the National Association of Social Workers*. Author.

Rawls, J. (1999). *A theory of justice* (Rev. ed.). Harvard University Press.

Skelton, R., & Miller, V. (2016). *The environmental justice movement*. Natural Resources Defense Council. https://www.nrdc.org/stories/environmental-justice-movement

Southern Poverty Law Center. (n.d.). *Economic justice*. https://www.splcenter.org/our-issues/economic-justice

United Nations. (2006). *Social justice in an open world: The role of the United Nations*. Author.

2

THEORETICAL AND CONCEPTUAL UNDERPINNINGS OF JUSTICE-DRIVEN PRACTICE

Diane N. Loeffler | Natalie D. Pope | Kalea Benner | Lenzi G. Dodgen

LEARNING OBJECTIVES

Students will be able to:

- Describe the five facets of oppression as outlined by Young (2004) and give examples of how these manifest in everyday life.
- Understand how the basic tenets of critical theories, critical race theory, and feminist theory inform justice-oriented social work practice.
- Explain the overlap between the person in environment perspective and critical theories, critical race theory, and feminist theory.
- Explain the role of unexamined bias in perpetuating injustice and oppression.

INTRODUCTION

What does it mean to be a justice-informed social work practitioner? How do you engage in just practice? In the first chapter of this text we introduced definitions of justice and equity, concepts that are important to understand when discussing justice-informed practice. Dr. Mit Joyner so eloquently stated in a thank you to all the well-wishers as she became the president of the National Association of Social Workers (NASW): as social workers, we are challenged to take "bold, intentional, deliberate actions to bend the arc of justice toward equity for all" (OUTPour LGBTQ Productions, 2020). In this chapter we start to examine the different ways in which social work practitioners can bend the arc, by engaging in practice that disrupts historic patterns of oppression and injustice and that builds toward a more just and equitable society.

At the time of this book's publication, stark examples of inequity and injustice are found all around us. The coronavirus disease 2019 (COVID-19) pandemic has further exposed inequalities across interrelated systems that are explored in depth in this volume. Within the text, experts provide robust discussion of *inequities* in the United States across many interrelated areas including the following:

- human rights
- education

- the criminal justice system
- poverty, wealth, and finances
- food security
- the environment, natural and human-made disasters
- health disparities, and
- housing

To be sure, injustice exists across *so many more* dimensions that are of critical importance to social workers. This volume stands as a starting point for dialogue, discussion, exploration, and critical analysis of practice arenas. You must, through education, dialogue, reflection, and understanding, determine how to bend the arc and how to ensure that your practice is just, equitable, anti-racist, and anti-oppressive. This is not easy and the way you go about practicing in these ways will depend a great deal on the unique context in which you practice.

CONTEXT FOR JUSTICE-INFORMED SOCIAL WORK PRACTICE

Context includes not only the current state of affairs but also the histories that have shaped our present reality. Context must also include an awareness and understanding of our own lived experiences, biases, values, and narratives that impact us and our relationships with others. Just as we social workers do, clients have their own context as well. As social work professionals, we cannot disregard the nuanced nature of each client's experience as we engage in helping processes. While we may never intentionally disregard, failing to acknowledge our client's lived experience is a form of disregard that we may not even realize. Being intentional in our interactions is the best way to engage clients in the context for change.

As professional social workers, we are called upon to utilize many different skills to engage in meaningful work—we act as brokers, educators, advocates, counselors, case managers, program developers, and evaluators, among others. In every action we take as a professional social worker we must ask whether the work we are doing is indeed done with a justice orientation.

While justice is a core component of social work professional identity and practice, that identification does not exclude us from being a part of systems that have inflicted harm and that have perpetuated systemic inequality. As we embrace our call to bend the arc toward equity, we must be aware of the gravitas required therein. An understanding of what oppression is, who is impacted by it, and how to address it in practice is essential. In Case Study 2.1, practitioner Lenzi Dodgen shares her journey and reflection on what it means to be a just practitioner. Her narrative reflects on her own personal experiences, challenges, and growth as a justice-oriented social worker.

CASE STUDY 2.1—JUSTICE IN SOCIAL WORK

by Lenzi G. Dodgen

Growing up on a thoroughbred horse farm settled in the grassy fields of gently rolling topography with striking hues of emerald green and sapphire blue in the horse-racing capital of the world sounds almost magical. My experiences with poverty and oppression amidst such beauty not only contributed to my path to social work but also shaped my value system, which is entirely juxtaposed from anything I was taught all those years ago in our tiny, substandard, shanty-style farm home.

(continued)

CASE STUDY 2.1—JUSTICE IN SOCIAL WORK (*continued*)

At some point, we must begin to honor our truth about history and our culture, even when it is painful and when we need to dismantle how it is oppressive to our growth and to those we serve. I will not allow myself to call that place magical when I know the horses' lives and well-being were blatantly valued more than my own.

Unpacking and unlearning years of programmed racism, sexism, capitalism, ableism, classism, and heterosexism began when I decided I was worthy of making a lofty investment in myself. As a radical feminist college student completing my undergraduate degree in social work, I now look back at the ways my White feminist lens excluded and erased the existence of many of the survivors with whom I now work. Now, I feel like those same power structures and systems that made me feel entitled were only tricking and victimizing me. When Audre Lorde (2007) said "I am not free when any woman is unfree, even when her shackles are very different from my own" (p. 126), I recognized that I have a responsibility to others, to myself, and to my legacy to honor this hard truth and stay committed to growth.

Dr. Ibram X. Kendi (2019) teaches us that we do not "become" racist or anti-racist, but rather we live our lives in moments in which our thoughts, words, behaviors, and choices are either racist or anti-racist. Practicing social work through an intersectional social justice framework means that we are never finished with The Work regarding social justice. Every single one of us sits in a position of power and privilege at different given moments. We are charged with the task of examining how this power and privilege serves our own needs and examining how this does not serve and protect others. If we want to practice just social work, we must tell ourselves these difficult truths and refuse to become paralyzed. We must instead catapult ourselves into radical action.

Further, radical action might look like existing and taking up space as your whole self in a family that wishes to deny you basic human rights, as it did for me on this path to honoring my truth.

Transforming is powerful, and yet power has an insidious agenda. Just as Paulo Freire warns of the oppressed becoming the oppressor, social work practitioners are uniquely situated in our society to have decision-making power regarding the health, safety, and well-being of others. There are profound and concrete reasons the NASW Code of Ethics places self-determination as a cornerstone of the practice. If I am honoring my truth genuinely and authentically, then I must with all sincerity provide my clients with the physical and emotional safety to explore what it may look like for them to navigate their lives by fully trusting them to be the experts. Any other alternative action requires swift, intense, and critical examination. Empowering others is justice, even if it may not look or feel like justice to me. We can dismantle power and control dynamics by recognizing that we wish to control what we do not trust. Love, compassion, and empathy are the opposite of control because they demand trust and truth. We need more radical truth-tellers who are willing to trust themselves and others even when it hurts. The world needs social workers who are out of control!

BENDING THE ARC

Our task as social workers is to bend the arc, to seek equity for our clients and equity in opportunities, in access, and in outcomes. Quality of life and well-being is constructed of both functioning and capability where functioning is the ability to do something or be something and capabilities are the opportunities to do that something. Often, our biggest challenges to achieving equity in functioning or capabilities often arise from the multitude of settings and systems in which our clients are engaged that often fail to share a common purpose of yielding transparent, equitable opportunities for all. As a result, our clients frequently experience disenfranchisement, a loss of power and privilege. When opportunities are not shared equitably, feelings of marginalization, particularly related to social and economic exclusion, will occur. These barriers are particularly important to understand as they relate to oppression.

OPPRESSION

Before we can truly engage in just and equitable practice, we must better understand what oppression is and how it shows up in our world and the world around us. While there is not one uniform definition of oppression that is used throughout social work or social science literature, Iris Young's conceptualization of oppression withstands the test of time and offers a helpful framework for understanding oppression, as it relates to injustice. Iris Young's work emphasizes that oppression is structural and is experienced differently by different people—and different *groups* of people. Young's conceptualization of oppression provides a set of "functional criteria" for understanding how oppression is experienced. Oppression, she explains, can be experienced through exploitation, marginalization, powerlessness, cultural imperialism, and violence (Young, 2004). This conceptualization of oppression helps us, as practitioners, to understand the effects of oppression on clients and client groups. Certainly her discussion of oppression is theoretically driven and richly contextualized. Reading her original work is warranted as this chapter's discussion borrows from her work but does not dive into the rich and nuanced discussion of Marxism, feminist theory, and political structure and society that makes her original conceptualization of these five facets of oppression so powerful.

Borrowing from Young's framework allows us to understand the numerous ways in which oppression is present in the lives of many. Key to understanding oppression is recognizing that social systems are comprised of groups that are the oppressor and groups that are oppressed. These are deeply rooted in history and in the perpetuation of treating certain groups of people as less than or less worthy. Examined as it pertains to racial oppression, this is abundantly clear. The legacy of slavery is ever present in our society and we have been complicit in creating systems that continue to oppress Black people in the United States. This oppression takes the forms of exploitation, marginalization, powerlessness, cultural imperialism, and violence. This oppression is cumulative and has devastating impacts with far-reaching consequences.

To be clear, oppression is experienced by all Black, Indigenous, and other people of color (BIPOC) in the United States. Oppression occurs when any group is subjugated by a group that has more power. In the United States the default group in power is, without a doubt, tied to race (White), gender (male), and wealth.

Let us turn to an examination of Young's five faces of oppression. Each examination provides only a cursory discussion that can be viewed as a starting point for deepening one's understanding of the concept of oppression.

Exploitation

Exploitation of a person—or group of people—is evident throughout history and around the world. Dominant groups rely on the labor of others for their own gains. Slavery, indentured servitude, and sharecropping provide a historical frame of reference for exploitation of labor, yet this practice continues today and is evidenced by the proliferation of low-wage service sector work, human trafficking, a lack of unionization and organization among many workers, and more. Exploitation of people also became uniquely visible during the COVID-19 pandemic in the United States when, for example, grocery store workers were deemed essential yet were working for subliving wages.

Exploitation may also occur when one group is valued less than another and expected to do the same job—we see this at play in the world around us today with gender wage gaps—especially when we examine gender wage gaps for BIPOC. Exploitation can also be viewed geographically—in the United States we need look no further than the poorest counties. Persistently poor counties in the United States are largely rural and are not coincidentally located in places where natural resource extraction has exploited the land (and the laborers there) for gain by others. These areas include Central Appalachia, the Lower Mississippi Delta, the Colonias, and Native/Indigenous lands.

Marginalization

Oppression through marginalization occurs when groups are deemed *unworthy* or *incapable* by the majority. When one is viewed as unable or undesirable and is sidelined from participation in society because of this, they are marginalized. Marginalization occurs in the labor force and often in meaningful participation in society. Marginalization shows up in the 21st century in the form of subminimum wages that are federally allowable. It is indeed still legal in many states to pay people with disabilities a subminimum wage; this is tied to the notion of limited productivity or value provided by that person. This practice is clear marginalization. Marginalization also shows up when, for example, race, gender, gender identity, sexual orientation, or other attributes of physical appearance are implicitly (or explicitly) used to exclude someone from the workforce. This is evidenced in the myriad studies that have demonstrated that employers will prefer those with "White-sounding" names over those with "Black-sounding" names when other qualifications are the same. This also appears in the overwhelming narratives from trans men and women in the United States who have been denied employment or been terminated without cause.

Powerlessness

One cannot have power if one's voice is not heard. Powerlessness, then, is a mighty oppressor. Consider, in the United States, the right to vote. Historically, when the United States was formed, White men who either owned land or paid taxes were the only citizens who had the right to vote. The Constitution's allowance for states to determine voting rights created a hierarchical system that disallowed the voices of many in the political process. Many states utilized land ownership as a criterion for voting, ensuring that only those with wealth/status would have a voice. While the 15th Amendment (1870) disallowed "race, color, or previous condition of servitude" as reasons to deny one the ability to vote, Black men and poor White men were still excluded from voting through a series of Jim Crow–era poll taxes, literary tests, and so on. Women were excluded from the right to vote until 1920. Details notwithstanding, it is safe to say that even after the passage of the Voting Rights Act in 1965 many groups were—and still are—excluded from voting in the United States. Voter ID laws are a modern example of this practice because they require a form of identification (that typically costs money) and documentation of residence and so may not be easily obtained by all.

Powerlessness is also evident when violence against Black men and women is silenced, when immigrant children are detained inhumanely and their stories are not heard, when transgender men and women are murdered (at rates much higher than cisgender men and women) but those murders go unnoticed by the media and the public at large. A lack of power creates a lack of ability to fully participate in society.

Cultural Imperialism

Cultural imperialism relates to the very way in which dominant groups and their narratives create a sense of otherness and minimized value by rendering oppressed groups invisible, exotic, or deviant. This strips people of their very humanity and even renders them invisible. In a culture where whiteness is dominant and maleness is connected to power and privilege, cultural imperialism plays a visceral role in the dehumanization and devaluing of those who are not male, of those who are not White. Powerful social constructs of race and gender create normative behaviors, appearances, and practices that are upheld as "good" or "successful" or "worthy" and penalize those whose behaviors, practices, and appearances fall outside of these norms. Examples of this cultural imperialism include preference for specific language and dialect, aesthetic standards that celebrate and value certain body and hair types and skin tones and subsequently shame others, and language that is far more derogatory toward women than men.

Violence

As a form of oppression, violence is all around us. When people—and systems—in power utilize force and brutality to demonstrate their power and render others silent, the consequences are far reaching. The history of violence against Black men and women in the United States is a shameful example of the oppressive nature of violence. At the writing of this chapter, Breonna Taylor's murder has yet to be acknowledged as such by the police in Louisville, Kentucky, and the police officers who committed her murder are still free citizens. BIPOC are not afforded the same rights as White people when simple acts—pumping gas, bird watching, driving to work, exercising in public—may put you in harm's way. For any group that has been marginalized, othered, rendered less than, violence has always been a part of that othering. Violence must be examined and understood as a forceful tool of oppression.

ADDRESSING OPPRESSION IN SOCIAL WORK PRACTICE

Oppression can take many forms and the preceding examples of the five faces are just that—examples. The complexity of oppression must not be undervalued by a social work practitioner. Further, it is important to understand that one's experience of oppression is uniquely their own and uniquely situated within the context of their identity or identities. Not only is oppression individually impactful but oppression can be experienced within entire groups and communities as well.

Systemic oppression occurs when actions and behaviors are codified by history, laws, policies, and cultural or societal norms that allow the perpetuation of othering and exclusion based on race, sex, gender, ability, religious beliefs and affiliations, country of origin, and more. Systemic oppression artificially dichotomizes identities (White vs. non-White, cis vs. transgender, etc.) and gives preference to the dominant identity while marginalizing others. Systemic oppression affects both the individual and the concomitant community.

INTERSECTIONALITY

Intersectionality is the systemic connectivity of oppression and the ways it is uniquely experienced by different people. Oppression is not a uniform experience, as discussed previously; rather, it is highly individualized and reflective of the person's context. Kimberlee Crenshaw's introduction of the term "intersectionality" into our lexicon has given voice to the extremely nuanced and specific ways in which forces of oppression disadvantage individuals and groups differently. Her work opened the door for us to deepen our understanding of how forces of oppression combine and compound. For example, the oppression that is experienced by Black transgender women in the United States is unique because of the intersection of two marginalized identities—Black and transgender—and the expressions of oppression that are specifically enacted upon this group are *different* from oppression enacted upon and experienced by Black women and by, as a comparison, White trans women.

This construct of intersectional oppression is particularly helpful to social work professionals who must be able to understand the context of each client's experience and who must be able to understand that experiences of oppression are as unique as each client. Here, "client" is used on the micro level, considering the experience of one client; we must allow the understanding of intersectionality to inform our practice with and for groups and communities as well. Intersectionality is experienced structurally, politically, and in ways that are representational (Crenshaw, 1989).

UNDERSTANDING AND MITIGATING BIAS

Our experiences shape who we are and how we respond to the world around us. Each facet of our lived experiences, including our own experiences with oppression, contributes to the specific way in which we view the world. Similarly, facets of our lived experience—how we have interacted with the ideas presented to us by others, to the media, to family and cultural influences—shape our value orientation and our own biases.

BIAS

Bias—whether implicit or explicit—is dangerous because it reinforces stereotypes that allow injustice and oppression to perpetuate. In comparison to the overtness of explicit bias, implicit bias is a result of internalized beliefs regarding others that unconsciously shape our interactions, our behaviors, and our perceptions of others. Both can be destructive to engaging others. As social workers, we must be willing to truly discover and acknowledge our biases, challenge them, and act upon or change them when realized. This process is one that continues throughout our careers and our lives.

Biases are powerful because, when unchecked, they allow us to be complicit in oppression. We must find ways to systematically and meaningfully engage with our subjectivities. When our biases remain unexamined, they lay beyond our control—we may notice them only when it is too late, such as when we have written a harsh account of a client session in our case notes or when we have made an unfair comment to our colleagues about a potential new hire. As just practitioners we must commit to the continual growth and necessary—and often uncomfortable—self-exploration and change that is required to ensure that we can commit to our clients and to our work in ways that are justice oriented.

TRAUMA-INFORMED PRACTICE

Trauma-informed practice is an important aspect of addressing the violence and subsequent trauma associated with oppression. Many of our clients experience trauma, which is commonly associated with violence, oppression, and/or racism and is caused by a sense of a physical or psychological threat that results in feelings of helplessness or fear (American Psychiatric Association, 2013). The National Council for Behavioral Health (n.d.) noted that 70% of adults in the United States have experienced at least one trauma event in their lives. Roberts et al. (2012) found that Black adults were also more likely to have experienced trauma in childhood. Two-thirds of children have experienced one traumatic event by 16 years of age, which is a risk factor for nearly all behavioral health and substance use disorders (Substance Abuse and Mental Health Services Administration, 2015).

Trauma disproportionately impacts individuals and communities of color and has long-term consequences if not addressed. For example, racism is associated with an increased risk of posttraumatic stress disorder (Williams et al., 2018) and adverse health conditions (Williams et al., 2019). Experiencing trauma also affects cognitive functions such as thought processes and ability to problem-solve (Blanchette & Caparos, 2016), personal and professional relationships, health, and emotional responses (National Child Traumatic Stress Network, n.d.). Substance misuse is also exacerbated by trauma as individuals suffering from substance misuse are more likely to have been exposed to or experienced trauma (Falvo & Schmid, 2018), with alcohol use associated with 41% of those who reexperience trauma, making substance misuse a risk factor for trauma recidivism (Nunn, Erdongan, & Green, 2016). The National Institute on Drug Abuse (n.d.) estimates that 80% of women who abuse drugs have also experienced trauma.

With the magnitude of these effects, social workers must employ trauma-informed practice to mitigate the negative impact. Trauma-informed practice ensures that social workers acknowledge the influence of trauma on the client, examine presenting problems within the context of the trauma experience, and recognize how trauma informs a client's "fundamental beliefs" (Levenson, 2017, p. 105) regarding perceptions of self and of their world, thus impacting functioning across all aspects of life. Utilization of trauma-informed practice strengthens the therapeutic alliance by implementing the core principles of safety, trust, collaboration, choice, and empowerment (Levenson, 2017). Social workers must ensure that trauma-informed practice is used as a foundation for all justice-informed practice.

In Case Study 2.2, social work practitioner and researcher Natalie Pope reflects on her research with older men experiencing chronic homelessness. Her reflection draws on the concepts discussed thus far in the chapter, bringing together the need to understand the intersectional nature of oppression, to be able to challenge and check our biases as practitioners, to be able to address needs related to trauma, and to challenge systemic barriers to client successes.

CASE STUDY 2.2—CHRONIC HOMELESSNESS AND STRUCTURAL OPPRESSION

by Natalie D. Pope

In my research interviewing older homeless men experiencing chronic homelessness, my colleagues and I heard participants recount stories of housing discrimination and unfair treatment by employees and volunteers charged with helping and supporting them in their quest to secure safe and stable housing. The recurrence of data about unfair treatment across institutions and interpersonal relationships suggests that these experiences were not single, isolated events. Many homeless, single men—at least the ones we spoke to—seem to face pervasive and systemic bias, oftentimes from people and institutions charged with

(continued)

CASE STUDY 2.2—CHRONIC HOMELESSNESS AND STRUCTURAL OPPRESSION (*continued*)

helping them. Men we interviewed described interactions with case managers that were often characterized by negativity and a lack of understanding. While it would be unfair to characterize all homeless service programs and providers in this way, in our research we did observe that some of the structures, programs, and people responsible for helping these men were retraumatizing them in ways that included restricted autonomy and choice in shelter settings and a lack of follow-through and perceived absence of empathy from service providers. A particular narrative stands out.

I met Evan in 2017 at a day center for homeless men in a midsouthern metro city. My interaction with him was about 90 minutes as he shared his story regarding experiencing multiple bouts of homelessness.

At the time of our interview, Evan was 56 years old and living on the streets or in emergency shelters when he was able. When he told me about working as a cook in a local restaurant, I was not surprised—something about his outfit of loose-fitting elastic waist pants and Crocs gave the appearance of a line cook. I was there to learn about why Evan, after being homeless and securing housing, had found himself homeless again.

Evan shared openly about his formative years, which were characterized by instability and inconsistent caregiving. He was one of 14 children, the oldest boy. He described his father, a captain in the air force, as consistently disengaged as both a husband and a father. With her husband gone all of the time, Evan's mom was not able to take care of him and his siblings. Eventually child protective services got involved. His childhood years were spent bouncing between seven boys' institutions and 13 foster homes. With little in the way of stability, support, or nurturance during the years he needed it most, Evan was arrested at age 18 for involuntary manslaughter; he served 4 years. After getting out of prison, Evan moved to the city in which he currently resides at the urging of an uncle who thought a change of scenery would be good for him. Unfortunately, when Evan relocated he "got mixed up with the wrong crowd" and ended up committing a crime that resulted in a prison sentence of more than 20 years.

After Evan served his sentence, he attended community college and earned an associate's degree in culinary studies. His cooking skills enabled him to work fairly consistently as a chef. Despite having steady employment, housing was expensive and he was frequently homeless.

Most recently, Evan was living in a three-bedroom apartment with two other sous chefs and had been living there for about 18 months. While he was in the hospital for pneumonia, he returned to his apartment only to find it locked and inaccessible. His two roommates had gotten into a fight, the police were called, and everyone was evicted. Because Evan's name was not on the lease, he was not allowed to get his things from the apartment, including his HIV medicines and a few important possessions.

Admittedly, Evan's story is a complicated one and—like many of the interviews I did that year with men experiencing chronic homelessness—it was sometimes hard to follow the events and episodes he described. But, there are central themes that unify his narrative.

First, Evan's childhood lacked consistent safety, comfort, and protection necessary to help him develop ways of coping to function as a healthy adult. He spent most of his adult life in prison.

(*continued*)

CASE STUDY 2.2—CHRONIC HOMELESSNESS AND STRUCTURAL OPPRESSION (*continued*)

He had never been married and indicated no consistent, meaningful relationships in adulthood. He was estranged from all of his siblings. During our interview, Evan smiled easily and I felt drawn to his likable demeanor. Despite this, he talked frankly about episodes of rage throughout his adult life, like when he rammed his boss's van into a wall after being docked in pay for something he did not do. I was struck by the pattern of broken relationships in his life. The culminating impact of adverse childhood experiences has had a lasting impact on Evan and cannot go unacknowledged in practice. Trauma, in all of its forms, is oppressive.

Second, I was struck too by what he did not say. He did not talk explicitly about his experience as a Black man in the South. He did not talk about how he contracted HIV or much about living with a stigmatized autoimmune disease. His experiences of poor healthcare, multiple interactions with the police, and a lack of sense of belonging in the community seemed to speak to these intersecting identities and intersecting oppressions. Intersectionality feels so important in making sense of Evan and his story exemplifies the importance of the unique modes of discrimination and oppression that clients experience.

Third, although Evan appeared healthy, he had several chronic health conditions that were likely tied to a lack of access to affordable and culturally competent care. While in prison he was diagnosed with HIV; he also had glaucoma and neuropathy in his feet. I thought about him working a job where he had to be on his feet all day. His homelessness made it nearly impossible to attend to his medical needs. When speaking about his HIV medication, Evan told me, "Because I'm homeless, there's no where I can take it regularly because I can't carry it with me." Given his inability to access preventive care and maintain ongoing contact with a physician, I also wondered what other potential medical issues he may have, but not yet know about.

In our short time together, Evan shared experiences that demonstrate the need for a justice-oriented approach to practice that understands and centers the experience of clients within the context of their own narratives. We must give space for clients to engage in self-exploration and give clients choice and agency whenever possible. From Evan's story, we can see that he has not always experienced self-determination, especially in the settings where he resided both as a youth and as an adult. However, as a central cornerstone of the social work profession, we must seek out opportunities to give power to Evan so that he can make decisions based upon his needs. We must also attend to intersecting identities and intersecting oppressions experienced uniquely by the clients we serve.

PERSON IN ENVIRONMENT EXPLORED

Evan is a product of his environment, and his adult life reflects much of the instability and insecurity experienced in his childhood. A hallmark of the social work profession is the value we place upon the person in an environmental perspective. Within social work practice, we often ascribe this to the ecological or systems perspective of practice. However, this person in an environmental framework stands on his own and is an important element of justice-oriented practice. Utilizing the person in an environmental perspective ensures we continually apprise and attempt to understand the impact of the social environment and the context that informs the client's experiences. By acknowledging and valuing the interplay between individuals and their broader environments, we recognize the multifaceted ways in which oppression can dramatically impact one's life and experiences. In this, we tacitly acknowledge the systemic foundations of inequity and injustice. This acknowledgment, however, is not sufficient. We must engage in work that seeks to disrupt structures that are oppressive and labor with others to dismantle these systems. We must do so, even when dealing with institutions from which we may have benefited ourselves.

EXAMINING THEORIES AS JUST PRACTICE

The person in an environmental perspective helps inform justice-oriented social work practice as does utilizing theoretical frameworks that speak to impact and change strategies. To understand and engage in practice that is just, it is important to have an understanding of theories used in social work that can help us to orient our work toward justice. Theories, generally speaking, help to explain and predict human behavior. However, depending on the assumptions, values, history, and culture that inform a theory, the utility of the theory may be limited in scope and applicability to justice-oriented social work practice. Just like people, theories are biased. They are biased by cultural norms and values, by the experiences and worldviews of their thought leaders, and by the history and context in which they developed and are used.

We must be cognizant of these limitations as we build tool kits to enable us to practice in a justice-informed manner. As we learn about and begin to utilize theory in practice, it is important to examine and understand the values and limits of theory as well as the ways that theory can be used as a tool for oppression. Because this is not a theory text, we cannot enumerate all of the theories that are taught and utilized within social work. We ask that, as you deepen your understanding and knowledge of theories, you do so with a critical lens, asking tough questions about the foundational assumptions and underpinnings of the theories you are utilizing in practice.

In the following, we will briefly introduce and explore Critical Theory, Critical Race Theory, Intersectional Feminism, Person-Centered Theory, and Anti-Oppressive Approaches as excellent frameworks for justice-informed social work practice.

Critical Theory and Critical Race Theory

Critical theory is an umbrella term that encompasses theories focused on issues related to power and oppression.

Just as social work is a values-oriented profession and practitioners come to their work with an appreciation of certain ideals (e.g., self-determination, dignity and worth of person, and respect), critical theorists prioritize a particular set of concepts. This theory, like feminist theories and others, is value laden. While an exhaustive discussion of critical theories is beyond the scope of this text, we will address some of the central tenets of critical theory, particularly as they relate to justice-informed practice.

Adopting a critical perspective in practice means that social workers attend to power structures and seek to change them in positive ways. For instance, social workers informed by critical theory, being highly sensitive to forms of exploitation and inequality, are wary of their own power in worker–client relationships. There is no doubt that many well-meaning social workers have exerted their own preferences, values, and ideals onto their clients. Paternalism is a real risk for social workers engaging with clients and violates the social work principle of the right to self-determination. Critical theory prompts us to be mindful of power imbalances and seek ways to partner with clients, rather than try to control them.

A critical approach to social work would avoid relying on purely psychological, or individual, explanations for client problems. Attention is given to the ways that social structures inhibit human potential. When employing critical theory, presenting problems from clients or client systems are conceptualized within their social, political, economic, and cultural contexts. Critical social work practice not only goes beyond assessing clients within their broader systems but also advocates for praxis and social change.

Another important aspect of critical theory is the emphasis on questioning assumptions about the existing social order. Those aspects of our society considered undesirable are not merely accepted but a critical approach to practice would involve questioning and combating the accepted status quo. In this way, critical theory aligns with the profession's emphasis on social justice and social change.

From a critical perspective, social workers are to assess client systems in light of power relationships in society. Knowledge regarding clients should be examined and reexamined with a recognition that reality and "truth" can be distorted by sexism, racism, heteronormativity, and colonialism. From a critical perspective, clients' truth is valued above all other forms of knowledge. Social workers would seek ways to include and incorporate multiple voices (especially those voices that are often stifled) into their work. In practice, a social worker conducting risk assessments in child welfare work would merge both objective and subjective sources of information (Houston, 2001). Critical theory would suggest that we use multiple sources and types of client data to inform our work and also deliberately question this information through ongoing reflection. In this way, we can hope to avoid the value-laden communications that are often present and may bias our work with clients.

Critical theories are relevant for social workers seeking to engage in justice-informed practice. From this perspective, we would intentionally work to deconstruct the authority of social institutions in maintaining the status quo and would shoulder the responsibility for social change.

Critical race theory uses race and racism as a central organizing principle to examine long-standing social disparities between dominant and marginalized groups of color. Critical race theorists include scholars and activists who seek to expose and disrupt the relationship between race, racism, and power. Like critical theory, critical race theory contains an element of activism. From this perspective, we must go beyond simply understanding the way society is structured, "around racial lines and hierarchy" (p. 3) but, seek to transform things for the better (Delgado & Stefancic, 2001).

Emerging in the 1970s, the genesis of critical race theory came from two movements—critical legal studies and radical feminism. Although starting in law and legal studies, critical race theory has now expanded to other disciplines such as social work, education, and political science. For instance, critical race theorists working in education might study racial inequities that exist in school funding, discipline policies, and standardized testing.

Critical race theory has been used to counter arguments against policies like affirmative action. This perspective would call our attention to types of internal colonialism where landfills, high-pollution industries, toxic waste sites, and sewage treatment plants are installed in communities of color or native lands. Critical race theory would recognize that poverty and race intersect in complex ways. This perspective would highlight how, although poverty exists among people of all races, the experience of poverty for people of color differs in profound ways from poverty among their White counterparts. More poor Black people live in concentrated poverty (in terms of neighborhoods) than poor White people. White poverty, even among immigrant families, often lasts for only one to two generations, unlike generational poverty among people of color.

Critical race theory aligns with the person in an environmental perspective, long adopted by social workers. Racism, according to critical race theory, is pervasive and ordinary. Racism would not be viewed individually or interpersonally; racism is seen as embedded in the structure of systems in which we engage every day: legal, educational healthcare, among others. Many of the social problems with which social workers deal on a daily basis reflect these systems, including availability and access to healthcare, mental healthcare, food, safe and stable housing, all of which stem from institutionalized racism. Therefore, we cannot adequately help any client without working to change the systems, policies, and practices that contribute to race-based marginalization and oppression.

A Feminist Lens

Feminist theory, like critical theory, is a broad umbrella term. Because this is not a theory text, the history and critique of theories that can be collected under a feminist umbrella cannot be discussed in depth. Butler-Mokoro and Grant (2018) provide an excellent and in-depth discussion of feminism and social work practice and they enumerate the waves of feminist thought and theory that have preceded the intersectional feminist perspective that is discussed here. In the evolution of feminist thinking, it is important to understand and acknowledge the criticism of feminism as being exclusionary—too White, too academic, and too focused on a narrow range of social issues related to reproductive health and freedom.

Feminist activism and theory have evolved during our generation, shaped by the work of powerful thought leaders like Kimberlee Crenshaw, Audre Lord, bell hooks, and Patricia Hill Collins who have challenged the discourse and dialogue and who have ensured that voices of marginalized and oppressed women are included in and amplified by feminist thought and action. Like many ideas introduced in this chapter, there is no singular definition of feminist theory. Foster (2018) provides an excellent description of feminist theory as seeking gender justice by presenting a comprehensive view of understanding how the social construct of gender intersects with systems of inequality (class, nationality, race) to create privilege, oppression, and hierarchies that "disadvantage" women as well as "some groups of men" (p. 34).

A 21st-century feminist orientation to social work practice inherently centers the lived experiences of individuals within the broader context of structural oppression. This too aligns with the person in an environmental perspective central to social work practice. A feminist lens for practice, then, will allow an understanding of the complex interplay between intersectional oppressions as well as the need for practice that disrupts the status quo and that demands liberation and equity for those who have been marginalized and oppressed.

Person-Centered Theory

Another body of theories that is particularly useful for working from a justice-oriented perspective is humanistic therapies that are inherently relationship oriented. Humanistic theories include existential and person-centered theory, among others. Person-centered theory, in particular, has applicability to engaging in just practice, albeit from more of an individual level than a macro level.

Carl Rogers, a psychologist who pioneered humanistic psychology, developed the person-centered theory, which posits that people have the capacity to effectively resolve problems and challenges in their lives without direct guidance from others (i.e., social workers, therapists, well-meaning friends). Rogers originally conceived this approach as client-centered therapy but later renamed his ideas as *person*-centered theory to highlight their applicability to *all* interpersonal interactions, not just interactions between a client and a clinician. He applied his system to education, politics, and international conflict.

According to person-centered theory, everyone has a core motive that drives their behavior—that of striving for self-actualization. We are all seen as experts on our own lives and can all resolve our own problems, as long as our core needs are met. Rogers argued that the foundation for behavioral change for all people included authentic relationships, unconditional positive regard, and empathy. Person-centered relationships characterized by these core conditions (or facilitative conditions) are the primary determinant of the change process. This approach assumes that people have the resources to effectively develop—to become the person they desire to be.

In our relationships, we are not to exert power over another and assume that we know what is best for anyone. Person-centered theory suggests we approach our relationships as a partner and collaborator, rather than the expert. We are to provide an environment where those around us are emotionally and physically safe to fully engage with their own experiences—where they are safe to be themselves and be fully accepted just as they are. Social workers operating from a person-centered philosophy would give thoughtful attention to personal empowerment with individual clients. Self-determination, personal agency, and free will are of high priority in person-centered interaction.

Anti-Oppressive Approaches

Emerging in the late 1980s and 1990s, anti-oppressive practice has been informed by the writings of Black feminist authors and other formerly nondominant voices. Anti-oppressive practice is informed by a person-centered approach in that relationships are managed in an egalitarian way so as to minimize the effects of structural inequalities and minimize social hierarchies and power differentials (Dominelli, 1996). Anti-oppressive practice investigates how such difference and discrimination lead to social divisions. This approach to social work also shares many of the ideals of critical traditions (i.e., critical theories, feminist theories, anti-racist practices).

Anti-oppressive social work attends to social divisions (based on race, class, disability, sexual orientation, etc.) and structural inequalities. This approach recognizes that groups who hold power in society maintain the status quo by creating negative stereotypes of marginalized groups who tend to have social identities that are linked to devalued characteristics. Anti-oppressive practice would emphasize combating those actions by groups in power through promoting social equality regarding rights of citizenship and social justice. Social work practice informed by anti-oppressive theory would prioritize social change, challenging inequalities at both macro and micro levels.

Strier and Binyamin (2010, 2014) speak to the ways an anti-oppressive approach might shape social work practice at the organizational/institutional level. These include creating "non-hierarchical work relations between clients and social workers ... acknowledging unequal power relations with clients, creating a non-bureaucratic [organizational] culture, developing alliances with clients and critical consciousness among clients and workers, as well as promoting reflexivity between workers and clients" (Strier & Binyamin, 2014, p. 2097).

These theories and strategies are not comprehensive but collectively serve to provide a robust framework for justice-informed social work practice.

CONCLUSION

Engaging in justice-informed social work practice has to be an intentional endeavor. We must understand the marginalization, disenfranchisement, and oppression, as well as the associated effects that occur with many of our clients, in order to implement effective practice. This chapter introduced a brief review of theoretical and conceptual underpinnings of justice-driven practice as well as examined the manifestation of oppression, specifically as it relates to social workers seeking to engage in justice-oriented practice. Young's five faces of oppression (exploitation, marginalization, powerlessness, cultural imperialism, and violence) were applied to understand the effects of oppression on client systems. This chapter also addressed the role of bias in reinforcing stereotypes that perpetuate injustice and oppression. We argue that social workers must practice meaningful and systematic assessment of our biases in order to effectively engage in justice-driven practice. Other aspects that inform social work's response to oppression were identified as trauma-informed practice and the person in an environmental framework to conceptualize strengths, resources, and needs. Finally, critical, critical race, feminist, person-centered and anti-oppressive theories were offered as relevant theories that provide a framework to this work.

DISCUSSION QUESTIONS

1. Consider the emotional and physical toll that experiencing oppression might take.
   a. What might this be like for clients?
   b. Consider the range of responses to oppression, whether anger, hopelessness, lack of trust, and so on. What might this look like in working with a social worker? What can you expect to encounter?
2. How can oppression be considered to be traumatic?
3. Explain the value of understanding different theoretical approaches to experiences of marginalization and oppression.
4. Think about you personally engaging clients who have experienced adversity due to race or gender or intersecting identities.
   a. How would you go about exploring the impact of identities on someone's lived experience? What would you specifically say?
   b. How would you address resistance from a client who states, "What do you know about my life? How are you going to help me change anything?"
   c. What will your biggest challenges be in exploring oppression with a client?

REFERENCES

Only key references appear in the print edition. The full reference list appears in the digital product on Springer Publishing Connect: connect.springerpub.com/content/book/978-0-8261-3539-1/chapter/ch02

Blanchette, I., & Caparos, S. (2016). Working memory function is linked to trauma exposure, independently of post-traumatic stress disorder symptoms. *Cognitive Neuropsychiatry*, 21(6), 494–509. https://doi.org/10.1080/13546805.2016.1236015

Butler-Mokoro, S., & Grant, L. (Eds.). (2018). *Feminist perspectives on social work practice: The intersecting lives of women in the 21st century*. Oxford University Press.

Crenshaw, K. (1989, May). Demarginalizing the intersection of race and sex: A Black feminist critique of antidiscrimination doctrine, feminist theory and antiracist politics. *University of Chicago Legal Forum*, 140, 139–168. https://chicagounbound.uchicago.edu

Foster, J. (2018). Key feminist theoretical orientations in contemporary feminist practice. In S. Butler-Mokoro & L. Grant (Eds.), *Feminist perspectives on social work practice: The intersecting lives of women in the 21st century* (pp. 33–58). Oxford University Press.

Levenson, J. (2017). Trauma-informed social work practice. *Social Work*, 62(2), 105–113. https://doi.org/10.1093/sw/swx001

OUTPour LGBTQ Productions. (2020, July 7). *Dr. Mit Joyner saying thank you for all the congratulatory messages* [Video]. YouTube. https://www.youtube.com/watch?v=Jdye9JWQ5pY&feature=youtu.be

Strier, R., & Binyamin, S. (2010). Developing anti-oppressive services for the poor: A theoretical and organisational rationale. *British Journal of Social Work, 40*, 1908–1926. https://doi.org/10.1093/bjsw/bcp122

Williams, M. T., Metzger, I. W., Leins, C., & DeLapp, C. (2018). Assessing racial trauma within a *DSM-5* framework: The UConn Racial/Ethnic Stress & Trauma Survey. *Practice Innovations, 3*(4), 242–260. https://doi.org/10.1037/pri0000076

Young, I. (2004). Five faces of oppression. In L. Heldke & P. O'Connor (Eds.), *Oppression, privilege and resistance* (pp. 39–65). McGraw-Hill.

FRAMING SOCIAL WORK PRACTICE IN THE HUMAN RIGHTS CONTEXT

Emily Bergeron

LEARNING OBJECTIVES

Students will be able to:

- Understand the history and evolution of human rights in the international and national context as well as what constitutes a human right.
- Assess how human rights impact global and local problems.
- Analyze social work strategies based on existing policy and practice in the context of human rights.

INTRODUCTION

Human rights laws and ethics are accepted worldwide, not as aspirational but as defining what is fundamental to being human and legally protected as such. Human rights address inalienable rights to culture, nationality, education, participation in government, housing, sustainable income, privacy, and much more, without regard to someone's gender, ethnicity, religion, origins, language, or any other associated status. The principles of human rights are reflected in the value base of social work and the mandate to seek social, economic, and environmental justice in social work practice. Social work aligns with the principles of human rights through actively seeking and promoting well-being across all aspects of personhood. Human rights provide the foundation for an existence in dignity, and thus provide a foundation for justice-informed social work practice. Human rights are steeped in the notion that people are central to decision-making regarding their lives and that justice is central to the tenets of social work practice.

CASE—A GLOBAL PANDEMIC ILLUSTRATES THE NEED TO PROTECT HUMAN RIGHTS

When the world began to face the coronavirus disease 2019 (COVID-19) pandemic, a global public health crisis was created, one that experts had previously predicted. A U.S. Department of Defense pandemic influenza response plan identified a novel respiratory illness as the "most likely and significant threat" in a pandemic situation (Slotkin, 2020, para. 2). Despite this foreshadowing, COVID-19 became a pandemic of such scale as had not been seen since the influenza epidemic from a century before. Millions of individuals were infected and hundreds of thousands of lives were lost.

The public health crisis quickly resulted in simultaneous economic, social, and human rights crises. While national and international emergencies sometimes limit the exercise of certain human rights, the scale and severity of COVID-19 occurred at a level where global restrictions were justified on the grounds of public health. However, those restrictions and unintended consequences compounded the effects of the disease and resulted in tremendous human suffering. Future intentional planning, based on human rights principles, can shape better responses.

From the outset, the virus's far-reaching economic, social, and political consequences were devastating. The priority of the global response was to save lives, necessitating that countries adopt extraordinary measures imposed on their own citizens as well as those from other countries living or traveling within their borders. Extensive lockdowns were implemented to slow transmission of the novel virus and prevent medical systems from being overwhelmed. The human rights implications of the disease were vast. Equality and nondiscrimination, core human rights that apply at all times, were accentuated as the pandemic showed clearly how inequality and discriminatory practices are unacceptable yet still present and ultimately impact everyone involved.

HUMAN RIGHTS AS A FOUNDATION TO UNDERSTAND THE IMPACT OF THE PANDEMIC

While the virus may not discriminate, its impacts do, and these devastating impacts hit vulnerable populations with much greater aggression, painfully and fatally exacerbating long-standing inequalities for people of color, immigrant communities, Indigenous peoples, the differently abled, the incarcerated or detained, and low-wage workers across all sectors. These groups already face the considerable, cumulative impacts of environmental and climate risks as well as a perpetual state of sanctioned violence.

COVID-19 disproportionately infects and kills people already subjected to systemic racism and the denial of self-determination throughout the United States. Black, Latinx, and Indigenous peoples including American Indians and Alaska Natives have suffered from higher rates of hospitalization and death from COVID-19 than White persons. Age-adjusted hospitalization rates have been highest among American Indian, Black or African American, and Hispanic or Latinx populations at a rate of 3.7, 2.9, and 3.1 times higher compared to white, non-Hispanic persons. Deaths in these populations have been 2.4, 1.9, and 2.3 times higher respectively (Centers for Disease Control and Prevention, 2020). COVID-19 has also swept through detention facilities with over 100,000 cases in the first 6 months of the pandemic alone, where distancing measures are impossible and, as a result, already vulnerable detainees are more susceptible to the disease (The Marshall Project, 2020).

Beyond the United States, high-risk areas included high-density informal settlements and refugee, internally displaced people (IDP), and migrant camps where physical distancing is challenging and access to health services is severely limited, thus creating additional populations especially vulnerable to any disease, in particular, COVID-19 (Wehrli, 2020). The connection between experiencing prior injustices and the increased risks and impacts of COVID-19 is not a coincidence.

In an effort to limit exposure and protect healthcare systems, shutdowns restricted freedom of movement (an acknowledged human right) and, consequently, freedom to enjoy many other human rights. This in turn impacted people's livelihoods and security, access to healthcare (beyond that needed for COVID-19), food, water and sanitation, work, education, and even leisure. The economic impact of these shutdowns was immediately significant and seemingly intractable. Many of the most visible losses associated with policies put in place to contain the virus began with organizations canceling or postponing events involving large crowds and escalated to include forcing nonessential businesses to close temporarily. Businesses were forced to reduce hours or close, furlough, or lay off workers, and many would eventually close permanently.

The poor and the vulnerable are not only at greater risk from the virus itself, they are most severely impacted by the procedures to control it. Shelter-in-place measures had a disproportionate economic impact on the poorest and most vulnerable populations that cannot work from home and live at subsistence levels. These costs gain perspective when compared to the potential costs of allowing the virus to spread rapidly, which would not only include significantly greater loss of life but could also disrupt the labor force, reduce productivity, weaken consumer demand, and potentially disrupt the supply chains for food, medical supplies, and other necessities.

Unemployment rates have increased across major economies as a result. Further, the *Global Economic Prospects* predicted the long-term damage to economic growth as a 5.2% contraction in global Gross Domestic Product (GDP) in 2020, which is the most severe global recession in decades (World Bank, 2020). This recovery is long-standing and ongoing for individuals, communities, organizations, and nations.

Both unemployment (Aaronson & Alba, 2020) and food insecurity (United Nations [UN], 2020) skyrocketed in many countries within a very short space of time. Lockdowns have also resulted in limited access to food, school, work, and basic services. The closure of schools has interrupted the education of more than 1 billion children worldwide (Psacharopoulos et al., 2020) and compromised many families trying to balance work, family, and virtual classes. The abrupt closure of care institutions and health services for children has also increased children's vulnerability to violence, exploitation, and abuse (Kamenetz, 2020; Woodall, 2020) as well as reduced opportunities for reporting abuse as schools went virtual, limiting access of children to school-based, mandated reporters.

Women shouldered a disproportionate burden of the family care work that has resulted, with additional impacts on their own rights to health. Those confined to home with their abusers now lack access to harm-reduction services and shelters, potentially facing greater risk of violence and causing rates of violence in the home to rise (Graham-Harrison et al., 2020). Older persons faced higher infection and mortality rates, as well as isolation, abuse and neglect, discriminatory healthcare choices, greater exposure and poor treatment in residential care institutions, and ageist commentary from the media and public. The situation for persons with disabilities, especially those with underlying health conditions or in institutions, was particularly grave, since it made it harder for them to take prudent steps to protect themselves. The outbreak also threatened their independence and created problems in accessing healthcare and addressing basic necessities.

HEALTHCARE AS A HUMAN RIGHT IMPACTED BY COVID-19

The response to COVID-19 and the right to well-being mandate that there is a duty to protect human life by addressing the general conditions in society that threaten it. State responses that incorporate human rights thinking consider a number of issues in responding to the pandemic, including physical, mental, environmental, and economic health. The right to health is inherent in the right to life; therefore, everyone, regardless of their social or economic status, should have access to the healthcare they need.

The International Covenant on Economic, Social and Cultural Rights (1976) as well as the United Nations Universal Declaration of Human Rights ([UDHR], 1948), among others, recognize the fundamental right to access appropriate healthcare. Health-associated human rights also extend to underlying health determinants such as safe water and sanitation, adequate and nutritious food, stable and secure housing, healthy living and working conditions, and appropriate and adequate health information.

However, during the COVID-19 pandemic, healthcare systems around the world were overtaxed, with some at risk of collapse. Strong, resilient healthcare systems are best equipped to respond to pandemic crises like COVID-19. In the United States, underinvestment in health systems has weakened the ability to respond to this pandemic and to provide other essential health services. At odds again, and highlighted by the pandemic, is the premise of universal health coverage (UHC) seen in other countries as an imperative in a nation that embraces human rights but not yet adopted in the United States. The UHC approach has been shown to promote strong and resilient health systems that are able to reach those who are vulnerable, providing access for everyone without discrimination. Such a system addresses basic measures that contain the spread of the virus including, but not limited to, testing, specialist care for the most vulnerable, intensive care, and vaccinations when available, regardless of the ability to pay.

HOUSING AS A HUMAN RIGHT IMPACTED BY COVID-19

Human rights also looks at generations of housing discrimination and segregation that have resulted in systemic disinvestment in health infrastructure and resources, chronic poverty, and environmental racism. This includes everything from disproportionate exposure to air and water pollution to a lack of fair compensation and inequalities in job opportunities. Environmental justice issues play a significant role in the impact of the disease. Communities denied the right to adequate housing for reasons often grounded in racism and xenophobia have been subjected to the clustering of environmental and public health risks, creating sacrifice zones.

COVID-19 again highlights the issue of human rights as strategies to contain the virus are nearly impossible for those without adequate housing. Air and water pollution, limited access to hospitals, restricted food options, lack of paid sick leave, and overcrowded housing conditions that limit social distancing have resulted from community disinvestment. Factors like the lack of access to clean air and water, healthcare or paid leave, or safe and healthy food, transportation, housing, and workplaces have led to disproportionate impacts. Research has shown COVID-19 death rates to be significantly higher in areas of even slightly elevated long-term levels of fine particulate matter air pollution (Friedman, 2020). Further, for nearly 3 billion people in the world, regularly washing hands is not an option because they have inadequate access to water in their homes (Otto et al., 2020). For 1.4 million in the United States who are homeless or have inadequate, overcrowded housing, physical distancing is simply not possible (Maxmen, 2020).

A HUMAN RIGHTS APPROACH TO ADDRESSING A GLOBAL PANDEMIC

Responses to the pandemic that are shaped by and respect human rights, from ensuring healthcare for everyone and preserving human dignity, sustenance, and income, will result in better outcomes in addressing the impact of COVID-19. Further, focusing attention on who is suffering most and asking why and what can be done about it will also help the world emerge from the crisis with more equitable and sustainable communities. COVID-19 illustrates perfectly the concept that the disease and its prevention are not about personal liberty or freedom but rather about human rights and addressing the needs of all, not just the affluent.

OVERVIEW OF HUMAN RIGHTS

More than 70 years ago, the UN emerged as a response to the needs of a generation left damaged by the atrocities of World War II and the Great Depression and committed to never again allow such suffering to occur. In 1948, the UN released the language of the UDHR as a promise made by global leaders to recognize and address the fundamental rights and freedoms of all of humankind. Multiple international covenants, laws, and institutional systems have since continued to address civil, political, social, economic, and cultural rights, promoting and protecting human rights as well as the values and commitments that are their foundation. This common, global vision of what makes us human is intended to inspire the pursuit of a better world for current and future generations and to provide the foundation for all of social work practice.

While certainly gains have been made that provide safer, longer lives and dignity in living them, people continue to face major challenges, and violations of human rights continue to be widespread. Many of the clients whom social workers serve experience these challenges. Increasing incidents of hate speech, misogyny, exclusion and discrimination, social polarization, environmental degradation, and disparate access to resources and opportunities plague citizens across the globe as people deal with climate change, population growth, and rapid urbanization (Guterres, 2020). As governments, academic institutions, corporations, and individuals move forward in addressing the pandemic and future similar events, the decision-making framework based upon the sanctity of human rights becomes increasingly relevant.

A common narrative of the pandemic, meant to empower and unify, was "*we are all in this together.*" The ways in which governments and individuals responded help to shape our collective future. The COVID-19 crisis has revealed weaknesses that a human rights orientation can help repair; weaknesses in how public services are delivered and inequalities that impede access to them. Human rights thinking can help create a social work response to immediate priorities and development of prevention strategies for the future. This thinking must be the foundation not only for government action but also for the actions of social workers and others who are dedicated to providing the services necessary for achieving equity. The principles of human rights must inform social work practice.

Law in particular has been a primary method for protecting people from human rights abuses. Human rights legislation, treaties, and conventions as well as human rights commissions heavily populated by legal experts promote this bias that law is the arbiter of human rights. However, social work is a human rights profession—steeped in the notion that people are central to decision-making and that social justice should be central to all activities. Social workers should have a basic understanding of the origins, evolution, application, and limitations of human rights policies and principles in order to employ justice-informed practice.

WHAT ARE HUMAN RIGHTS?

Human rights are the values that shape norms in determining treatment of people. Human rights promote the dignity fundamental to being human, and include freedom from oppression, opportunities for fairly compensated work, and rights associated with an appropriate standard of living. These rights are universally accepted across the globe and serve to better the lives of all. Human rights acknowledge the relationships between "political, social, economic and cultural" aspects of life (Human Rights Institute, 2010, p. 3). Upholding the human rights principles ensures governments will respect and protect these rights (Human Rights Institute, 2010).

Human rights are those rights held by individuals by virtue of being human. These universal rights are based on the principle of respect for the individual and are shared equally by all people, regardless of gender, race, nationality, ability, age, religion, economic background, or other status. They ensure that people are protected against actions that interfere with their fundamental freedoms and dignity through human rights laws that have been stipulated in treaties and international law, as well as other sources of regulation. In order to achieve dignity, equality, and freedom, a broad range of rights, initially set out in the UN's UDHR, are protected, specifically placing an obligation on governments, in partnership with communities and practitioners, to respect and protect these rights for all individuals without discrimination. These human rights connect directly with the professional values and practice imperative of the social work profession.

The UDHR created the right to a life lived in freedom and safety. It prohibits slavery, torture, and unfair detainment and requires a right to a fair trial, including the presumption of innocence, and equal protection under laws regardless of nation of origin. Individuals are also entitled to a right to privacy as well as freedom to marry and have a family. The document also creates a right to a nationality and to take part in the government through democracy as well as freedom of movement. Communication is also protected through freedom of thought, expression, and public assembly. Finally, dignity is ensured with the right to affordable housing, medicine, education, food, childcare, and sufficient compensation for sustainable living. Each individual and nation is required to protect the rights and freedoms that should be shared by all people, rights grounded in the social work professional value of respect for the dignity and worth of every person. Human rights in application are not without limits. For example, the human right to free speech is limited by libel or slander. These rights, however, are universal, inalienable, indivisible, interrelated, and interdependent and provide the context for all of social work practice.

HISTORY OF HUMAN RIGHTS

The concept of human rights is often traced back to 539 BCE, when Cyrus the Great, the first king of ancient Persia, conquered Babylon (Finkel, 2012). Rather than enslaving the people or worse, he freed them and, among other rights, gave them the right to choose their religion and provided for racial equality. This decree was baked onto a clay cylinder with cuneiform script. The Cyrus Cylinder is often thought of as the first charter on human rights and has many parallels to the first Articles of the UDHR. From there, human rights ideals spread to India, Greece, and Rome where the concept of "natural law" arose, promoting notions of equality, justice, and the idea that justice is based on the inborn qualities of being human (Wronka, 1998).

Also considered significant in the evolution of the concept of codifying freedoms, the Magna Carta has been argued to have led to the creation of constitutional law in the English-speaking world. The Great Charter (as it was also known) was created in 1215 in response to King John of England's violation of ancient laws and customs by which the country had traditionally been governed (Linebaugh, 2008). The king's subjects mandated his signature on a document establishing what were essentially human rights including the right of the church to be free from governmental interference, the rights of all free citizens to own and inherit property and to be protected from excessive taxes. Women were considered in the document that established the right of widows who owned property to choose not to remarry. It also established principles of due process and equality before the law and included provisions forbidding bribery and official misconduct.

A nascent United States would also contribute significantly to the progression of human rights thinking. On July 4, 1776, the U.S. Congress approved the Declaration of Independence. The statement pronounced that the American Colonies were no longer a part of the British Empire and stressed the exercise of individual rights and the right of revolution, ideas that would spread rapidly across the globe. These rights asserted by the Declaration of Independence were followed by the nation's Constitution (1787) and subsequent Bill of Rights (1791), both of which defined the principal operations of American government and the legally protected, basic rights of citizens.

In particular, the Bill of Rights would limit the powers of the federal government in order to protect the rights of citizens, residents, and visitors in the American territory. The Bill of Rights protects freedom of speech, freedom of religion, the right to keep and bear arms, the freedom of assembly, and the freedom to petition. It also prohibits unreasonable search and seizure, cruel and unusual punishment, and compelled self-incrimination. It prohibits the government from depriving any person of life, liberty, or property without due process of law. In federal criminal cases it requires indictment by a grand jury for any capital offense or infamous crime, guarantees a speedy public trial with an impartial jury in the district in which the crime occurred, and prohibits double jeopardy, being charged for the same crime again after being acquitted for it already.

Many of these elements would appear again in the language of the UDHR. It is crucial to note, however, that the protections afforded to the people in the United States were very limited. Women, African Americans, and Indigenous Native Americans were provided little to no protection under these instruments, making the Declaration of Independence, Constitution, and Bill of Rights influential in the evolution of the ideas behind what are considered modern-day human rights, but not human rights instruments themselves as they failed to protect every human being equally.

UNITED NATIONS'S UNIVERSAL DECLARATION OF HUMAN RIGHTS

The UDHR emerged after World War II. In 1945, toward the end of World War II, cities across Europe and Asia were in ruins, millions of people were dead, and millions more were homeless or starving. As a result, delegates from 50 countries met in San Francisco to establish an international body whose mission would be to promote peace and prevent future wars. Thus, the UN was formed (Meisler, 2011). The UN established an Economic and Social Council (ECOSOC) to address economic and social needs while promoting the protection of human rights.

By 1948, the UN's new Human Rights Commission, under the dynamic leadership of the recently widowed Eleanor Roosevelt, drafted the UDHR. Resulting from the atrocities and loss of life during the war, the UDHR established for the first time universal protection for fundamental human rights. Rather than the idea of being equal before the law, people were granted the equal protection *of* the law, making common humanity, not citizenship or other legal status or social identity (e.g., gender or ethnicity), the basis of protection. This is an important distinction for social work practice as equality is rarely achievable nor is it commonly a practical goal. However, equal protection is, and often results in seeking equity in opportunities and resources, a hallmark of justice-informed social work practice.

Human rights law has gradually expanded to assert standards and protection for women, children, persons with disabilities, and other groups vulnerable to oppression and discrimination. The 1976 International Covenant on Economic, Social and Cultural Rights included protections regarding the rights to work in just and favorable conditions, to social protection, to an adequate standard of living, to the highest attainable standards of physical and mental well-being, to education, and to the enjoyment of benefits of cultural freedom and scientific progress. In 2006, the General Assembly created the Human Rights Council to replace the UN Commission on Human Rights.

WHAT CONSTITUTES A HUMAN RIGHT?

The history and evolution of these rights and the documents that support them provide an overview of what generally these conventions are intended to stand for. It still begs the question, however, what exactly is a human right? Not all "rights" are human rights. There are a number of things that people assert as rights (e.g., the right to smoke, which has unsuccessfully been claimed as a first amendment right in the United States); however, people often conflate their wants with rights. Human rights define the core legal status of the individual human—providing for protection against arbitrary government interference, preserving things like human life, bodily integrity, and physical freedom.

Human rights are predominantly seen as legal rights or state obligations. Rights generally exist to the extent that they are protected by the law; this represents a positivist approach to human rights where the norms and social influences are valued more than the merits of the law (Ife, 2014). For example, after the September 11, 2001, attacks on the United States, the U.S. government authorized the use of "enhanced interrogation techniques" on terrorism suspects in U.S. custody. However, the majority of Americans think that the interrogation techniques used on terrorism suspects after the September 11, 2001, attacks were justified, even though about half agreed that the treatment amounted to torture (Goldman & Craighill, 2014). This is an example of where the ends (safety, security) are seen as justifying the means (torturous interrogation techniques); such strategies are prohibited under numerous human rights conventions in addition to international law.

HOUSING AS A CULMINATION OF HUMAN RIGHTS

It is important to recognize that human rights are intersectional—for example, the rights to privacy and dignity overlap. Perhaps one of the clearest examples of the intersectionality of the various human rights is explained through the human right to housing. Home is more than just a place of shelter—where we live influences every aspect of our lives. Housing quality can impact physical health. Substandard housing can lead to lead poisoning, lack of access to clean water, asthma, and bodily injury, such as falls which are the leading cause for hospitalization among older adults. The cost burdens associated with housing reduce the income otherwise available for additional necessities like food and healthcare.

Physical neighborhood attributes like walkability, proximity to traffic and public transportation, access to green space, and potential food desserts impact mental and physical health, safety, and nutrition. Concentrated areas of poverty, environmental safety, and segregation concerns, as well as other social and community attributes, further contribute to stress and deterioration of health. Social workers must attend to the impact of location, which also influences individual and community identity, the quality and quantity of public services available and received, social networks, exposure to crime and violence, physical distance and isolation, and other stressors and contextual factors that are supportive of physical and emotional well-being.

Adequate housing as a human right is a widely recognized concept. The right is protected in Article 25 of the UDHR and is also included as an element of the UN Sustainable Development Goals. Goal 11 seeks to ensure urban communities are "inclusive, safe, resilient and sustainable" (para. 7) to address the shortage of adequate, affordable, and appropriate housing. Urban communities are expected to continue to grow in the next decade, particularly in Asia and Africa, exacerbating access to essential resources such as clean water and associated waste water management, potentially threatening public health (UN, 2015).

The profession of social work is intimately involved with human rights. When considering adequate housing as an example of human rights, social workers understand that housing is essential to human well-being and dignity and is intimately connected to the realization of other equitable necessities. These necessities of employment, health, education, exposure to violence, privacy, and social relationships are all significantly impacted by lack of access to adequate and available housing. Social work must see housing as a human rights issue, one that encompasses social, economic, and environmental justice. Lack of affordable housing forces already vulnerable groups to choose between meeting basic human necessities such as food, healthcare, or clothing and a place to live. There is a gap between human rights recognized on the international stage and the current housing and housing rights framework that exists in the United States, a disturbing notion in light of the country's wealth and economic power. Legislation protecting people against certain housing abuses do exist, and many battles have been waged in the courts. These laws are, unfortunately, inadequate to address the profound problems faced by so many people.

While housing is recognized as a universal human right, the U.S. government does not currently recognize a human right to housing and few advocacy organizations within the United States have attempted to address these issues using the international human rights framework. Further, the adoption of retrogressive laws and cuts in social and welfare benefits continue to erode the social safety net of those individuals in the greatest need. In many ways, this represents the crux of the challenge of justice-informed social work practice: we must seek justice within systems that do not always produce just results.

CASE STUDY 3.1—INTERSECTING NEEDS AND HUMAN RIGHTS

Eugenio is a 34-year-old who is on a temporary work permit for a job in the United States. Eugenio was recruited from Chihuahua where he was seeking employment and experiencing overwhelming poverty. He was provided transportation to the job location and was told that housing would be available as a result of his employment. Once he arrived, the manager kept Eugenio's documentation of his work visa and told him that it will be returned when the job is over. Eugenio shares a three-bedroom apartment with six other male employees and sleeps on the couch. He is lonely, misses his family, and is being told to speak English in the apartment so he can learn it more quickly. The apartment is owned by his employer and Eugenio's rent is taken out of his paycheck and is approximately a third of his overall paycheck. His travel expenses are also being deducted from his paycheck at $50 each check and he is uncertain when that will end. Eugenio's employer does not provide a paycheck but instead gives employees the options of a direct deposit into the bank or adding his biweekly paycheck to a declining balance on a Visa card. Eugenio does not have a green card and could not set up a bank account without his documentation, so he uses the Visa option. However, to be able to send cash home to his wife and support his family, Eugenio must pay 8% in fees to access the cash on the Visa card. He is happy to be working and able to support his family, but feels like his employer takes most of his paycheck for rent, taxes, and fees. Eugenio has considered looking for other jobs that would allow him to pay less rent but needs documentation of his legal status in the United States, and he does not have that because his employer is holding his work visa for him. Eugenio knows that as much as he is being taken advantage of in his employment situation, he thinks it is better than having no job and no income or ability to support his family.

There are a number of conflicting human rights concerns that Eugenio is experiencing. First, the overwhelming poverty that he is experiencing leads him to seek employment in a different country. He willingly traveled with no guarantees, no assurances, just the promise of income that would let him support his family. Additionally, the fact that his employer is holding his documentation is a concern. We would likely need more information to know if the housing and travel fees are appropriate but regardless, Eugenio does not feel they are. And while being encouraged to speak English may have had good intentions, the right to culture and language is a basic human right that feels compromised for Eugenio. He sees these as sacrifices that he is making in order to economically support his family. These compromises of intersecting needs and basic human rights are exactly what the UDHR attempts to address so that people can meet their needs while doing so within the human rights context.

ENVIRONMENTAL JUSTICE AS A CULMINATING EXAMPLE OF HUMAN RIGHTS

Human rights is also closely connected to the justice issue of environmental health. The constitutions of over 100 developing and developed nations have provisions for the protection of the environment for the sake of human life, creating human right entitlements to clean air, water, and soil (Jeffords, 2009). Although U.S. federal law exists to protect the environment and human health, U.S. law does not per se provide a legally enforceable human right to a clean environment.

Despite improvements in the nation's environmental protection framework, millions of Americans continue to live in unsafe and unhealthy physical environments, exposed to more significant health hazards in their homes, on the job, and in their neighborhoods than their more affluent counterparts (Bullard & Johnson, 2000). People of color, impoverished persons, and Indigenous Native Americans have borne greater environmental and health risks than society as a whole, meaning the same communities that face the burden of discriminatory practices also often live where they must bear a disproportionate burden of environmental problems. For social work, the concept of environmental justice sits at the intersection of human rights, infrastructure, and community.

The concept of environmental justice as a human right is based on the notion that environmentally hazardous sites, representing the worst of industry from toxic waste dumps to leaky pipelines, are more often situated in vulnerable communities. Further, these communities are more severely impacted by environmental problems due to the systemic issues associated with race and poverty. For example, people of color in the Northeast and mid-Atlantic live with substantially more air pollution, which has been found to increase incidents of lung and heart ailments, asthma, diabetes, developmental problems in children, and premature death. African Americans are exposed to 61% more pollution from burning gasoline emanating most typically from trucks in comparison to White individuals while Asian Americans are exposed to 73% more, and Latinx to 75% more (Holden, 2019).

One of the worst cases reflecting the disproportionate burdens of environmental contamination coupled with the political and legal failures in addressing these burdens is the health crisis created when Flint, Michigan, switched its water source, exposing nearly 100,000 residents to lead-tainted drinking water. Not only has the state failed to find any official accountable, but the Department of the Attorney General dropped all charges related to the investigation—including one involuntary manslaughter charge against a top health official. This intersectionality reflects the need for justice-informed social work practice; injustice can be perpetrated by the very systems designed to protect citizens.

HUMAN RIGHTS IN THE UNITED STATES

Despite the United States's founding documents being steeped in ideas that would lead to the UDHR, our country's history with human rights is complicated. The United States played a key role, for example, in the drafting of human rights treaties like the Convention on the Elimination of Discrimination Against Women and the Convention on the Rights of the Child (Human Rights Institute, 2012). However, neither of these have been ratified by our country. Further, expressions of support for human rights have repeatedly been made by U.S. politicians. Notably, President Franklin Delano Roosevelt's 1941 State of the Union stated that people everywhere are entitled to freedom of speech and expression, freedom of worship, and freedom from fear; President James Carter urged the country to respect human rights as a moral example to other nations; and President George H.W. Bush recognized the connection between democracy and human rights, noting the importance of providing global influence to ensure human rights principles were realized across international communities.

However, the United States has had contradictory behaviors toward human rights as we have signed, but not ratified, treaties on women's rights, children's rights, and the rights of persons with disabilities. Being a signatory, however, means only that the country will not actively contravene the treaty's object and purpose in comparison to actually enforcing those associated rights of children, women, and persons with disabilities.

The U.S. legal system has arguably failed to address mounting social and economic inequality, potentially attributable to the country's failing to adopt human rights thinking. Disparities in health, education, employment, and more persist across racial, economic, and gender lines, leaving one of the wealthiest countries in the world with some of the worst social indicators among countries that are part of the Organisation for Economic Co-operation and Development (OECD)—particularly failing with gender and racial disparities (Center for Economic & Social Rights, 2010).

The American public widely supports the notion that it is the government's responsibility to protect and provide human rights for people in the United States. Those efforts occur across federal, state, and local governments. Cities such as Pittsburgh, Washington, DC, Eugene, Carrboro, and Chapel Hill have all passed resolutions or proclamations recognizing and committing to human rights principles, adopting the title "human rights cities." Other places have sought to adopt certain provisions or conventions that exist at the international level or their own interpretation of human rights ideas. For example, resolutions in support of the Convention on the Rights of the Child were passed by Hawaii's House of Representatives and Los Angeles's City Council while Vermont and Connecticut created state-wide universal healthcare legislation reflective of human rights principles.

In addition to governments, global companies and transnational corporations have taken a role in the human rights narrative. These multibillion dollar entities exert significant enough power that the role of governments to shape economic and social actions has become just one form of enforcement, leaving democratic control more closely tied to spending than voting. Some companies, such as Patagonia and L'Oreal, have adopted corporate policies supportive of dealing with both the environment and human rights, recognizing that such an approach may ward off costly, time-consuming remediation, unhappy stakeholders, and angry (potentially boycotting) consumers. In this way, through their consumption and spending, consumers can express support for those companies with sustainable policies and practices reflective of human rights principles.

FROM THE FIELD 3.1

ENFORCING HUMAN RIGHTS

Many larger communities in the United States have established Commissions on Human Rights to protect residents. These commissions are seen as neutral parties that can investigate allegations of discriminatory practices related to hiring and employment, educational access, housing practices, and so on. Communities are essential in the pursuit of human rights since supporting and enforcing human rights must occur within the local context. Many communities have established commissions or similar agencies that are responsible for investigating allegations, educating businesses on implementing policies in a human rights context, and helping to mediate solutions when concerns or violations exist. An example of this is housing evictions. When a landlord sells a home that has an existing contract, or if a tenant fails to make timely payments, the eviction process is complicated. With housing as a recognized human right, the process of removing someone from housing must be compliant with existing law as well as hopefully within a social justice lens. Local Commissions on Human Rights are responses to help ensure that human rights are not usurped by policies and practices within the community and that citizens are treated fairly by those existing policies.

Social workers should be aware of the local and state agencies responsible for protecting human rights. These commissions can be allies in seeking justice for our clients and in implementing justice-informed social work practice.

HUMAN RIGHTS AS JUSTICE-INFORMED SOCIAL WORK PRACTICE

The principles of human rights, which address fairness, dignity and well-being, freedom from oppression, and access to opportunities, provide a powerful framework for social work practice. The social work profession recognizes the need for unilateral human rights yet readily acknowledges many of our clients fail to have those rights protected. Justice-informed social work practice must understand that human rights equates to human dignity, a core value of the social work profession.

The principle of human rights is also a mandated competency for all social work education programs. The Council on Social Work Education (2015) identifies "advancing human rights" (p. 7) as a competency that is integrally connected to social, economic, and environmental justice. A fundamental understanding of human rights is integral to social work education and subsequent practice, and must accompany an understanding of the policies and resources that exist in local communities, and must support social workers in identifying and meeting client needs.

The principles of human rights have also been used in advocating for client needs. Human rights are closely tied to civil rights, those rights afforded by the governing law, in comparison to human rights which are those afforded simply by being human. Social workers have used these shared values to seek change in the legal system related to the age at which juveniles can be charged as an adult. Human rights have been used to change city zoning laws to allow for more affordable, multifamily housing areas when those prior policies contributed to homelessness as a result of a lack of affordable housing. Examples in which social workers rely upon human rights to seek justice for our clients are numerous and inextricably linked to change advocacy.

Social workers advocate for protection based on the UDHR and must always include essential elements of human rights principles in assessing and identifying interventions with clients.

A few of these elements would include aspects of safety and security, adequate employment and/or income, housing, oppression, violence, and community and environmental supports such as access to appropriate food and clean water. Justice-informed social work practice can be attained only by ensuring these elements inform the process of identifying client needs, and subsequent interventions designed to identify requisite changes that must be addressed.

CONCLUSION

Human rights, their implementation, and interpretation have significantly changed since the UDHR in 1948 and will continue to evolve—likely at an accelerated rate—as issues like COVID-19 persist. Climate change is another significant, imminent challenge that the global community now faces and is likely one of the greatest threats to human rights of current generations. This force of man and nature will require communities to address issues ranging from forced migration to economic inequality in the crucial years ahead. While issues of human rights are most often considered as legal issues—this is after all where standards are created—it is at the level of the social work practitioner where the implementation of these principles must occur.

DISCUSSION QUESTIONS

1. In what ways do human rights intersect with social, economic, and environmental justice? Provide an example for each.
2. Think about your community's response to COVID-19. How did your community react to restrictions associated with civil rights (e.g., employment, restriction on travel, wearing masks, etc.)? How would you explain the variety of responses across the United States?
3. The United States has a complex relationship with human rights and the UN. What do you think might contribute to the United States supporting covenants but not ratifying them?
4. How can social workers use human rights to frame client needs?
    a. What allies might be brought into the role of advocacy when using human rights to implement justice-informed social work practice?

REFERENCES

Only key references appear in the print edition. The full reference list appears in the digital product on Springer Publishing Connect: connect.springerpub.com/content/book/978-0-8261-3539-1/chapter/ch03

Bullard, D., & Johnson, G. S. (2000). Environmentalism and public policy: Environmental justice: Grassroots activism and its impact on public policy decision making. *Journal of Social Issues, 56*(3), 555–578. https://doi.org/10.1111/0022-4537.00184

Center for Economic & Social Rights. (2010). *Visualizing rights: Fact Sheet No. 11: United States of America.* https://www.cesr.org/sites/default/files/USA_Web_final_0.pdf

Centers for Disease Control and Prevention. (2020, June 25). *COVID-19 in racial and ethnic minority groups.* Retrieved March 12, 2021, from https://www.cdc.gov/coronavirus/2019-ncov/need-extra-precautions/racial-ethnic-minorities.html

Friedman, L. (2020, April 07). New research links air pollution to higher coronavirus death rates. *New York Times.* https://www.nytimes.com/2020/04/07/climate/air-pollution-coronavirus-covid.html

Guterres, A. (2020). *The highest aspiration. A call to action for human rights.* United Nations.

Human Rights Institute. (2010). *State and local human rights agencies: Recommendations for advancing opportunity and equality through an international human rights framework.* Columbia Law School.

Meisler, S. (2011). *United Nations: A history.* Grove Press.

United Nations. (2015). *Sustainable development goals.* Retrieved September 6, 2020, from https://www.un.org/sustainabledevelopment

United Nations. (2020, June). *Policy brief: The impact of COVID-19 on food security and nutrition.* https://www.un.org/sites/un2.un.org/files/sg_policy_brief_on_covid_impact_on_food_security.pdf

Wronka, J. (1998). *Human rights and social policy in the 21st century: A history of the idea of human rights and comparison of the United Nations Universal Declaration of Human Rights with United States federal and state constitutions.* University Press of America and state constitutions. University Press of America.

4

POVERTY AS THE GREAT OPPRESSOR

Shiyou Wu

LEARNING OBJECTIVES

Students will be able to:

- Articulate poverty-related concepts and measures.
- Assess the consequences of poverty and the inequality of poverty across different populations.
- Recognize how social workers can respond to poverty and advocate for the poor at micro, mezzo, and macro levels.

INTRODUCTION

Although the United States is one of the richest countries in the world, poverty is still a pervasive social problem with significant, long-lasting consequences. Indeed, the right to a minimal standard of living is a universal human right. Social work has sought to address the causes and consequences of poverty since the beginning of the profession in the United States. Namely, social work's advocacy for social reforms has continually targeted the relentless effects of poverty. Social workers from across the globe actively play an important role in fighting poverty and mitigating its negative effects.

However, poverty is an extremely complicated concept (Carney, 1992), given its many domains, numerous causes, and multitude of consequences. This complexity is one reason poverty has been so intractable and resistant to intervention efforts. To address the complexity, first we must understand how poverty is defined.

DEFINITIONS OF POVERTY

There are many definitions of poverty. In a *general sense*, poverty connotes a living status or condition lacking the minimum standard of living needs such as shelter, food, healthcare, and safety (Bradshaw, 2007). Poverty thus defined is also called "absolute poverty." The United Nations (1995) defines absolute poverty as "severe deprivation of basic human needs" (p. 57). This definition of poverty is seen as *objective*, which means using statistical measures to indicate whether a person's total annual household income is under a given threshold, such as a poverty line (Bradshaw, 2007).

Using a *social* or *relative* definition, however, poverty implies "relative deprivation" (Valentine, 1968), which compares an individual's needs and situation to others at the same time and from the same society (Walker & Smith, 2002).

The definition of poverty can also be a *political act* in which those in power "neutralize the poor and disadvantaged" (O'Connor, 2001, p. 12). Solutions to poverty are typically identified in the political realm. In this way, poverty is always political, those who are impoverished have little power, political or otherwise, and decisions are often made without the consent or input of those experiencing poverty. Therefore, the definition of poverty includes not only individual, household, and societal components but also economic and political elements.

MEASURES OF POVERTY

A poverty line is often used as a measure of absolute poverty. In the United States, to determine whether a person is living in poverty, two factors are taken into consideration: household size and household annual income. Household size includes all the related number of adults and children in a family that live together. *Household annual* income includes the total household annual before tax, monetary income from all family members. Specific types of income (before taxes) are used to compute poverty status such as earning, unemployment compensation, and worker compensation. Other types of income such as capital gains, non-cash benefits (e.g., public housing subsidies, Medicaid, and food stamps), and tax credits (U.S. Census Bureau, 2019a) are not used to calculate income. Poverty thresholds vary by the total household size, household member age (e.g., children [<18 years] or elders [≥65 years]), and total household income (U.S. Census Bureau, 2019a).

The current U.S. official poverty thresholds are known as the federal poverty level (FPL) and were developed by Mollie Orshansky, a staff economist at the Social Security Administration in the mid-1960s (Fisher, 1997). Using a simplifying assumption and a "food-costs-to-total-expenditures procedure," Orshansky calculated the poverty thresholds by estimating the minimum cost of food for a hypothetical average (i.e., middle-income) family multiplied by three to cover the cost of all other nonfood expenditures (Fisher, 1992). The resulting poverty threshold calculation was then used to guide the determination of eligibility for certain federal subsidies and aid such as the Children's Health Insurance Program (CHIP), the National School Lunch Program, Food Stamps, Medicaid, and Family and Planning Services.

However, Orshansky's calculation of poverty thresholds considered neither the cost of child/medical care and housing, nor did it consider the significant geographical variation of these costs across the country, except for Alaska and Hawaii given the cost of living in these two regions is much higher (U.S. Department of Health and Human Services [U.S. DHHS], Office of the Assistant Secretary for Planning and Evaluation [ASPE], 2019). Given the limitations and the lack of applicability of the thresholds developed in the 1960s, economists and researchers are advocating for the development of a new poverty measure with a broader coverage of basic needs (Banerjee et al., 2006; National Research Council, 1995). These needs include food, clothing, shelter (including utilities), and limited other needs (e.g., personal care, transportation, and household supplies). Therefore, to address the main limitations of the current FPL discussed previously, the U.S. Census Bureau also reports a supplemental poverty measure each year to consider necessary expenses (e.g., child and medical care) and government welfare benefits (e.g., Women, Infants, and Children [WIC] and Food Stamps benefits), as well as to include the foster children and unmarried partners, and to consider the variation of housing costs from different regions (Haveman et al., 2015).

In addition, some welfare programs use different percentages of the FPL to allow expanded eligibility for more recipients. For example, the Supplemental Nutrition Assistance Program (SNAP; formerly known as "food stamps") uses gross monthly income under 130% of the FPL (USDA, 2019) and Medicaid uses 138% of the FPL as the threshold (HealthCare.gov, n.d.). The Premium Tax Credits and the Affordable Care Act insurance subsidies are also available to families whose gross monthly incomes are between 100% and 400% of the FPL (HealthCare.gov, n.d.).

Table 4.1 shows the U.S. poverty thresholds for 2019. Based on the size of the family unit and the number of related children under 18 years, families with total incomes below the corresponding poverty threshold can be considered to live in poverty (U.S. Census Bureau, 2019b). For example, in 2019, a family comprising two parents and two children has a poverty threshold of $25,926. However, a family of four without any related children has a threshold of $26,370.

CASE STUDY 4.1—COMPUTING A FAMILY'S POVERTY STATUS

Steps of Computing a Family Poverty Status

Situation: Family A has five members: two children, one mother, one father, and one grandmother.

Step 1: Determine the family's poverty threshold for that year.

The family's 2019 poverty threshold (see Table 4.1) was $31,275.

Step 2: Calculate the total family income for the same year.

Suppose the members' incomes in 2019 were:

- Child 1: $0
- Child 2: $0
- Mother: $9,000
- Father: $13,000
- Grandmother: $10,000

Thus, Family A's total income for 2019 was $32,000.

Step 3: Compare the family's total income with the poverty threshold.

The difference in dollars between family income and the family's poverty threshold is called the "Income Deficit" (for families in poverty) or "Income Surplus" (for families above the poverty threshold).

$$\text{Income} - \text{Threshold} = \$32{,}000 - \$31{,}275 = \$725$$

Conclusion

Since Family A's total income was greater than its poverty threshold, it is considered not "in poverty" according to the official definition.

SOURCE: U.S. Census Bureau. (2019). *How the Census Bureau measures poverty*. https://www.census.gov/topics/income-poverty/poverty/guidance/poverty-measures.html

Absolute Poverty and Relative Poverty. When poverty is defined using fixed standards or thresholds, such as the official U.S. poverty thresholds discussed previously, it is also called "absolute poverty" (Eskelinen, 2011). Most countries in the world use an absolute poverty threshold

TABLE 4.1 Poverty Thresholds for 2019 by Size of Family and Number of Related Children Under 18 Years

SIZE OF FAMILY UNIT	NUMBER OF RELATED CHILDREN UNDER 18 YEARS								
	NONE	ONE	TWO	THREE	FOUR	FIVE	SIX	SEVEN	EIGHT+
One person (unrelated individual):									
Under age 65	13,300								
Aged 65 and older	12,261								
Two people:									
Householder under age 65	17,120	17,622							
Householder aged 65 and older	15,453	17,555							
Three people	19,998	20,578	20,598						
Four people	26,370	26,801	25,926	26,017					
Five people	31,800	32,263	31,275	30,510	30,044				
Six people	36,576	36,721	35,965	35,239	34,161	33,522			
Seven people	42,085	42,348	41,442	40,811	39,635	38,262	36,757		
Eight people	47,069	47,485	46,630	45,881	44,818	43,470	42,066	41,709	
Nine people or more	56,621	56,895	56,139	55,503	54,460	53,025	51,727	51,406	49,426

SOURCE: U.S. Census Bureau. (2019). *Poverty thresholds.* https://www.census.gov/data/tables/time-series/demo/income-poverty/historical-poverty-thresholds.html

to measure poverty. Additionally, the World Bank uses an absolute poverty measure to estimate the global poverty rate by setting an absolute international poverty line (IPL). Beginning in 1990, to measure global extreme poverty, the World Bank used an income of $1 per day per person of purchasing power parities (PPPs) as its IPL for calculating extreme global poverty, and used an income between $1 and $2 per day per person as the means for calculating a moderate poverty rate around the world (Sachs, 2005; World Bank, 1990). In 2008, the World Bank raised the IPL from $1 to $1.25 a day at 2005 PPP rates (Ravallion et al., 2008). Almost a decade later in 2015, the IPL was further updated by using a daily per capita of $1.90 at 2011 PPP rates. This 2015 figure was taken by the World Bank as the new global absolute minimum living standard for measuring global poverty (Ferreira et al., 2016).

In contrast to the United States, many Eastern European Union (EU) countries (e.g., Bulgaria, Czech Republic, Estonia, Hungary, Latvia, Lithuania, Poland, Romania, Slovak Republic, and Slovenia; Feng & Nguyen, 2014) use a poverty threshold for calculating poverty rates called "relative poverty." This measure defines a family as living in relative poverty if the household income falls below a given cutoff point value (e.g., using 60% of the median income distribution in the EU as the threshold; Feng & Nguyen, 2014) of a country's overall income distribution.

Because relative poverty compares a family's poverty status relative to other members in the same social context, this approach to measuring poverty reflects the income inequality and social exclusion in a specific time and within a specific place (Marx & van den Bosch, 2007). This relative poverty measure is commonly used by many global organizations such as the United Nations Development Program (UNDP), the United Nations International Children's Emergency Fund (UNICEF), and the Organisation for Economic Co-operation and Development (OECD).

POPULATIONS AND THE CONTEXT OF POWER, OPPRESSION, AND PRIVILEGE

As one of the most pervasive and long-lasting social problems in the United States, millions of Americans face poverty as a fact of life. In 2018, about 38.1 million (11.8% of the total U.S. population) lived in poverty (Poverty USA, n.d.). There are wide disparities in the occurrence of poverty according to gender, geography, age, and racial/ethnicity due to the inequity of power, inclusion, and privilege for people from different social classes, origins, and identities (U.S. Census Bureau, 2018).

Specifically, women experience higher poverty rates than men. Additionally, Southern and Western states have higher average poverty rates compared to the Northeast and Midwest; children under the age of 18 have higher poverty rates than adults; and people of color (e.g., Black, Indigenous, and Latinx people) have higher poverty rates than White people (Chaudry et al., 2016; U.S. Census Bureau, 2018). This section focuses on the key characteristics of Americans defined as living in poverty. Table 4.2 demonstrates the trends in poverty across the past few generations and by gender, region, age, and race/ethnicity.

Poverty Rates in the United States

Based on the U.S. Census Bureau statistics (see Table 4.2), millions of Americans experience poverty every year. While poverty has been decreasing in recent years, the U.S. population has been increasing so that, from 1978 to 2018, the number of Americans living in poverty increased from about 24 to 38 million. In addition, about 17 million (5.3% of the total U.S. population) lived in extreme poverty (under 50% of the FPL) in 2018.

Who Is Poor in the United States?: A Snapshot of 2018

Around 12.9% (21.4 million) women lived in poverty. As shown in Table 4.2, the data demonstrate that from 1978 to 2018, females experienced higher poverty rates than males. In 2018, approximately 16.8 million (10.6%) males lived in poverty, a staggering 4.6 million less than American females in the same situation. Further, the U.S. Census Bureau (2018) statistics show that there appear to be no differences in the poverty rate between female and male children (<18 years; same poverty rate of 16.2%). However, adult females (18–64 years; 12.3% vs. 9.0%) and senior females (>64 years; 11.1% vs. 8.1%) have higher poverty rates than their male counterparts.

Poverty disproportionately affects women in the United States, which is also known as the "feminization of poverty" (McLanahan & Kelly, 2006; Pearce, 1978; Starrels et al., 1994). McLanahan and Kelly (2006) summarized three possible explanations for the feminization of poverty in the United States: First, changes in the family, including the delay in the age of first marriage for both men and women, can contribute to increased poverty among women. The increasing divorce rates along with the decreasing marriage rates have also resulted in higher poverty for women as single women have a higher risk of being poor than single men. The rising numbers of children born outside marriage have resulted in more single mothers at higher risk of living in poverty. The increasing numbers of one-person (or nonfamily) households and the increases in life expectancy have also contributed to women having higher rates of poverty.

Second, women on average make 81 cents for every dollar that a man makes (Sheth et al., 2020) when comparing similar experiences, qualifications, and so on. Even with changes in the

TABLE 4.2 **Poverty Rates in the United States (1978–2018)**

		1978	1988	1998	2008	2018
Overall	100% Federal Poverty Level	11.4	13.0	12.7	13.2	11.8
Gender	Male	9.6	11.5	11.1	12.0	10.6
	Female	13.0	14.5	14.3	14.4	12.9
Region	Northeast	10.4	10.1	12.3	11.6	10.3
	Midwest	9.1	11.4	10.3	12.4	10.4
	South	14.7	16.1	13.7	14.3	13.6
	West	10.0	12.7	14.0	13.5	11.2
Age	<18	15.9	19.5	18.9	19.0	16.2
	18–64	8.7	10.5	10.5	11.7	10.7
	>64	14.0	12.0	10.5	9.7	9.7
Race/ethnicity	White, non-Latinx	7.9	8.4	8.2	8.6	8.1
	African American	30.6	31.3	26.1	24.7	20.8
	Asian and Pacific Islander	–	17.3	12.5	11.6	9.8
	Latinx	21.6	26.7	25.6	23.2	17.6

SOURCE: U.S. Census Bureau. (2018). *Historical poverty tables: People and families—1959 to 2019.* https://www.census.gov/data/tables/time-series/demo/income-poverty/historical-poverty-people.html

economy, such as increasing female participation in the labor force, with earnings below that of their male counterparts, income opportunities remain limited.

Third, changes in public benefits occurred that resulted in a reduction of benefits for women who become divorced, single, or reach retirement age. As safety nets for families, particularly single mothers, were eliminated, benefits have been reduced such as limiting Temporary Assistance for Needy Families (TANF) to a maximum of 5 years in comparison to prior benefits which were not time restricted.

Approximately 13.6% (16.8 million) of people from the South lived in poverty. Overall, the Southern states have had the highest poverty rates, followed by the West (see Table 4.2). Historically, the Midwest and the Northeastern states were among the lowest poverty rate regions, while historically and geographically the Southern states included a number of severe poverty clusters including the Southeastern Cotton Belt, the Mississippi Delta, and the central Appalachia regions (Partridge & Rickman, 2006; Figure 4.1). People from these areas often experience higher poverty rates concomitant with poor health, lower levels of educational attainment, high unemployment rates, high crime rates, and poor public schools. In addition, the negative effects of urban sprawl in Southern regions exacerbate poverty (Jung, 2009). In these areas, racial discrimination, gentrification of urban areas, and reduced educational and economic opportunities increase poverty (Bullard et al., 1999; Colby, 2006; Dalaker, 2001; DeNavas-Walt & Proctor, 2014; Wiewel & Schaffer, 2001).

Around 16.2% (11.9 million) children lived in poverty. As can be seen from Table 4.2, between 1978 and 2018, children (<18 years) experienced the highest poverty rates by age. Historically, senior citizens (>64 years) experienced higher poverty rates than adults (18–64 years). However, since 1993 this situation has been reversed. Adult groupings, on average, have experienced higher poverty rates than seniors. In 2018, nearly one child in every six lived in poverty, whereas about 21.1 million (10.7%) adults, and 5.1 million (9.7%) senior citizens lived in poverty.

Statistics and research also show that children of color, immigrant children, children from single-mother families, and children whose parents had lower educational levels experience disproportionately higher poverty rates (Chaudry et al., 2016; Koball & Jiang, 2018; McCarty, 2016; Tienda & Haskins, 2011). To illustrate, in 2016 children of color experienced an estimated poverty rate three times higher than White children (Koball & Jiang, 2018). Moreover, according to the 2014 American Community Survey data, McCarty (2016) found that Latinx children had even higher poverty rates (4.9 million) compared to Black children (3.9 million). One possible explanation for this is the rapid growth in recent years of immigrant children, the majority of whom are Latinx, with nearly 40% coming from Mexico alone (Hanson et al., 2014; McCarty, 2016). It should also be noted that previous research has frequently found that many children experience intergenerational poverty, that is, children from low-income families often inherit their parents' poverty status due to the lasting effects of social, economic, and environmental deprivation as they grow up (Bird, 2013; Sharkey, 2008; Wagmiller & Adelman, 2009).

Figure 4.2 examines poverty by age group, again illustrating the increased rates of poverty for children under age 18.

Around 20.8% (8.9 million) Black Americans lived in poverty. According to the U.S. Census Bureau statistics from 1978 to 2018, people who are Black had the highest poverty rates across racial/ethnic groups over time. Latinx group had slightly lower poverty rates than African Americans, but with a larger overall population living in poverty. The majority of those living in poverty were White (15.7 million or 8.1%) although by proportion, Black people had the higher percentage in poverty as about 8.9 million (20.8%) were impoverished compared to 10.5 million (17.6%) Latinxs, and 2.2 million (9.8%) Asian and Pacific Islanders.

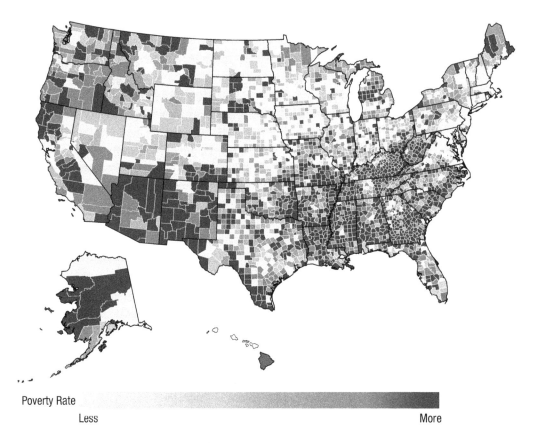

FIGURE 4.1 2018 U.S. poverty rates by regions.

SOURCE: Reproduced with permission from Poverty USA. (2018). *2018 U.S. poverty rates by regions*. https://www.povertyusa.org/data/2018

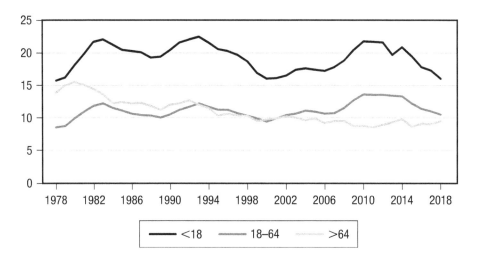

FIGURE 4.2 Poverty rates by age groups from 1978 to 2018.

SOURCE: U.S. Census Bureau. (2018). *Historical poverty tables: People and families—1959 to 2019*. https://www.census.gov/data/tables/time-series/demo/income-poverty/historical-poverty-people.html

Gradín (2012) found that people of color generally have higher poverty rates due to more dependent children, lower levels of education, and lower labor force participation. Other work in this area found racial segregation to be positively related to concentrated poverty, meaning that the incidence of poverty is highly concentrated in specific neighborhoods (Iceland & Hernandez, 2017). Research also suggests that the increasing number of immigrants (e.g., Latinxs) contributes to higher poverty rates among people of color (Elmelech & Lu, 2004).

CASE STUDY 4.2—ARIANA'S STORY

Ariana (24 years old) is a Latinx single mother with two children from Phoenix, Arizona. Her parents were originally from a poor town in Nogales, Mexico. They came to the United States for the first time after they got married. They arrived legally using a tourist visa and then they decided to stay in the United States as undocumented migrants because they wanted to find jobs and have a better life.

Two years later, Ariana was born as a U.S. citizen. She grew up in a Latinx community in Phoenix. When she was young she could speak only Spanish. She started to learn English after she went to kindergarten, which was a transitional bilingual kindergarten offering both Spanish and English in the Latinx community where she grew up. The majority of Ariana's classmates and friends were Latinxs.

She dropped out from high school when she found out that she was pregnant with her first child. The child's biological father left her when he found she was pregnant and moved to another state. Ariana raised her child with the help of her parents.

Ariana got married when she was 22 years old and gave birth to another child a year later. Recently she became divorced because her husband was a drug abuser who also abused her. Ariana has worked as a cashier, a dishwasher, a food preparation assistant, and a waitress in a Mexican restaurant. Now she works as a housekeeper because the job is more flexible. Her income is approximately $1,800 a month now.

Imagine that you are a social worker from an agency that provides services to Ariana's community. Consider the following questions:
- Is Ariana living in poverty?
- From individual, peer, family, community, and societal and structural levels, evaluate the potential barriers contributing to Ariana's current life status.
- What strengths exist that could assist Ariana in changing her life circumstances?

MAGNITUDE AND SCOPE OF POVERTY

In general, poverty is linked to adverse living conditions such as homelessness, unsafe neighborhoods, substandard housing, food insecurity, malnutrition, poor education, unemployment, illness, disability, and lack of access to healthcare (Cohen et al., 2017; Kim & Chan, 2013; Torpy et al., 2007). Several theories can be used to help us better understand poverty from the individual, cultural, and structural perspectives. In this section, we review poverty theories, including the effects and consequences of poverty.

Theories of Poverty

A variety of theories have been used to explain poverty, especially why the United States has such a high poverty rate. The first one—now largely disenfranchised—suggests that the poor themselves are to blame, attributing "inferiority ... or bad personal choices" (Eitzen & Smith, 2009, p. 13) as the cause of poverty. Individual theories of poverty argue that individual deficiencies cause poverty because the poor do not work hard or make poor life choices (Bradshaw, 2007). People who follow this line of thought often use Social Darwinism to explain why some people are rich and some people are poor. Basically, Social Darwinism purports that people need to compete for status and wealth, with the best and the brightest being the upper social class whereas the weak fall to the bottom levels of society. This perspective—characteristic of Nazi Germany in World War II—also argues that people who are unhealthy or disabled must make room for fitter people (Eitzen & Smith, 2009). This theory is not acceptable as a scientific explanation for poverty but does still have some social gravitas, meaning many still believe it.

The second perspective on poverty is based on the concept of culture. The culture of poverty theory suggests that poverty arises because of lifestyles that reduce productivity, such as having an inability to delay gratification through a strong present-time orientation resulting in a lack of planning for the future. Additionally, according to this view, subcultures of children who grow up in a poor community may develop the feelings and beliefs of marginality, helplessness, and dependence, which in turn make it hard for them to escape poverty as adults (Asen, 2002; Eitzen & Smith, 2009; Murray, 1984). The culture of poverty as a theory has been challenged as well and does not acknowledge those who have not persisted in a generational cycle of poverty nor does it acknowledge the systemic and structural discrimination which can serve to maintain people in the cycle of poverty rather than support changes.

The third theory of poverty is structural in nature. Instead of individualizing the causes of poverty, structural theory suggests that poverty derives mainly from economic, political, and societal factors. From this perspective, poverty exists because of inequalities and discrimination in society—structural factors—that limit resources and opportunities for some people (Bradshaw, 2007; Eitzen & Smith, 2009). Specifically, the economic structure of poverty indicates that the capitalist system accelerates inequality in the economic system. The U.S. labor market has a minimum wage and labor unions to ensure everyone gets fairly paid and lives above the poverty line, but a low minimum wage and weakened labor unions create the same structural forces that produce poverty (Brady, 2009; Russell, 2011).

At the political level, the government does not spend enough on social welfare—such as income supports, public housing, childcare subsidies, and national health coverage—to counterbalance structural inequities. In the United States, high poverty rates are also partially due to the ineffectiveness of governmental public policies, such that many impoverished people cannot secure sufficient resources and opportunities to get out of poverty (Block et al., 2006). At the societal level, society does not provide equal opportunities for all citizens in terms of education, jobs, healthcare, and incomes. For example, in the United States, because of societal barriers (e.g., social class, location, gender, and racial/ethnicity), some groups such as Black people and women are more likely to be unemployed, to be paid less, and to fail to be promoted in the labor market, which causes disproportionately high poverty rates among these groups.

Consequences of Poverty

Living in poverty has direct and indirect, short-term and long-term consequences. In addition, the sequelae of poverty are often reciprocal and interrelated. For example, numerous studies have found people living in poverty are more likely to experience adverse conditions such as homelessness, unsafe neighborhoods, food insecurity, and inadequate healthcare (Andrews et al., 2000; Coleman-Jensen et al., 2014; McBride Murry et al., 2011; Nunez, 1996; Smith et al., 2000), and therefore they are more likely to have health, mental health, and behavioral health problems (Moore et al., 2009; Wu, Wang, et al., 2018).

Poverty traps many families and their offspring in a cycle of adversities. For example, people living in poverty often have a higher prevalence of infectious and chronic diseases, child mortality, and maternal health issues (Raphael, 2011; Spencer, 2008). In addition, poverty, especially the stigma of poverty, negatively affects mental health (e.g., depression; Mickelson & Williams, 2008; Reiss, 2013; Wu, 2017; Wu, Wu, et al., 2018). Impoverished children often have lower self-esteem and confidence, and feel stress, anxiety, and fear being bullied by richer peers (Hooper et al., 2007; Ridge, 2002, 2005, 2009). Research also found that poverty is highly related to poor behavioral health outcomes, such as substance abuse, criminal offending, and criminal victimization (Brill, 1993; Ceccato, 2017; Kramer, 2000; Lee, 1996; Smyth & Kost, 1998; Wu et al., 2016; Zerden et al., 2019).

As one of the most vulnerable populations, children who are raised in poverty are at higher risk for poor academic achievement and school dropout, as well as short- and long-term problems in the areas of behavioral, psychosocial, physical, and mental health (Brooks-Gunn & Duncan, 1997; Casey et al., 2004; Smith et al., 2000; Wu, 2017; Wu, Fraser, et al., 2018; Wu et al., 2020). We should note that all of these risks contribute to poor economic outcomes as adults.

Brooks-Gunn and Duncan (1997) conducted a review of studies to identify the effects of poverty specific to child outcomes. They analyzed six large, nationally representative data sets to compare the outcomes of children (birth–17 years) from poor and nonpoor households while controlling for other family characteristics (e.g., gender of household head, mother's age and education). The results showed that as compared with their nonpoor counterparts, children from poor families had worse outcomes, especially in the domains of physical health, behavioral health, cognitive development, and academic achievement. Specifically, living in poverty contributed to poor physical health outcomes, which were measured using indicators of chronic asthma, low birth weight, the incidence of lead poisoning, and growth stunting. Brooks-Gunn and Duncan (1997) also found that poor children had worse cognitive outcomes (e.g., developmental delays and learning disabilities) as well as worse emotional and behavioral outcomes. In turn, these poor outcomes contributed to the finding that children living in poverty have lower academic achievement, including higher rates of grade repetition, expulsion, and high school dropout rates. Additionally, Brooks-Gunn and Duncan (1997) found children living in poverty had other poor outcomes such as elevated rates of adolescent pregnancy, single parenthood, inability to maintain employment by the age of 24 years, and food insufficiency. The long-term consequences of poverty are devastating for children and can serve to maintain the cycle of poverty. Social workers must know these consequences in order to address the causes and preempt the consequences.

Poverty Alleviation Through Policy in the United States

In response to high poverty rates, the U.S. federal government has a long history of implementing policies and programs aimed at assisting impoverished and low-income people in meeting basic needs. These programs are often referred to as the "social safety net." Most U.S. government welfare programs are means-tested programs, meaning individuals must qualify based upon meeting established minimum income or asset levels. These programs provide cash assistance, food resources through Supplemental Nutrition Assistance Program (SNAP) and others such as the free breakfast and lunch programs, educational assistance, vocational training, medical assistance, childcare and development, and other social services for the poor. The social safety net also includes programs covering workers' compensation as well as unemployment insurance. In addition, the social safety net includes some universal or unconditional benefits such as the social security retirement income, Medicare, veterans' healthcare, and access to public education.

In 2012, approximately 21.3% (52.2 million people) of the U.S. population participated in one or more of these welfare programs each month (Irving & Loveless, 2015; U.S. Census Bureau, 2016), and Markus et al. (2013) found that Medicaid paid for half of all U.S. births. In total, about 67.9 million Americans are receiving some form of governmental welfare benefits, which includes about 41.2 million recipients of SNAP, 10.2 million recipients of unemployment insurance, 7.7 million recipients of housing assistance, 4.3 million recipients of TANF benefits, and 4.5 million recipients of other types of general welfare benefits. In addition, about 70.5 million people were enrolled in Medicaid (Statistic Brain Research Institute, 2016). In 2012, children represented approximately 75% of TANF recipients; about half (50.9%) of these TANF families had one child, 26.9% had two children, and 20.3% had three or more children (U.S. DHHS, 2014).

Means-tested programs. Means-tested programs provide benefits conditioned on specific criteria (e.g., federal poverty line) to determine whether a person or family is eligible to receive the benefits. Back in the 1930s, President Franklin Roosevelt proposed a series of New Deal programs that ushered the nation into the era of the modern welfare state (Moffitt, 2015), with its unique melding of democracy, welfare, and capitalism (Marshall, 1950). The New Deal aimed to create a safety net of programs to improve the lives of those suffering the effects of the Great Depression. These programs focused on high rates of unemployment (about 25%), food insecurity and hunger, inability to afford medical care, and poor housing and homelessness. Specifically, the Social Security Act of 1935 (Public Law 74-271) was enacted to provide general welfare to needy populations (e.g., older adults, the blind, and dependent children).

In the decades that followed, this Act and its subsequent amendments served as a catalyst for the expansion of welfare coverage and eligibility (e.g., the Medicare program of 1965 that provides medical insurance to adults 65 years and older). The design and development of various federal welfare programs serve as meaningful milestones for charting the process of establishing the modern-day U.S. welfare system.

Title IV of the 1935 Social Security Act created the federal assistance or "welfare" program known as Aid to Families with Dependent Children (AFDC). AFDC was administered through

CASE STUDY 4.3—DO YOU KNOW?

Harry Hopkins (1890–1946) was appointed as the director of the New York State Temporary Emergency Relief Administration by then governor but soon to be president, Franklin Roosevelt. As a social worker, Hopkins brought the ideology of relieving unemployment through federally sponsored programs such as those that built bridges, hospitals, and schools across the country as a means of employing Americans while building much needed infrastructure. As one of the engineers of the New Deal, Hopkins continued in his advisory role with President Roosevelt throughout World War II. Hopkins exemplifies how social workers conceptualize the role of policy in poverty alleviation (Encyclopaedia Britannica, n.d.).

Harry Lloyd Hopkins

the U.S. DHHS, and was designed to provide cash welfare payments to children who did not have parental support due to the parents' absence from the home, death, disability, or unemployment (U.S. DHHS, ASPE, 2009). Over time, eligibility restrictions evolved, which led to dramatic increases in the number of welfare recipients. AFDC had no time caps, and reliance on welfare became a way of life for some families (Maynard et al., 1998). AFDC operated until 1996, when President Bill Clinton signed the Personal Responsibility and Work Opportunity Reconciliation Act (PRWORA; Public Law 104-193), that created the current TANF mode. TANF shifted the U.S. social welfare policy from "welfare" to "workfare"; that is, changed from a program of unconditional means-tested cash assistance to a program requiring work participation or participation in job-training programs. TANF introduced other reforms such as lifetime participation limits which are federally capped at 5 years lifetime assistance with some states capping assistance at 2 years.

Healthcare programs. Welfare programs, particularly health-related welfare programs, play important roles in the lives of vulnerable, impoverished populations. Healthcare programs are designed to allow the economically disadvantaged and other vulnerable populations to have access to basic healthcare. Healthcare systems take many forms around the world. Different from most of the developed countries that have implemented systems of universal access (i.e., providing all citizens access to basic medical care), the U.S. healthcare is based on a fee-for-services model with payment through a third-party (i.e., insurance, which can include Medicaid or Medicare) or out-of-pocket payment by patients without insurance. Federal healthcare spending is targeted at those who are impoverished and older adults. Historically, middle- and working-class Americans relied on healthcare insurance that was available through their employers (Garfinkel et al., 2010), but the escalating cost of insurance has led many employers to curtail or eliminate this benefit. The costs of healthcare through employer-provided health insurance are considerably higher than the costs of equivalent care through a universal healthcare system. In fact, although the United States spends more on healthcare than any other nation, the financial investment in healthcare still yields health disparities within the United States as well as in comparison to countries with differing healthcare system approaches.

The U.S. system of healthcare has led to high rates of uninsured or underinsured people who have to forego or delay needed medical care because they are unable to afford the cost (Baribault & Cloyd, 1999). To be sure, providing all people with access to healthcare while controlling costs is a complex and difficult issue. Across the globe, healthcare systems have advantages and disadvantages. Since the inception of the first income-assistance and medical care programs in America, the debate among researchers and politicians has been ongoing regarding the optimal design of health and social welfare programs.

Statistical data from Western countries have shown welfare programs such as old-age pensions and unemployment compensation have been effective in helping some of the most vulnerable to maintain a basic standard of living when they become too old to continue in the workforce or face temporary unemployment (Piven & Cloward, 1993). In the United States, healthcare-related welfare programs such as Medicaid and CHIP through Medicaid provide health insurance to more than 70 million economically disadvantaged or disabled Americans (Centers for Medicare & Medicaid Services [CMS], 2017). A centerpiece of the 2010 Patient Protection and Affordable Care Act (2010) was the expansion of health coverage through Medicaid and CHIP. Although only 31 of 50 states chose to expand Medicaid, this expansion reduced the percentage of uninsured Americans from 16% in 2010 to 8.9% in 2016 (CMS, 2017). At this time, the Affordable Care Act is in jeopardy, and if the Congress repeals the Act or the courts find it unconstitutional, millions of Americans who have access to affordable health coverage are likely to lose that care.

The total federal and state government spending on all the welfare programs in 2011 was about $1.03 trillion (U.S. Senate Budget Committee, 2012). However, despite spending over $1 trillion each year on more than 126 welfare programs to fight poverty, these antipoverty programs have been ineffective in reducing poverty rates (Tanner, 2012), and the current U.S. poverty rate remains one of the highest among developed countries (OECD, 2017). In fact, the U.S. poverty rate has remained higher than 10.5% since 1964 when President Lyndon B. Johnson declared an "unconditional war on poverty in America" (Johnson, 1964, §III, para. 2).

In the two decades since the 1996 welfare reforms, the United States has reached new highs for both national and child poverty rates (Proctor et al., 2016). The data suggest that antipoverty policy in the United States has failed to have a sustainable effect. In addition, an increasing number of studies have found strong associations between participating in welfare programs and risk factors, such as being overweight and/or obesity (Baum, 2011); marginalized and unsafe neighborhoods (Massey et al., 1991; Oreopoulos, 2003); and elevated exposure to crime (e.g., high crime rates in public housing units; Oreopoulos, 2003). In addition, the social stigma of receiving welfare can lead to higher rates of depression in individuals and higher rates of tension in communities with marked disparities in wealth or access to resources (Morton, 2014).

ROLE OF SOCIAL WORK TO IDENTIFY UNMET SYSTEMIC NEEDS

Relying on existing governmental welfare programs is not sufficient to be above the poverty line. As a helping profession, social work arose from efforts to address poverty and the vulnerabilities that it creates (Stuart, 2013). The core mission of the social work profession reflects the commitment to addressing poverty, stating social work must seek to improve well-being and empower individuals, in particular those who are "vulnerable, oppressed, and living in poverty" (National Association of Social Workers [NASW] Code of Ethics, 2017). The Council on Social Work Education (CSWE, 2015, p. 5) further affirms that mission, stating the social work profession seeks social and economic justice through "elimination of poverty," thus enhancing well-being for individuals and the communities that support them.

To address poverty and its related issues, social work was formally and professionally developed in the United States in the late 1800s and early 20th century. Several periods or threads of activity characterize the profession's development and growth. In the latter part of the 19th century, derived largely from the industrialization of American society, many social problems emerged in the urban cities. These social problems included unemployment, child abuse, child neglect and abandonment, chronic disability, immigration, juvenile delinquency, and poverty. To address the contradiction of the overwhelming poverty despite the "productive and prosperous economy" (Stuart, 2013, p. 1), the charitable organization society (COS) movement and the settlement house movement jointly contributed to the development of social work as a helping profession.

These two movements advocated for social reforms, especially for the poor and for poor children (Lundblad, 1995). For example, social work pioneers including Jane Addams and Ellen Gates Starr initiated in Chicago the first U.S. settlement house, Hull House, in 1889. In contrast to COS, Addams recognized that the social environment was the main reason why so many people were trapped in poverty. She argued for social structural change and reform, not simply reinforced moral teachings that were the hallmark of the COS (Lundblad, 1995). The aims of Hull House, which is located in Chicago, were to "improve conditions in industrial districts" through incorporating civic and social engagement and educational opportunities, particularly for children (Addams, 1912, p. 112).

By 1920, the number of settlement houses had increased to nearly 500 in the United States (Johnson, 2004). From Hull House and other reforms of the era (e.g., the start of juvenile courts in 1899 in Chicago), social work expanded its scope and purview of service and began to focus on many other problems facing children and families.

As poverty became widespread in the late 1920s to 1930s, due to the market crash and economic collapse of the Great Depression, the social work profession refocused on poverty. Public agencies offered unemployment and supported work assistance services (Swift, 1934). Along with the enactment of the Social Security Act (1935), welfare systems were expanded, providing job opportunities for social work graduates working in federal and state welfare systems across the country. Today, large numbers of social workers continue to be employed by federal and state agencies.

After World War II, the social work profession shifted its main focus from poverty to mental health, due to the high demand for inpatient and outpatient mental health services for veterans and others. However, poverty became the main focus of the social work profession again in the 1960s, with the enactment of the 1963 Public Welfare Amendments to the Social Security Act (PL 87-543) by the Kennedy administration. These amendments utilized federal funds for programs identified and implemented at the state level, as well as increased educational opportunities for social workers who were then to be employed in state public welfare programs in addition to providing funds for state employees to become educated as professional social workers (Stuart, 2013).

Within welfare systems, social workers provide therapeutic and case management interventions (Gates et al., 2017). These interventions, though probably helpful, were still not seen as effective in changing the direct financial circumstances of poor people (Eamon et al., 2012; Gates et al., 2017; Hawkins, 2005; Krumer-Nevo et al., 2009). Since 1994, Michael Sherraden, founder of the Center for Social Development (CSD) at the Brown School of Social Work at Washington University in St. Louis, has attempted to address that problem by designing novel social work programs to address both the financial assets and social development of people living in poverty.

Different from the previous poverty practices, which rely on income assistance and the consumption of services, the CSD approach focuses on asset-based policies and interventions, to help people with low income increase savings and investments for the future. CSD also noted that changing the current social policy and policy structures is also important for poverty alleviation. For example, Sherraden (1991) advocated implementing asset-building policies such as having universal and progressive saving accounts for all newborns, a program called "Child Development Accounts" (CDAs).

> **Definitions:**
> *Child Development Accounts (CDAs)* are savings or investment accounts that begin as early as birth. In many cases, public and private matching funds are deposited into these accounts to supplement savings for the child. The goal of CDAs is to promote savings and asset building for lifelong development. Thus, CDAs may be targeted at postsecondary education for youth, and home ownership and enterprise development in adulthood.
>
> **Key structural features of CDAs:**
> *Restricted:* With few exceptions, savings accumulated in CDAs can be used only for approved purposes. These commonly include postsecondary education (college or vocational school), down payment on a starter home, and seed capital to start a small business, among others.
>
> *(continued)*

> *Designed to encourage savings:* As an incentive to save, most CDAs are "seeded" with an initial deposit of around $500 to $1,000, and deposits made by children and their parents are matched, often at a 1:1 ratio up to a certain annual or lifetime limit.
>
> *Progressive:* Recognizing the difficulty of saving for low-income households, the accounts of lower income children receive additional financial assistance. This assistance may take the form of a larger initial deposit, a higher match, or a grant.
>
> *Universal:* Ideally, CDAs are universal—available to all—in the same way that public education is universal. Universality ensures that all children are included, and that all children benefit.
>
> *With public support:* As the public now supports saving in 401(k)s and many other types of accounts, the government should support saving in CDAs, particularly for households with low-to-moderate incomes. In this regard, CDAs usually provide an initial deposit and sometimes matching funds. These funds are usually offered as a grant or subsidy, though a recent proposal in the United States would offer the initial deposit and match funds as a long-term, low-interest loan.
>
> *Part of a larger financial education program:* CDAs often include mandatory financial education for children and their families that may be offered at school or online. Classes cover topics such as how to create a budget, how to write a check or make a deposit, how to distinguish "needs" from "wants," and how to read a bank statement. Hands-on management of their accounts appears to provide equally important learning to children and their parents.
>
> So far, Canada, Singapore, the United Kingdom, and Israel have instituted national CDA policies. In the United States, Maine implemented the first statewide CDA.
>
> SOURCE: Center for Social Development. (n.d.) *Child development accounts.* https://csd.wustl.edu/child-development-accounts

Asset Effects Model: A New Approach to Help the Poor

The asset effects model was largely derived from the work of Michael Sherraden (1991), who introduced the idea that asset ownership has economic, social, and psychological effects. Assets were defined financially as bank accounts, stocks, bonds, and pensions plus nonfinancial tangible assets, such as homes, cars, and small businesses or self-employment (Lerman & McKernan, 2008; Sherraden, 1991). From this perspective, four major effects derive from holding assets: (a) economic well-being, (b) social well-being and civic engagement, (c) child well-being, and (d) health and psychological well-being.

According to the asset effects model, Lerman and McKernan (2008) argue that, theoretically, holding assets reduces material hardship and improves economic well-being, including income, consumption, future assets, and self-sufficiency. Financial assets produce cash income by earned interest, dividend payments, and capital gains when the value of stocks and bonds increases. In addition, nonfinancial tangible assets can raise incomes by paying less services fees (e.g., owning a car allows people to not use Uber). Moreover, having assets (e.g., car) helps individuals broaden job searching and availability, which in turn, potentially influences higher future incomes. Assets have potential effects on raising the level of consumption and decreasing the variability of material hardship, for example by avoiding paying extremely high interest rates of borrowing. Assets, when they accrue sufficiently, also increase self-sufficiency and self-efficacy.

Regarding social well-being and civic engagement, asset ownership has positive effects on household and residential stability (Lerman & McKernan, 2008). Higher household and residential stability typically increase participation in neighborhood activities, which in turn helps individuals to increase social capital. From this perspective too, asset holding, especially property ownership (e.g., home ownership), may provide incentives to become involved in civic organizations in order to maintain or increase property values. Higher residential stability is usually associated with better child schooling outcomes (e.g., Zhan & Sherraden, 2003). Residential stability also helps children maintain their friendships and become more involved in extracurricular activities (Lerman & McKernan, 2008), thus promoting social stability for children.

Asset holding is also positively associated with physical and mental health outcomes (Bynner & Despotidou, 2001; Lerman & McKernan, 2008). For example, having assets may decrease the worry and reduce the stress of sudden income losses and can help people meet unanticipated healthcare costs. People may also feel happier or more satisfied when they have a sense of economic security (Lerman & McKernan, 2008).

In the model of asset effects, asset ownership is conceptualized as promoting a foundation for hope and aspirations for well-being (Schreiner & Sherraden, 2007). Psychologists have found that the ability to accumulate assets is influenced by personal characteristics, such as thrift, conscientiousness, emotional stability, autonomy, extraversion, inflexibility, and tough-mindedness (Nyhus & Webley, 2001; Wärneryd, 1996).

The asset effects model also helps to explain the indirect effect of household assets on children's educational expectations. Children who are raised in households that own assets develop high educational expectations (Ansong et al., 2015). They believe that pursuing education is a possibility, that is, assets are available to pay for tuition, books, and school-related expenses (Elliott, 2008). In turn, expectations for academic achievement are thought to promote positive comportment and study habits in school (Mau & Bikos, 2000). In a cognitive sense, then, household assets are thought to lead to better educational outcomes such as higher grades (Ansong et al., 2019; Elliott, 2009; Fang et al., 2020).

STRATEGIES FOR ENGAGING IN "JUST" POVERTY PRACTICE

Poverty is a form of structural inequality and injustice (McCartan et al., 2018). As social workers, we advocate for social justice for everyone regardless of their race/ethnicity, gender, or social class. The 2015 Educational Policy and Accreditation Standards (EPAS) by CSWE identified social, economic, and environmental justice as a core competency in social work education and is expected of all social work students seeking bachelor's (BSW) and master's (MSW) degrees. They should be able to understand social, economic, and environmental justice, and know how to apply justice orientations in practice. In addition, social work students need to understand strategies for eliminating oppressive barriers at the structural or system level (CSWE, 2015).

Grand Challenges for Social Work: Just Society

In 2013, the American Academy of Social Work and Social Welfare (AASWSW) named reducing extreme income inequality and building financial capability for all as two of its 12 Grand Challenges for social work. Consistent with a structural perspective, the AASWSW pointed out that without changing the structure at the societal level, it is almost impossible to eliminate poverty, and people from families living in poverty will be trapped in the cycle of poverty. In order to reduce extreme economic inequality, social workers can participate in the design of social policies that increase income and assets for the impoverished members of society and that reduce inequalities in income and wealth (Elliott et al., 2016).

In order to build financial capability and assets for all, social workers should focus on ways to strengthen financial capability and build assets, to allow all families access to the policies, practices, and consumer protections that benefit privileged families, and to promote the development of universal and progressive CDAs (Huang et al., 2016).

To achieve the goals of building financial capability and assets and eliminating extreme economic inequality, it is important to make systematic changes at both the individual and structural levels. Relying on individual financial education alone to improve financial capability is not sufficient and, because programs to change structural inequalities have failed to do so and hence have failed to reduce poverty, it is critical that social workers develop programs for economically vulnerable populations at micro, mezzo, and macro levels.

Micro Strategies

Financial literacy training/education. Social work can help improve individual economic self-sufficiency and empowerment by providing financial literacy training or financial literacy education programs (Dodaro, 2011; Gudmunson & Danes, 2011; Gutter & Copur, 2011; Huang et al., 2016; Joo & Grable, 2004; Rothwell & Wu, 2019; Sherraden et al., 2015). Economic self-sufficiency requires sustainable income generation and sufficient financial capability. Sustainable income generation requires that individuals have the skills, knowledge, and opportunities to be paid in a manner sufficient to maintain a secure livelihood. Sufficient financial literacy means

> **Definitions:**
>
> *Income generation* refers to the *skills and knowledge* needed to make money including the ability to develop a career plan, manage the conflicting demands of life circumstances and expectations of employment, learn the relational competencies needed to be a successful worker, know workers' rights and employer responsibilities as mandated by law or formal workplace policies, or be aware of sources of social support in and outside of the workplace. It also includes the *opportunities* to secure a livelihood such as exposure to diverse career options; access to opportunities for career exploration (e.g., internships, apprenticeships); access to workforce development providers and training and education programs, recruitment and hiring pools, employer-based benefits and diversity policies and practices, and support services needed to make work possible (e.g., financial, childcare, eldercare, health/mental health); or protections of employment by federal mandate.
>
> *Financial capability* includes financial literacy and financial inclusion (Johnson & Sherraden, 2007; Sherraden, 2013). *Financial literacy refers* to the knowledge and skills needed to manage financial resources effectively, including budgeting, financial planning, cash management, saving, investing, establishing credit, managing debt, obtaining insurance or retirement, and estate planning.
>
> Financial capability also requires *financial inclusion*, and refers to the access and opportunity to act to best meet one's financial interests such as the opportunity to access appropriate and affordable banking products and services, for example, a place to deposit money, store savings, secure credit, and obtain insurance.
>
> SOURCE: Gates, L. B., Koza, J., & Akabas, S. H. (2017). Social work's response to poverty: From benefits dependence to economic self-sufficiency. *Journal of Social Work Education*, 53(1), 99–117. https://doi.org/10.1080/10437797.2016.1212752

that individuals are knowledgeable and skillful in managing financial resources effectively for now and for the future, and have the access and opportunity for their financial activities and interests (Huang et al., 2016; Sherraden et al., 2015). Financial literacy training often includes knowledge and skills regarding budgeting, financial planning, cash management, banking, and retirement planning (Jacob et al., 2000).

Skills training and job readiness programs. In addition to financial literacy training, skills-training and job-readiness programs are intended to improve individual financial well-being through increasing employability and earning potential. These programs include both hard-skills (e.g., specific skills required for a job) and soft-skills training (e.g., interpersonal communication, teamwork; Galley, 2015; Jackson, 2007). Typically, training is offered through life skills, vocational skills, and educational workshops. Skills training to increase employability is also intended to increase lifelong earning potential and the potential to accumulate wealth, improve financial capabilities, and enhance economic well-being (Gutter & Copur, 2011; Jackson, 2007; Joo & Grable, 2004).

Mezzo Strategies

At the mezzo level, social workers can help impoverished families by providing an asset-based family intervention. These interventions offer a matched-savings account in conjunction with financial literacy training. They are intended to help families accumulate assets by (a) providing access to financial services, (b) encouraging savings behaviors through incentives, and (c) acquiring experience in managing and planning household finances (Chowa et al., 2010; Filmer & Pritchett, 2001). Participation in asset-based intervention can help families develop greater expectations for attaining financial security (Elliott, 2009; Zhan & Sherraden, 2011). Research has shown that having higher financial expectations encourages families to plan for their future and to implement actions toward accumulating assets needed to carry out those plans (Chowa et al., 2010). The belief that a family is going to have more money allows family members to plan for future life choices. When families have increased levels of life expectation, they rethink their attitudes toward the future and the importance of saving (Cook et al., 1996; Elliott & Beverly, 2011; Elliott et al., 2010; Mau & Bikos, 2000). These higher expectations are thought to motivate action for life change, which is critical to break cycles of poverty. The effects of an asset-based intervention are expected to be seen in outcomes such as improved financial security and economic well-being of participants, reduced rates of poverty, improved quality of life, and an environment of greater justice and equality (Chowa et al., 2010).

In addition, providing microcredit and entrepreneurship programs can help economically disadvantaged families move out of poverty by providing access to small loans, financial training, and small business supports. Researchers have found microcredit or entrepreneurship programs can be effective in reducing poverty (Islam & Choe, 2013). Findings suggest the programs have positive effects on health (Fawole et al., 2004), life trajectories (Müller, 2010), and educational outcomes (Maldonado & González-Vega, 2008).

To address asset losses and the concentration of poverty in some rural low-wealth communities, social workers can take a leadership role in state coalitions to provide job development, smart growth, sustainable development, and asset building in these communities (Otabor & Gordon Nembhard, 2012). In addition, outreach or street work may be helpful for social workers to reach the often socially excluded populations such as people living in poverty and immigrants (Szeintuch, 2015).

Macro Strategies

At the macro level, social workers play an active role in advocating for policy changes at both the state and federal levels. For example, at the state level, social workers can advocate for the state governments to transform current 529 college-savings plans into progressive asset-building programs (e.g., the CDAs) for low- and moderate-income families (Clancy et al., 2004). Social workers also can be actively engaged in developing and changing national policies such as the development of the Assets for Independence Act of 1998 (2013; Sherraden, 2011) and the Refund to Savings (R2S) initiative (Grinstein-Weiss et al., 2014). The AASWSW also provides policy recommendations to guide social workers to respond to each of the challenges associated with reducing economic inequality and building financial capability for current and future social work practices (see Table 4.3).

Given economic inequality, social workers can also engage in advocating for policy reforms related to low-wage employment, including increased earnings, guaranteed minimum hours and pay for reporting, and on-call time at local, state, and federal levels (Lein et al., 2016). For example, as the Earned Income Tax Credit (EITC) became the main income-support policy for poor families, social workers can also advocate to expand the EITC coverage so that low-income families can get greater assistance. Social workers can also promote the expansion of childcare policies at both state and federal levels so that low-income families can claim childcare supports

TABLE 4.3 **Policy Recommendations to Guide Social Workers**

	REDUCE EXTREME ECONOMIC INEQUALITY[1]	BUILD FINANCIAL CAPABILITY AND ASSETS FOR ALL[2]
1	Strengthen labor standards and reform employment policies	Support a strong Consumer Financial Protection Bureau (CFPB) to help ensure the transparency, safety, fairness, and affordability of financial products and services
2	Expand active employment creation through public programs and support for business start-up and capitalization	Start lifelong asset building with universal and progressive Child Development Accounts (CDAs)
3	Expand the Earned Income Tax Credit (EITC)	Create a web-based financial capability gateway to build financial capability for all
4	Expand child care access to enable stable employment in the context of healthy child development	Prepare social workers and human service practitioners to build financial capability and assets for all
5	Create new, lifelong policies for inclusive and progressive wealth building	

[1]Elliott, W., III, Henly, J. R., Lambert, S. J., Lein, L., Romich, J. L., Shanks, T. R., & Sherraden, M. (2016). *Policy recommendations for meeting the Grand Challenge to Reduce Extreme Economic Inequality* (Grand Challenges for Social Work Initiative Policy Brief No. 10). American Academy of Social Work & Social Welfare.

[2]Huang, J., Sherraden, M. S., Clancy, M. M., Sherraden, M., Birkenmaier, J., Despard, M., Frey, J. J., Callahan, C., & Rothwell, D. (2016). *Policy recommendations for meeting the Grand Challenge to Build Financial Capability and Assets for All* (Grand Challenges for Social Work Initiative Policy Brief No. 11). American Academy of Social Work & Social Welfare.

from the government. To reduce the economic inequality of the U.S. society, social workers can also advocate for building universal and progressive asset-building policies (Lein et al., 2016; Sherraden et al., 2015).

In addition, social workers in poverty alleviation fields or welfare departments should be aware of the stigma when providing services to clients. Stigma should never be a barrier to keep people from seeking and receiving supports from the government. As the NASW (2017) stated, social work practitioners seek to "expand choice and opportunity for all." Social workers—when implementing and delivering welfare programs and services—also need to be aware of how to reduce the effects of stigma on welfare recipients. For example, Barr (2000) listed several ways of reducing welfare stigma, such as renaming Medicaid and CHIP welfare programs as "Public Health Coverage," training eligibility staff to provide high-quality customer service and to treat all recipients as valued account holders, improving provider reimbursement rates to attract more high-quality providers to the system, simplifying the application and redetermination process, and adopting payment formats in welfare coverage similar to those in the private market. Eliminating the stigma associated with receipt of welfare at the societal level is critical to ensuring the well-being of vulnerable groups that goes beyond providing assistance with basic needs. Also critical is the need to find appropriate ways to eliminate the stigma of the effects of welfare recipients and put these efforts into consideration when policy makers design welfare programs. In addition, social workers can address stigmas that provide barriers to accessing other types of services such as the negative stereotype connected with mental health treatment, and can continue to reduce such stigmas and stereotypes through public education.

CONCLUSION

Poverty in the United States continues to be a major social problem. However, poverty varies significantly by racial/ethnicity, gender, and social class. Such injustices require social workers—as professional helpers—to consistently pay attention to the circumstances surrounding poverty. This helps our profession to better respond to poverty issues past, present, and future. As social work students, in order to better assist the poor, we need to be familiar with basic poverty-related concepts and measures. We also need to understand poverty alleviation history, the form of public policy debates, and welfare programs. Most importantly though, we need to be aware that poverty has structural as well as individual causes. Therefore, the ideal of poverty alleviation is best achieved by change at both individual and structural levels.

DISCUSSION QUESTIONS

1. What are some reasons that the United States uses a relative measure of poverty rather than an absolute measure?
2. Why do social workers need to know the policies and historical approaches associated with trying to eliminate poverty?
3. Explain the difference between individual and structural causes of poverty.
4. What theoretical causes of poverty best reflect your knowledge of, and experiences with, poverty?

REFERENCES

Only key references appear in the print edition. The full reference list appears in the digital product on Springer Publishing Connect: connect.springerpub.com/content/book/978-0-8261-3539-1/chapter/ch04

Ansong, D., Chowa, G., Masa, R., Despard, M., Sherraden, M., Wu, S., & Osei-Akoto, I. (2019). Effects of youth savings accounts on school attendance and academic performance: Evidence from a youth savings experiment in Ghana. *Journal of Family and Economic Issues, 40*(2), 269–281. https://doi.org/10.1007/s10834-018-9604-5

Bradshaw, T. K. (2007). Theories of poverty and anti-poverty programs in community development. *Community Development, 38*(1), 7–25. https://doi.org/10.1080/15575330709490182

Chaudry, A., Wimer, C., Macartney, S., Frohlich, L., Campbell, C., Swenson, K., Oellerich, D., & Hauan, S. (2016). *Poverty in the United States: 50-year trends and safety net impacts.* U.S. Department of Health and Human Services.

Elliott, W., III, Henly, J. R., Lambert, S. J., Lein, L., Romich, J. L., Shanks, T. R., & Sherraden, M. (2016). *Policy recommendations for meeting the Grand Challenge to Reduce Extreme Economic Inequality* (Grand Challenges for Social Work Initiative Policy Brief No. 10). American Academy of Social Work & Social Welfare.

Gates, L. B., Koza, J., & Akabas, S. H. (2017). Social work's response to poverty: From benefits dependence to economic self-sufficiency. *Journal of Social Work Education, 53*(1), 99–117. https://doi.org/10.1080/10437797.2016.1212752

Koball, H., & Jiang, Y. (2018). *Basic facts about low-income children: Children under 18 years, 2016.* National Center for Children in Poverty, Columbia University.

McCartan, C., Morrison, A., Bunting, L., Davidson, G., & McIlroy, J. (2018). Stripping the wallpaper of practice: Empowering social workers to tackle poverty. *Social Sciences, 7*(10), 193. https://doi.org/10.3390/socsci7100193

McCarty, A. T. (2016). Child poverty in the United States: A tale of devastation and the promise of hope. *Sociology Compass, 10*(7), 623–639. https://doi.org/10.1111/soc4.12386

Proctor, B. D., Semega, J. L., & Kollar, M. A. (2016). *Income and poverty in the United States: 2015.* United States Census Bureau. https://www.census.gov/content/dam/Census/library/publications/2016/demo/p60-256.pdf

Sherraden, M. S., Huang, J., Frey, J. J., Birkenmaier, J., Callahan, C., Clancy, M. M., & Sherraden, M. (2015). *Financial capability and asset building for all* (pp. 1–29). American Academy of Social Work and Social Welfare.

U.S. Department of Health and Human Services, Office of the Assistant Secretary for Planning and Evaluation. (2019). *2019 poverty guidelines.* https://aspe.hhs.gov/2019-poverty-guidelines

Wagmiller, R. L., & Adelman, R. M. (2009). *Childhood and intergenerational poverty: The long-term consequences of growing up poor.* National Center for Children in Poverty, Columbia University.

Wu, S., Wang, X., Wu, Q., & Harris, K. M. (2018). Household financial assets inequity and health disparities among young adults: Evidence from the National Longitudinal Study of Adolescent to Adult Health. *Journal of Health Disparities Research and Practice, 11*, 122–135. https://www.ncbi.nlm.nih.gov/pmc/articles/PMC6590690

Wu, S. (2017). Welfare participation and depression among youth and young adults in the United States and China (Doctoral dissertation). Retrieved from ProQuest Dissertations Publishing (No. 10619248).

5

SOCIAL AND ECONOMIC DISPARITIES WITHIN THE EDUCATIONAL SYSTEM

Shantel D. Crosby | Kristian Jones | Angelique G. Day

LEARNING OBJECTIVES

Students will be able to:

- Articulate the historical context of educational disparity in the U.S. educational system.
- Identify the systemic barriers that contribute to educational disparity and the various populations of students who are vulnerable to this injustice.
- Recognize how social workers can address and advocate for just educational practice in schools.

INTRODUCTION

Educational schooling in the United States has had a troubling and complicated history, leading to the perpetuation of systemic barriers for certain youth populations in our country. This has had a long-standing negative impact on the schooling experience of many young people in contemporary school settings. There are a number of disparities related to education, particularly connected to social class and being a youth of color as well as other factors such as being gender expansive, homeless, or system involved, all of which can result in lower academic outcomes and higher negative outcomes in school settings. Lack of educational achievement and attainment has significant consequences that extend into adulthood, in particular related to economic opportunities.

HISTORY OF EDUCATIONAL DISPARITY

Throughout history, the U.S. educational system has been driven by oppressive policies and practices, racialization, and racism (Kohli et al., 2017). Early examples of this include the Americanization schools (Cody, 1918) and American Indian boarding schools (Adams, 1995) which spanned much of the 19th and 20th centuries. Later examples include the persistent socialization of inferiority in segregated schools serving African American and Mexican American students (Powers, 2008), demonstrating a legacy of students of color being subjected to institutionalized conditions that contradict their interests and humanity (Kohli et al., 2017). To better understand modern-day issues of educational disparity in the United States, it is important to unpack the historical evolution of schooling and the early policies that continue to have influence. In this section, we provide a snapshot of this history to provide a foundational context for the current state of our educational system.

HISTORY OF PRIMARY EDUCATION IN THE UNITED STATES

Formal K–12 education in the United States began mostly as homeschooling, where families hired private tutors to teach their children in-home (Popa, 2016). Due to the financial burden of homeschooling, this was generally a luxury enjoyed primarily by affluent families (Popa, 2016). In the early 17th century, the first public schools began functioning, as the Boston Latin School—the first public school—opened its doors in 1635 (Popa, 2016). During this time, the colonial period, and through the early 19th century, public schools were locally controlled and designed to meet the needs of the local community or members of the church (Parkerson & Parkerson, 2017). These schools required families to pay for enrolling their children, which significantly limited opportunities for youth from lower socioeconomic backgrounds to participate (Popa, 2016). Educational standards also varied greatly in different regions of the country, as children in New England and New York received basic education through schools, Pennsylvania and New Jersey utilized churches for educating their children, southern colonies relied on private schools and private tutors, and more rural regions had very little access to education at all (Parkerson & Parkerson, 2017).

In addition to financial costs being a barrier to families, schooling was also limited in most schools to male-only institutions, leaving out girls and young women (Popa, 2016). As a result, the illiteracy rate among women remained high, as girls were systematically barred from formal education due to the enforcement of oppressive, patriarchal beliefs and norms (Parkerson & Parkerson, 2017). During the American Revolution and the period of Enlightenment, notions of female intellectual inferiority began to change and young women were eventually allowed into schools in most communities. Still, there continued to be limitations on the types of courses in which they could participate, as they were often denied the opportunity to take courses in math or science. By the end of the Civil War, between 60% and 70% of all young girls in Northern states were attending school—the same rate as their male counterparts (Parkerson & Parkerson, 2017). Today, women attend primary schools at all levels at rates comparable to men and in the case of college or university study, women outnumber men.

In many places in America, especially in the South, youth of color were banned from education altogether (Popa, 2016). Affluent Black Americans also had difficulty receiving education, even in the few cases where they could pay for homeschooling. As a result of tremendous discrimination, Black children in southern parts of the United States were forced to rely on private philanthropy or churches in their community to receive an education (Parkerson & Parkerson, 2017). While the educational opportunities in northern states may have been somewhat more accessible, segregation persisted throughout the nation during this period. For mainstream society, cultural deprivation and the idea that people of color were intellectually inferior were prominent theories used to uphold racial inequity in schooling (Kohli et al., 2017). Progress was made only through a bitter civil rights struggle that mobilized the Black community and democratic reformers throughout the country (Parkerson & Parkerson, 2017). Through court decisions and legislation, and direct action by the Black Americans and their allies, public education gradually became more inclusive for Black children (Parkerson & Parkerson, 2017).

In 1954, the landmark case *Brown v. Board of Education of Topeka* changed public education in America forever; the Supreme Court acknowledged the great importance of providing all children with an appropriate education and ensured the rights of marginalized groups in urban and other settings, regardless of race, ethnicity, language, or disability (Talbert-Johnson, 2004). The case determined that separate public educational institutions for Black and White students were unconstitutional, triggering a monumental shift in public education (Popa, 2016). As a result of this legislation, government-mandated desegregation programs were subsequently implemented across the United States, which included policies that involved busing and ultimately removed many children in urban communities from their neighborhood schools, requiring travel to other community schools (Talbert-Johnson, 2004). One unintended consequence of this decision was increased difficulty for parental involvement because of the increased distance to schools in unfamiliar areas of the city (Talbert-Johnson, 2004). Another was the wholesale closure of Black schools and the resultant decimation of the numbers of Black school administrators. Between 1954 and 1964, the number of African American principals was reduced by 90% (Smith, n.d.). This trend has continued for several decades and into the 2000s, causing issues of underachievement of students from diverse cultural and linguistic backgrounds in comparison to their mainstream peers. This continues to be a pervasive problem, particularly in urban education (Talbert-Johnson, 2004), yet there has been a lack of urban policy urgency or legislation that has truly addressed these disparities.

CONTEMPORARY EDUCATION IN THE UNITED STATES

On January 8, 2002, President George W. Bush reauthorized the Elementary and Secondary Education Act and signed into law the No Child Left Behind (NCLB) Act of 2001. The federal education act signified a historic reform of the public education system in America based on four key pillars: flexible usage of federal funds, accountability, school choice, and an emphasis on utilizing scientifically based research to validate and justify practices and programs deemed to be effective in public education.

However, the focus on standardized test scores also intensified and led to the use of testing as the primary indicator of school performance (Nichols & Valenzuela, 2013). This approach resulted in punitive measures being imposed on school districts when scores did not meet the standard and thus created a pressure-packed environment for teachers and students to achieve high test scores (McNeil, 2000). If schools did not make satisfactory yearly progress after 5 years, the school would be mandated to make drastic changes to the way it was being run or be at risk of being closed, with parents having the option to transfer their children from the failing school to charter schools or schools performing better on standardized tests.

Similarly, the Race to the Top legislation, implemented by the Obama administration, impacted education in a number of ways. This education policy focused on establishing charter schools, increasing teacher accountability through standardized testing, and incorporated policies that fostered the use of surveillance and unwarranted policing to feed punitive reform measures. The legislation ultimately sought to solve educational problems through the diversion of funds from public entities to private corporations, thereby increasing high-stakes outcomes and curricular co-opting, despite the fact that these provisions proved unsuccessful under NCLB (Croft et al., 2015).

Specifically, researchers have established that privatization practices are associated with increases in racial disparities in K-12 school settings, and the insurgence of charter schools has led to school closures that have disproportionately and negatively affected urban, Black neighborhoods (Kohli et al., 2017). These policies contain severe implications for schools in ethnic minority communities in particular, as these communities have historically been disproportionately underfunded and understaffed (Nichols & Valenzuela, 2013). As schools are often considered an extension of communities, "killing a school equates to killing a community" (Kohli et al., 2017, p. 188). Furthermore, as the United States becomes more diverse, ethnically and culturally, as a result of immigration from Asia, Latin America, and the Middle East, consistent calls for English-only instruction and opposition to bilingual education also present additional obstacles for the equal education of immigrant children (Parkerson & Parkerson, 2017).

POPULATIONS AND CONTEXT OF POWER, OPPRESSION, AND PRIVILEGE

Considering the challenging past of the American school system, power, oppression, and privilege have always played critical roles in the ways in which youth find academic success or are alternately failed by an unfair educational system. Research has consistently shown that youth from lower socioeconomic backgrounds consistently have lower academic outcomes (i.e., test scores, graduation rates, college enrollment) and higher negative outcomes in school settings (i.e., problem behaviors, suspension, expulsion, dropout rates) compared to youth from higher socioeconomic backgrounds (American Psychological Association, Presidential Task Force on Educational Disparities, 2012; Coleman, 1966; Quintana & Mahgoub, 2016; Reardon, 2011). These rates are exacerbated when other identities are considered such as race/ethnicity, immigration status, sexual orientation, juvenile justice or foster care involvement, or a variety of other identities. We recognize that there are various factors at play that dynamically influence a child's experience of oppression or privilege in school. In this section, we highlight some—not all—of the identities that can impact the experience of a child in our educational system, recognizing that the populations described in the following are in no way meant to be an exhaustive or complete list of groups impacted by educational inequity.

SOCIAL CLASS IN SCHOOL SETTINGS

Educational research continues to highlight the importance of one's social class as one of the most powerful predictors of academic achievement (Aud et al., 2010; Reardon, 2011). Associations have been found between living in poverty and childhood deficits in cognitive development and educational performance, beginning as early as the second year of life (Campbell et al., 2001) and extending through the elementary and high school years. In fact, the educational achievement gap between youth from high- and low-income families has grown significantly in recent decades (Reardon, 2011). From using outdated textbooks to having teachers who are less experienced and qualified, youth in schools in lower socioeconomic settings need additional supports that are often unavailable due to the scarcity of resources. Also, the parents of these youth may not have additional resources or expendable income to invest in their child's education. They also may have jobs that are less flexible, limiting their ability to attend school meetings, conferences, and other events. Research has found that families with higher incomes tend to have caregivers who are highly educated and are able to invest more in the academic success of their children in both early childhood and throughout their school experience (Lareau, 1989; Reardon, 2011). This has significant implications for youth living in poverty, who not only have less access to quality education but also have less ability to invest more into their educational future.

CASE STUDY 5.1—NICHOLAS SAMUELS

Nicholas (Nick) Samuels is a White adolescent from a low-income, rural town, finishing his first semester in the ninth grade. He is in danger of failing his ninth-grade algebra class and has spent the last 2 days in in-school suspension (ISS) due to being late to class more than three times in a week. Nick is the oldest of four siblings and is responsible for getting his siblings to school in the morning when his father is called in for work early in the mornings. Nick has always struggled in math classes, despite being a student who devotes significant time to his academics. However, missing time makes it difficult for him to keep up in class. Nick excels in art and photography and also tends to perform better in his core academic classes when he feels comfortable with the teacher. However, he does not ask for help from his algebra teacher because he does not feel much of a personal connection with her because of the types of "real-life" examples she uses in class.

While Nick was in ISS, he was given class assignments but could not figure out the math concepts by himself. When he asked the ISS teacher for help, the teacher simply explained that he himself had not seen any of that type of math before and would be of no help to Nick. When Nick returned to class after being in ISS for 2 days, the class was assigned a pop quiz—he scored a 30 out of 100. When he asked the teacher for extra help, the teacher responded that he should have shown more initiative earlier in the week before she assigned the pop quiz. At the end of the class, Nick's teacher announced that the class was going to be given a test on the same material tomorrow. Unfortunately, due to his father's work schedule, Nick would have to assist with childcare at home that evening and was concerned about being able to study for the exam. Nick currently had a D in the class and was only a few points away from having a failing grade. After the test tomorrow, there would be only one more test left in the semester. Nick is worried that he will fail the upcoming test, which will lower his grade point average, making him ineligible for the art program for which he would like to apply in the upcoming summer.

Nick is an example of a student who has additional family responsibilities that interfere with his ability to devote time to his academic responsibilities. But Nick's personal situation is compounded by the school response. In what ways are school-level and structural barriers contributing to Nick's experience in school? How might these barriers impact his educational progress long term? What can be done so that Nick's school setting can better support his goal to enter the art program?

YOUTH OF COLOR IN SCHOOL SETTINGS

Despite the amount of progress that has been made in the American educational system, there are still a number of disparities faced by youth of color in America. Pervasive racial and ethnic educational disparities exist, in which African American, American Indian, Latinx and Southeast Asian groups underperform academically, relative to Caucasians and other Asian Americans (American Psychological Association, Presidential Task Force on Educational Disparities, 2012). For example, McFarland et al. (2019) reported that American Indian/Alaska Native youth had the lowest rate of high school graduation (72%), followed by African American youth (78%), and Hispanic youth (80%)—all falling under the national average (85%) in contrast to their White and Asian/Pacific Islander counterparts (89% and 91%, respectively). Additionally, this report also showed American Indian/Alaska Native youth as having the highest rate of high school dropout

(10.1%), followed by Hispanic youth (8.2%), and African American youth (6.5%)—again, much higher than their White and Asian/Pacific Islander counterparts.

Youth of color from lower socioeconomic statuses are especially susceptible to negative outcomes in educational settings, as the American Psychological Association (2012) noted the significant overlap between racial/ethnic disparities in social class and in educational achievement. While being a racial/ethnic minority does not necessarily equate to having lower socioeconomic status, a disproportionate amount of youth of color resides in and attends schools in lower socioeconomic neighborhoods. Youth of color are often relocated to schools with fewer resources, as research has found schools with 90% or more students of color spend $733 less per student than schools with 90% or more White students per year (Spatig-Amerikaner, 2012). Given these inequities in school resources, it is not surprising that, on average for children who are Black, one out of every four boys and one out of seven girls repeat a grade during their K–12 school careers (National Center for Education Statistics, 2010). This proportion is significantly higher than the proportion found among White students (i.e., 1 out of 20).

However, socioeconomic status is not the only consideration in the examination of these disparities. Scholars have described the ways in which these disparities have been a by-product of the legacy of disadvantage encountered by many generations of racial/ethnic minorities, including American slavery, school segregation, and teachers' biases and villainizing of certain racial/ethnic minority student groups (Quintana & Mahgoub, 2016; Rausch & Skiba, 2004). Therefore, one of the most challenging factors contributing to educational inequity is the differential treatment of students based on race/ethnicity, as seen in the gap in school discipline experienced by youth of color (Crenshaw et al., 2015; Quintana & Mahgoub, 2016). Black students spend less time in the classroom due to discipline and are nearly two times as likely to be suspended without educational services as White students (American Psychological Association, Presidential Task Force on Educational Disparities, 2012). Furthermore, Black students are 2.3 times more likely to receive a referral to law enforcement and be subject to a school-related arrest as White students (U.S. Department of Education Office for Civil Rights, 2016). A meta-analysis found support across multiple studies for teachers holding higher academic expectations for and being more positive and encouraging to White and Asian American students in comparison to Black and Latinx students (Tenenbaum & Ruck, 2007). Research has also consistently demonstrated that youth of color experience discrimination in school settings (Boccanfuso & Kuhfeld, 2011; Dupper, 2010; Kayama et al., 2015; Rausch & Skiba, 2004) that translates into unfair interactions between their teachers and greater chances of having lowered educational achievement (McKown & Weinstein, 2008; Quintana & Mahgoub, 2016). Some scholars have argued that instead of helping students to be successful, the disciplinary practices in the educational system are actually preparing Black, Latinx, and Native American students for prison more so than higher education (e.g., Skiba et al., 2014).

IMMIGRANT YOUTH IN SCHOOL SETTINGS

Approximately 20% of children in the United States have parents who have immigrated from other countries around the world (Suárez-Orozco et al., 2010). Families often immigrate to the United States in an effort to provide a better chance for their children to be successful in life. Despite the ambition and perseverance displayed by many immigrant families, they often have to face myriad barriers because of their immigrant status. Commonly, the issues and challenges of immigrant students may be conflated with issues of race and ethnicity in school settings. However, the experience for immigrant youth or those with parents who have immigrated to the United States is uniquely different, warranting particular consideration. It is also important to consider the different experiences of youth and their families in relation to their particular country of origin. For example, immigrant students from China tend to perform better on U.S. standardized tests in comparison to immigrant students from Mexico (American Psychological Association, Presidential Task Force on Educational Disparities, 2012; Schwartz & Stiefel, 2011).

Research has found that Black and Latinx immigrants in New York City are much more likely to be in lower socioeconomic settings than White immigrants from Eastern Europe and are also more likely to attend elementary and middle schools with native-born Black and Latinx students who are from lower socioeconomic backgrounds (Schwartz & Stiefel, 2011). Research has also found that students who are English learners are at risk for a variety of educational disparities compared to students who are native English speakers, even after receiving educational services (American Psychological Association, Presidential Task Force on Educational Disparities, 2012). The likelihood of experiencing educational disparities is increased when the parents of immigrant youth are not knowledgeable about the U.S. educational system and do not have a high school education (American Psychological Association, Presidential Task Force on Educational Disparities, 2012). Additionally, the xenophobia (i.e., fear of and prejudice against immigrants) directed toward certain immigrant groups, in addition to anti-immigrant legislation and pervasive negative stereotypes about immigrants have created experiences of deep fear and social isolation for immigrant youth in schools (Suárez-Orozco et al., 2010), further widening the educational gap.

SEXUAL MINORITY AND GENDER-EXPANSIVE YOUTH IN SCHOOL SETTINGS

Sexual minority youth includes young people who identify as lesbian, gay, bisexual, transgender, questioning (LGBTQ), and/or any identity that is not heterosexual. "Gender-expansive" refers to individuals who do not identify their gender as male or female, but rather outside of the binary gender system. Schools can be a hostile environment for sexual minority and gender-expansive students (Kosciw et al., 2014), often leading to higher rates of school-induced anxiety, depression, and suicide ideation among this population (Garofalo et al., 1999; Hatzenbuehler, 2011; Marshal et al., 2011). Research has consistently demonstrated that these youth experience bullying at greater rates than their gender-conforming and heterosexual peers, and they also have to navigate unique social challenges in school settings (Abreu et al., 2016; Birkett et al., 2009; Black et al., 2012; Cochran et al., 2002; D'Augelli et al., 2002; White et al., 2018). Heteronormative practices and policies in schools perpetuate their experiences of oppression, creating socioemotional challenges for these students as they struggle to feel included and connected within their school environment. Additionally, the bullying that they endure from their peers (and sometimes school staff as well) has implications for their overall school success, as research has shown bullying to hinder their academic performance, decrease academic achievement (Kosciw et al., 2015), and increase truancy and school dropout (Aragon et al., 2014; Birkett et al., 2014). Research has also found that although antibullying policies and laws appear to exist across the country, they are not addressing the specific needs of sexual minority and gender-expansive students (Abreu et al., 2016).

HOMELESS AND SYSTEM-INVOLVED YOUTH IN SCHOOL SETTINGS

There are an estimated 3.5 million youth in the United States who experience homelessness in any given year (Morton et al., 2018). Being without a consistent place to live creates many significant educational barriers for young people. For example, one study reported that approximately 57%

of homeless youth were enrolled in school (National Coalition for the Homeless, 2007). This means that over 40% are not even registered to attend school in their district.

System-involved youth—those in the foster care and/or the juvenile justice system—are also some of the most commonly documented youth populations that become vulnerable to the inequities of the U.S. educational system. Research has consistently shown that system-involved youth often have lower grade point averages (Hurt et al., 2001), high school graduation rates (Courtney et al., 2009; Kirk & Sampson, 2013), and academic achievement test scores (Courtney et al., 2004; Pecora et al., 2005) than their counterparts. They also receive much higher referrals for special education programs (Macomber, 2009), are programmed into punishment facilities rather than into treatment, and are given more pathological labels than warranted (Talbert-Johnson, 2004). They also experience significant school instability, changing schools with much greater frequency than their peers (Avery, 2001; Burley & Halpern, 2001).

Youth who experience homelessness or system involvement have often had encounters with abuse, neglect, or violence exposure (Dierkhising et al., 2013; Gaetz, 2004; Kidd, 2003) that contribute to their traumatic histories and overall well-being as well as the ways in which they respond to triggers in the school setting (Cook et al., 2005). However, schools have not historically made disciplinary decisions with this trauma in mind when these students have a difficult behavioral moment in class. Instead, they are often suspended or expelled from school rather than being provided with supportive services. In fact, these young people are more likely to be suspended and receive lengthier suspensions (Burley, 2010; Courtney et al., 2004; Zajac et al., 2015), creating a direct pathway for these youth to the school-to-prison pipeline as well as missed opportunities for learning (Ferguson, 2016).

There is an urgent need for teachers and school administrators to develop more appropriate ways to manage discipline to divert these students away from punitive treatment and into programming that will help them to successfully graduate. Under the circumstances, it is not surprising that these young people enroll in postsecondary institutions at much lower rates (Randolph & Thompson, 2017). For those who are able to matriculate into a postsecondary institution, there are lower college retention and graduation rates (Randolph & Thompson, 2017), and students are less academically prepared to be successful in college when compared to the general population of young adults exiting high school (Unrau et al., 2012).

CASE STUDY 5.2—CLAUDIA MELENDEZ

Claudia Melendez is a Dominican teenager from Brooklyn, New York. She is in the 10th grade at an academically rigorous school outside of her neighborhood and was recently released from juvenile justice court supervision for chronic truancy. She dislikes her school, has struggled to make friends, and feels like she cannot relate to anyone since she is the only Dominican in her class—one of the only three Latinx students in the entire school. Claudia is often teased for her accent, glasses, and clothes, which has led her to verbal arguments, physical fights with other students, and skipping school. As a result, Claudia has received multiple in-school suspensions and has also been suspended twice. If Claudia is suspended again for fighting, she is in danger of being expelled and potential juvenile justice reentry.

When Claudia is in class, she excels with her classwork despite the rigorous curriculum. Claudia is especially interested in science and wants to attend New York University (NYU) to pursue a career as an engineer. Claudia is from a tight-knit family and is the middle of three

(continued)

> **CASE STUDY 5.2—CLAUDIA MELENDEZ (*continued*)**
>
> sisters. Claudia describes a loving father who works 7 days a week, but spends time with his daughters when possible. She also has a mother who works multiple jobs. Claudia gets along with her sisters and also has an especially close relationship with her grandmother, someone who was a big advocate for Claudia to attend the school. As much as she hates to admit it, Claudia happens to enjoy the challenges of the academics of her school. Claudia does not want to get expelled from school and does not want to have to go back to court, which would disappoint her family, especially her grandmother, but she hates her current school and wants to be in a setting with people who "get her."
>
> Claudia is an example of a student who has multiple educational vulnerabilities. In what ways are school-level and structural barriers contributing to Claudia's experience in school? How might her interactions with the juvenile justice system be impacting her progress? What can be done so that Claudia's school setting can better support her goal to attend NYU?

INTERSECTIONALITY IN SCHOOL SETTINGS

Overall, youth from each of these populations face a variety of obstacles that can impede their ability to be successful in formal school settings. However, it is important to view these identities in the context of one another—from an intersectional lens—recognizing that people are made up of more than one social identity, which all intersect to shape the social experience for that individual (McCall, 2008). Intersectionality is vital when advocating for marginalized groups and the resources that they may need to counteract negative experiences of oppression (Jackson et al., 2016). For example, a student who is a heterosexual, Filipino, male from a lower socioeconomic, single-parent household may have completely different needs and school experiences than a student who is bisexual, Filipino, and from an upper-middle-class, two-parent household, where both parents have advanced degrees. The nuances of how these various identities intersect to create both privilege and disadvantage in the lives of young people should be carefully considered when examining the ways in which a school setting may or may not contribute to inequity.

MAGNITUDE AND SCOPE OF EDUCATIONAL DISPARITY

Addressing educational disparities is not simply an individual problem, but rather a national crisis. Research has shown that dropping out of high school is associated with lower chances of later employment and various other negative life outcomes (Child Trends Databank, 2015). Youth who are transitioning into adulthood without a high school diploma are unlikely to have the necessary skills to function in today's increasingly technology-dependent workplace if they do not receive the knowledge and skills provided in formal school settings. Research has also consistently shown that lower educational attainment is associated with lowered chances of financial stability for young people in a rapidly growing and globally competitive environment.

Schools can be viewed as a strong source of immediate safety for youth as well as a future pathway to economic empowerment and mobility (Crosby et al., 2019). However, the systemic structures that are prevalent within our schools can make this less of a reality for the most vulnerable populations of students. There is pervasive evidence of structural and institutional racism, particularly as it has manifested in differential access to high-quality and equitable educational opportunities (Aleman et al., 2011).

ACHIEVEMENT GAP DIFFERENCES

There are many reasons for achievement gap differences, commonly including racial, environmental, and other institutional causes. First, we know that poverty constitutes the most significant sociocultural cause of the academic achievement gap. However, Black and Latinx children are disproportionately impacted by this, as they make up 60% of all children living in poverty (Ferguson, 2016; Talbert-Johnson, 2004).

Second, students of color and their families are often blamed for a lack of academic success. This is often connected to an ideology that promotes a shift in individual student behavior as the solution (i.e., reminding parents about the need to read to their children, advocating for programs designed to teach a growth mindset), rather than suggesting changes to structures and policies that systematically impede the academic success of students of color (Kohli et al., 2017). However, the philosophy of blaming marginalized students for their educational inequality erases institutional responsibility and further perpetuates the inequity.

Third, Black children enrolled in urban schools are also subject to school practices of tracking and ability grouping, both of which result in highly disproportionate numbers of these children being placed in low-ability and special education classrooms (Talbert-Johnson, 2004). The overrepresentation of Black and Latinx students in special education is often guided by assumptions of cultural deficits and racist assumptions about ability, as well as exposure to teachers who lack behavioral management skills that result in misguided conceptualizations of disability and prevent these students from reaching their academic potential (Ferguson, 2016; Kohli et al., 2017).

Fourth, urban schools are often home to students whose lives and experiences are vastly different from those of their teachers who are often White, middle class, monolingual English speakers (Talbert-Johnson, 2004). Many of these teachers lack cultural responsiveness and, as a result, are more inclined to approach Black students more aggressively because of group reputations for defiant behavior. Anticipated hostility on the part of both teachers and students in encounters with each other can produce spiraling escalation of misbehavior and excessive discipline (Ferguson, 2016).

Fifth, schools in racially diverse communities require leaders and models of leadership that reflect the racial, cultural, and ethnic makeup of the school community. However, shortages of qualified teachers (of any race/ethnic background) in urban school settings have translated into the hiring of teachers with alternative certificates and the overreliance on the use of substitute teachers (Talbert-Johnson, 2004). Teacher shortages in urban schools have also translated into the need for enlarged class sizes, lack of access to higher level courses, and poor teaching. In addition to teacher shortages, additional structural barriers that disproportionately impact children of color include enrollment in larger schools and school overcrowding. Large schools are impersonal and bureaucratic; research on school size suggests that small schools have at least one major advantage over large schools—relationships among school members and students are more personal (Ready et al., 2004). Lower achievement in overcrowded schools is a result of many causes including increased stress among students and teachers and deteriorated conditions of school facilities (Ready et al., 2004). These structural problems lead to high teacher turnover and students who disengage from school.

ROLE OF SOCIAL WORK TO IDENTIFY UNMET SYSTEMIC NEEDS

Overall, when considering the historical context of schooling in conjunction with all of the aforementioned factors prevalent in the current educational landscape, social work professionals are imperative and should lead the charge for eradicating this equity crisis. Social workers in schools often help teachers to recognize high-risk student behaviors and consult on how to best meet these students' needs (e.g., implementing trauma-sensitive and culturally attuned interventions). It is essential that social workers advocate for and serve as allies to marginalized youth, recognizing intersectionality to assist youth who are often systemically vulnerable to academic and vocational failure. Social workers are critical sources of support who can help link youth to needed resources, provide social support and guidance, and work with the family and community to provide youth with the best chance of being successful in school. Social work professionals in schools operate in a number of varied capacities, ultimately with the goal of helping students to reach their academic and behavioral goals in the school setting. To accomplish this, school social work professionals often work collaboratively with students, parents, and teachers to address issues and barriers to student academic performance and overall well-being. They may be involved in facilitating psychosocial assessments of students; identifying issues of student trauma and well-being; developing treatment plans and overseeing treatment implementation; directly providing case management, therapeutic services, or crisis management; working collaboratively with teachers, parents, or other service providers to meet students' needs; providing training and support to teachers and parents (e.g., trauma-informed practice training); as well as addressing ethical issues and advocating for students (NASW Center for Workforce Studies & Social Work Practice, 2010).

Given the unique role of social work professionals in school settings, as well as their intentional focus on advocacy and ethics, the values that guide the social work profession are vital to this work. While all school practitioners (i.e., teachers, school administrators, etc.) should have a focus on, training in, and skills related to youth well-being, social workers operate with six crucial values that position them at the forefront of educational justice in schools. The National Association of Social Workers highlights these six values in the profession's Code of Ethics, as follows: service, social justice, dignity and worth of the person, importance of human relationships, integrity, and competence (NASW, 2017). For social workers practicing in schools, these values directly call social workers to serve as advocates for the educational well-being of young people in schools. In particular, social workers should unravel systems of social injustice by seeking to serve and advocate for the most vulnerable students like those previously discussed. They should also acknowledge and elevate these students' dignity and worth, even when they may be considered the "problem student" by others in the school setting. This critical work is conducted primarily by engaging in healing and transformative human relationships with students, engaging them ethically and with integrity, and operating competently in these endeavors.

CASE STUDY 5.3—RENEE SHAW

Renee Shaw is a Native American middle school student, currently living with her maternal grandmother. Almost 1 year ago, Renee's mother left the home, leaving her in the care of her grandmother and aunt. While Renee usually received passing grades in school, she has recently been struggling to concentrate, complete assignments, and focus while in class. Her sixth-grade teacher became concerned about her performance and recommended that she be evaluated for attention deficit hyperactivity disorder (ADHD) and placed on medication, given her disengaged/withdrawn behavior in class. Renee's grandmother struggles with the idea of giving her granddaughter medication, especially since she has no behavioral issues at home. Given the teacher's difficulty with convincing the grandmother of her ADHD concerns, the school social worker, Ms. Bailey, was consulted and asked to intervene.

(continued)

CASE STUDY 5.3—RENEE SHAW (*continued*)

Ms. Bailey held two meetings with Renee—one to simply get to know the child and another meeting to discuss the challenges that she has had in class. Renee described herself as feeling sad since her mother left and not being interested in the work that her teacher gives her in class. Given the social worker's knowledge of trauma and trauma-informed practice, she also conducted a trauma screening, which resulted in positive posttraumatic stress disorder symptoms. Ms. Bailey brought this information to the attention of Renee's grandmother and convened a meeting between Renee, her grandmother, her teacher, and herself. While facilitating the meeting, she recognized the specific concerns that the grandmother reported about using medication and provided psychoeducation about ways to deal with trauma that did not require medication. She also assisted the teacher in understanding ways that her curriculum and behavior management techniques may not have been culturally relevant or stimulating to Renee. After the meeting, Renee and her grandmother decided to utilize a trauma-specific youth group provided in the school to address Renee's emotional well-being. The teacher also made intentional efforts to include diverse reading material and class examples to better engage Renee and her other non-White peers. The teacher also incorporated the use of storytelling to teach right and wrong ways of behaving, as this aligned more with historical ways of culturally grounded learning. After several weeks, Renee was beginning to focus better in class and reported feeling more engaged. She also reported talking to her grandmother more about her feelings at home.

Given our professional values, and specific attention to social, economic, and environmental justice, social workers can uniquely serve as resources in school settings, providing consultation to and in collaboration with teachers, administrators, and other school personnel. This means navigating school structures, policies, and infrastructures that often disempower youth or ignore youth's voices and perspectives—especially when the youth in question have demonstrated problematic behavior in school—and serving as a mediator between them and those aforementioned structures. Additionally, social workers can serve the role of advocate to youth in schools who feel disempowered in the multiple contexts of their lives as well as by the systemically unjust structures present in their school environment.

FROM THE FIELD 5.1

by Jackie Jones, LCSW

Jackie Jones is a 32-year-old African American social worker who has worked for a community-based nonprofit for 6 years. Her agency provides outpatient therapy and services to youth who live in foster care in a mid-sized city in the Midwest. Jackie has been in her position as community support therapist for just over a year. Initially, Jackie thought that most of her job would consist primarily of cognitive behavioral therapy with youths and revolve around providing the youths she serves with consistent emotional support. However, Jackie has found one of the most important and difficult aspects of her job includes working with the many different adults in the youths' lives and ensuring that the youths receive the services they need and deserve,

(*continued*)

FROM THE FIELD 5.1 (*continued*)

particularly in regard to education. Jackie has found that if she does not request or advocate for educational services, her clients may not receive them.

Jackie has found that she spends a lot of time educating teachers and administrators in local schools on psychological trauma and how it can manifest in a variety of ways for different types of students. Jackie has also spent a significant amount of time advocating for certain accommodations in student individual education plans (IEPs) to account for their needs and to ensure their success in the classroom. For example, she often advocates for clients with difficulties concentrating—she coordinates with school staff to make sure that they provide extra time for classroom exams or other graded in-class assignments. Jackie reports that being consistently present in the schools has increased her visibility and allowed her to build rapport and credibility with the school staff and administration.

Jackie has found different professionals in varying disciplines use their own unique language to talk about the same concept or idea. Oftentimes, because of this, Jackie finds herself translating for foster parents, teachers, administrators, judges, lawyers, and the youths themselves. Working with youth in foster care has made Jackie realize the importance of advocating for youth who may not have adults in their lives to advocate for them in their current settings. Her work experience thus far has also made Jackie realize the importance of educating people from different backgrounds (i.e., education, medical, and criminal justice) on the importance of mental health considerations and the importance of social justice.

STRATEGIES FOR ENGAGING IN JUSTICE-INFORMED SOCIAL WORK PRACTICE IN SCHOOLS

Social workers are often at the forefront of current and emerging intervention strategies for advocacy and the promotion of social justice in multiple sectors. In the educational system, the function of social workers is no different. In this section, we describe several of these intervention strategies as examples of how social workers can engage youth and work across system levels to provide corrective and healing experiences for students.

Micro Strategies

Racial literacy. In classrooms, culturally responsive teachers are generally more cognizant of the academic and behavioral needs of diverse students (Talbert-Johnson, 2004). There are areas in the country that have had great success in improving educational outcomes through rich professional development opportunities for teachers. These solutions take into account an acknowledgment of poverty and violence that students may have experienced and bring to school with them (Croft et al., 2015). For teachers, racial literacy and an understanding of implicit bias—internalized beliefs founded on social constructs of identities—can substantially shift the problem of racial inequity in education from an individualized problem to an institutional analysis of racism (Kohli et al., 2017). Specifically, research has demonstrated that a teacher's racial literacy made a considerable difference in students' ability to process and confront racism (Kohli et al., 2017). Strategies to promote racial literacy include the provision of spaces for students to dialog about race, using storytelling to critically engage students in discussion around race, and the use of theater and arts to teach students about human rights and internalized racism (Kohli et al., 2017; Richards-Schuster & Aldana, 2013). Social workers can lead the effort toward racial literacy in school settings, utilizing such strategies with students, advocating for resources focused on racial literacy, and helping teachers and other school personnel improve their cultural responsiveness and unpack their own personal issues of bias.

Trauma-informed practice. Trauma-informed school practice is another approach that can provide support to marginalized youth, as it promotes social justice in educational settings (Crosby et al., 2018). Trauma-informed practice includes recognition of the prevalence and impact of psychological trauma, as well as multilevel responses that do not retraumatize (Substance Abuse and Mental Health Services Administration [SAMHSA], 2015). This includes ongoing professional development for school staff focused on childhood trauma and trauma-informed responses (Day et al., 2015), trauma-sensitive school discipline practices rather than punitive exclusionary methods like suspension and expulsion (Baroni et al., 2016), promoting strong and supportive relationships between students and teachers, and teacher flexibility in classroom management and instructional practices (Cole et al., 2005). Models of trauma-informed school practice focus on empowering students who have been traditionally disempowered by prioritizing critical recognition of the trauma that students encounter and the ways in which systems, both inside and outside of the school, perpetuate that trauma and retraumatize students (Crosby et al., 2018). Research has demonstrated the promise of this school strategy for reducing student trauma symptoms (Day et al., 2015), as well as student suspension and expulsion rates (Baroni et al., 2016). Social workers can serve as advocates for trauma-informed practice in schools and also provide critical education on trauma to school personnel who often do not enter the educational field with such training.

Restorative practice. Restorative practice, developed out of the Restorative Justice model, focuses on the ideology of reintegrative shaming, where individuals who commit offensive acts are both held accountable and also welcomed back into the community (Braithwaite et al., 2005). In schools, restorative practice seeks to build relationships among students and school staff, reduce incidences of student violations, and also repair the harm done when offensive student behavior takes place (Payne & Welch, 2015), while also addressing institutional power dynamics that influence students' feelings about their school's disciplinary practices and overall climate (Ginwright & Cammarota, 2002). Restorative practice has a developing body of evidence to support its use in school settings, including reductions in student suspensions (González, 2012). Social workers can work in conjunction with school staff to integrate restorative practices into their school's disciplinary structure, educating school staff on power dynamics that might perpetuate negative student–teacher relationships, and facilitating restorative practices when serious student violations occur. This may also include developing school-based opportunities for students to explore and discuss challenges occurring in their school, to employ community-organizing strategies, and to establish restorative procedures that would meet everyone's needs in order to ultimately leverage their power to create change in their school setting.

Preservice and in-service teacher professional development training. Schools of education need to develop strategies to provide professional development that prepares educators to teach diverse audiences. The most effective professional development approaches include clear goals, ongoing feedback to teachers on their performance, personalization and targeted supports for students, data-based decision-making, high standards for students, and relentless commitment to continuous quality improvement (Ferguson, 2016). A well-qualified teacher should also possess an empathic disposition, which manifests itself in teachers' caring relationships with students (Talbert-Johnson, 2004). Empathic teachers are caring, compassionate, competent, and flexible in their interactions with students, while addressing not only academic concerns but the emotional, behavioral, and social characteristics of students as well (Talbert-Johnson, 2004). Additionally, teachers should include a rich repertoire of resource materials across content areas that are reflective of all cultures. Low expectations, negative stereotypes, biases and prejudices, and cultural misconceptions held by teachers must be identified, challenged, and reconstructed (Talbert-Johnson, 2004).

Mezzo Strategies

Considering past and current inequities, it is important for social workers to be mindful of the barriers faced by marginalized youth and the importance of coordination with parents to engage in planning to keep them informed and aware of issues that may impact youth. It is also critical for social workers to work with teachers and administrators as a collaborative team to provide support and education to school staff, and to connect all available resources to meet students' needs. This is especially important in scenarios where youth are coming from underfunded and underresourced schools or where youth of color are one or few in their academic environment.

When working with youth in school settings, it is important to consider the socioeconomic background of the individual student and the type of resources the school has available. These factors can play a pivotal role in the experience of youth in school settings. Social workers can also play a pivotal role in helping youth of color advocate for themselves, when appropriate, using an assets-based approach to bridge the gap between the youth's family and the school the youth attends. It is also important for social workers to work with youth and families of immigrant status to ensure they have the best chance to overcome system-level barriers, viewing cultural capital and family stability as strengths to improve students' educational well-being. Social workers must account for possible language barriers that may impede their ability to best serve immigrant youth and be willing to problem-solve solutions to address this challenge.

Social support has been consistently identified as a protective factor that can help youth of sexual minority and gender expansive identities find success in school despite the risk factors they may face. It is important for social workers to work as allies with youth and families from this population and check their own biases that may impede them from providing the best service possible. It is also important for social workers to challenge heteronormativity and promote empathy among students, teachers, and administrators through social justice education and professional development to make sure students with sexual minority and gender-expansive identities feel safe and included in their school environments.

It is also imperative for social workers to work across systems to advocate for homeless and system-involved youth, whether checking to make sure students are given their school assignments after having to miss class for mandated court dates or collaborating with the caregivers and case workers to make sure the youths are receiving all of the recommended accommodations they need to be academically successful. Along with trauma-informed care, social workers will need to be aware of their own biases, privileges, and power when interacting in these various systems to empower youths who have had their choice and power systematically stripped in multiple areas of their lives. It is essential that social workers work with caregivers or residential placement staff (i.e., foster home, group home, or residential center), case workers, mental health professionals, and biological parents, if possible, to ensure that everyone is coordinated in the youth's care.

Macro Strategies

There are many strategies that can be employed to address structural racism at the policy and macro practice levels. First, the Every Student Succeeds Act (ESSA), which was signed into law in 2016 by President Obama, represents a unique opportunity for the federal government, states, districts, and schools to equitably design educational systems to ensure that students who have been historically underserved receive an adequate education that prepares them for the demands of the 21st-century service economy (Cook-Harvey et al., 2016). Specifically, the ESSA contains specific provisions that can be utilized to address educational inequities for students of color, English learners, students with disabilities, and those who are homeless or in foster care. Under this new law, education leaders have great flexibility to define student success and to design their own systems and programs to ensure education equity, a paradigm shift that allows policymakers to develop comprehensive strategies that take into account all aspects of student learning and development, including socioemotional skills (Gayl, 2017). Although ESSA is still primarily a test-based accountability system, one indicator of accountability includes a measure of school quality or student success that is not related to test scores. Specifically, this nonacademic indicator could include any of the following: student engagement, educator engagement, postsecondary readiness, and school climate and safety (Penuel et al., 2016). The use of these nonacademic indicators provides for the first time in federal law an opportunity to shed light on the opportunity gaps that create and exacerbate achievement gaps. Nonacademic indicators can signal a move away from punitive, high-stakes testing and toward a more holistic and equitable understanding of what helps students and teachers thrive in school settings. In addition to these new measures of school success, ESSA also provides new financial resources for teacher professional development in techniques and supports for referring at-risk students to mental health services, as well as how to address safety, peer interaction, drug and alcohol abuse, and chronic absenteeism (Gayl, 2017).

From a practice perspective, the most appropriate response to overcrowding is to build more schools; unfortunately, the costs associated with major construction are prohibitive (Ready et al., 2004). A less common response to overcrowding is to rearrange school calendars so that not all students are in the building at the same time (Ready et al., 2004). The drawback of this solution is that it can limit student access to cocurricular and extracurricular activities and sports, which tend to be offered based on traditional school calendars. A much more recent educational reform initiative has been to break large high schools into smaller subunits, or schools within schools (Ready et al., 2004). At present, there is very limited research that documents the overall achievement gains of this method. Finally, in communities where children do not have access to stable housing, and employment and other opportunities are denied to their families, the provision of health, social, medical, and dental support becomes essential. It is particularly important for schools in these communities to develop strong and mutually respectful partnerships with community-based organizations that can address these student needs (Mathis & Trujillo, 2016).

Constitutionally, the U.S. government cannot mandate state adoption of educational reform initiatives (Croft et al., 2015). However, federal dollars are a powerful decision-making factor in state education policy, and access to these resources can be made contingent on a state's implementation of educational reform. Unequal education treatments are not inevitable. All children should have access to high-quality schools, and policymakers have a social imperative to enact policies that actualize this goal.

CONCLUSION

Academic skills are a major contributor to income earnings and quality of life, especially for marginalized populations in our country. More importantly, every child deserves a learning environment where their experiences are recognized and valued. While our educational system may have a checkered past and a pervasively unjust present, there are opportunities for hope that our nation can do better for our most vulnerable groups of youth. Educational justice is a national challenge, and our work as social workers lies at the center of this challenge, moving the needle forward so that all young people will one day have an opportunity to learn and thrive in their school setting and beyond.

DISCUSSION QUESTIONS

1. What are some of the consequences of losing Black administrators in school settings?
2. School is a universal experience although how school is experienced varies dramatically. Explain how intersectionality might further compound outcomes for vulnerable children.
3. Identify the critical connections between school achievement and economic justice.
4. How would you recognize if a school is not able to meet a child's educational needs? What would you see in the child? What would you look for in the school?

REFERENCES

Only key references appear in the print edition. The full reference list appears in the digital product on Springer Publishing Connect: connect.springerpub.com/content/book/978-0-8261-3539-1/chapter/ch05

Aleman, Jr., E., Salazar, T., Rorrer, A., & Parker, L. (2011). Introduction to post-racialism in US public school and higher education settings: The politics of education in the era of Obama. *Peabody Journal of Education, 86*(5), 479–487. https://doi.org/10.1080/0161956X.2011.616129

Birkett, M., Espelage, D. L., & Koenig, B. (2009). LGB and questioning students in schools: The moderating effects of homophobic bullying and school climate on negative outcomes. *Journal of Youth and Adolescence, 38*, 989–1000. https://doi.org/10.1007/s10964-008-9389-1

Boccanfuso, C., & Kuhfeld, M. (2011). *Multiple responses, promising results: Evidence-based, nonpunitive alternatives to zero tolerance* (Research Brief 2011-09). http://childtrends.org/wp-content/uploads/2011/03/Child_Trends-2011_03_01_RB_AltToZeroTolerance.pdf

Cole, S. F., O'Brien, J. G., Gadd, M. G., Ristuccia, J., Wallace, D. L., & Gregory, M. (2005). *Helping traumatized children learn.* Advocates for Children.

Coleman, J. S. (1966). *Equality of educational opportunity [summary report]* (Vol. 2). U.S. Department of Health, Education, and Welfare, Office of Education.

Cook-Harvey, C. M., Darling-Hammond, L., Lam, L., Mercer, C., & Roc, M. (2016). *Equity and ESSA: Leveraging educational opportunity through the Every Student Succeeds Act.* Learning Policy Institute.

Crosby, S. D., Howell, P., & Thomas, S. (2018). Social justice education through trauma-informed teaching. *Middle School Journal, 49* (4), 15–23. https://doi.org/10.1080/00940771.2018.1488470

Ferguson, R. F. (2016). *Aiming higher together: Strategizing better educational outcomes for boys and young men of color* [Research Report]. Urban Institute.

González, T. (2012). Keeping kids in schools: Restorative justice, punitive discipline, and the school to prison pipeline. *Journal of Law and Education, 41*(2), 281–335. https://www.restorativeresources.org/uploads/5/6/1/4/56143033/thalia_gonzalez_school_to_prison_pipeline.pdf.

Kohli, R., Pizarro, M., & Nevarez, A. (2017). The "New Racism" of K-12 schools: Centering critical research on racism. *Review of Research in Education, 41*, 182–202. https://doi.org/10.3102/0091732X16686949

McKown, C., & Weinstein, R. S. (2008). Teacher expectations, classroom context, and the achievement gap. *Journal of School Psychology, 46*(3), 235–261. https://doi.org/10.1016/j.jsp.2007.05.001

Reardon, S. (2011). The widening academic achievement gap between the rich and the poor: New evidence and possible explanations. In G. Duncan, & R. Murnane (Eds.), *Whither opportunity?: Rising inequality, schools, and children's life chances* (pp. 91–116). Russell Sage Foundation. http://www.jstor.org/stable/10.7758/9781610447515.10

Zajac, K., Sheidow, A., & Davis, M. (2015). Juvenile justice, mental health, and the transition to adulthood: A review of service system involvement and unmet needs in the U.S. *Children and Youth Services Review, 56*, 139–148. https://doi.org/10.1016/j.childyouth.2015.07.014

6

JUSTICE-INFORMED SOCIAL WORK PRACTICE WITHIN THE CRIMINAL JUSTICE SYSTEM

Karen M. Kolivoski

LEARNING OBJECTIVES

Students will be able to:

- Describe the general characteristics of the criminal justice system, including demographics of those involved.
- Define mass incarceration.
- Explain the historical and contemporary connection between social work and the juvenile and criminal justice systems.
- Assess pervasive and structural barriers for people involved in the criminal justice system.
- Articulate a justice-informed social work approach to practicing in criminal justice.
- Explain the interconnection of criminal justice with other systems, including child welfare.

INTRODUCTION

Social work practice in the criminal justice system encompasses all access points from the initial contact, to arrest, through the court system, into correctional confinement, and those on probation or parole. Social workers are unique in that we support victims as well as offenders. Understanding the system of law in determining what is legal or not is essential to social work practice. Additionally, justice-informed social work practice in the criminal justice system must acknowledge and address the disparities that impact people and communities of color, and women, and place children in foster care and educational disciplinary systems at increased risk for engaging in the criminal justice system. Social work in the criminal justice system encompasses both micro and macro aspects to address the existing structural discrimination that creates enduring consequences long after incarceration, impacting individuals, families, and communities with life-altering consequences.

OVERVIEW OF THE CRIMINAL JUSTICE SYSTEM IN THE UNITED STATES

The criminal justice system in the United States collectively refers to the agencies and institutions aimed at reducing crime and addressing accountability for people who violate the law. The criminal law determines what acts and behaviors are legal and illegal and, for those deemed illegal, outlines punishments for people found guilty as well as due process to ensure that people accused of violating the law receive fair treatment.

The major entities in the criminal justice system include those who make the law, enforce the law, and interpret the law. Law originates from a variety of documents, including the U.S. Constitution, as well as state and local laws that determine which acts and behaviors are illegal. Often overlooked are the roles of policy and lawmakers as key components of the criminal justice system. Police are responsible for conducting investigations into who may have committed illegal acts, and arresting people deemed as suspected of violating the law. The courts are responsible for furthering the criminal justice process through determining if charges should be filed, deciding if a person accused of breaking the law is guilty, as well as for determining the appropriate sentence, punishment, and/or rehabilitation. Some courts, such as the U.S. Supreme Court, are also responsible for hearing cases to decide if they are constitutional or unconstitutional, which then sets legal precedent.

The "front end" of contact with the criminal justice involves that initial interaction with legal authorities, which is typically an arrest by police. Once a person is convicted of a crime, on the "back end" of the criminal justice system, a correctional agency is responsible for ensuring that the sentence from the courts is properly carried out. This may include housing people found in violation of the law, such as in jails or prisons, or in community-based settings where a person fulfills their sentence while living in their home of origin.

The Reality of the Criminal Justice System in the United States

As just described, the criminal justice system is responsible for identifying people who have violated laws and determining the appropriate punishment for illicit actions. It all sounds simple: there are the so-called "good guys" in charge of overseeing and correcting the behaviors of the so-called "bad guys." Although the description of the criminal justice system in the United States sounds on the surface like one that is fair and just, there are many, many issues with it, both historically and in the present. Because of these issues, many would argue that the criminal justice system is anything but one defined by justice.

For people in the public who may not have many substantial interactions with the criminal justice system or know someone who is under its surveillance, there may be differing perceptions that are not based on reality. For example, the general public oftentimes gets its information about the criminal justice system from crime drama series, yet such shows typically ignore structural criminal justice issues such as racial bias, and erroneously reinforce policies and beliefs about the system that are most detrimental to Black people, other people of color, and women (Jones, 2020). Additionally, crime dramas typically portray a criminal court process, yet 94% of state-level and 97% of federal criminal convictions derive from guilty pleas, rather than trials (Yoffe, 2017).

Public perceptions of crime are seldom related to actual crime rates (Gallup, 2020). Although the crime rate has dropped substantially in the last two decades prior to 2020, people often report their perceptions that crime is increasing (Color of Change and The USC Annenberg Norman

Lear Center, 2020; Lafree, 2018). One way of providing evidence to support this is to acknowledge that many people who do not have direct contact with the criminal justice system gain their beliefs about it from crime drama series which often misrepresent the reality of the criminal justice system. In a study of 353 episodes from scripted shows during the 2017 to 2018 television season, findings included that racist, and at times illegal, practices and the need for accountability of police misbehavior are largely unaddressed or even allowed and sometimes even justified, and that most of the people behind such shows (e.g., creators and writers) are White (Color of Change and The USC Annenberg Norman Lear Center, 2020).

The reality of the criminal justice system varies widely from what is typically portrayed on television or the perceptions of people not directly involved in it. The idea of locking people up and throwing away the proverbial key is not a realistic criminal justice system policy. More than 95% of people serving time in state prisons will be released (Hughes & Wilson, 2002). This means that re-entry for people who have been incarcerated is a necessity, yet few supportive resources are provided which increases the risk of return.

People may think that prisons are made up of "the worst of the worst" in terms of their offenses, such as homicide, aggravated assault, and kidnapping. However, according to data from the Federal Bureau of Prisons, drug offenses are the most common category of offenses (45.4%), and homicides and related offenses constitute 3.2% of inmates (Federal Bureau of Prisons, 2020).

There are approximately 630,000 people in jails on a given day, and 70% are in pretrial detention, meaning that they are being detained prior to their trial or court hearing. According to the Sixth Amendment of the U.S. Constitution, when a person cannot afford an attorney, one is assigned to them. However, many public defenders are overworked and carry unreasonably high caseloads (Schoneman, 2018) that make this unfeasible.

CASE STUDY 6.1—THE CRIMINAL JUSTICE SYSTEM FAILURES

Kalief Browder is a tragic example of the realities—and failings—of the U.S. criminal justice system. He was a Black man from Bronx, New York who was arrested in May 2010 after being accused of stealing a backpack. Because he was on probation at the time of his arrest, Browder was not released and was charged with second-degree robbery. Prior to his court trial, he was held at a jail on Rikers Island until 2013, with 2 years of that in solitary confinement. Browder was finally released after the prosecutor did not have sufficient evidence and a key witness was no longer in the United States. Two years later, in 2015, Browder committed suicide, thought to be due largely to the many abuses he sustained while incarcerated.

Mass Incarceration

Mass incarceration is a broad term used to describe the American phenomenon of using high imprisonment rates associated with typically young, Black men from communities that have been historically disenfranchised. Mass incarceration is a key driver quest for criminal justice reform and is associated with the current, highly criticized state of the criminal justice system. Mass incarceration is typically thought of as starting with the War on Drugs and punitive drug policies in the 1980s. As a result, the number of people incarcerated for drug offenses has dramatically escalated, with more people incarcerated for drug offenses than the total number of people in jails or prisons for any type of crime altogether in 1980 when the punitive drug policies were introduced (The Sentencing Project, n.d.).

The United States is the home of mass incarceration, the social phenomenon which refers to the sheer numbers of people who are under the surveillance of the criminal justice system in some form, and many would argue unjustly or unnecessarily so. More than 6.7 million people are under some form of criminal justice system control, including probation and parole (Carson, 2018). The United States incarcerates more people than any other nation in the world—more than China, Brazil, and the Russian Federation, which are in the second, third, and fourth spots, respectively (Prison Studies, n.d.). In a global context, the United States comprises about 5% of the world's population, yet has nearly 25% of the world's prison population (American Civil Liberties Union [ACLU], n.d.). This growth has been especially pronounced since the 1970s, when the number of incarcerated people increased by 700%, with approximately 2.3 million people incarcerated at present, which exceeds population growth and crime rates (ACLU, n.d.).

The incarcerated population includes the wide array of correctional entities in the country: 1,719 state prisons, 109 federal prisons, 1,772 juvenile correctional facilities, 3,163 local jails, and 80 jails in Indigenous communities, as well as military prisons, immigration detention facilities, civil commitment centers, psychiatric hospitals, and prisons in territories of the United States (Sawyer & Wagner, 2019). More than 10 million Americans have an immediate family member in jail or prison (FWD.us, 2018). These incredible numbers compose what is known as "mass incarceration," where not only is the overall trend that the United States is overincarcerating, but is overincarcerating those who are most vulnerable and marginalized. Moreover, this over-incarceration has not been shown to drastically reduce future crime as was intended.

As a social worker, it is important to engage critically with statistics like these and question why things might be this way. For instance, do you think the disproportionally large number of U.S. citizens in prison, compared to people across the world, is because Americans actually commit more crime? Or maybe it is because other countries are "soft" on crime and do not take it as seriously as the U.S. government? Probably not. Likewise, think about how people of color—especially Black and Latinx people—are overrepresented in jails and prisons across the United States. What structures exist that result in these numbers that are unique to the United States?

FROM THE FIELD 6.1

SAY THEIR NAMES: THE STORIES OF VIOLENCE AGAINST BLACK PEOPLE PAST AND PRESENT

The history of the criminal justice system with people of color, and particularly Black people, is one of systemic injustices and brutality whose impact on individuals and communities continues to the present day. With increases in technology, such as the internet, social media, smartphones, and police-worn body cameras and cameras mounted on police car dashboards, there is also rising attention to these atrocities. However, with constant turnover in the media and the public's attention, and unceasing stories of police brutality, the people behind the headlines may be lost. This is especially true for Black women, often ignored due to the intersection of race and gender, which fueled the #SayHerName campaign launched by the African American Policy Forum (AAPF) and the Center for Intersectionality and Social Policy Studies in

(continued)

FROM THE FIELD 6.1 (continued)

2014 (AAPF, n.d.). To amplify their stories, as well as draw attention to the larger issue of Black women experiencing violence at the hands of the police, it is important to know the stories of who these women are. For all people affected by police violence, one trend is to include their names as hashtags in social media platforms such as Twitter.

The Say Her Name campaign reflects the key ethical principles of the National Association of Social Workers (NASW) Code of Ethics in recognizing and honoring the dignity and worth of a person. Acknowledging the people behind the need for reform and advocacy is critical to humanize issues and to drive the changes needed for a more socially just society. Moreover, a critical piece to realize in these modern movements is that many of the injustices against Black people from the police and legal authorities are not new, but have been occurring for centuries.

To know the issues it is crucial to know the stories. Unfortunately, there are countless Black people who suffer at the hands of professionals in the criminal justice system whose names do not make headlines or whose stories we may never know. That does not dismiss the need to learn and honor the people whose stories we do know. In addition to Kalief Browder's story described in this chapter, additional contemporary names, people, and stories of which to be knowledgeable include: Sandra Bland, Trayvon Martin, Tamir Rice, Ahmaud Arbery, Freddie Gray, Michael Brown, Philando Castile, Tanisha Anderson, Rekia Boyd, and Breonna Taylor. Note: this list is not exhaustive nor comprehensive but does provide some context related to the need for criminal justice reform.

Last, it is also important that any social work professional, particularly those interested in criminal justice, be aware of names of Black people throughout history who have also not received justice. The most famous case may well be Emmett Till, a 14-year-old Black boy brutally murdered in Mississippi in 1955 after allegedly offending a White woman. His mother's decision to have an open casket funeral, in which her young son's mutilated body was on display, helped draw outrage to the injustice. Other stories may be less known yet remain important for people to know. These include James Earl Chaney, one of three civil rights workers murdered in 1943 by the Ku Klux Klan in Mississippi; 14-year-old George Stinney, Jr., executed by electric chair in 1944 and the youngest American sentenced to death and executed (and whose case has been revisited); Hayes and Mary Turner, their newborn baby, as well as their unborn baby (Mary was 8 months pregnant), all lynched in 1918 after Hayes was accused of murder and Mary was vocal against the accusation and his lynching; Jesse Washington, a 17-year-old accused of raping and murdering a White woman, and whose death at the hands of a mob included being stabbed, castrated, and his body put on public display in Waco, Texas; and the 1959 lynching of Mack Charles Parker, accused of raping a pregnant White woman, kidnapped from jail by a mob before his trial, and beaten and shot to death.

These examples are generationally traumatic and highlight how historical suffering continues into the present day with the continued violence against Black men and women. We cannot overestimate the impact that this history of violence has in continuing to inform the present-day context. Certainly, we can see how distrust, cynicism, anger, and outrage originated, both in the sense of an expectation of fair treatment and the lack of ability to trust in the criminal justice system.

Demographics of People in the Criminal Justice System

To understand the criminal justice system, particularly from a social work perspective, it is important to know the general demographics of who is most affected by it, especially for those historically oppressed and/or marginalized populations. Racial and ethnic disparities are one of the defining features of people involved in criminal justice system control. People of color comprise 37% of the population in the United States, but more than two-thirds of the prison population (The Sentencing Project, n.d.).

Disparities exist at various points of contact within the criminal justice system: from the initial point of contact, to arrest, through the court system, into correctional confinement, and on probation or parole. In a study of more than 100 million traffic stops, police were more likely to pull over Black drivers, and Black and Latinx drivers were more likely to experience a search for contraband, even though White people were more likely to have contraband (Pierson et al., 2019). People who are Black are more likely than people who are White to be arrested and convicted (The Sentencing Project, n.d.).

In terms of gender, of people who are incarcerated, women make up the fastest-growing portion of the population (Kajstura, 2017). Since 1978, the incarceration of women has risen at twice the rate of men (Sawyer, 2018). More than 80% of women in jails are mothers (McCampbell, 2005).

People who are LGBTQ or transgender are also an especially vulnerable population as related to the criminal justice system (National Center for Transgender Equality, 2018). The 2015 Transgender Survey cites that more than half of people who are transgender are afraid of contacting the police when needed (James et al., 2016).

The criminal justice system also is overwhelmingly disproportionate in its representation of people in poverty. Millions of people in the United States are involved in the criminal justice system due to being poor (Capeheart, 2018). The percentage of people of color and people who are poor within the prison population has risen compared to previous decades (Lynch, 2007).

These descriptive demographic numbers and categories of groups of people help give a sense of "who" is involved in the criminal justice system, but it is also important to acknowledge that placing people into categories such as these does not address the intersectionality with which they operate. For people involved in the criminal justice system, being a member of more than one group mentioned may mean increased bias from the justice system, as well as the need to pay attention to unique experiences based on these intersecting identities (Teti, 2017).

Lastly, although numbers can give context about who are the people in contact with the criminal justice system, any statistics need to be interpreted with caution. For example, the overrepresentation of people of color in the criminal justice system needs to take into consideration the racial bias inherent in criminal justice and racist history of legal authorities, particularly for Black people in the United States. On the surface, the criminal justice system may seem to be fair and just, often meaning that it is considered to be blind to one's position of race/ethnicity or class status. Viewing the criminal justice system in this manner assumes that justice occurs equally regardless of one's position in society. However, this perspective lacks awareness and can worsen the bias in the system because it is never addressed. According to Cole (2001), while we want society to believe that our criminal justice system protects citizens and our legal rights, in practice the reality is that the "law enforcement prerogatives" (p. 27) continue to be prioritized over the rights of the individual, particularly when that individual is a person of color.

OVERVIEW OF THE CRIMINAL JUSTICE SYSTEM AND SOCIAL WORK

Social workers are needed in criminal justice settings at both the micro and macro levels. Micro social work practice provides direct services to individuals and families affected by justice system contact and implements and assesses interventions for positive outcomes for clients. Macro social work practice informs policy reforms to address the disparities, inequities, and inadequacies in the system as well program reforms such as ensuring a successful reintegration into society. A social worker should have many qualities to bring about positive changes in the criminal justice system, including recognizing the inherent dignity and worth of people whom others may view as unworthy of help; recognizing that a person does not exist in isolation, but is a part of the broader environment; and recognizing the need to work on the individual client level as well as to advocate for broad system reforms (Kolivoski, 2017).

Social workers in criminal justice settings are equipped for many roles and may conduct mental health assessments with law enforcement or work in their domestic violence enforcement units, oversee diversion or re-entry programs, act as probation or parole officers, work in court settings, or with prosecuting attorneys as a victim advocate, and a multitude of other roles to apply their social work expertise in ways in which others are not trained. Finally, social workers may work as policy advocates or research analysts on juvenile and criminal justice issues. Law enforcement, city and county jails, state and federal correctional facilities, court systems, nonprofits that serve people who were formerly incarcerated, drug courts, mental health courts, and behavioral healthcare providers are all potential settings for a social worker interested in criminal justice.

Social work has also been fundamental to the crisis intervention team (CIT) program, an alliance between law enforcement and behavioral health professionals to provide better responses to people who interact with the criminal justice system, in particular at the point of engagement. Social workers are integral to the CIT programs in providing mental health assessments and recommendations for treatment-based outcomes. CITs have received support for their potential to improve ways to respond to people's mental health needs before, in lieu of, or beyond arrest as the solution (Watson & Fulambarker, 2012).

The American Academy of Social Work and Social Welfare (AASWSW) has identified what are known as the 12 Grand Challenges of social work to meet the greatest needs in society, with "promoting smart decarceration" as one that directly addresses people and families impacted by the criminal justice system (AASWSW, n.d.).

Social work and criminal justice have had a shifting relationship throughout U.S. history. On the one hand, numerous social workers operate within various aspects of the criminal justice system, including specialty courts, and in overall positive ways, such as in drug courts (Roberts et al., 2014) and mental health courts (Greville, 2016).

Social Work and Criminal Justice: An Uncomfortable Partnership?

In 2020, national and international public demonstrations in response to police violence against numerous people of color, notably George Floyd in Minnesota and Breonna Taylor in Kentucky, sparked a wave of media attention, and facilitated dialogue on reforms for the criminal justice system and prompted policy actions. Among these were a push for increased funding for social services as well as for social workers to play a more prominent role in responding to issues in which police are often the first responders, such as homelessness. For example, New York City is identifying and implementing better ways to respond to people in crisis, which include amplifying the role of social workers in the process and recognizing the unique skills and knowledge they bring to such issues (Cline-Thomas, 2020).

President Trump signed an Executive Order in June 2020 on police reform (Executive Order on Safe Policing for Safe Communities, 2020), and a prominent piece included calling on police departments to include social workers and other behavioral health professionals in responses to people presenting with behavioral health needs (Kelly & Naylor, 2020). In recognizing that many of the calls to which police respond are nonviolent and may overlap with social work's traditional clients and presenting issues, this may seem like a logical response and one that exists in some communities but not all. So it is seen as an improvement over the normal current police practices. Inclusion of social work has become the standard of care for those engaging with law enforcement.

However, many argue that these reforms do not address the heart of the issues regarding police brutality and systemic racism within the criminal justice system. The NASW released a response to the executive order that referred to it as inadequate, noting that many of the identified concerns, such as use of force, chokeholds, and no-knock warrants that allow police to enter a home without knocking, as well as disparities that place Black people at increased risk of engaging with the criminal justice system, were not addressed (NASW, 2020).

In addition, such reforms and others like them are not without controversy regarding the uneasy relationship between social work and criminal justice. Any reform needs to be critically evaluated. Recognizing the historical role of social work, some argue that having social workers respond to issues instead of police does not fundamentally change the systems within which the U.S. society operates (Foiles, 2020). Although social workers on the individual level may operate with well-meaning intentions, it is often social work as a profession itself that is seen as one that reproduces the same inequities it purports to seek to eradicate. Social work and social service agencies are not immune to institutional racism and other structural-level issues and, like law enforcement and the criminal justice system, need to be examined with a critical eye and are potentially in need of reform as well (Marwell & Mosley, 2020).

Some argue that social work's partnerships with law enforcement reinforce the profession's uneasy, and questionable, role as authorities enforcing social control, and not fundamentally questioning and changing social service and criminal justice systems (Vakharia, 2020). This is an issue not limited to the criminal justice system, as scholars such as Dorothy Roberts have drawn attention to the problems within the child welfare system, which she refers to as the "family regulation system," designed to penalize Black people and vulnerable groups while maintaining society's status quo (Roberts, 2020, para. 3). Proposed reforms asked of the criminal justice system that include calls to abolish or defund the police, or to have social workers replace police, need to also come with a critical self-reflection of the social work profession itself.

Social Work in Criminal Justice—Employment and Education

There is a demonstrated need for social workers in criminal justice settings, and the profession has identified criminal justice as one of 12 Grand Challenges facing our nation. However, the criminal justice system as a place of employment is not commonly identified by social workers. Most frequently, the top area of identified social work practice is mental health (37%), followed by health (13%) and child welfare/family (13%) with only 2% of social workers in criminal justice settings (NASW Center for Workforce Studies, 2006). Notably, each of these areas intersects significantly with criminal justice practice. More recently, a survey of 2018 social work graduates found that 3.2% described criminal justice as their primary setting (The George Washington University Health Workforce Institute, 2019).

This reduced presence of social workers in criminal justice settings is also reflected in social work education. Few schools of social work have distinct concentrations or courses specific to criminal justice, although there are roots of criminal justice's presence in social work education. In 1959, the Council on Social Work Education published a volume, part of a set of 13, by Studt (1959) that focused on teaching correctional social work. This resulted in several major schools of social work offering correctional social work courses (Roberts & Brownell, 1999).

However, in the present day, criminal justice–specific classes, concentrations and content (i.e., not including classes on social work and law) are offered at just 22% of Master of Social Work (MSW) programs, less than 5% have a concentration or specialization in criminal justice, and only 1% offer all three: dual or joint degree, concentration/specialization, and coursework (Epperson et al., 2013). Further, only six MSW institutions have a dual degree (e.g., criminal justice/criminology; Epperson et al., 2013).

A related topic to criminal justice social work is forensic social work, which centers on the intersections of social work and the law and covers topics such as a criminal defendant's competency, mitigation services, child abuse and custody issues, and so on. A 2019 review of master's programs found that only eight programs had a concentration on forensics or a forensic social work postmaster's certificate program (Kheibari et al., 2019). Although there is a lack of specific concentrations and courses on criminal justice in many MSW programs, nearly all MSW programs offer students field placements in various criminal justice–related settings (Epperson et al., 2013). Exposing students to criminal justice topics through field placements as well as coursework are strategies to foster students' interest in this area. The lack of a strong presence of social work within criminal justice employment settings and within the social work education realm remains a challenge, yet one with many areas for growth opportunity.

History of the Role of Social Work in Juvenile Justice

Historically, social work has had a prominent presence within criminal justice. Presumably, this presence will again be bolstered by emerging criminal justice reform policies. A specific area of attention within the criminal justice system has been that of juvenile justice. The social work profession was crucial in establishing the juvenile court system. This history includes familiar social work pioneers such as Julia Lathrop, Lucy Flower, Edith Abbott, Grace Abbott, and Jane Addams (Tanenhaus, 2002). The contributions of these women continue to be evident in the present juvenile justice system, recognizing that youth needed a separate court from adults, focused on rehabilitation and treatment. The next section is not an exhaustive history of the intertwining relationship between juvenile and criminal justice and social work, but offers some key highlights related to the waxing and waning relationship between them.

The origin of social work and criminal justice in the United States precedes the first juvenile court established in 1899, and has persisted since. In the 1800s, early social reformers worked in prison, juvenile, and reformatory settings (Gibelman, 1995). John Augustus, considered the "father of probation," was an early version of a social worker, as well as boot maker, who in 1841 worked with Boston courts to agree to release some offenders to him as an alternative to their incarceration. He successfully did this work until his death in 1859 (Lindner, 2006). The overlap of social work and criminal justice also has roots in the National Conference of Charities and Corrections, formed in 1879, with Jane Addams as its first woman president (Roberts & Brownell, 1999; Solomon, 1994).

With the establishment of the first juvenile court in Cook County, Illinois in 1899, the role of early social workers with the justice system was solidified. The Chicago Woman's Club started a distinct organization called the Juvenile Court Committee that ran a detention home and employed 15 probation officers, with Julia Lathrop as its first president (Tanenhaus, 2002). Jane Addams wrote in 1935 of the shifts in the juvenile court as separate from the adult system, noting that when a child was brought in front of a judge, the conversation was not about guilt or innocence, but focused on what could be done to improve their life outcome (Tanenhaus, 2013).

Social work also continued to influence the adult criminal justice system, as in the early 1900s, Women's Bureaus were founded in police departments to serve as advocates, and there were police social workers in 175 cities in the United States (Roberts, 1997), although the Great Depression ultimately ended this funding. In 1945, *Social Service Review* published an article by Pray and Towle that called on social workers to be more involved in criminal justice and to help people in the rehabilitation process, which further fueled interest in this area. From the 1950s through the 1980s, social workers led reform efforts at most stages of the criminal justice system and were crucial to developing policies on the national level to decrease incarceration and poverty while also advocating for education, employment resources, and community-based treatments (Miller, 1991; Rosenheim, 2002; Sarri & Shook, 2005). Among social work professionals in criminal justice, many were employed as administrators and policy makers, both nationally and at the local level (Sarri & Shook, 2005, p. 212).

However, in the 1980s and 1990s, there was an overall decline of social work's presence in juvenile and criminal justice. In the juvenile justice system, a primary reason was that social work professionals opposed being employed in settings deemed coercive and with mandated clients (Sarri, 2000). Peters (2011) echoes this, and also states that social workers fell out of favor in these settings due to the preference of men as probation officers while women served as social workers and the emphasis on providing services as a prevention for delinquent behavior, rather than working to address the system itself. As a result, many social workers withdrew from criminal justice settings, largely in part due to the broader criminal justice system shift toward more punitive policies and away from rehabilitation and treatment. Other reasons included less funding to support social worker training, courts and human rights attorneys stepping up to act as advocates for vulnerable people, and some professional organizations arguing that social work could not function in a system where the key goal was punishment and control (Sarri & Shook, 2005). In response to this trend, social work programs offered fewer training opportunities specific to criminal justice, and there was a decline in criminal justice research among social work faculty (Sarri & Shook, 2005). In 2004, Reamer lamented that the social work profession had, "largely abandoned the criminal justice field" (p. 213).

Since this statement, many in social work and criminal justice would argue that we are now undergoing a modern-day resurgence, and are rising to the Grand Challenges related to the justice system. This movement is due to many factors, including the increased awareness and attention to police brutality against people of color, rising mass incarceration, and calls for social work and similar fields to handle some issues for which police are typically called upon but may not be necessary. As Pettus-Davis and Epperson (2015) note, due to our history of leading reform efforts, the omnipresent context of justice-informed practice and attention to structural solutions, social workers are eminently "qualified to lead the decarceration effort" (p. 3). In the juvenile justice system, too, social work is once again establishing the substantial role played in its reform (Reardon, 2019). Social workers need to learn about the history of the profession as it relates to juvenile and criminal justice, and understand the unique strengths we bring in working toward social justice in the area of criminal justice.

PERVASIVE AND STRUCTURAL BARRIERS

As discussed in the previous sections, historically, some social workers have left work in the criminal justice system in part due to not wanting to operate within a system that reinforces inequalities and promotes social control. This leads us to discuss the role and purpose of the U.S. criminal justice system, and to critically reflect on the role of social workers within the criminal justice system. "We," as a collective society in the United States, decide what constitutes a crime, what does not, how to address issues when they arise, and on what to focus criminal justice, safety, and legal efforts. The Constitution, federal laws and statutes, and state and local laws and ordinances all are outward products of what the collective "we" value as right and wrong. The criminal justice system, then, is based on what is valued.

Magnitude and Scope of Barriers

With mass incarceration in the United States, one needs to explore the additional political, economic, and cultural forces at play that prevent the United States from having a more equitable criminal justice system. Sentencing policies, implicit racial bias, and socioeconomic inequities all contribute to racial disparities that exist at every stage in the criminal justice system today (The Sentencing Project, n.d.). To truly understand today's issues in the criminal justice system, the history of it in the United States needs to be acknowledged. Prior to the Civil War, slave patrols, early police-like groups that existed primarily in the South, were used to hunt and return slaves to owners as well as scare people and discourage any uprisings among slaves (Hansen, 2019). After the war, terrorizing policing of Black people continued in other forms, including the Ku Klux Klan's lynchings and destruction of property, unnecessary police force during peaceful Civil Rights demonstrations in the 1960s, and the targeted strategy to hurt Black communities with President Nixon's War on Drugs (Philimon, 2020). The ripple effects of such decisions have enduring effects on people involved in the criminal justice system.

More recently, policies such as the 1994 Violent Crime Control and Law Enforcement Act (Public Law 103-322; informally known as "the crime bill"), the largest crime bill in the history of the United States, is a central aspect of the genesis of our current problem with mass incarceration. It included measures to encourage the building of prisons and jails, place more police officers out on the streets, provide "truth in sentencing" which increased lengthy prison sentences, ban 19 types of semiautomatic assault weapons, allow for the death penalty for new definitions of federal crimes, institute a federal "three strikes and you're out" law, and yet only marginally improved public safety (Chung et al., 2019; Eisen & Chettiar, 2016).

Crimes such as murder, rape, and robbery dominate the local news as they are more tangible and sensationalized, whereas white-collar crimes such as embezzlement and corporate fraud are often viewed as less of a priority, despite the significant costs to individuals and society. In a study by Michel (2015), participants were presented with violent crime as well as white-collar crime scenarios, and they viewed violent crime scenarios as more serious and were less punitive to the people involved in white-collar crimes.

One goal of the criminal justice system is to have a deterrent effect, in other words, to not have people commit new crimes, or recidivate, and enter the system again. However, within 3 years of being released from prison, almost 68% of people are rearrested, and within 5 years, more than three-quarters are rearrested (James, 2016). With such high numbers, this opens up the criminal justice system to criticism in terms of its ability to prevent new crimes from being committed.

Due to broad legal and societal barriers, people who are part of re-entry back into the general population after involvement in the criminal justice system face a staggering number of obstacles that may encourage recidivism. Compared to people without criminal justice system histories, it can be much harder to find meaningful employment, stable housing, and become a fully functioning member of society; the punishment and stigma from being in contact with the criminal justice system endures long after incarceration (Simmons Staff, 2016).

When a person is involved with the criminal justice system, having that history despite "serving their time" can have long-lasting detrimental effects as they try to re-enter society. Until recent reforms, most states allowed asking about criminal conviction histories on job applications as well as conducting background checks at the initial point of applying for a job (Avery, 2019). Millions of people are excluded from voting due to their criminal justice system histories (Brennan Center for Justice, 2019). It is estimated that disenfranchisement due to felony convictions have risen from 1.17 million in 1976 to 6.1 million at present (Uggen et al., 2016). Some argue that modern-day felony disenfranchisement has racist roots in similar efforts to ban racial minorities from voting, especially as Black Americans represent 2.2 of the over 6 million who cannot vote; this number is four times the rate of other racial groups combined (Taylor, 2018).

"Treating" Social Problems With the Criminal Justice System

In the U.S. criminal justice system, many social problems are addressed or "treated" by the criminal justice system, and all too often inadequately. Society's values shape law, and laws determine what behavior is illegal and legal, which typically has negative repercussions for vulnerable populations. Additionally, the criminal justice system is largely focused on punitive responses, and is overall less equipped at effectively handling cases with a treatment and rehabilitative emphasis. Homelessness, immigration, mental illness, substance use, poverty, and prostitution are all social problems in the United States for which the criminal justice system has often inadequate responses. In dealing with our social problems in the criminal justice system, and not reserving it for people who do commit heinous crimes without remorse, society is not effectively addressing public safety, crime, and recidivism, and not allocating resources and taxpayer dollars as effectively as it could. As Jones and Sawyer (2019) summarize, when our criminal justice system, particularly police and jails, are charged with public safety but then are asked to interface with economic and behavioral health-related needs, but continue to use the measures and strategies associated with social control, this results in our jail systems being overwhelmed with people who have associated needs that go well beyond what can be met in an incarceration system.

Is It Really a "Justice" System?

Given the evidence of how the U.S. criminal justice system has failed many vulnerable populations, and the structural barriers that prevent positive and fulfilling lives despite justice system contact, the question arises about the broader purpose of the system and whether it really is a "justice" system. The philosopher Michel Foucault is famous for his criticisms of prisons and the justice system, and asking critical questions about the role of such systems as a form of social control (Foucault, 1975). In an interview in the *New York Times* in 1975, in response to the criticism of prisons producing new criminals, Foucault asserted that they have been largely successful as that is what they have been asked to do (Droit, 1975).

Social work is well-suited to raise questions about the nature and purpose of the criminal justice system on behalf of vulnerable and oppressed populations, and should know that such conversations are not as dominant in criminal justice. "Critical criminology" is the term within criminal justice that refers to raising broad questions about the criminal justice system's role in reproducing inequities, and radical social workers within criminal justice question these same perspectives, yet within the criminal justice field such broad analysis and critiques are not prominent (Cox & Augustine, 2017).

Three areas of specific focus highlighted by Cox and Augustine are: (a) how those with power and wealth create and enforce what is considered a crime to serve self-interests; (b) the ways that criminal justice system does not adequately recognize or sanction corporate, climate, or state crimes; and (c) how definitions of crime target vulnerable groups which then furthers divisions in race, class, gender, and religion. Specific to racial disparities, scholars such as Alexander (2010) point to how inequities reproduce themselves but in different forms, such as segregation and dehumanization in the forms of slavery, to Jim Crow laws, to racial disparities in mass incarceration of Black people in the United States. Through the lens of critical race theory, the ways in which the criminal justice system is used to maintain the status quo of racial inequities is shown (Delgado & Stefancic, 2007).

Critics of the criminal justice system, including Angela Davis, argue that prisons are not needed as they reproduce society's adverse issues rather than solving them; this is part of the broader prison abolition movement (Washington, 2018). Words matter, and even the terms used to describe systems broadly are subject to critique. Although the term "U.S. criminal justice system" is still a common way of defining the system, others use the term "American legal system" to indicate the lack of true justice within it.

What Would a Socially Just Criminal Justice System Look Like?

There are seemingly endless critiques of the current U.S. criminal justice system and its failings, particularly for vulnerable and oppressed groups of people. Thinking broadly and into the future, it is worthwhile to consider: What would a socially just criminal justice system look like? How would it be structured? How could society ensure that people are being treated fairly, both in terms of due process as well as with the outcome of their criminal justice system contact?

One scholar, John Rawls, first wrote a book in 1971, *Theory of Justice* (2003), in which he offers his perspective on a socially just society. His theories are based on egalitarianism and libertarian principles, which appeal to many Americans (Caravelis & Robinson, 2015). According to Rawls (2003), social justice concerns equal protection to freedoms and rights while also paying attention to the needs of vulnerable and oppressed people. One concept Rawls asserts is the "veil of ignorance." For example, consider the current racial and ethnic disparities in the criminal justice system, as well as the adverse treatment of groups based on sexual orientation/gender identity, socioeconomic status. If you did not know into what position in society you would be born—you would not know to which racial or ethnic group you would belong; not know what your sex, sexual orientation, or gender identity would be; and not know whether you would be born into a rich or poor family: What would you want the criminal justice system to be? How would it operate? The idea behind the veil of ignorance, as applied to the criminal justice system, is that if a person did not know which characteristics they would have in society, then they would not be motivated by self-interests and would ideally design a system to be beneficial for all individuals as well as the larger society.

FROM THE FIELD 6.2

RESTORATIVE JUSTICE

In critically thinking and analyzing how the current U.S. criminal justice system could be reimagined, "restorative justice" is often a buzzword that emerges in the dialogue, but sometimes with little description of its substantive meaning. In simple terms, restorative justice involves a response to crime that involves the person or persons who received harm, the person or persons who imposed harm, and often the broader community that weighs in on the recommended outcome to repair the issue. Communities and countries have applied restorative justice practices throughout history. The modern term likely originated from Albert Eglash when he described multiple approaches to justice, including the concept of restorative justice that would have a foundation of restitution that included the voices of the parties involved, for example, the victim, offender, community, and so on (Van Ness & Heetderks Strong, 2010). Howard Zehr is a pioneer of popularizing restorative justice, and its meaning over time has evolved beyond victim/offender mediation at an individual level to one of system rethinking how the U.S. criminal justice system could shift from one that is an adversarial process (i.e., one in which there is plaintiff, defendant, and judge who decides the outcome) to one informed by restorative justice principles. With restorative justice, the focus shifts away from an offender receiving their "just desserts" and swift punishment, and toward recognizing that such actions are typically ineffective (Zehr, 2018). Instead, restorative justice's goals include repairing harm from crime by having offenders acknowledge what occurred, taking steps to correct it, and involving members of the community in the process (Zehr, 2018). Contemporary scholars such as Mariame Kaba have been influenced by such restorative justice philosophies to advocate for prison abolition and emphasize that community needs need to be met in better ways than through the current, retribution-focused criminal justice system (Hayes, 2019).

STRATEGIES TO EFFECT CHANGE

To effectively implement a true justice-oriented approach for social workers interested in working with people who have had contact with the juvenile or criminal justice systems, grounding one's work in the core values of the profession is necessary (NASW, 2017). Social work has many unique qualities to offer regarding helping individuals and communities affected by the criminal justice system, as well as to affect broader policy and systemic reforms. For professionals employed directly in criminal justice settings, such as jails or a parole office, fellow colleagues may not necessarily have similar, social work backgrounds. Given the relatively small numbers of social workers employed in such agencies, you may be the only social work voice at your agency or place of employment. A well-prepared social worker will be confident in the expertise that the field brings, and learn how to work with people from other disciplines. For example, with the field of criminal justice being more focused at the present on theories of rational choice for explaining law-violating behavior, a social worker can analyze an issue from a person-in-environment perspective and see the role that family violence and trauma have played in limiting life opportunities for an individual. Through addressing such root issues related to being involved in the criminal justice system, the hope is not only to reduce recidivism but also to provide for a better life outcome for that individual person. More broadly, a social worker recognizes the role of racial profiling and racial disparities on people of color, and can work to advocate for reforms that prevent unnecessary justice system contact in the first place.

CROSSOVER YOUTH

In recent years, increasing scholarship and research has led to a rise in attention toward the school-to-prison pipeline, in which schools and the educational system act as referrals for the juvenile and criminal justice systems. In addition to the need to address this specific way in which youth may be unfairly funneled into these systems, and with adverse life outcomes because of it, other avenues that feed into the juvenile and criminal justice systems also merit attention, advocacy, and policy and practice change. This includes the child welfare system, and a special population of young people known as "crossover youth" or "dually involved youth" due to their shift between the child welfare and justice systems; they are children and youth who have experienced abuse or neglect and engage in delinquency (Herz et al., 2010). This issue is also referred to as the "foster–care-to-prison pipeline" (Juvenile Law Center, 2018).

With both the school and foster care pipelines deeply entrenched in the justice systems, it is not surprising to add that the number of police officers in U.S. schools has dramatically increased while social services and supports have been reduced (Johnson, 2020). With statistics from 2016, 1.7 million students go to school where there are police but not counselors, 3 million students attend school with police but not nurses, and 10 million students are enrolled in schools with police, but no social workers (Johnson, 2020). Thus, the necessity for social work to work toward prevention and early intervention of this vulnerable group of young people is critical.

Crossover youth are simultaneously viewed as a victim due to the trauma and maltreatment that they have experienced, as well as an offender from committing a status offense or breaking a law. Compared to young people in the general population (i.e., without any system contact), crossover youth have worse long-term outcomes related to contact with the criminal justice system, recidivism, behavioral health outcomes, and education and employment outcomes. By some estimates, crossover youth are as prevalent as 50% of maltreated youth being referred for delinquency (Halemba et al., 2015). In terms of demographics, research generally indicates that youth of color and Black girls are overrepresented among samples of crossover youth.

For a social worker interested in disrupting the pipeline from the child welfare and educational systems to the juvenile and criminal justice systems, there are several action steps to be taken from both micro and macro social work practice (Kolivoski et al., 2017). At the micro level, when assessing a youth's assessment, it is important to ask them about the multiple providers and professionals with whom they interact. Understandably, the social worker might have to do some sleuthing to piece together who a person is, and a youth might remember only the person's name or agency. However, this step can help provide a foundation for coordination across systems. Some agencies allow the option to search for youth across systems, so that a child welfare worker can assess if a foster care youth has been arrested or referred to the juvenile justice system. Individuals working in these systems can also check their agency, local, state, and other relevant policies related to information sharing for case-planning purposes. There may be a memorandum of understanding already in place that allows for this. Agencies can also foster improved relationships with one another by having cross-trainings on each system, such as a "Child Welfare 101" or "Juvenile Justice 101" training to learn about the different philosophies, jargon, timelines, and so forth of other professions. At the macro levels, more formalized trainings and technical assistance, such as the Crossover Youth Practice Model (Center for Juvenile Justice Reform, 2020), can provide structure to changing practices and policies. Additionally, policies addressing placing supports in educational systems would help divert students from the justice system by addressing needs.

SOCIAL WORKER PERSPECTIVE 6.1

MACRO SOCIAL WORK IN ACTION—CROSSOVER YOUTH

by Macon Stewart, MSW, Deputy Director for Multi-System Operations, Center for Juvenile Justice Reform, McCourt School of Public Policy, Georgetown University

Working with vulnerable populations is a role that many social workers play. The work I am blessed to do as a social worker combines research, policy, advocacy, and training in a manner that seeks to improve the experiences of vulnerable young people and their families. This work recognizes that youth involved with either child welfare or juvenile justice are more vulnerable to entering a second system of care if their needs are not addressed appropriately. With that in mind, I have had the pleasure of co-authoring and supporting countless communities in the implementation of the Crossover Youth Practice Model. This model seeks to address the risk factors that make youth involved with child welfare more likely to become involved with juvenile justice, and conversely youth involved with juvenile justice are at a greater risk of involvement with child welfare. The model recognizes that the system's attempt to reduce harm and support youth well-being is often not enough, and the consequences of its failures lead to these youth becoming adults that are dependent upon or involved within governmental systems. The Crossover Youth Practice Model (CYPM) was developed in 2010 at the Georgetown University McCourt School of Public Policy Center for Juvenile Justice Reform. Since its inception, the CYPM has been implemented in 120 counties in 23 states within the United States. The model supports three pillars of systems integration: Prevention, Information Sharing, and Interagency Collaboration. The model is implemented (in a community) as a result of collaboration between behavioral health, child welfare, family courts, education, and juvenile justice. While the work of the CYPM is challenging, it is seeing success in many communities in pursuit to prevent youth's system involvement and enhance collaboration when involvement is necessary that will mitigate risk factors, improve youth and family outcomes, and maximize how systems functions collaboratively.

CONCLUSION

The criminal justice system has been robustly criticized due to the disparities that exist at various points of contact within it from the initial point of contact, to arrest, through the court system, into correctional confinement, and to those on probation or parole. People of color make up 37% of the population in the United States, but more than two-thirds of the prison population, while women are the fastest-growing portion of the prison population. More than 6.7 million people are under some form of criminal justice system control, including probation and parole, with drug-related offenses as the most common reason for incarceration. Social work in the criminal justice system encompasses both micro and macro aspects to address the existing structural discrimination that reinforces inequalities and promotes social control. The punishment, disenfranchisement, and stigma from being in contact with the criminal justice system endures long after incarceration, impacting individuals, families, and communities with life-altering consequences.

DISCUSSION QUESTIONS

1. What would a socially just criminal justice system look like? Whose needs would have to be addressed? How would it be structured?
2. Who should be prioritized in a socially just system? The victim? Or the offender?
3. How could society ensure that people are being treated fairly, both in terms of due process as well as with the outcome of their criminal justice system contact?
4. What might motivate you as a social worker to practice in the criminal justice system? What concerns would you have and how would you address those?

REFERENCES

Only key references appear in the print edition. The full reference list appears in the digital product on Springer Publishing Connect: connect.springerpub.com/content/book/978-0-8261-3539-1/chapter/ch06

American Academy of Social Work and Social Welfare. (n.d.). *Promote smart decarceration.* https://grandchallengesforsocialwork.org/promote-smart-decarceration

James, N. (2016). *Offender reentry: Correctional statistics, reintegration into the community, and recidivism.* https://fas.org/sgp/crs/misc/RL34287.pdf

Juvenile Law Center. (2018, May 26). *What is the foster care-to-prison pipeline?* https://jlc.org/news/what-foster-care-prison-pipeline

Kolivoski, K. M. (2017, June). What social work uniquely provides to criminal justice. *Smart Justice Blog.* https://medium.com/smart-justice/the-impact-of-mass-incarceration-on-people-of-color-michelle-alexanders-the-new-jim-crow-and-acc9f2a8baac

National Association of Social Workers. (2020, June 18). *NASW says Trump Administration's police reform executive order is inadequate.* https://www.socialworkers.org/News/News-Releases/ID/2196/NASW-says-Trump-Administrations-police-reform-executive-order-is-inadequate

Pettus-Davis, C., & Epperson, M. W. (2015). *From mass incarceration to smart decarceration.* American Academy of Social Work and Social Welfare. https://grandchallengesforsocialwork.org/wp-content/uploads/2015/12/WP4-with-cover.pdf

Reardon, C. (2019). Juvenile justice journey—Social work role returns in new era of reform. *Social Work Today, 19*(5), 12. https://www.socialworktoday.com/archive/SO19p12.shtml

Sarri, R. C., & Shook, J. J. (2005). The future for social work in juvenile and adult criminal justice. *Advances in Social Work, 6,* 210–220. https://doi.org/10.18060/92

Sawyer, W., & Wagner, P. (2019, March 19). *Mass incarceration: The whole pie 2019.* https://www.prisonpolicy.org/reports/pie2019.html

Teti, I. F. (2017, February 12). *Intersectional oppression in America's criminal justice system.* Penn State Presidential Leadership Academy. https://sites.psu.edu/academy/2017/02/12/intersectional-oppression-in-americas-criminal-justice-system

The George Washington University Health Workforce Institute. (2019, April). *From social work education to social work practice: Results of the survey of 2018 social work graduates.* https://cswe.org/CSWE/media/Workforce-Study/2018-Social-Work-Workforce-Report-Final.pdf

The Sentencing Project. (n.d.). *Criminal justice facts.* https://www.sentencingproject.org/criminal-justice-facts

HEALTH DISPARITIES AND SOCIAL JUSTICE

Kathryn M. Cardarelli | Rafael E. Perez-Figueroa | Brendan Mathews

LEARNING OBJECTIVES

Students will be able to:

- Describe health disparities in the United States.
- Discuss the impact of health disparities on populations and communities occupying unequal positions in society.
- Articulate the relationship between health disparities and different social determinants of health.
- Outline strategies to address health disparities through justice-informed practice.

INTRODUCTION

Social workers are commonly employed in health and behavioral health settings where our clients are often impacted by health disparities. Health is the complex interplay between biological, behavioral, social, and structural factors and is subjected to influence by social and structural injustices such as poverty, unemployment, underfunded and poor education, inadequate housing, poor public transportation, interpersonal violence, and decaying neighborhoods, all of which contribute to health disparities. Health disparities result in discrepancies in disease prevalence, treatment access, utilization and outcomes, and mortality. Largely, health disparities are influenced by social determinants of health, the conditions in which people live, learn, work, and play. Social workers play a key role in addressing and mitigating health disparities, both with the individual and in implementing policy changes that reduce poverty and increase access to healthy, affordable food; stable housing; and sustainable employment income, all of which are impactful in improving the fundamental determinants of health. Justice-informed social work practice is fundamental to implementing and sustaining the key factors for successful reduction of health disparities.

OVERVIEW OF HEALTH DISPARITIES IN THE UNITED STATES

Over the past three decades, a rapidly expanding body of scientific evidence has documented disparities in health status across different groups in the United States. Health disparities are differences that exist among specific population groups in the attainment of their full health potential that can be measured by variations in incidence, prevalence, mortality, burden of disease, and other adverse health conditions (National Institutes of Health, 2002). Health disparities exist across many dimensions including race, ethnicity, gender, sexual orientation, disability, socioeconomic status, and geographic location (Adler & Rehkopf, 2008). African Americans, Latinx/Hispanics, American Indians and Alaska Natives, sexual minorities, and disabled persons are among the groups that experience disparities in their burden of disease and death in the United States. Unjust disparities have been documented in almost every aspect of health, including quality of healthcare, access to health and social services, utilization of healthcare, and health outcomes. Health disparities can be prevented and addressed. Social workers play a critical role in reducing health disparities.

In most cases, health disparities stem from health inequities—systematic differences in the health of groups and communities occupying unequal positions in society that are avoidable and unjust (Graham, 2004). The root causes of health inequities are historical and ongoing institutional and societal structures, policies, practices, and norms that oppressively shape the experiences of disadvantaged groups and communities in the United States. Only part of a person's health status depends on their biology, behavior, and choice. Social and structural injustices like poverty, unemployment, underfunded and poor education, inadequate housing, poor public transportation, interpersonal violence, and decaying neighborhoods contribute to health inequities. The social determinants of health are the conditions in the environment in which people live, learn, work, play, worship, and age (World Health Organization [WHO], 2009). These conditions affect a wide range of health, functioning, and quality-of-life outcomes and risks. The interplay between biological, behavioral, social, and structural factors is diverse, complex, evolving, and interdependent in nature.

During the past three decades, *Healthy People* has been the main governmental agenda for preventing and addressing health disparities in the United States. This strategy intends to identify the most significant preventable threats to health nationally and to establish goals to reduce these threats. In 2010, the Department of Health and Human Services launched *Healthy People 2020* (Koh et al., 2011), which had four overarching goals: (a) attain high-quality, longer lives free of preventable disease, disability, injury, and premature death; (b) achieve health equity, eliminate disparities, and improve the health of all groups; (c) create social and physical environments that promote good health for all; and (d) promote quality of life, healthy development, and healthy behaviors across all life stages. *Healthy People 2020* contains the Leading Health indicators, a targeted set of 12 topics containing 26 objectives to advance action in high-priority health issues (Institute of Medicine, 2011). This coordinated national strategy encourages collaborations among communities and sectors to address health disparities and serve to measure the impact of prevention activities in the nation.

THEORETICAL FRAMEWORKS FOR THE STUDY OF HEALTH DISPARITIES

Multiple frameworks have been used to examine how different arrangements of biological, behavioral, social, and structural factors influence healthcare access and utilization, health status, and health outcomes. A life-course perspective is useful to understand the varying health needs and experiences of populations that are harmed by health disparities over the course of their lives (Elder, 1998). This framework posits that the experiences of individuals at every stage of their lives influence subsequent experiences. This interrelationship among experiences starts before birth and transcends generations. A life-course framework has four key dimensions: (a) social relations influence individuals' perspectives; (b) significant events and experiences have a distinctive effect at various developmental stages; (c) the social and structural environment influence choices; and (d) the historical context influences how different groups experience health events. These four dimensions consider a range of issues that influence the outcomes of different populations experiencing health disparities.

An intersectional perspective is also helpful because it acknowledges simultaneous dimensions of inequality and emphasizes understanding how those dimensions are interrelated and compound one another. Intersectionality encompasses a set of foundational tenets and principles for understanding health inequities and its relationship with marginalized statuses based on dimensions of race, ethnicity, sexual orientation, and social class among others (Crenshaw, 1989; Dill & Zambrana, 2009; Weber, 2010). These include the following: (a) structural inequities are socially constructed—the experiences of marginalized groups can be understood only in the context of institutionalized patterns of unequal control over the distribution of valued goods and resources; (b) to understand health disparities we need to examine the full range of historical and social experiences with respect to class, gender, race, ethnicity, and geographical location; (c) the social positioning of marginalized groups is associated with institutional practices and policies; and (d) the way in which these groups are represented is intricately related to structural, political, and economic factors. An intersectional approach to the study of health disparities recognizes that group identities are complex and dynamic. At different points in life some statuses might be more relevant than others. Individuals cannot be examined as a monolith, but must be understood as shaped by multiple identities and simultaneous intersections of many characteristics.

The minority stress model conceptualizes how groups that are harmed by health disparities are exposed to chronic stress as a result of stigma and discrimination (Brooks, 1981; Meyer, 1995, 2003). In the context of individual environmental circumstances, there are distal and proximal stress processes. In this model, proximal stress processes are subjective and depend on an individual's perspective (e.g., perceived stigma, internalized homophobia, concealment). Distal processes are objective stressors that do not depend on a personal perspective or appraisal (e.g., discrimination, violence). This model, grounded in social psychology, is particularly helpful for explaining the high prevalence of mental health disorders and psychosocial conditions among minority groups as caused by excess in stressors related to stigma and discrimination. Social workers can use this framework to attend to interventions going from the individual to the structural level.

Finally, the theory of fundamental causes can be helpful to understand how some social factors or circumstances remain persistently associated with health disparities over time despite dramatic changes in diseases, risk factors, and health interventions (Hatzenbuehler et al., 2013; Phelan et al., 2010). This theory was initially developed to explain the association between socioeconomic status and health disparities (Link & Phelan, 1995). However, it is relevant to other social conditions such as stigma, racism, ethnocentrism, and homophobia.

Health disparities persist because fundamental causes have certain characteristics. First, a fundamental social cause influences multiple health outcomes through different mechanisms. Second, it involves access to material resources (e.g., money, knowledge, power, social capital) that can be used to avoid risks and minimize the consequences of diseases. Third, across time and place the association between social conditions and health is reproduced via the replacement of intervening mechanisms. This theory highlights the need of addressing the fundamental social causes of oppression through policies and interventions, rather than the recognized mechanisms that link the condition to health.

HEALTH DISPARITIES IN UNIQUE POPULATIONS

Health disparities in the United States manifest in unique ways across vulnerable and marginalized groups, shaping the ways in which they achieve optimal health. When considering the term "health disparities," it is often used to reflect upon differences in health status across racial and ethnic identity groups; however, the impacts of health disparities permeate across multiple dimensions of identity. The burden of health disparities harms Black, Latinx/Hispanics, American Indians and Alaska Natives, sexual minorities, and disabled persons in unique ways. This injustice must be considered to guide best health practices in social work.

Racial and Ethnic Health Disparities

Health disparities for communities of color assume many forms in the United States. In many cases, communities of color experience higher rates of chronic diseases, such as cancer, diabetes, overweight/obesity, cardiovascular disease, and HIV/AIDS, with Black people disproportionately shouldering the majority of these burdens compared to the majority of White communities (Levine et al., 2001). Additionally, these health disparities mean that many communities of color die prematurely at higher rates than their White counterparts (National Center for Health Statistics [NCHS], 2016).

These disparities across racial and ethnic groups also affect infant health outcomes. The United States has some of the highest infant mortality rates among industrialized nations, largely attributed to the infant mortality rates in communities of color. Nationally, Black women experience the highest rates of preterm delivery, and Black infants are more than twice as likely to die than their White counterparts (NCHS, 2016). American Indians and Alaska Natives also shoulder a disproportionate burden in infant mortality, as rates of infant death in these communities are 60% higher than those of White communities (Office of Minority Health, 2019). Finally, while rates of low birthweight have remained constant for White populations since 2015, Black and Latinx communities have seen increases in their rates of preterm birth (NCHS, 2016).

Homicide, unintentional injury, and mental health-related deaths also show sharp disparities across racial and ethnic lines. Homicide rates are the highest in Black communities, followed by Indigenous and Latinx populations (Centers for Disease Control and Prevention [CDC], 2013a). Indigenous populations experience the highest rates of both intentional and unintentional injury-related deaths (CDC, 2013a). Overall, these data on racial and ethnic health disparities must be evaluated with caution, though, as communities of color are rapidly growing, and further studies must be conducted to reveal how these disparities affect communities across the nation.

Gender-Based Health Disparities

When discussing gender-based health disparities, it must be acknowledged that many of these disparities are rooted in socially constructed conditions including income, education status, cultural norms that lead to drastic differences in life expectancy, substance use and abuse, mental health issues, and victimization by violence.

On average, women in the United States can expect to live approximately 5 years longer than their male counterparts, as the average life expectancy for women is 81.1 years while it is only 76.1 years for men (NCHS, 2016). When stratified by race and ethnicity, these gaps in life expectancy vary drastically. The average life expectancy for Black women, for example, is 78.5 years while it is only 71.9 years for Black men. In Hispanic/Latinx communities, average life expectancy is higher than White communities, with Hispanic/Latinx women living an average of 84.3 years and Hispanic/Latinx men living an average of 79.1 years (Arias & Xu, 2019). Studies show that this life expectancy gap may be closing, which seems like a positive trend; however, this is likely to be attributed to increasing rates of early death for women experiencing chronic health conditions (Arias, 2016). Research suggests that women are increasingly dying from unintentional drug overdoses (related to the current opioid epidemic), suicide, smoking-related chronic health conditions, and obesity (Astone et al., 2015).

With regard to mental health, women are significantly more likely to report some mental health conditions, such as major depression, posttraumatic stress disorder, and anxiety (Eaton, 2012). Men are more than four times as likely to die by suicide than women (CDC, 2013b). Men are also more likely to report higher rates of alcohol and illicit substance use disorders than women (Eaton, 2012). Mental health disparities must be studied further. People underreport mental health conditions, making it difficult to quantify the true nature of these disparities (Eaton et al., 2012).

Finally, victimization by violence affects men and women in very different ways. Men are more likely to be victims of assault (Morgan & Oudekerk, 2019) or die from assault than women (Prevention Institute, 2011). However, women are significantly more likely to experience, report, and sustain sexual assault (Morgan & Oudekerk, 2019) and/or injury from intimate partner violence (Tjaden & Thoennes, 2000) than men. Research also suggests that sustaining injury from intimate partner violence has many negative long-term health effects for women, as they become more likely to develop chronic conditions, such as arthritis, experience increased rates of sexually transmitted infections, increased mental health issues, and severe gynecological complications (Campbell & Boyd, 2000).

Sexual and Gender Minority Health Disparities

The term "sexual and gender minority" is used to refer to individuals whose sexual identity, orientation, or practices differ from those who identify as heterosexual. This term is used to refer primarily to lesbian, gay, bisexual, and transgender individuals; it can also refer to queer, intersex, and asexual persons. Sexual and gender minorities experience the health disparities faced by society as a whole, while also bearing disproportionate burdens for many other health conditions, such as HIV/AIDS, mental health issues, substance use and abuse, and violence.

Many of these health disparities occur throughout the life course, as the experience of certain forms of violence, such as bullying or being kicked out of their home, leads to poor mental health, substance use and abuse, and physical and/or sexual violence (Robinson & Espelage, 2013). Additionally, some sexual and gender minorities are more likely to engage in risky sexual behaviors, which have been associated with higher risk of HIV and other sexually transmitted infections (Garofalo & Bush, 2008).

Sexual and gender minority individuals experience unique health disparities. Although the term "sexual and gender minority" or the acronym LGBTQ+ is used as an umbrella term, different subgroups represent distinct populations with their own health risks. For example, lesbians are more likely to experience preventable diseases that could have been detected early by health screenings, and also are more likely to experience higher rates of smoking, obesity, and certain forms of cancer (O'Hanlan & Isler, 2007). Gay men experience the highest rates of HIV/AIDS, and also experience many mental health disparities, such as increased body image issues, eating disorders/disordered eating behaviors, and depression (Burns et al., 2015). Bisexual persons often report high rates of intimate partner and physical violence (Brown & Herman, 2015), though overall health disparities for bisexual persons are poorly understood due to lack of population-level research. Transgender persons, particularly transgender women, experience some of the most striking health disparities in the United States. Persons who identify as transgender face high rates of physical and intimate partner violence, mental health issues, substance use disorders, HIV/AIDS, and other sexually transmitted infections, as well as the potential side effects of hormonal therapy (Lawrence, 2007).

Overall, health disparities among sexual and gender minorities must be looked at through the lens of intersectionality, as many of these disparities also result from lack of adequate access to healthcare, racial discrimination, and income inequity. In order to best study these disparities, quantify their effects, and tailor interventions to promote health equity in these communities, further and more rigorous research must be conducted.

Disability Status and Health Disparities

Disability, whether acquired at birth or obtained throughout the life course, can manifest in physical, mental health–related, or cognitive capacities that ultimately affect health outcomes. People living with disabilities represent almost 20% of the U.S. population (Brault, 2012). There is a large body of evidence that suggests that disability status is directly correlated with overall poor health outcomes (CDC, 2013c), although until recently people living with disabilities were routinely excluded from health data collection and analysis.

In addition to increased reporting of fair or poor health, people living with disabilities, particularly those belonging to other marginalized identity groups, are at an increased risk for developing many chronic health conditions (Krahn et al., 2015). Persons living with disabilities, particularly cognitive disabilities, report higher rates of obesity, cardiovascular disease, and diabetes than the rest of the population. People living with disabilities are often more likely to report decreased rates of physical activity and increased rates of smoking and smoking-related health conditions (Reichard & Stolzle, 2011). Overall, future population-level health research should include this population to determine the breadth of these disparities and to guide public health and social work interventions.

STRUCTURAL FACTORS AND HEALTH DISPARITIES

When analyzing health disparities, it quickly becomes clear that many groups are exposed to multiple co-occurring forms of systemic oppression based on the power dynamics connected to their identities. The intersection of lower ranks of socioeconomic, political, and cultural/normative hierarchies of power results in structural vulnerability (Holmes, 2011; Quesada et al. 2011). This structural vulnerability exposes individuals to discrimination and social marginalization which increases health risk and constrains access to needed healthcare services and the unobstructed pursuit of healthier lifestyles (Botticelli & Koh, 2016; Bourgois et al., 2017).

Structural Inequity

Structural inequities in the United States manifest through personal, interpersonal, institutional, and systemic drivers, such as racism, sexism, homophobia, and transphobia, that affect the fair distribution of health opportunities and overall health outcomes. These structural inequities typically follow individuals and communities throughout the course of their lives, often impacting the health of individuals from birth until death. The effects of interpersonal, institutional, and systemic biases in policy and practice-based decisions—structural inequities—are key determinants of health.

For example, policy decisions that determine to which school a child goes is based on their geographic location (i.e., children in high-income neighborhoods attend well-resourced schools and children in low-income neighborhoods attend under-resourced schools) which affects their educational attainment and subsequently their future ability to access high-income jobs with health benefits, their overall ability to access quality healthcare, and their ability to relocate to a healthier geographic location later in life (Woolf et al., 2007). These structural inequities also give rise to disparities in an individual's ability to have a voice in policy-making conversations, reducing their access to provide insight on how a policy may affect them and their communities, which gives rise to the cyclic nature of oppression and structural vulnerability (Robert Wood Johnson Foundation, 2009).

Racism

Inequities rooted in biases toward certain racial and ethnic identity groups are some of the most pervasive and difficult to address. "Racism" is an umbrella term used to describe the interpersonal, institutional, and systemic bias perpetrated against people of color in nearly every facet of our society. Whether it is through racist policies, such as stop-and-frisk, implicit biases in healthcare decision-making by providers, or interpersonally mediated acts of violence through hate crimes, racism can directly and/or indirectly affect health outcomes.

There is a growing body of empiric evidence that suggests that being targeted by racism is linked to mental health, birth, chronic disease, and other health outcomes, in addition to the consistent physical threats due to interpersonal violence (Gee et al., 2009; Uniform Crime Report, 2015). Finally, although racism is often studied and conceptualized through the unique experience of Black individuals, the effects of racism are pervasive across all communities of color in the United States.

Discrimination

The manifestations of discrimination in society can impact health outcomes both overtly through conscious, intentional poor treatment of certain groups, as well as inadvertently through implicit biases that systematically function to suppress and oppress certain groups. Overt acts of discrimination, such as hate crimes and the intentional poor treatment of others based on their identities, can have direct physical impacts on health (i.e., through physical violence) and also can impact mental health outcomes (Sue et al., 2007). Chronic exposure to discrimination may result in stress-induced physiological effects, such as hypertension, increased risk for substance use, poor birth outcomes, and mental health issues, disproportionately affecting marginalized communities (Alhusen et al., 2016; Sims et al., 2012).

Inadvertent forms of discrimination, implicit biases, affect health outcomes often through the lens of patient–healthcare provider interactions (van Ryn & Fu, 2003). If a patient from a marginalized identity group seeks care, the implicit biases held by a provider toward that group may subconsciously affect the type of care that patient receives. For example, some healthcare providers may hold the implicit bias toward Black women that they have a higher pain tolerance, thus leading them to not take the concerns of these women seriously after labor and delivery, resulting in higher rates of maternal mortality from preventable causes (Louis et al., 2015). Discrimination, whether inadvertent or overt, must be addressed at every level of our society to promote health and equity for all populations.

Income Inequality

There is a vast body of evidence that characterizes the implications of income inequality on health and health disparities (National Academies of Sciences, Engineering, and Medicine, 2015). Income inequality drastically impacts women and people of color in the United States, as pay gaps across racial and gender lines are pervasive at every level of educational attainment in almost every job role, and both directly and indirectly influence individual and population-level health outcomes (Zonderman et al., 2016). The vast majority of low-wage, part-time, and hourly paid jobs are held by women and people of color in the United States, which drastically limits socioeconomic standing, ability to access and pay for quality healthcare, and to take time off from work to meet health needs (Clougherty et al., 2010). Income inequality also impacts an individual's ability to live in well-resourced geographic locations, typically leading to socioeconomic segregation, which perpetuates the previously discussed cyclical nature of structural inequity in our society (Roberto, 2008).

HEALTH DISPARITIES AND SOCIAL WORK PRACTICE

Social workers are the nation's largest group of mental health service providers working in the medical, social service, and public health sectors (U.S. Department of Labor, 2020). They play an essential role serving clients experiencing health disparities. Those working in healthcare systems witness daily the impact of psychosocial and material deprivation on poor health. It is critical for them to be vigilant of how economic changes, healthcare policy, unemployment, and structural injustice exacerbate pathways for health disparities (Mitchell, 2012). Social workers participate in improving the quality of patient care, facilitate communication in the healthcare system, advocate for patients' rights, ensure treatment compliance, safeguard patient-centered care, and inform the process of decision-making (Auerbach et al., 2007; Zimmerman & Dabelko, 2007). Social workers are in a key position to assist marginalized and targeted groups in accessing and better utilizing healthcare services.

Social workers face important challenges working in healthcare systems. These challenges might constrain the ability of social workers to draw connections between individual patient experiences and well-recognized population patterns of health disparities. Social workers report a lack of adequate time for counseling, role ambiguity, constraints of resources, difficulties managing conflicts with other medical team members, ethical dilemmas, and low levels of recognition as part of a medical team (Allen et al., 2007; O'Donnell et al., 2008). Linking the social work practice experience with broader population-based knowledge on health disparities, evidence-based interventions, and culturally and linguistically responsive behavioral practices is fundamental to reduce the burden of health inequities.

In recent years, there is a growing recognition of the role of integrated care systems on health equity (Holden et al., 2014; Hough et al., 2011; U.S Department of Health and Human Services & Hogg Foundation for Mental Health, 2012). Social workers play a key role in integrated healthcare systems. Healthcare systems must be patient centered, value cultural humility among providers, and be implemented in physical environments that respect and appreciate patient diversity and represented cultures (Tucker et al., 2007, 2011). These factors facilitate a greater degree of trust among patients, healthcare providers, and staff. In addition to working as mental health providers, social workers coordinate patient needs, monitor health outcomes, and ensure efficiency across care systems (Hogg Foundation for Mental Health, 2008; U.S Department of Health and Human Services & Hogg Foundation for Mental Health, 2012). Emphasis has been placed on developing a national strategy to improve integrated healthcare for populations that experience health disparities in the United States (Center for Integrated Health Solutions, 2012). This strategy would utilize social workers and demand training with the associated skills to use integrated healthcare service delivery approaches to address health disparities.

A core strategy for addressing health disparities is training healthcare professionals on cultural and linguistic competency (Barksdale et al., 2017). Cultural competency refers to behaviors, attitudes, and policies on a continuum to ensure that systems, agencies, programs, and individuals function effectively and appropriately in diverse cultural interactions and settings (Selig et al., 2006). Given the complexity of multiculturalism, it is important to understand cultural competence as a process rather than an end product.

"Cultural humility" refers to a process-oriented approach to cultural competency, defined as the ability to maintain an interpersonal stance that is open to others in relation to aspects of cultural identity (Hook et al., 2013). A culturally humble approach involves an ongoing commitment to self-evaluation and a desire to fix power imbalances, starting with oneself (Tervalon & Murray-García, 1998). A healthcare provider might have a body of knowledge critical to health, but the patient is an expert on their life, symptoms, meaning attributed, and strengths. Both must collaborate and learn from each other to achieve the best outcomes. Cultural humility involves examining social norms, policies, institutions, and community practices. Social workers must recognize and value diversity, acknowledging that structural change is needed to achieve health equity.

STRATEGIES TO ADDRESS HEALTH DISPARITIES

Factors that contribute to health disparities occur at multiple levels. The socio-ecological model (Bronfenbrenner, 1977; McLeroy et al. 1988) recognizes that influences on individuals can be much broader than the immediate environment. Intervening on individual- and population-level determinants of health represents opportunities to address health disparities. This model graphically depicts these different levels (Figure 7.1).

The socio-ecological model considers multiple levels, each of which influence individuals who experience health disparities. Beyond the individual, these may include interpersonal relationships, community, and society. The overlapping nature of the model demonstrates how factors at one level influence those at another.

FROM THE FIELD 7.1

USING A SOCIO-ECOLOGICAL MODEL TO ADDRESS HEALTH DISPARITIES

Many chronic health disparities can be linked to smoking, the leading cause of preventable death and more common in those with lower educational attainment and socioeconomic status (CNN Money, n.d.). A social worker can implement a program to reduce smoking behavior (individual level) which would impact that individual's health outcomes. Or, a social worker could intervene in a clinical setting to reinforce healthcare provider recommendations for smoking cessation (interpersonal), thus impacting those clients who participate in that clinical setting. Use of the socio-ecological model would ensure that larger resources are used as well. A social worker could implement changes to modify the point-of-sale environment at gas stations, to reduce smoking advertising influences (community), or could address smoking as a health disparity through policy changes and seek to increase cigarette taxes (societal). Ideally, social workers should address health disparities from each of these levels of intervention.

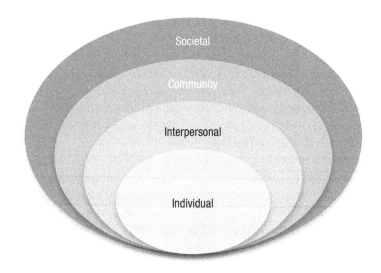

FIGURE 7.1 Socio-ecological model.

The socio-ecological model is helpful in conceptualizing that behaviors both affect the social environment and are affected by it. Intervening on more distal factors (e.g., community, society) can provide an even greater impact than intervening at the individual level (Cardarelli et al., 2005). For example, neighborhood conditions, poverty, and lack of affordable food, community and societal level factors are significant drivers of behaviors and, consequently, health disparities.

Recognizing the fundamental role of social determinants of health on health disparities by intervening on community and societal factors would mitigate health inequities (Cardarelli et al., 2005). Policy focused on the nonmedical determinants of health has substantial impacts on health disparities, including policy focused on housing, education, the environment, transportation, and the economy. There is scientific evidence to demonstrate that investments in early childhood education; stable, affordable housing; income enhancements; and community development can improve health and reduce health disparities (Thornton et al., 2016).

The federal government has developed multiple action plans to address health and healthcare disparities nationally. For example, the U.S. Department of Health and Human Services (DHHS) released an action plan in 2011 that explicitly built on the *Healthy People 2020* goal to eliminate disparities (U.S. DHHS, 2015). In response to the objectives set in that report, multiple federal agencies have engaged in activities to advance health equity, including expanding access to healthcare, and strengthening the healthcare workforce (U.S. DHHS, 2015).

For example, the CDC funds the High Obesity Program (CDC, 2020), which supports efforts to advance policy, systems, and environmental interventions to make healthy choices such as being physically active and eating more fruits and vegetables. The CDC High Obesity Program focuses on communities with a prevalence of adult obesity of 40% or greater and intentionally employs a community-engaged approach to reduce obesity. In rural Kentucky, the program resulted in increased fruit and vegetable consumption over a multiyear period (Gustafson et al., 2019).

Most notable among federal efforts to reduce health disparities is the Patient Protection and Affordable Care Act (ACA, sometimes referred to as "Obamacare"), a comprehensive healthcare reform law that was passed in 2010. The primary goal of the ACA was to enhance access to health insurance, and one of the primary components was the expansion of Medicaid to include nonelderly adults whose income falls below 138% of the federal poverty level. This resulted in new health insurance options to individuals in low- and middle-income households, a group in which Black and Latinx people are overrepresented (McMorrow et al., 2015).

Although Medicaid expansion was intended to be national in scope, the Supreme Court in 2012 ruled that states could opt out of this expansion. Since its implementation in 2014, the ACA was associated with statistically significant reductions in probabilities of being uninsured, delaying healthcare, and forgoing any needed healthcare. It was also associated with increasing physician visits, compared to pre-ACA implementation. Racial and ethnic minority populations were particularly more likely to gain access to health insurance and needed healthcare after ACA implementation (Chen et al., 2016).

The ACA included specific provisions to reduce disparities, such as creating Offices of Minority Health within U.S. Department of Health and Human Services agencies to coordinate federal health disparity reduction efforts (Andrulis et al., 2010). The ACA promoted workforce diversity, increased funding for cultural competence training and educational materials, and strengthened data collection and research efforts. Finally, it permanently reauthorized the Indian Health Care Improvement Reauthorization Extension Act of 2009, a bill by the Senate Committee on Indian Affairs that strengthened and improved healthcare for American Indians and Alaska Natives. Many ACA provisions have been eliminated under the Trump administration, including the tax penalty for not having health insurance. Other provisions are currently being challenged in courts, including the work requirement for Medicaid recipients and the individual mandate that encourages young and healthy people to get or stay insured.

Efforts among the states to reduce health disparities vary considerably, which is not surprising given how heterogeneous public health is organized and delivered at the state level. Less than half of all states or territories have a strategic plan addressing health disparities (Office of Minority Health, 2018). Many of those plans that do exist include data collection and analysis; Medicaid expansion; immunization programs; and chronic disease management efforts (Office of Minority Health, 2018). Additionally, many states' health disparity reduction efforts focus on particular populations, such as children, refugees, and/or individuals experiencing homelessness (Office of Minority Health, 2018).

Notable for social work practice, efforts to reduce health disparities should include expanding and diversifying the workforce to increase access to culturally and linguistically appropriate care. Evidence suggests that racial and ethnic minority practitioners are more likely to practice in medically underserved areas and provide healthcare to large numbers of racial and ethnic minorities who are uninsured and underinsured (Smedley et al., 2001). This strategy includes actions to increase the diversity of social workers to address the compelling need for reductions in health disparities (Office of Minority Health, 2018). Additionally, we must increase the availability, quality, and use of data to improve the health of marginalized populations. That is, we must ensure that data collection standards for race, ethnicity, gender, sexual orientation, primary language, and disability status are implemented in activities, and surveys.

KEY ELEMENTS FOR SUCCESS

The Committee on Community-Based Solutions to Promote Health Equity in the United States (National Academies of Science, Engineering and Medicine, 2017) has suggested three key elements for successful mitigation of health disparities: (a) creating a shared vision of health equity; (b) building community capacity for health promotion and disease prevention; and (c) fostering multisector collaboration. Each of these is detailed in the following.

First, in order to foster sustainable change in a community, several approaches are important. Two examples are creating a shared sense of urgency around health disparities (including the use of community health data) and reinforcing solutions that come from and involve community members. Articulating the shared purpose and identifying one or more champions can also bolster sustainable change. Such champions need not be elected officials, but they should be trusted, well-respected individuals in a community who can communicate with elected officials.

Second, another important approach to reducing health disparities is building community capacity for prevention. Defined by Wallerstein and Duran (2010) as the intersection of science and practice to improve health equity, community-based participatory research (CBPR) employs an approach to research that pairs community engagement and social action. CBPR employs tactics that combine research methods and community capacity building to bridge the gap between knowledge produced by research and interventions or policies (Lantz et al., 2006). CBPR requires equitable contributions by community members and investigators and can be particularly important when conducting research to reduce health disparities.

FROM THE FIELD 7.2

BUILDING COMMUNITY CAPACITY FOR PREVENTION

The Dallas Cancer Disparities Coalition worked with academic investigators to identify cancer health priorities in South Dallas, which faced disproportionately high levels of cancer death relative to other areas of Dallas or Texas. Using a CBPR approach, investigators and community members co-designed and piloted a breast cancer prevention program (Cardarelli et al., 2011). The program was found to be effective in increasing knowledge of risk factors for breast cancer and in increasing uptake of screening mammography. Furthermore, healthcare system-level barriers were identified and addressed in subsequent years. In this project, community members reviewed data, designed a focus group moderator guide, analyzed and interpreted data, codesigned an intervention, and assisted with dissemination of study findings. Community members were instrumental in providing community context, history and perspectives of feasibility, and acceptability for the intervention. Furthermore, they enhanced their research skills and provided a built-in dissemination mechanism for reporting back the findings of the study. Ongoing CBPR collaborations have the potential to mitigate mistrust of institutions and build sustainable partnerships to collectively address health disparities.

As From the Field 7.2 illustrates, community partnerships are an integral component of addressing health disparities and considered one of the most effective ways to do so. Understanding data-related health disparities is an important component of the process and sets the stage for the needed interventions.

Finally, bringing together nonhealth sector partners to contribute to health disparity reduction efforts is critical. Given that factors such as transportation, education, community development, and environmental quality all impact health and health disparities, it makes sense that collaboration from these sectors will contribute to the reduction of health disparities. This requires a clear articulation of shared values, successful working relationships, and usually a lead organization from health or public health to guide the collaborations. Collective impact represents one approach to a multisector collaboration for health (Kania & Kramer, 2011). Collective impact projects typically represent long-term commitments from multiple partners to solve a common problem.

CONCLUSION

Despite some progress in the United States, additional efforts are urgently needed to reduce health disparities. In particular, policy changes that reduce poverty and increase access to healthy, affordable food, stable housing, and employment with increased minimum wages will be most impactful in improving the fundamental determinants of health. These root causes of health disparities are deeply entrenched in the U.S. society and will take collective community and elected officials' will to address. Solutions that include direct input and leadership from affected health disparity populations will likely be most sustainable. Social work practice has an important role in implementing and sustaining the key factors for successful reduction of health disparities.

DISCUSSION QUESTIONS

1. Identify two ways in which intersectionality impacts health disparities.
2. How can policy efforts reduce health disparities?
3. Describe how only part of someone's health depends on their biology, behavior, and choices.
4. How will your own health and health-related decisions impact how you engage clients regarding their health?

REFERENCES

Only key references appear in the print edition. The full reference list appears in the digital product on Springer Publishing Connect: connect.springerpub.com/content/book/978-0-8261-3539-1/chapter/ch07

Andrulis, D., Siddiqui, N. J., Purtle, J. P., & Duchon, L. (2010, July). *Patient Protection and Affordable Care Act of 2010: Advancing health equity for racially and ethnically diverse populations*. Joint Center for Political and Economic Studies. https://nashp.org/wp-content/uploads/sites/default/files/files/webinars/joint.center.ppaca_.health.equity.report.pdf

Barksdale, C. L., Rodick, W. H., 3rd, Hopson, R., Kenyon, J., Green, K., & Jacobs, C. G. (2017). Literature review of the national CLAS standards: Policy and practical implications in reducing health disparities. *Journal of Racial and Ethnic Health Disparities, 4*(4), 632–647. https://doi.org/10.1007/s40615-016-0267-3

Bourgois, P., Holmes, S. M., Sue, K., & Quesada, J. (2017). Structural vulnerability: Operationalizing the concept to address health disparities in clinical care. *Academic Medicine: Journal of the Association of American Medical Colleges, 92*(3), 299–307. https://doi.org/10.1097/ACM.0000000000001294

Cardarelli, K. M., de Moor, J. S., Low, B. J., & Low, M. D. (2005). Fundamental determinants of population health. In: L. A. Aday (Ed.), *Reinventing public health: Policies and practices for a healthy nation*. Jossey-Bass Publishers.

Chen, J., Vargas-Bustamante, A., Mortensen, K., & Ortega, A. N. (2016). Racial and ethnic health disparities in health care access and utilization under the Affordable Care Act. *Medical Care, 54*(2), 140–146. https://doi.org/10.1097/MLR.0000000000000467

Hatzenbuehler, M. L., Phelan, J. C., & Link, B. G. (2013). Stigma as a fundamental cause of population health inequalities. *American Journal of Public Health*, *103*(5), 813–821. https://doi.org/10.2105/AJPH.2012.301069

Koh, H. K., Piotrowski, J. J., Kumanyika, S., & Fielding, J. E. (2011). Healthy people: A 2020 vision for the social determinants approach. *Health Education & Behavior*, *38*(6), 551–557. https://doi.org/10.1177/1090198111428646

Office of Minority Health. (2018). *State and territorial efforts to reduce health disparities*. U.S. Department of Health and Human Services. https://minorityhealth.hhs.gov/assets/PDF/OMH-Health-Disparities-Report-State-and-Territorial-Efforts-October-2018.pdf

Phelan, J. C., Link, B. G., & Tehranifar, P. (2010). Social conditions as fundamental causes of health inequalities: Theory, evidence, and policy implications. *Journal of Health and Social Behavior*, *51*(Suppl.), S28–S40. https://doi.org/10.1177/0022146510383498

Robert Wood Johnson Foundation Commission to Build a Healthier America. (2009). *Beyond health care*. Robert Wood Johnson Foundation. https://www.rwjf.org/en/library/research/2009/04/beyond-health-care.html

Thornton, R. L. J., Glover, C. M., Cene, C. W., Glik, D. C., Henderson, J. A., & Williams, D. R. (2016). Evaluation strategies for reducing health disparities by addressing the social determinants of health. *Health Affairs*, *35*(8), 1416–1423. https://doi.org/10.1377/hlthaff.2015.1357

8

DISPARITIES IN MENTAL HEALTH SERVICES: A MATTER OF JUSTICE IN THE CLINICAL SETTING

Martha J. Markward | Kalea Benner

LEARNING OBJECTIVES

Students will be able to:

- Articulate the history of mental health services in the United States.
- Define the types of social justice philosophies that can be used in understanding the disparities in mental health services.
- Recognize the disparities that exist in mental health services and the magnitude of consequences on the individual and society.
- Identify the roles of social work in eliminating disparities in mental health services.

INTRODUCTION

Social workers are currently challenged to address the disparities in the provision of mental health services. Social workers provide the majority of mental healthcare, outnumbering all other mental health professions combined (National Association of Social Workers [NASW], n.d.). As such, social workers must acknowledge that any disparity in the provision of mental health services is a matter of social justice, especially when the disparity is associated with social determinants external to individuals. In so doing, social workers can begin to address the service barriers that many members of ethnic/minority groups encounter when they seek help for mental health issues. By taking advantage of the opportunities to eliminate the gaps in services for particular populations of individuals and groups, social workers can contribute to a more just provision of mental health services.

MEANING OF MENTAL HEALTH

According to the American Psychiatric Association (APA, n.d.), mental illness is a health disorder characterized by emotional, behavioral, and/or cognitive changes. In turn, those changes are associated with distress and problems that interfere with an individual's ability to function properly in daily activities.

Szasz (1961) disagreed with conceptualizing mental illness as a disorder and argued that individuals with problems in daily functioning should not be identified as ill (mentally or otherwise) and doing so is a disservice to the patient as the diagnosis fails to identify a disease or provide a clear treatment path (Benning, 2016). Szasz strongly opposed identifying emotions or thinking or behavior as abnormal, believing that it was a form of social control that pathologized the client rather than providing a medically based disease diagnosis.

In response to the criticism of disorder versus disease, Wakefield (1992) suggested that mental illness is made up of harmful dysfunctions predicated upon the individual's social determinants, such as the cultural values and norms in the individual's community. Incorporating the individual's culture not only helps to eliminate bias that may exist in diagnosing but also simultaneously presents criteria that allow others to influence perceptions of health or mental well-being. Reliance upon others to determine what is healthy or appropriate for the individual interjects elements of subjectivity and adds another potential aspect of injustice.

Uncertainty in diagnosis—disorder versus disease versus dysfunction—compounds the disparities experienced in the provision of mental health services because less than half of those who meet criteria for a diagnosis actually receive care (APA, 2017). This has obvious justice implications for our clients who deserve some level of objectivity in diagnosing and treating mental illness. By any definition, Parekh (2018) noted that problems in daily functioning can be treated so that individuals can engage adequately and appropriately in all aspects of daily living and be able to adjust to or cope with challenges that arise. This brings into question how problems in daily functioning have been treated in the provision of mental health services over time.

Currently, the meaning of mental illness is classified in the *Diagnostic and Statistical Manual of Mental Disorders* (5th ed.; *DSM-5*; APA, 2013), which was developed for the purpose of classifying mental health "disorders" (APA, n.d.). The classification of "disorders" is by definition prevalence, etiology, and criteria for diagnosis, which also provides insight into cognitive, emotional, and behavioral features of identified disorders. As such, it allows clinicians to have a common language regarding mental disorders that allows better communication about and identification of diagnoses to guide congruent treatment. However, the *DSM* has been criticized for a number of reasons.

First, the purpose of professionals discussing disorders from the same reference points is often to justify the end goal of funding for services. Second, it allows for labeling certain behavior as deviant, such as the homosexual label until 1973. Third, the *DSM* fails to fully acknowledge the impact of social determinants of mental health disorders, such as socioeconomic status, community disadvantage, and lack of health insurance. Last, clinician bias in interpreting the criteria for diagnosing particular disorders can interfere with accurate and unjust treatment, as well as impact data on prevalence. In this manner, the *DSM* might contribute to the disparities in the prevalence of mental health disorders and, in turn, in the need of particular populations for services and treatment.

HISTORY OF MENTAL HEALTH SERVICE PROVISION

Historically, there have been important changes in the provision of mental health services in the United States. During the 1800s, the number of large institutions and asylums was expanded as a humane means of providing services to those with mental illness. To be consistent with moral treatment and care, the intent in those institutions was to provide individuals who had mental disorders or those who were considered "insane" with a safe environment in which to live. Despite this intent, those institutions tended to become more like prisons for patients and many had a horrific history of abuse and neglect (Goldman & Morrissey, 1985; Morrissey & Goldman, 1984).

Into the 20th century, the focus was on prevention and a scientific orientation that included the introduction of psychotropic drugs, as well as the use of debatable interventions, such as lobotomies (Goldman & Morrissey, 1985; Morrissey & Goldman, 1984). To address what they perceived to be inhumane treatment of patients in the asylums, physician Philippe Pinel and social worker Dorothea Dix also advocated for psychiatric hospitals to address the needs of many who still resided in jails and poor houses (Tiffany, 1891). The care provided in many psychiatric hospitals became questionable if not inhumane, and subsequently, those with mental illness began to be visible in the community setting.

Within the context of social integration and deinstitutionalization, President Harry S. Truman signed the National Mental Health Act in 1946, an act that provided funding for education and research on mental illness and led to the establishment of the National Institute of Mental Health in 1949. In 1955, Congress mandated an assessment and evaluation of services for those with mental illness (Accordino et al., 2001), and in 1963, the Community Health Centers Act gave impetus to the provision of mental health services in the community (Accordino et al., 2001).

Since 1975, the mental health movement has encouraged the integration of services in the community. As such, mental illness is addressed as a social welfare problem that warrants attention to basic living needs as a means to enhancing mental health that includes housing and employment (Goldman & Morrissey, 1985). While Presidents Nixon and Carter advocated for additional mental health funding, the Omnibus Budget Reconciliation Act passed during the Reagan administration reduced all domestic funding, which included services for mental health treatment and resulted in the deinstitutionalization of many who had resided in hospital settings for decades.

As the 21st century began, the number of patients diagnosed with mental illnesses, including substance use disorder, continued to increase. In 2003, President George W. Bush increased funding for community health centers (CHCs), which in turn increased the number of services for outpatient settings. Although the funding for mental health services in the community continues to be a priority, there continues to be a paucity of resources for the provision of services at the clinical level to increase the ability of citizens to access mental health services. Given the need to find the balance between service provision and service use, Bruckner et al. (2019) noted that CHCs have targeted underserved communities wherein a disproportionate number of persons with an untreated mental disorder reside.

These researchers explored the mental health services provided in CHCs between 2007 and 2015 and found that mental health service provision in CHCs outpaced general CHC growth. This likely reflected federal efforts to integrate behavioral health with primary care, including (a) behavioral health integration grants distributed throughout the nation, (b) the Mental Health and Parity and Addiction Equity Act that expanded access to mental health services for those with private insurance, and (c) the Medicaid initiatives in the Patient Protection and Affordable Care Act that allowed more persons to access mental health services. With this said, however, Bruckner et al. (2019) concluded that more research is needed to understand the extent to which mental health services in CHCs are effective in addressing disparities in mental health services.

It is especially important to note that despite the growth in service provision via the CHCs, Mongelli et al. (2020) highlighted that correctional facilities provide services to inmates, 50% of whom have a mental health diagnosis, and 25% of those inmates have been diagnosed with a serious mental illness. In considering those percentages, It is noteworthy that one-third of Black men will be imprisoned in their lifetime, which has unintended consequences with regard to services for their partners and children. Wildeman and Wang (2017) noted that parental incarceration leads to increased substance use and abuse among their children.

Equally important to note is that, over time, deinstitutionalization has been a response to deplorable conditions in residential facilities, with new medications being the hope for allowing persons with mental illness to function effectively in their communities at a manageable cost. This movement has been criticized because many individuals with severe mental illness are homeless or in jails as a result of inappropriate behavior. Unfortunately, medications have not improved functioning even when symptoms are addressed, and as a result, community mental health centers have been overwhelmed and unable to meet the needs of those with severe mental illness (Yohanna, 2013).

SOCIAL JUSTICE AND MENTAL HEALTH SERVICE

Rawls (1971) proposed the most familiar philosophy of social justice and the one that is currently used to determine what is and is not socially just in society, justice as fairness. Rawls proposed that social justice is contingent on a least common denominator of need, which is the criterion for the distribution of goods and services that provides a safety net for those in need in a society. While the major proposition in the philosophy is that goods and services should be redistributed to help those individuals in most need, what constitutes goods and services is less clear. In addition, the distinction between want and need warrants attention.

Relative to the Rawlsian philosophy of social justice, the libertarian and utilitarian philosophies of social justice warrant attention. The libertarian philosophy of social justice is focused on the notion of individual rights and the argument that whatever one has achieved or acquired is "just" without any interference from other citizens or the government (Nozick, 1974). Based on this philosophy of social justice, it would be just for an individual to not wear a mask during a worldwide pandemic. The assumption is that the individual would ask for no interference if they were to become sick as a result of a pandemic situation.

By comparison, the utilitarian philosophy of social justice suggests that justice considerations "maximize happiness for the greatest number" (Mill, 1863). For example, utilitarianism suggests that it is socially just to identify persons in neighborhoods who have served time for sexual crimes, presumably to maximize safety and happiness for the majority. However, this philosophy also justified the creation of public education as a means of providing an enlightened citizenry. In sum, utilitarianism posits that although what is just for the majority may not be just for a minority of individuals in a society; it maximizes happiness for the greatest number in society.

In building on the ideas of Rawls, Wakefield (1988) argued that a central organizing value of social work is distributive justice (Rawls, 1971). In this regard, therapeutic service is important in redistributing justice when the goods and services are related to psychological needs. Wakefield contended that clinical social work could be construed as psychological intervention intended to "impart justice related traits" to those who lack the traits they need in order to function fairly in society (p. 354), and those traits include individual and social traits, such as socioeconomic status and neighborhood residence. Unfortunately, many nonclinical professionals engage in labeling those with mental illness.

Prevalence of Mental Health Disorders

Data from the 2019 National Survey on Drug Use and Health show the magnitude and scope of disparities in service use, primarily by gender, age, and race/ethnicity (Substance Abuse and Mental Health Services Administration [SAMHSA], 2020). Fifty-one million persons in the United States experienced a mental health disorder of any type, which was slightly more than 20% of the population. Of those persons, 25% were female compared to 16% male. According to SAMHSA (2017), 26% of individuals between 18 and 25 years of age experienced mental illness compared to 22% of individuals between 26 and 49 years of age and 14% of individuals 50 years of age and older. By race/ethnicity (SAMHSA, 2020), 22% of White/non-Hispanic individuals experience mental health disorders compared to 17% of Black, 19% of American Indigenous and Alaska Native, 18% of Latinx, and 14% of Asian populations. Thirty-two percent of persons reporting two or more races experienced mental illness.

Treatment of Mental Health Disorders

In terms of treatment, approximately 20% of persons with mental illness disorders receive treatment (SAMHSA, 2020). Females are more likely to receive treatment than males, with nearly 50% of females receiving treatment compared to 37% of males who had a disorder (SAMHSA, 2020). By age, 39% of persons between 18 and 25 years of age received services compared to 44% of persons between 26 and 49 years of age and 47% of persons 50 years of age and older. By race/ethnicity (SAMHSA, 2020), the following percentages show the difference in the use of mental health services: White (48%), Black (30.6%), Hispanic (32.6%), and Asian (20.2). These data show the disparities in the use of mental health services by race and ethnicity.

These statistics worsen when moderate to severe mental disorders are considered (SAMHSA, 2020). The lack of treatment is more problematic relative to particular mental health disorders, specifically major depressive disorder and substance use disorder. Fifty-six percent of those with a diagnosis of major depressive disorder and nearly 90% of those with substance use disorder receive no treatment. In considering the differences in members of communities of color receiving treatment relative to the White population, these diagnoses affect members of those populations disproportionately.

IMPACT OF UNTREATED MENTAL ILLNESS

Mental illness is one of the leading causes of disability and premature death and is one of the conditions most costly to treat as well (APA, 2017). In addition to the devastation that an individual with a mental illness experiences, society is impacted by an economic toll associated with addressing mental illness. Nearly $1 trillion annually is associated with mental healthcare, criminal justice system costs, and loss of productivity; specifically nearly half the persons with mental illness are unemployed (McCance-Katz, 2020).

The consequences of mental illness disproportionately impact members of racial and ethnic groups. Members of racial and ethnic minority groups are more likely to experience a disability as a result of mental illness and more likely to experience persistent mental illness (APA, 2017). For this reason alone, it is especially relevant and important to understand how the disparities in the delivery of mental health services impact minority populations. It is noteworthy that trauma may be a consequence of untreated mental illness in many communities of color and neighborhoods, which, in turn, may result in more mental health problems.

DISPARITIES IN MENTAL HEALTH SERVICES AND SOCIAL JUSTICE

A disparity or gap in treatment is the difference in the proportion of people who have a disorder and those who receive care (Mongelli et al., 2020). Taken together, people of color make up a considerable proportion of the entire population in the United States, but they also tend to lack access to mental healthcare, and the care to which they have access is often of poorer quality

(Maura & Weisman de Mamani, 2017). Relative to prevalence of mental illness, it is important to recognize the disparities in mental healthcare that people of color experience because those disparities also include the disparities by gender, age, and diagnosis. With that in mind, this section addresses disparities in service provision in terms of (a) access to services, (b) utilization of services, (c) the therapeutic alliance/engagement, and (d) interventions/treatment.

Access to Service

Cost is one of the most well-documented barriers to accessing mental health services. In addition to cost, the lack of services for children, neighborhood, and/or community influences the need for navigators; and the lack of trauma-informed systems contributes to the access problem for particular populations.

COST

The first aspect of the mental health system to examine is access to the system of care, and the National Conference of State Legislatures (NCSL, 2018) found that 44% of those with mental illness noted cost as the greatest barrier to accessing service. In terms of cost, persons who are members of racial/ethnic groups are less likely to be insured or have a primary care provider, which can lead to little access to services, especially preventive measures. Approximately 20% of persons on Medicaid experience mental illness, but the expenditures on mental illness account for nearly half of all Medicaid expenditures. Given the cost, it seems likely that some individuals will go without the services they need. In addition, cost is associated with other reported barriers to accessing care, such as the lack of transportation and childcare needed to access care, as well as the flexibility to take time away from work.

LACK OF SERVICES FOR CHILDREN

Although disparities in adult access to mental health services are problematic, children's access to mental health services is of particular concern relative to all populations of children, and especially to children of color. Whitney and Peterson (2019) used data from the 2016 National Survey of Children's Health to identify the extent of mental health problems among children. To collect data, a parent proxy approach was used wherein parents of children younger than 18 years of age responded about their child's mental health. In relying on several means used to survey parents, the response rate was 41% overall ($N = 50,212$). A key finding in the study was that of the nearly 8 million children in the United States with a treatable mental health disorder, only half receive treatment from a mental health professional, though this statistic varies by state.

NEIGHBORHOOD/COMMUNITY DISADVANTAGE

Glasgow et al. (2019) noted that neighborhoods influence the access of Black children and adolescents to mental health services. Those children and adolescents disproportionately reside in chaotic neighborhoods yet have a low rate of mental health diagnoses. The low rate of diagnoses among Black children who reside in these neighborhoods suggests that those children have little or no access to screening and diagnostic services. Likewise, Baams et al. (2019) highlighted how instability of residency also limits the access of LGBTQ youth to mental health services, many of whom are members of racial/ethnic groups.

Children who experience trauma lack access to trauma-informed care. In particular, Black children experience disproportionate adverse childhood events (ACEs), such as divorce, economic hardship, or an incarcerated parent, compared to other populations (Sacks & Murphey, 2018). Sixty-one percent of Black children experience at least one ACE compared to 40% of White non-Hispanic children. The prevalence of two or more ACEs is highest among Black children in all regions of the country (Sacks & Murphey, 2018). Because the ACEs often occur in the neighborhood or home, they go unaddressed in terms of trauma.

Children who are trauma affected often display behaviors that typically mimic attention deficit hyperactivity disorder (ADHD) and oppositional defiant disorder in the educational process (Walkley & Cox, 2013), though they may actually be in a perpetual "fight or flight" or a "freeze" state (Perry, 2006). Behavior associated with those emotional states may result in Black students receiving punitive disciplinary actions. Unfortunately, punitive disciplinary actions may further intensify the impact of trauma among Black students and may retraumatize them repeatedly (Walkley & Cox, 2013). Without access to appropriate intervention, the emotional dysregulation associated with trauma will carry over into adulthood.

NEED FOR NAVIGATORS

The access of children and youth to mental health services can be enhanced with the assistance of a family navigator (Godoy et al., 2019). Navigators are individuals who have experience with and understanding of mental health systems in particular locations, for example, neighborhoods, communities, and states. While navigators have been used to help adults access the mental health services they need, the authors suggest that navigators in pediatric primary care settings could help both children and youth access mental health services.

Utilization of Mental Health Services

Utilization and engagement contribute to disparities in mental health services in general. Alegria et al. (2020) noted that structural barriers that include communication, limited times available for care, and poor quality of services influence engagement of people of color in utilizing services. For example, Benuto et al. (2019) noted that in the case of Latinx, interventions targeting the stigma associated with seeking and utilizing mental health treatment that could reduce disparities in behavioral health service utilization are lacking.

Community disadvantage is an important consideration in assessing the utilization of mental health services. Pulsifer et al. (2019) highlighted that the lack of quality services for residents in low-income, urban communities creates a gap in services for both children and adults. Likewise, Acevedo et al. (2018) found that community disadvantage results in Black and Native American/American Indians who are substance misusers not initiating or engaging in treatment as compared to non-Latinx White users.

Therapeutic Alliance/Engagement

The therapeutic alliance is often lacking in the therapeutic relationship when clinician and client do not share social backgrounds. There is a need for the clinician to find common ground with regard to clients' respective backgrounds, but unfortunately, the clinician is the one perceived to have the knowledge (Alegria et al., 2020). As such, the clinician identifies the goals and objectives for treatment and engagement that may lack meaning for members of race/ethnic groups, which is complicated by the clinician not listening to what is meaningful to those consumers. For example, Galvan and Gudiño (2019) identify caregiver acculturation is often lacking in terms of addressing internalizing versus externalizing need among Latinx clients.

Interestingly, Hall et al. (2020) noted that it is important to focus on external social determinants of mental health problems among Black persons rather than on disease. Within the context of the therapeutic alliance, the diagnosis is also a most relevant component to consider. Moreno and Chhatwal (2020) noted that Black patients are less likely to receive a bipolar diagnosis and more likely to receive a schizophrenic spectrum disorder. Proportionately, Black consumers are also likely to have higher rates of severe depression than White individuals. One explanation for this is clinician bias in their interpretation of symptoms (Moreno & Chhatwal, 2020).

Treatments/Intervention

Collaborations and partnerships with primary care physicians are needed to address the lack of mental health services, especially in rural areas where many persons with mental health disorders live and are areas officially identified as having a shortage of professionals (Guilbault & Vinson, 2017). Kohn et al. (2018) pointed out that although primary care physicians see 60% of persons with a mental health disorder in these areas, the service they provide is often minimal (Butler et al., 2018). Physicians themselves have identified their lack of confidence in addressing the mental health problems of patients (Butler et al., 2018). Providing mental healthcare that is integrated in primary care settings destigmatizes seeking help, increases treatment availability and access options, as well as improves patient outcomes (American Psychiatric Association & Academy of Psychosomatic Medicine, 2016).

CASE STUDY 8.1—JALIL

Jalil is 16 years of age and lives with his maternal grandmother after his mom was murdered when he was 13 years of age. His dad lives in the same community and visits frequently. Grandma is concerned because Jalil is supposed to be released from juvenile justice custody when he turns 17, but she knows he is smoking weed and that he will fail a drug test if one is administered.

Grandma describes the loss of her daughter with tremendous grief, describing Jalil as: "He was just beyond me at that point, so angry and defiant. No one knows what losing his mama did to that boy. He's not like that now, he just seems to think it's ok for him to smoke 'cause everyone is. But not everyone is trying to get out of the system. It's different for him."

Experiencing his mother's murder and the subsequent investigation that ultimately ended in a guilty plea by the defendant took a tremendous toll on Jalil. He was angry and resentful and found it hard to focus in school. His grandma knew he needed help and took him to talk to the youth minister but did not have insurance to pay for healthcare, medication, or therapy. Ultimately, Jalil got into a fight after school at a middle school football game that resulted in his arrest, due largely to his noncompliance with the responding officers. The recommendation was that Jalil needed intensive treatment (psychological, behavioral), and so he was placed in lockdown at a residential facility at the age of 14. Jalil was released after 6 months to his grandmother's physical custody, but the state retained legal custody.

(continued)

CASE STUDY 8.1—JALIL (*continued*)

Jalil went into custody because he experienced unresolved trauma that resulted in unmet mental health needs. Many of our youth become system involved as a result of needing mental health treatment. The inability to access professional mental healthcare had serious consequences for him and his relatively brief time in the system demonstrates his ability to succeed if given the right resources. His grandmother is rightly concerned about getting him released from the criminal justice system and his drug use is jeopardizing that release.

1. Why might accessing mental health services for Jalil be difficult for his grandmother?
2. Explain how providing mental health services for children, especially children who are members of racial/ethnic minority groups, is in the best interest of society.
3. Why is it important to identify how the trauma of his mother's murder is important relative to Jalil being diagnosed with mental health disorders?
4. How can a *DSM* diagnosis result in mental health services that are different for Black consumers than for White consumers?
5. Why is integrated healthcare important in destigmatizing mental health services for persons of color?
6. Based on statistics, how would Jalil's experience with substance abuse and mental health services likely compare to that of a White counterpart?

SOCIAL JUSTICE CONCERNS AND DISPARITIES IN MENTAL HEALTH SERVICES

In most discussions of social justice, the discussants reference John Rawls and the notion of social justice as the redistribution of goods and services to provide a safety net for those most in need. And as Wakefield (1992) suggested, Rawls's notion of social justice is applicable when the goods and services are related to psychological and mental health needs. However, when one considers the disparity in mental health services, the utilitarian notion of social justice warrants consideration of what is just; in this case, what is *just* is also for the greater good. From this perspective, it seems that addressing the disparity in mental health services for children and adults would literally and figuratively maximize happiness in terms of mental health for the greatest number in society as a whole. With both notions of social justice in mind, it is important to articulate the social injustices that seem apparent in the provision of mental health services to members of racial/ethnic groups.

- There is a clear gap between prevalence and treatment for people and communities of color.
- The *DSM* may actually be used to diagnose mental health disorders in ways that fail to recognize behavior that is normative rather than pathological, for example, depression may be a normative response to practices that a member of a racial/ethnic group perceives to be racist rather than a disease or disorder.
- Economic justice is lacking for people of color who have mental illness because the goods and services related to psychological needs in their neighborhoods and communities fail to provide them with a safety net to access mental health services at minimal cost.

- When children, especially Black children, lack the services they need in particular neighborhoods and under certain circumstances, it is impossible to maximize the happiness of the greatest number in society because children take their unmet psychological needs into adulthood.
- Trauma-informed care is lacking for Black children who experience the behavioral effects and emotional dysregulation associated with trauma that results from ACEs.
- When clinicians and practitioners fail to engage members of racial/ethnic groups in the therapeutic process in such a way that gives meaning to the process for them, those individuals receive unjust treatment, which makes it impossible to maximize what is in the best interest of society.
- When clinicians and practitioners fail to diagnose particular disorders among members of racial/ethnic groups, such as major depressive disorder and substance use disorder, or misdiagnose one disorder for another, there is a need for justice.
- Given the sum of disparities in addressing the mental health needs of racial/minority populations, it is important to examine all possible opportunities for addressing those disparities.

CASE STUDY 8.2—JUANA

Juana is 68 years of age and resides with her son Juan, his wife Maria, and their three children who are 8, 6, and 4 years of age. The family lives in a small house in a neighborhood that is predominantly Latinx. Juan and Maria have become increasingly concerned about what they perceive to be Juana's "crazy spells." During these spells, Juan and Maria say it is like she loses touch with reality.

Before Juana lived with Juan and Maria, she lived with her husband who was quite abusive and, on several occasions, nearly beat her to death. Given the loyalty to her husband, it took her many years to leave him and later divorce him. After she divorced, she took a job with a cleaning company and proceeded to earn enough to survive.

Unfortunately, Juana began to have slight spells on the job, and her coworkers on cleaning jobs became a bit frightened because they could not understand what was happening when she had the spells. In addition, considering her age, she was let go from her cleaning work. At that point, Juan and Maria invited Juana to live with them and the children.

Maria has become particularly concerned about Juana's hysterical outbursts that are sometimes directed at the children. The outbursts are often focused on her childhood in Mexico, her husband's abusive treatment of her, and her inability to support herself. Juan has tried to find mental health services for Juana, but Juana has no retirement of any kind, and he and Maria cannot afford to pay for services out of pocket. This is complicated by the fact that English is a second language for Juana, and Juana is not a citizen of the United States.

1. Consider how social, economic, or environmental justice, or a combination of the three, is important in keeping Juana from accessing the mental health services she needs.
2. Consider how diagnoses that do not take into account social determinants, such as Juana's position as a cleaning lady with no access to retirement funds, create an injustice in mental health treatment.
3. Explain how goods and services related to psychological needs and the provision of a safety net for mental health services are relevant to Juana's situation.
4. To what extent might English as a second language be important in finding the right clinician?

ADDRESSING SOCIAL JUSTICE CONCERNS IN MENTAL HEALTH SERVICES

Although there are disparities in mental health services that warrant attention in terms of social justice, several researchers have identified opportunities for addressing those disparities, especially for members of racial/ethnic groups.

1. With regard to access, Whitney and Peterson (2019) concluded that both state policies and practices play a role in the mental healthcare needs of children and their use of services. In this regard, Dopp and Lantz (2020) contended that more focus is needed "upstream" at the public policy and community levels to address the determinants of children's mental health disorders. For example, numerous researchers have found that health insurance does result in access to mental health services for racial/ethnic minority groups, particularly the positive influence of the Patient Protection and Affordable Care Act (Cook et al., 2018; Lee-Tauler et al., 2018; Novak et al., 2018).

2. In particular, Black children need access to trauma-informed care, especially in the school setting, as well as in the child welfare and juvenile justice systems of care. Those children are disproportionately represented in the latter two systems. Trauma-informed care in the school setting might address the behaviors of Black students who are associated with trauma events, resulting in fewer disciplinary actions and a more compassionate approach taken toward those students. The first step in trauma-informed care involves parents/guardians in the therapeutic process and their understanding of ACEs.

3. Both adults and children who are members of communities of color could benefit from a family navigator to help them access mental health services in particular neighborhoods and communities. Corrigan et al. (2017) noted that peer navigators can help persons negotiate the mental health system because they have empathy and are able to listen to patients and clients, especially African Americans who have a severe mental health disorder and are homeless.

4. In terms of utilization of mental health services by members of racial/ethnic groups, stigma is an important issue that must be addressed. Mowbray et al. (2018) contended that even when there is utilization and engagement, there is a need to simultaneously address the stigma attached to individuals actually engaging in mental health treatment. Even during engagement, the stigma can result in the consumer leaving or ending treatment early. In addition, integrated physical and mental health in CHCs may reduce the possibility of stigma (Lee-Tauler et al., 2018).

5. In terms of engaging clients, Alegria et al. (2020) identify recommendations that are helpful in addressing the "ethnic, economic, or political hierarchy" that clinician and client might experience based on their respective characteristics, for example, age, gender, and education. The researchers provide three recommendations for addressing the differences in clinician and client within the therapeutic relationship.

    First, it is helpful for the clinician to use shared decision-making that engages the client in making decisions about their treatment. This may include using "we" and "us" in discussing the session agenda, which allows the client input into setting the agenda (see also Lee-Tauler et al., 2018).

    Second, it is important for the clinician and client to establish goals and objectives that are important to the client and that have meaning in their life. The clinician can ask the client how they see the problem and its cause, as well as use the client's own language in discussing the problem. In working with children and their parents, it is especially important to give children a voice and to hear their language regarding the problem.

The third recommendation for engaging clients who are members of communities of color is to facilitate exchanges that focus on the clinician sharing who the client is and asking the client about their experiences. This can allow for learning about the client's cultural background, as well as how a client sees the world. More important, an open dialogue that allows for both clinician and client to share who they are can result in a focus on their similarities rather than differences, which takes on particular salience in changing perceived differences in their respective social backgrounds and experiences. For example, Galvan and Gudiño (2019) identify caregiver acculturation as important to address internalizing versus externalizing need among Latinx clients. Interestingly, Hall et al. (2020) noted that it is important to focus on external social determinants of mental health problems among Asian Americans rather than on disease.

6. Alegria et al. (2020) also emphasize the importance of systemic changes in addressing the disparities in mental health services for clients who are members of communities of color. Systemic changes might include more clinical training that utilizes the previous recommendations, developing different modes of treatment, such as by phone or online modalities, establishing flexible hours, and meeting in a variety of settings that are comfortable for clients. Of particular importance is the value of integrating into mental healthcare the various social determinants that contribute to mental health problems, for example, socioeconomic status, neighborhood and community of treatment, meeting in more comfortable settings, and being flexible in meetings.

7. Collaborative care utilizes a team approach in a medical setting to address mental health issues, which is an approach embraced in CHCs and has been supported in the ACA. Mongelli et al. (2020) described a patient-centered medical home model wherein the team approach is intended to treat the "whole person." In this model of service delivery, the team works to provide comprehensive behavioral health intervention in a medical setting with social services, as well as dental care in some cases. These types of models have provided mental health services in underserved areas for the past two decades.

8. Task sharing is a strategy intended to include a wide variety of professionals to be involved in meeting the needs of persons with mental health disorders, including nurses, nurses' assistants, and pharmacists (Kazdin, 2017). The persons involved in task sharing may be from different sectors in the community, which allows for a more interpersonal approach to service delivery. In this regard, Whaley (2019) suggested the need to also involve "Indigenous healers" in addressing mental disorders. With more task sharing, more persons can become aware of mental illness and destigmatize it so more individuals will seek treatment (Barnett et al., 2018; Castillo et al., 2019).

9. There are innovations in addressing the service gap in urban areas as well as in rural areas. Mobile outreach teams can be used in a city to bring services to those in need of mental health services, and in general, the move toward the individuals who need the service is a thoughtful practice (Hwang & Burns, 2014). Broadly speaking, mobile outreach is an important means of engaging persons who need mental health services, especially children and adolescents. Along with mobile outreach, Corrigan et al. (2017) noted that peer navigators can help persons negotiate the mental health system because

they have empathy and are able to listen to patients and clients, especially African Americans who have a severe mental health disorder and are homeless.

10. Technology is the newest means of addressing mental health services with the caveat that a broadband connection is unavailable in many areas of the nation. Despite the in-person human contact, both clinicians and clients/patients from various backgrounds and with different diagnoses have reported a high level of satisfaction with videoconferencing (Chakrabarti, 2015). In addition to providing services to clients/patients, technology can be used for training as well. For example, Extension for Community Healthcare Outcomes (Project ECHO) is a training program for clinicians that provides weekly sessions on a variety of topics with intent of enhancing clinician competence (Hager et al., 2018).

CASE STUDY 8.3—JAMES

James is a 10-year-old in fourth grade and was referred for disciplinary action for slamming another child's head into the hand dryer in the elementary school bathroom. James displays considerable aggression at school, primarily with peers but also with staff on a rare occasion. His mother has a history of drug use and has been incarcerated repeatedly as a result. The first time his mother was incarcerated, James was 6 years of age when he lived with his 18-year-old brother until his mother was released.

After 6 months, his mother violated her parole by failing a drug test so she returned to prison, and James then lived with his aunt and uncle in another town, which necessitated him changing schools. Mom was eventually released once more on parole and James returned to live with her, once again changing towns and schools. He knows she has been using again because he sees her using, and that she had an appointment to see her parole officer that day. James is terrified that she will fail her drug test and return to prison. He says he's "too much trouble," and that no one wants him to live with them. His mom said that if she went back to prison, then he would have to go to foster care.

At school, James is aggressive, both verbally and physically. He can also be loving and seems to crave attention. James has few friends and seems to struggle with building any connection—let alone a relationship. He is typically withdrawn from others except for when he demonstrates attention-seeking behaviors that are typically followed by aggression, most frequently toward his peers, never toward his teachers, and once toward a bus driver who asked him if his mama was out of prison yet.

In the latest incident, James hurt his peer significantly enough that the child had to have stitches in his face from the impact with the metal hand dryer. James is defiant, shows little remorse, and insists the other child deserves it because he was telling others that James was going to have to go to foster care. The school stated they had no other recourse but to call the police. They feel his behavior has escalated and that his peers are at risk if he remains in the school system.

James is a clear example of a traumatized child who needs mental health treatment but will likely receive it in the juvenile justice system, if at all. James's lack of stability, the disruptive living situation, lack of a stable caregiver, and drug abuse in the home are all adverse child

(continued)

> **CASE STUDY 8.3—JAMES (*continued*)**
>
> conditions which place him at increased risk of mental illness. The understandable emotional and behavioral dysregulation that results from these conditions places him at increased risk for involvement in the legal system. Failing to address and resolve James's mental health needs will likely have lifelong consequences for him.
>
> 1. How important is the environment in helping James address his issues compared to social and economic issues?
> 2. Explain why parents/guardians of Black children must understand ACEs in order to help provide trauma-informed care in the home and school settings.
> 3. How can a navigator be useful in enhancing services for both James and his mother?
> 4. To what extent might James engage more enthusiastically with a Black, male clinician?
> 5. How can task sharing be used to help James in the home and school setting?

IMPLICATIONS FOR SOCIAL WORK PRACTICE

In order to address disparities in mental healthcare services among racial/ethnic minority populations, social workers today must reflect the professional perspectives of both Jane Addams and Mary Richmond. Like Jane Addams, social workers must be aware of the social determinants of mental health disorders among racial/ethnic minority populations, especially in neighborhoods and in communities. Like Mary Richmond, they must also be interested in assessment, which includes diagnosing, as well as using social histories and background information to better understand the mental health issues of individual patients/clients who are members of ethnic minority groups. They must also use their assessment skills to better understand how neighborhoods and communities contribute to disparities in mental health services. Based on the literature reviewed and referenced herein, there are areas where social workers can contribute to reduce racial/ethnic disparities in mental health services and to enhance social justice for society as a whole.

Community Health Services

Social workers should consider how they can become involved in community-based programs. For example, they should make efforts to practice in outpatient pediatric and family medicine settings that provide services to underserved populations of children and families. This could create a model of practice that allows social workers to partner with physicians, nurses, nurse assistants, and other professionals to connect children's physical and mental health in the context of the family system. This partnership could be expedited if schools of social work explore and negotiate practicum experiences in those settings. At the very least, social workers might seek positions in CHCs.

Shared Decision-Making

Social workers at the community and individual levels must be skilled in assessment in order to understand the social determinants and background experiences that have contributed to the mental health problems of clients. In terms of culturally sensitive practice, social workers must go beyond awareness and be able to use strategies that include clients/patients in decision-making at all points in the therapeutic process. In recognizing social determinants, such as stigma about mental health treatment, social workers must consider seeing clients in environments where they are more comfortable and when treatment is more convenient for them, which might warrant social workers' home visits for service provision or working with children in their school settings if appropriate. In considering shared decision-making, narrative and solution-focused approaches might be better choices than cognitive behavioral therapy as a means of empowering disenfranchised clients/patients.

For a social worker, the ultimate goal in providing mental health services is to ensure appropriate access to and utilization of treatment while subsequently ensuring that treatment outcomes are equitable as well. Merced et al. (2020) found that the provider plays a significant role in determining adherence to treatment plans and that a perceived lack of inclusivity, biased messaging (unintentional or otherwise), and other factors such as locale can all contribute to whether a client engages in treatment.

Use of Technology

The worldwide pandemic occurring as this chapter was written has expedited the use of telemedicine and telebehavioral health to address both health and mental health problems. Based on the efficacy of providing treatment via videoconferencing, social workers can and should begin using technology to reach underserved populations, especially in rural areas. Equally important, social workers can and should advocate at the national level for all citizens to have broadband so all may access and utilize telemedicine and teletherapy more equitably. With thoughtfulness, social workers can use technology as a means of addressing the mental health needs of adolescents in schools who are members of racial/ethnic groups, which would address the fear of social stigma and fears related to loss of privacy.

Trauma-Informed Care

Given the number of adults and children who are affected by traumatic events and subsequent mental health disorders, specifically posttraumatic stress disorder and anxiety, it seems critically important that social workers become involved in addressing those disorders. They can also advocate upstream to the state and national levels for funding that is needed to provide services to both adults and children who are members of racial/ethnic groups and who have experienced more trauma than other groups. In particular, as practitioners in education, juvenile justice, and child welfare systems, social workers must give voice to the need for trauma-informed care in those systems where there is none.

Clinical social workers in private practice should continue to diversify their client populations whenever possible to provide members of racial/ethnic minorities with access to their services. In all clinical settings, it will be important for clinicians to consider how the behaviors and emotions associated with the effects of trauma may or may not warrant a diagnosis of a mental health disorder. When a label is unnecessary, it should not be assigned; when it is necessary, a diagnosis should be assigned so that the best, most evidence-based intervention can be implemented.

Teaming/Task Sharing

There are two important ways that social workers can team and task share in order to address disparities in the mental health services for members of racial/ethnic minority groups. In some communities, there are those residents who are perceived to have special powers and wisdom, especially among indigenous populations. Social workers can collaborate with those individuals to explore how best to address the mental disorders of residents.

Social workers in clinical settings can also collaborate with "navigators" to ensure that patients who are members of ethnic minority groups know how to access and utilize the mental health system at the community, state, and national levels. Social workers must also collaborate and team with professionals in a variety of settings to understand all perspectives on what mental health services are needed and how barriers to those services can be removed.

CASE STUDY 8.4—LATONYA'S CASE REVISITED

Remember Latonya? Latonya is a Black woman, 37 years of age, married, and a mother of two who is employed on the assembly line at a local Toyota plant. Latonya scheduled an appointment with a social worker but had to wait 3 weeks to be able to have an appointment after her work hours. She uses public transportation and the bus took over an hour to get there and required two bus changes. Upon her arrival, right at the appointed time, the receptionist jokingly told her that she was lucky to get an evening appointment. The receptionist gave her paperwork to complete while stating that the appointment could not start until the paperwork was completed but that her appointment would not be extended for the time the paperwork took.

The social worker noted that Latonya was reserved and seemed hesitant to engage, which the social worker identified as reluctance. When the social worker inquired about the possibility of medication, Latonya said she was hoping to avoid taking medication because she experienced considerable side effects in prior instances and wanted to start with therapy instead. When the social worker sought to establish buy-in and have Latonya agree to return, Latonya was cautious and asked if it would take another 3 weeks to get in. The social worker assured her that she had appointments available the following week and she could schedule one with the receptionist on the way out. When Latonya scheduled the appointment, the next one available outside of her working hours was 2 weeks away. The social worker was not surprised when Latonya failed to show up for that appointment.

1. In what ways could the social worker have been more culturally sensitive to Latonya?
2. Should the social worker have collaborated with a service provider who prescribes medicine to help Latonya find a medication with minimal side effects to consider, given the new medications on the market?
3. How could the social worker have explored Latonya's situation to make it easier for her to access services closer to her home and/or work?
4. To what extent is it important for social workers to consider all options for meeting clients where they are in terms of time and place?
5. How could the social worker use good assessment skills with Latonya, especially to assess the cause of the depression?

CONCLUSION

This chapter focused on disparities in the mental health services. Within the context of mental illness and social justice, the prevalence of mental health disorders in the United States was presented relative to the treatment that members of minority populations clearly receive compared to members of the White population. With this in mind, the main objective of this chapter was to identify disparities in service provision that result in the lack of treatment for members of racial/ethnic groups. Those disparities were transferred into social justice concerns and recommendations were made for addressing those concerns. With recommendations for change in mind, the implications for social work practice were highlighted and articulated. Social workers have the opportunity to reduce the disparities in mental health services via multifaceted, flexible social work practice that will result in more just service experiences for members of racial and ethnic groups at various points in the service delivery system.

DISCUSSION QUESTIONS

1. Consider Wakefield's definition of mental illness as a harmful dysfunction as determined by someone's culture. What might be ways in which it is appropriate to deviate from cultural norms?
2. How important is the environment in helping clients address mental health issues compared to social and economic issues?
3. Explain why social workers must be adept at understanding disparities in mental health treatment access as well as utilization.
4. Think about engaging clients who have chronic or severe mental illness. What are your greatest concerns and how will you cope with those?

REFERENCES

Only key references appear in the print edition. The full reference list appears in the digital product on Springer Publishing Connect: connect.springerpub.com/content/book/978-0-8261-3539-1/chapter/ch08

Barnett, M., Gonzales, A., Miranda, J., Chavira, A., & Lau, A. (2017). Mobilizing community health workers to address mental health disparities for underserved populations. *Administration and Policy in Mental Health and Mental Health Services Research, 45*, 195–211. https://doi.org/10.1007/s10488-017-0815-0

Corrigan, P., Pickett, S., Schmidt, A., Stellon, E., Hantke, E., Kraus, D., Dubke, R., & Community Based Participatory Research Team. (2017). Peer navigators to promote engagement of homeless African Americans with serious mental illness in primary care. *Psychiatry Residency, 255*, 101–103. https://doi.org/10.1016/j.psychres.2017.05.020

Dopp, A., & Lantz, P. (2020). Moving upstream to improve children's mental health through community and policy change. *Administration and Policy in Mental Health and Mental Health Services Research, 47*, 779–787. https://doi.org/10.1007/s10488-019-01001-5

Godoy, L., Hodgkinson, S., Robertson, H., Sham, E., Druskin, L., Wambach, C., Beers, L. S., & Long, M. (2019). Increasing mental health engagement from primary care: The potential role of family navigation. *Pediatrics, 143*(4), e20182418. https://doi.org/10.1542/peds.2018-2418

Hall, G., Berkman, E., Zane, N., Leong, F., Hwang, W., Nezu, A., Nezu, C., Hong, J., Chu, J., & Huang, E. (2020). Reducing mental health disparities by increasing the personal relevance of interventions. *American Psychologist*. Advance online publlication. https://doi.org/10.1037/amp0000616

Kohn, R., Ali, A., Puac-Polanco, V., Figueroa, C., López-Soto, V., Morgan, K., Saldivia, S., & Vicente, B. (2018). Mental health in the Americas: An overview of the treatment gap. *Rev Panam Salud Publication*, *42*(1), e165. https://doi.org/10.26633/RPSP.2018.165

Maura, J., & Weisman de Mamani, A. (2017). Mental health disparities, treatment engagement, and attrition among racial/ethnic minorities with severe mental illness: A review. *Journal of Clinical Psychology in Medical Settings*, *24*, 187–210. https://doi.org/10.1007/s10880-017-9510-2

McCance-Katz, E. F. (2020). *The National Survey on Drug Use and Health: 2019*. Substance Abuse and Mental Health Services Administration. https://www.samhsa.gov/data/report/dr-elinore-f-mccance-katz-webcast-slides-national-2019

Merced, K., Imel, Z. E., Baldwin, S. A., Fischer, H., Yoon, T., Stewart, C., Simon, G., Ahmedani, B., Beck, A., Daida, Y., Hubley, S., Rossom, R., Waitzfelder, B., Zeber, J. E., & Coleman, K. J. (2020). Provider contributions to disparities in mental health care. *Psychiatric Services*, *71*(8), 765–771. https://doi.org/10.1176/appi.ps.201800500

Mongelli, F., Georgakopoulos, P., & Pato, M. (2020). Challenges and opportunities to meet the mental health needs of underserved and disenfranchised populations in the United States. *Focus*, *18*(1), 16–24. https://doi.org/10.1176/appi.focus.20190028

Novak, P., Anderson, A., & Chen, J. (2018). Changes in health insurance coverage and barriers to health care access among individuals with serious psychological distress following the Affordable Care Act. *Administration and Policy in Mental Health and Mental Health Services Research*, *45*, 924–932. https://doi.org/10.1007/s10488-018-0875-9

Pulsifer, B. H., Evans, C. L., Capel, L., Lyons-Hunter, M., & Grieco, J. A. (2019). Cross-sectional assessment of mental health and service disparities in a high-risk community. *Translational Issues in Psychological Science*, *5*(4), 365–373. https://doi.org/10.1037/tps0000211

Substance Abuse and Mental Health Services Administration. (2020). *2019 National Survey of Drug Use and Health (NSDUH) releases*. Author.

Whitney, D., & Peterson, M. (2019). US national and state-level prevalence of mental health disorders and disparities of mental health care use. *JAMA Pediatrics*, *173*(4), 389–391. https://doi.org/10.1001/jamapediatrics.2018.5399

9

ENVIRONMENTAL JUSTICE AND DISASTERS: SOCIAL WORKERS' ROLE IN COMBATING STRUCTURAL INEQUALITIES

Allison Gibson

LEARNING OBJECTIVES

Students will be able to:

- Summarize factors that contribute to environmental injustice.
- Assess the structural barriers that harm various groups' (older persons, poor families, and Indigenous tribal communities) experience in being able to adequately prepare, respond to, and recover from disasters.
- Articulate the skills that social work professionals use to partner with communities to combat structural inequalities in improving disaster preparedness, response, and recovery.

INTRODUCTION

Communities across the globe face unprecedented environmental challenges, increasing population, and devastating pollution. These challenges threaten individuals and communities' health and quality of life. Environmental pollution hurts individuals and communities, forcing them to breathe unhealthy air, drink tainted water, or ingest toxic chemicals. These challenges disproportionately impact some segments of the population who are more likely to be affected as a result of socioeconomic status or locale. Social workers must address these aspects of environmental justice in order to meet client needs associated with health and behavioral health outcomes, employment, housing, and safety.

ENVIRONMENTAL JUSTICE AND THE ENVIRONMENTAL MOVEMENT

Health is significantly impacted by where one lives (Braveman et al., 2011). Prior research has highlighted the importance of the geographic factors in one's health outcomes (e.g., health opportunity, health equity) in understanding the social determinants of health (Anderson et al., 2003; Yen & Syme, 1999). Environmental inequities are also social inequities, resulting in health and economic disparities (Bullard, 2005).

Environmental challenges and pollution disproportionately affect people of color and poor communities, which then creates additional disparities in employment and income, food insecurity, and securing affordable housing (Bullard & Johnson, 2000). Moreover, the World Commission on Environment and Development (WCED) has identified a self-reinforcing, circular relationship between poverty and environmental pollution (WCED, 1987). Frequently, people in poverty inadvertently engage in environmentally destructive activities because they have no other choice to survive (Bullard, 2008; Bullard & Johnson, 1997). For example, someone living with limited income might hold on to a car that is less efficient and contributes more harmful emissions into the air instead of purchasing a newer, "greener" car that burns less fuel or runs on an alternative fuel such as electricity.

In many ways, environmental pollution keeps individuals in poverty. People with limited income tend to live on the poorest quality land, breathe the least healthy air, and drink contaminated water, all of which contribute to high rates of illness and disease, which further impact their ability to access sustainable employment and education (Bullard, 2005). Environmental justice, therefore, aims to achieve "equitable" distribution of pollution and reduce disparities of environmental degradation.

National conversations about the impact of environmental degradation began in the United States in the 1980s (Bullard & Johnson, 2000), although Indigenous populations have expressed concern far before then. The environmental justice movement was focused on identifying, documenting, and addressing the inequalities that stemmed from human settlement (i.e., colonialism, imperialism, globalization, etc.) and industrial development. Robert "Bob" Bullard, a key voice in the movement, called on communities to educate and assist groups in organizing and mobilizing. He worked to empower people to take charge of their lives and their communities (Levy & Patz, 2015). The environmental justice movement and the efforts of Bullard focused on addressing power imbalances, developing political enfranchisement, and redirecting resources for establishing healthier and more equitable communities (Bullard & Johnson, 2000).

In 1983, the U.S. General Accounting Office (GAO) found three out of four of the offsite commercial hazard waste landfills were located in predominantly African American communities (GAO, 1983; Bullard & Johnson, 2000). Then, the newly formed Commission for Racial Justice determined that race was the strongest variable in predicting the location of waste facilities (Bullard & Johnson, 2000). This finding led to the study of environmental racism, which is a form of racist discrimination in environmental policy-making and enforcement of regulations and laws (Mohai et al., 2009).

In 1991, these efforts resulted in the first summit on environmental justice in Washington, DC, where the 17 Environmental Justice Principles document was developed (Bullard, 2001). This document helped shape the Environmental Justice movement in the United States. Following the summit, the Environmental Protection Agency (EPA) responded with a definition for environmental justice (1991):

> Environmental Justice is the fair treatment and meaningful involvement of all people regardless of race, color, national origin, or income with respect to the development, implementation, and enforcement of environmental laws, regulations, and policies. EPA has this goal for all communities and persons across this Nation. It will be achieved when everyone enjoys the same degree of protection from environmental and health hazards and equal access to the decision-making process to have a healthy environment in which to live, learn, and work. (U.S. EPA, 2018, para. 1)

Since then researchers, professionals, and policy makers have explored the disparate impact of the environment on communities. Well-known impacted communities include Cancer Alley in Louisiana (Blodgett, 2007; Singer, 2011), the Flint Michigan water crisis (Campbell et al., 2016; Rosner, 2016), areas differentially impacted by disaster events such as Hurricane Katrina (Bullard, 2008; Johnson & Rainey, 2007), and mountaintop removal in Appalachian coal communities (Barry, 2012).

CLIMATE CHANGE AND DISASTERS

It is imperative that social work professionals attend to the needs of individuals and communities disproportionately affected by climate change. Evidence is mounting that the rise in frequency of natural disasters is likely due to the Earth's climate change (U.S. Geological Survey, 2020). Environmental disasters can be naturally occurring or man-made. Man-made events include accidents such as the British Petroleum oil spill in the Gulf of Mexico in 2011 and deliberate events such as the terrorist attacks of September 11, 2001, or the November 2015 Paris attacks.

Natural disasters, on the other hand, can occur because of climate or weather events or can occur as a result of natural processes such as the movement of Earth's tectonic plates. The occurrence of disasters, large events that threaten lives and/or possessions of those in affected areas, is on the rise (Mooney & Dennis, 2018; National Oceanic and Atmospheric Administration [NOAA], 2020). Disasters often bring catastrophic destruction including loss of life, homes, economic opportunities, and property. The disaster science literature documents threats to health and well-being for directly affected individuals during the period immediately following the impact.

Each year, people all over the world experience various natural and environmental disasters—ranging from weather events such as hurricanes, floods, earthquakes, and fires to oil spills, and leakage of nuclear materials. With climate change, the number of natural disasters is on the rise, with record incidences occurring during each of the past few years (NOAA, 2020). In 2017, the United States broke previous records with 16 major weather and climate disaster events (NOAA, 2020). Internationally, 1.7 billion individuals were impacted between 2005 and 2014, and the damage from natural and environmental disasters was $1.4 trillion (United Nations Office for Disaster Risk Reduction, 2018).

DISASTERS IN THE CONTEXT OF POWER, OPPRESSION, AND PRIVILEGE

Understanding dynamics of power, privilege, and oppression against minorities is necessary to break the cycle of environment-based health disparities (Gee & Payne-Sturges, 2004; Gibson, 2019; Mostofi & Brown, 2020). Globally, minority status is associated with increased risk of impact associated with disasters (Bethel et al., 2013; Smid et al., 2018). For generations, many groups of people have endured bias, prejudice, discrimination, and violence on the basis of their identity (Goosby & Heidbrink, 2013; Ortiz & Telles, 2012). Specifically, ethnic minorities often experience increased interpersonal stress due to marginalization, discrimination, immigration status, limited social support, language barriers, and acculturation issues (Cleveland et al., 2014; Drogendijk et al., 2011, 2012; Smid et al., 2018). People exposed to certain historical events (e.g., previous disasters, war, financial depression, redlining practices) or social forces (e.g., discrimination, racism, cis-heterosexism, micro-aggressions) may have different perceptions of and responses to disasters (Brown, 2008).

Hurricane Harvey is one such example, hitting the Houston, Texas, area in August 2017 with the storm and its aftermath disproportionately affecting immigrants. A Migration Policy Institute report cites a 2017 survey of 24 Texas counties, including Houston's Harris County (Wu et al., 2018). The report found that 64% of the region's immigrants reported job or income loss following the storm. More than half surveyed had already been below 200% of the federal poverty threshold and did not have much of a social safety net. Further, among the respondents who reported damage to their homes, only 40% of immigrants applied for assistance and only 41% had flood insurance, compared to 64% and 55% of U.S. citizen residents. Almost half of immigrants whose homes were damaged in the storm said they had not asked for assistance because they were worried about alerting authorities to undocumented family members (Wu et al., 2018).

Using Theory to Understand Disproportionate Impacts of Disasters

This kind of disproportionate impact has led to a recent shift in framing disasters, emerging from the social vulnerability theory of disaster (see Phillips et al., 2010; Wisner et al., 2004). Social vulnerability theory recognizes that power relations in society determine how people experience disasters. Marginalized and oppressed populations (due to racism, capitalism, ageism, ableism, etc.) are more vulnerable and likely to experience negative consequences during and after disasters because they often are in more vulnerable positions than their counterparts before the disaster (Wisner et al., 2004).

Phillips et al. (2010) suggest that while disaster scholars have generally accepted the role social inequity plays in disasters, popular culture and media representations continue to portray disasters as "Acts of God," which shifts blame from power structures to processes outside of human influence. Thus, mainstream media and popular discourse tend not to challenge the balance of power after disasters, which perpetuates public opinion that "nothing else could have been done to prevent such a tragedy." In fact, it is very likely that a good deal could have been done to reduce the negative impacts of a disaster among marginalized groups within our communities. Social workers must advocate alongside communities and work diligently to disrupt the dominant narrative.

PERVASIVE AND STRUCTURAL BARRIERS IN DISASTERS

One way to conceptualize how pervasive and structural barriers affect our clients during a disaster is through a socio-ecological framework. This framework can be used to explore the multiple systemic levels (individual, family, and community) involved in responding to the disparities that occur in planning, responding, and recovering from a disaster event. The socio-ecological framework lends itself well to this discussion because it highlights the transactional interaction between individuals and their environment (Andrew & Keefe, 2014). Further, this framework has consistently been a central feature of social work theory and practice (Kemp et al., 1997; Saleebey, 2004). Disaster preparedness and interventions are predicated on the idea that the disaster will alter existing relationships between systems and strain the ability of those systems to cope with the impact of the disaster. The following section focuses on three populations—older adults, individuals with limited income, and Indigenous people—to illustrate how existing structural inequalities shape how certain groups experience more negative consequences in health and well-being from disasters as compared with more privileged groups.

Vulnerability of Older Adults

As a biological construct, chronological age is the length of time someone has existed, which has implications for one's developmental needs and capacities. As a social construct, age informs the cultural context, social norms, expectations, and meanings that are associated with one's age group (Field & Syrett, 2015). Disasters happen to people of all ages and disrupt the social and interpersonal context and routines in which they function (Brown, 2008; Freeman et al., 2015; Heath et al., 2009). Older people have a lifetime of experiences that makes their perceptions of disasters unique (see Gibson et al., 2018a; Mostofi & Brown, 2020). Even still, older adults (i.e., adults aged 65 years or older) are an age group that is at great risk during and after disasters (Brown, 2008; Field & Syrett, 2015; Gibson et al., 2018a; Substance Abuse and Mental Health Services Administration [SAMHSA], 2014). While age itself does not guarantee someone will be more vulnerable in times of disaster, other factors that typically affect older persons do increase their exposure to harm. Such factors include physical frailness or limited mobility, isolation, or being homebound due to chronic or terminal conditions (Gibson et al., 2019).

Older adults who experience financial difficulties, physical limitations, frailty and mobility issues, and diminished sensory or cognitive capacities can have a difficult time preparing for and recovering from a disaster (Aldrich and Benson, 2008; Dyer et al., 2008; Walsh et al., 2016). Because of these age-related risks, older persons are often exposed to a greater level of danger, are likely to encounter life-threatening challenges when trying to evacuate or relocate, are less likely to receive disaster warnings, and usually experience greater financial losses related to a disaster (Acierno et al., 2006; Aldrich & Benson, 2008; Sakauye et al., 2009).

Certain aspects of aging may exacerbate mental health vulnerabilities in older adults. For some, aging may bring loss of functional capacities and increased dependence on others (Brown, 2008; Colón-Emeric et al., 2013). Further, a major source of anxiety for this population is the fear of not being able to evacuate during a disaster or terrorist attack, due to immobility or infirmity (Monahan & Lurie, 2007; Gibson et al., 2018b).

CASE STUDY 9.1—CLIENT PERSPECTIVE

Mrs. Bailey is a White woman who lives alone in a small cabin just outside the Umpqua National Forest in Oregon. She and her husband of 36 years, who died just under 9 months ago, moved there so they could be closer to Crater Lake National Park. This was their favorite place to visit when they would vacation together over the years. Today, Mrs. Bailey has been watching the news about the spread of wildfires in her area. She has never considered what she would do if she had to leave her home suddenly. Mrs. Bailey still drives on occasion, but she is hesitant to evacuate her home. She is not currently in an area that is under mandatory evacuation, but she knows that could change quickly if the wind picks up. Mrs. Bailey has some concerns about evacuating to a shelter that may not be ready to support her needs, but she does not have enough money to go stay in a hotel. Mrs. Bailey has arthritis in her hands and feet, a weak back, and diabetes—which she manages with insulin. She also has two Persian cats that she does not want to leave behind. She is worried that if she goes to the shelter, it will be difficult for her to take care of herself. She has heard that shelters often provide only cots and limited essentials. She worries the poor support on the bed will throw out her back and also wonders if she will be able to replenish her limited supply of insulin. Further, Mrs. Bailey is worried that if a healthcare professional or social worker sees that she is having trouble getting up from her cot, they might not let her come back to live on her own in the cabin. Mrs. Bailey has no other family, and she is fearful of losing her independence.

Mrs. Bailey is an example of how the elderly may be particularly vulnerable to the effects of a disaster, with health and behavioral health consequences in addition to concerns regarding transportation, mobility, safety, and security. We will return to the narrative of Mrs. Bailey later in our discussion. Next, let us consider how the experience of disasters may be different for a poor family.

Impoverished Families

Socioeconomic status (i.e., social class) is typically defined as a location in the social and economic hierarchy that reflects a combination of income status, educational attainment, and occupational prestige (Kraus et al., 2017). Social class can also include the presence of social capital, which refers to resources (e.g., information, influence, financial capital, emotional support) available through a person's networks (Manstead, 2018; Pitkin Derose & Varda, 2009). While multiple social classes may characterize an individual during their lifetime, socioeconomic status often has long-lasting effects on people's personal and social identity. Class influences a person's thoughts, emotions, and behaviors in response to social environment (Dorius, 2018; DuPont et al., 2015; Kraus et al., 2017; Manstead, 2018). For example, evidence suggests that individuals with lower income are less likely to invest in renters' or homeowners' insurance (Insurance Information Institute, 2019), which most certainly would affect their ability to recover from a natural disaster.

Families with limited income typically struggle to prepare for, respond to, and recover from disasters (Brown, 2008; SAMHSA, 2017). Not surprisingly, because they lack financial resources, these families are not likely to have extra food or supplies on hand when a disaster hits. They may also have inadequate resources, such as a personally owned vehicle or money to pay for travel, to evacuate when needed. Like older adults, people of low socioeconomic status will be less prepared for disasters, unable to respond to official warnings about disasters, and more vulnerable to adversity during the recovery phase (Al-Rousan et al., 2014; Fothergill & Peek, 2004; SAMHSA, 2017). As mentioned, families with limited income may be unable to afford sufficient insurance that would support them in rebuilding their homes following a disaster. The inability to rebuild increases their risk of homelessness or dislocation (Brown, 2008; SAMHSA, 2017). Losses that cannot be replaced can cause families extreme distress and feelings of hopelessness (U.S. Department of Health and Human Services [DHHS], 2003; SAMHSA, 2017).

CASE STUDY 9.2—THE JALEES FAMILY

The Jalees family is living in Houston, Texas, where a Category 4 hurricane has devastated their community. Ms. Jalees, a single, heterosexual mother, prepared to stay at home with her three children to ride out the storm. Earlier in the season, a Category 5 hurricane was expected to hit Houston, but ultimately it did not even come near the city. At that time, Ms. Jalees and her children had evacuated to her sister's home in Wichita Falls, Texas, about 5 hours from Houston. The cost of gas for this trip depleted her monthly budget and she ended up missing 4 days of work, which greatly impacted the family's income. The Jalees family almost lost the lease on their home when Ms. Jalees could not meet the deadline for rent. Given the consequences of the last time the family evacuated, Ms. Jalees was determined to ride out this storm by any means necessary. In preparation, she and her children went to the store to purchase water jugs and canned food in case they lost electricity or running water. They expected to shelter-in-place for 4 to 5 days. However, the flooding that occurred was more than she expected and now Ms. Jalees is concerned they will not have enough food or water. She has tried reaching out for help, calling 9-1-1 as well as family and neighbors, but for the time being, it appears that they are stuck until the flooding subsides.

Ms. Jalees and her children's situation just described is not unlike what happens for individuals who reside in communities frequently affected by natural disasters like hurricanes. We will table Ms. Jalees's situation for now, but let us move on to talk about how communities of people, such as Indigenous tribal communities, may experience disasters.

Indigenous Tribal Communities and Nations

Race and ethnicity are two separate yet closely related macro-level categories of culture that have long been employed to describe human ancestry (Mersha & Abebe, 2015). "Race" refers to a selective set of visually obvious phenotypic characteristics such as bone structure and skin, eye, and hair color that have a high degree of variation and often reflect natural selection to specific geographic regions (Brown, 2008; Feliciano, 2015; Relethford, 2009). "Ethnicity" is defined as the shared cultural heritage or national ancestry of a group of people that includes common history, language, and preferences for food and music (Brown, 2008; DHHS, 2003; Ford & Harawa, 2010). Although empirical evidence has confirmed that race does not have any biological meaning, it continues to be a commonly used social construct with very real implications (Brown, 2008; Smedley & Smedley, 2005). Both race and ethnicity are fundamental elements of sociocultural identity and often profoundly impact the ways in which people are forced to respond to and cope with disasters (DHHS, 2003).

People with Indigenous heritage (i.e., aboriginal, native) are the ethnic group known as "the original inhabitants of a region" (Currie et al., 2018). Their shared histories of being colonized often involved land theft, enslavement, and acts of genocide (Brown, 2008). In particular, trauma has been a ubiquitous personal and communal reality of many native people.

Globally, ethnic and racial minority status is associated with increased risk (i.e., less likely to receive assistance, poorer quality of health, higher incidences of posttraumatic stress disorder [PTSD]) following disasters (Bethel et al., 2013; Smid et al., 2018). For generations, many groups of people have resisted and endured bias, prejudice, discrimination, and violence on the basis of their phenotype (Goosby & Heidbrink, 2013; Ortiz & Telles, 2012). Ethnic minorities often experience increased interpersonal stress due to reasons such as marginalization, discrimination, immigration status, limited social support, language difficulties, and acculturation issues (Cleveland et al., 2014; Drogendijk et al., 2011, 2012; Smid et al., 2018).

The high poverty rates among Indigenous tribes is of particular concern because poverty is one of the main factors that renders groups vulnerable in a disaster (Fothergill & Peek, 2004). Government resources are strained following disasters and those who depend on government aid may be left with no support network (Burnette & Renner, 2017; Tobin-Gurley et al., 2011). Costs of home repair may spiral out of control or the wait for insurance payouts may be lengthy. In the meantime, finding adequate shelter to preserve health and safety in the wake of a disaster becomes precarious due to escalating demand (Peacock et al., 1997) and who is prioritized.

Previous research with Indigenous tribes has found that disasters result in loss of identity, challenges to safety and well-being, poor health outcomes, loss of land/place, and trauma (Cutter et al., 2003; Elliott & Pais, 2006; Figley & Burnette, 2017; Liddell et al., 2020; Norris & Alegría, 2008; Public Health Emergency, 2018; Rabalais et al., 2002; Reilley et al., 2014; Ryder, 2017; SAMHSA, 2017). The ability for Indigenous tribes to recover postdisaster is also affected by a lack of federal tribal recognition for tribe, heirship property, and lack of representation in the recovery process (Miller Scarnato et al., 2020).

American Indian tribal recognition in the United States most often refers to the process of a tribe being recognized by the U.S. federal government. The Federal Register maintains a list of eligible tribes to receive assistance from the U.S. Bureau of Indian Affairs (2019). Recognition is important, as it can ultimately determine the eligibility for services that tribal members can receive, particularly following a natural disaster.

Within the United States, there are an estimated 40% of Native American/American Indians who do not have an affiliation with a federally recognized tribe (Thornton, 1997). Reasons for not having federal recognition include: smaller tribes after the 1900s lacked government involvement; some tribes elected to limit political influence over its members; there was a lack of eligible members to constitute a federal tribe. Most federally recognized tribes require their membership to have lineage descent (documentation that they are the direct descendent of another tribal member) or a minimum blood quorum of Indigenous ancestry. Blood quorum laws represent a significant contemporary issue that has contributed to a lack of eligible members (Miller, 2004; Thornton, 1997). For example, the Omaha Nation requires a blood quantum of 1/4 Native American and descent from a registered ancestor for enrollment (National Indian Law Library, 1983). As Indigenous marriage and partnership practices have expanded outside of one's own tribe, children may be born only 1/2 Indigenous. Within another generation, that now grown adult may also have a child with a nontribal member—with that next child being only 1/4 Indigenous. Thus, the likelihood of Indigenous children being born within minimum blood quorums has decreased in recent generations (Maher, 2018).

As a related issue, heirship property refers to land that is transferred between family members where an affidavit is a sworn statement used to establish ownership of property when the original owner dies intestate and the estate is not worth more than a statutory amount, rather than a deed or will. This was a common, historic practice among Indigenous tribes and family members. In times of disaster, this can be particularly problematic because it is not apparent who originally owned the land, and lack of clear documentation can further blur the recovery process (Miller Scarnato et al., 2020), particularly in regard to accessing federal and local recovery resources that are dependent upon documentation of ownership of the impacted property.

FROM THE FIELD 9.1

PINE RIDGE RESERVATION

The Pine Ridge Reservation is located in what is known as South Dakota and is frequently exposed to blizzards, heavy rainfall, and flooding. In the spring, residents were stranded in their homes for over 2 weeks following a blizzard that then melted into severe flooding. Many Lakota citizens were caught off guard by the storm, with limited food or medication on hand for the duration of being homebound. Many parts of the reservation's backcountry are accessible only by horse, boat, or helicopter, and most of these methods of access became nearly impossible as the floodwaters rose. Officials who administer resources to the reservation lacked the "training, manpower, and equipment" (Smith, 2019, para. 6) to address the crisis and much needed rations were slow to arrive. One year later, tribal citizens are meeting to discuss how the event impacted their tribe and what can be done in the future to prevent such hardships for their people.

The Pine Ridge Reservation is an example of how unpredictable disasters can create immediate health and safety crises. The next section discusses the role of social workers in addressing unmet systemic needs and how they work to provide appropriate justice-informed social work services.

ROLE OF SOCIAL WORKERS TO ADDRESS UNMET SYSTEMIC NEEDS

"Disaster" is a broad term that captures a diverse range of circumstances (i.e., tornados, nuclear explosions, virus pandemics, mudslides [Pourhosseini et al., 2015]). Although the effects of some disasters can be prevented or mitigated, most people will be affected by a disaster during the course of their lives. Disasters have the potential to destroy the physical environment and adversely impact the health of large numbers of people in a brief period of time (Math et al., 2015).

Because most disasters occur with little advance warning and result in widespread damage, post-event communities require urgent support that often exceeds local resources. Disaster responders and recovery teams from unaffected areas have to be mobilized quickly to provide aid and assistance to affected populations (Wells et al., 2013). Given that social workers work with vulnerable populations, they serve an important role in disaster preparedness, response, and recovery. While social workers in the United States may not receive specific training in disasters, their experiences working with community strengths and needs, responding in crises, and mobilizing disparate groups have prepared them to contribute to municipal disaster planning (Gibson et al., 2019; Kusmaul et al., 2018). In fact, social workers account for approximately 50% of responders postdisaster (Naturale, 2018) through both their existing roles and as disaster-specific responders (National Association of Social Workers [NASW], 2017a). Social workers have long understood that where people live influences how they live, which has profound implications for equity and social justice (Kemp, 2011).

ENGAGING IN ENVIRONMENTAL JUSTICE-ORIENTED SOCIAL WORK PRACTICE

The NASW finds disaster response "compatible with social work epistemology" and expresses that assistance must be holistic in nature and address the health and behavioral health, social, cultural, and spiritual needs of individuals and communities impacted by the disaster (NASW, 2017a, p. 75). While some social workers trained in disaster response and recovery work with agencies like the Red Cross, still other social workers are employed within agencies called to take action in the event of a disaster, such as healthcare organizations, emergency shelters, food banks, and county social services. Let us revisit Mrs. Bailey, the Jalees Family, and the Pine Ridge Indian Reservation to understand the work social workers provide in times of disaster within these various groups.

Application With Mrs. Bailey

CULTURAL COMPETENCE AND ASSESSMENTS

By 2050, one of five Americans will be 65 years and older (Murdock et al., 2015). To provide appropriate services to the growing older adult population, social workers must develop a basic understanding of the unique needs of older adults and integrate this into disaster preparedness work (Mostofi & Brown, 2020). In disaster situations, age-related changes can predispose older adults to serious threats to health and safety. Factors that contribute to the vulnerability of older adults during a disaster include frailty, cognitive impairment, hearing or visual impairments, being dependent on medication, special nutrition, and medical supplies and equipment to manage health problems.

For older people living in poverty or older adults of color, these health-related age changes intersect with structural inequalities, creating a disproportionate impact. Vulnerable older adults are found to have an increased risk of illness, injury, or death during disasters (see Gibson et al.,

2019; Kusmaul et al., 2018). Furthermore, older adults who are socially isolated, even in large communities, are less apt to receive timely warnings, ask for help, or evacuate, which can leave them "virtually invisible" to rescue and recovery efforts (Banks, 2013). This would be especially true for Mrs. Bailey, who appears to be quite isolated in her cabin.

In working with older adults during disasters, age cohort effects are another important factor for social workers to consider. Cohort differences exist because of experiences and circumstances unique to the generation to which one belongs (Bell & Jones, 2015).

Finally, older adults often have limited financial resources and decreasing social support networks that may be further depleted by disasters (Malik et al., 2017; Shih et al., 2018). Given that many older persons are retired beginning in their mid-60s or early 70s, they are often on a fixed income and have a limited time horizon with limited savings to meet their financial needs (Walsh et al., 2016).

EDUCATION ON PREPAREDNESS AND RESOURCES

Educating others on an individual and community level is another important way that social workers can engage in environmentally conscious social work practice. Given that two-thirds of older adults do not have an emergency plan for handling disasters and most have not participated in any educational programming related to disasters nor know where to find resources (Al-Rousan et al., 2014), targeting older adults in education efforts is paramount. Topics important to cover would include what supplies to have on hand during a disaster and what resources are available for assistance. Data from a national sample of seniors indicate that one-third did not have basic supplies (e.g., food, water, medical supplies) available in the event a disaster would occur, and about 14% would require electricity to keep medical devices working (Al-Rousan et al., 2014). One practical suggestion for social workers would be to encourage their older clients to maintain an up-to-date list of their medications and keep the list in their wallet or purse to ensure preparedness during disaster evacuations. Practitioners could also provide clients with a list of reputable resources, including governmental and nongovernmental sources, which could assist with disaster planning (Banks, 2013).

Even when people receive timely and accurate warnings of natural disasters, many may not choose to evacuate for a variety of understandable reasons. For older adults, there are many reasons they might choose not to evacuate—one such explanation is to remain with one's pets. Individuals who do not have the means to transport or shelter with their animal may be reluctant to abandon their home (Torgeson & Kosberg, 2008). This was a consideration for Mrs. Bailey when she was debating whether or not to leave her cabin. The many questions Mrs. Bailey had about what resources were available in a shelter to accommodate her unique needs suggest that the community should do more to inform the public about what to expect in a shelter setting and what resources are included. Further, shelters are now required by law to provide rescue, care, shelter, and essential needs for individuals with household pets and service animals and to the household pets and animals themselves following a major disaster or emergency (PETS Act of 2006 which authorizes the Federal Emergency Management Agency [FEMA]). If Mrs. Bailey could have received this information in a timely manner, she might have felt comfortable evacuating her cabin ahead of the wildfires.

DEVELOP A DISASTER PLAN

Social workers should also assist older individuals in establishing a disaster plan, something every household should have. Such efforts can be part of social work educational outreach. Mrs. Bailey was unsure if or when she should evacuate, under what circumstances, or even where she would go.

While the role of families and other informal supports is important in disaster planning for older adults, the reality is that many older individuals do not have relatives or other support persons to assist them in disaster events (Banks, 2013). As such, social workers should take into account that informal supports or neighbors could be involved in an individual's disaster plan. Disaster plans are especially pertinent, and social workers could encourage them to make arrangements with neighbors to check-in, particularly during times of difficult weather and disaster situations, on the older adults who may live alone (Gibson et al., 2019).

COMMUNITY REGISTRY

One additional resource that could be of use to Mrs. Bailey is requesting that she be listed on the special needs registry, if it is available in her community. In some areas, older adults and people with disabilities can sign up for a registry so that emergency operations managers know how and where to find these individuals in times of emergency (Kusmaul et al., 2018).

Social workers can help connect individuals, especially those who are socially isolated and have identified risk factors making them vulnerable to serious threats to health and safety during a disaster, to these registries (Gibson et al., 2019). It is important to note, however, that many individuals, particularly marginalized groups such as individuals with disabilities, may be hesitant to be labeled as such. Further, people who are undocumented may be hesitant to invite public services into their personal lives. Given violence and targeting of people of color, some groups, understandably, may be cautious or even afraid to list their personal health information on a government registry. Fear for their safety may therefore result in not reaching out for formal support. Understanding the privacy and confidentiality aspects of these registries, which may be a deterrent for many individuals, such as Mrs. Bailey, who are concerned with how the personal health information could be used against them, would be helpful for social workers in order to more effectively ensure clients are a part of these registries. Social workers also respect the autonomy of a client and realize that some may simply not want to be on any registry. One response would be for social workers to ensure that the strengths, diversity, and heterogeneity of those listed on these registries are highlighted, which could help to avoid discriminatory, stereotypical, or stigmatizing responses from the officials and the public regarding those listed (Elmore & Brown, 2007).

Application With the Jalees Family

With the Jalees family, many of the same steps could be taken by social workers to assist the family in planning and preparing for a disaster, perhaps well before an impending hurricane warning.

CULTURAL COMPETENCE AND ASSESSMENT

Cultural competency for social workers requires awareness about classism (i.e., bias, prejudice, discrimination, and stigmatization based on social class; Fuller-Rowell et al., 2012; Simons et al., 2017). Classism has previously been documented as a barrier to disaster recovery (Weber & Hilfinger Messias, 2012). Attending to clients' subjective experiences of classism (i.e., perceived or internalized classism) with awareness of intersectionality related to their social identities can promote empowerment and resilience in times of disaster planning, response, and recovery (Schwarzbaum & Thomas, 2008).

THE ROLE OF EVACUATION ORDERS AND SUPPORT

As highlighted from the Jalees family's story, there are numerous reasons why one might choose not to evacuate their home during a disaster. Sometimes it can be due to lack of financial resources.

For this reason, it is important that communities provide free or low-cost transportation options and advertise them widely. Decisions about disaster response and evacuations can also be influenced by individuals' values, beliefs, and life experiences. If one has successfully sheltered-in-place previously, they may be less likely to evacuate. Other times individuals may not leave due to perceptions of risk. They may have a sense of false security that they are not in danger from storms. Further, if residents have evacuated before and it turned out to be unnecessary, this experience can contribute to a perception of feeling safer than one really is. Not surprisingly, many people are more likely to respond to a mandatory evacuation order than a voluntary evacuation request (Gibson et al., 2019; Gray-Graves et al., 2011). Further, there are data that even suggest people are more likely to take the threat of storms seriously if the storm is named after a man versus a woman, for example, Hurricane Marco was taken as a more serious threat than Hurricane Fay (Jung et al., 2014).

LINKING FAMILIES TO SHELTERS

When deciding whether to evacuate or shelter-in-place, an individual needs to consider both the perceived threat to their area and where they would shelter and how to get there. This information must be made readily available in the community to help inform families that may be reliant on social supports or external resources (Gibson et al., 2019). Had Ms. Jalees and her children been aware of shelter resources in or nearby their local community, they may have elected to evacuate to a shelter where there was adequate food and water. Engaging with a social worker to help the family establish a disaster plan might have empowered the Jalees family to evacuate to a safe, local location. Further, this would have been a more affordable option than to drive to her sister's house that was 5 hours away. Social workers must advocate for community education regarding resources available in shelter and disaster recovery settings (Kusmaul et al., 2018).

ASSESSING IMPACT OF DISPLACEMENT AND RELOCATION

Social workers have unique responsibilities when it comes to providing care to individuals and families during disasters. It is critical for emotional well-being and recovery that social workers remind individuals and families that they need to maintain normalcy and routine (Naturale, 2018). Displacement and relocation are also common processes for many following a major disaster. While it is unclear at this time if the Jalees family will have to relocate, it is possible their home may be damaged from the flooding, forcing them to leave their home while repairs are made.

A common concern for poor families is that, should they have to relocate, they may not be able to find adequate and affordable housing for their family (SAMHSA, 2017). Relocation after natural disasters can trigger long-term stressors, with disruption of a family's lifestyle relationships and connection with their community and their sense of safety (Chao, 2017; Norris et al., 2002; Watanabe et al., 2004). While some families have the ability to return home following the rebuilding of houses or the community postdisaster, it is common for individuals and families to permanently relocate to a new community (Binder et al., 2015). Social workers may need to be cognizant of prelocation stressors when they encourage a newly relocated family in their community that was displaced because of a disaster event.

ASSESSING AND TREATING TRAUMATIC STRESS

Immediately postdisaster, it is important to offer a "compassionate presence" to those recovering from the grief and trauma of a disaster (Naturale, 2018). Being trapped by floodwater and/or running out of food and water can be traumatic for both adults and children, such as in the case of the Jalees family. Social workers must be familiar with the mental health consequences that often accompany trauma from natural disasters and should have a general understanding of how trauma responses might differ across cultural groups. It is well documented that exposure to a disaster increases risk for PTSD (e.g., Galea et al., 2008; Pietrzak et al., 2012). While disaster survivors often experience temporary distress following disasters, a small percentage (estimated between 6% and 20%), without appropriate intervention, will have long-term debilitating trauma symptoms frequently associated with PTSD (Breslau et al., 1998; Brewin et al., 2002; Kessler et al., 1995).

Clinical social workers are well poised to provide affected populations with PTSD treatment using evidence-based approaches such as cognitive processing therapy and prolonged exposure therapy (Cox & D'Oyley, 2011; Jeffreys et al., 2014; Lopes et al., 2014) and acceptance and commitment therapy (Petkus & Wetherell, 2013). Despite the existence of effective, trauma-informed treatment, social workers must recognize that poor families may be hesitant to seek out services because of trust/safety issues, concerns about costs, or barriers to travel to/from such services (Brown, 2008).

Assessing Financial Stress

Financial stress can also play a role in the emotional well-being of families in the wake of disasters (Al-Rousan et al., 2014; Fothergill & Peek, 2004; SAMHSA, 2017). While families that experience disasters may have time to rebuild, poor families are likely unable to get back to their predisaster financial state. Poor families are often unable to afford insurance sufficient to allow them to rebuild their homes, which increases their risk of homelessness or dislocation (Brown, 2008; SAMHSA, 2017). Social workers are well suited to assist families in identifying support and resources to help fill the gap of financial need and to advocate alongside them for federal and state programs that can assist the unique needs of poor families (Gibson et al., 2019).

Application With the Pine Ridge Reservation

With the Pine Ridge Reservation, many of the same steps could be taken by social workers to assist this community in planning and responding to the disaster.

Cultural Competence and Assessment

Cultural competence is especially important for social workers providing services to communities where there have been generations of discrimination, oppression, and trauma. Understanding the dynamics of power, privilege, and oppression against groups that have been historically and systematically marginalized (e.g., communities of color, colonized groups, people denied citizenship) and engaging these populations in interventions that promote increased social connectedness and restoration of cultural meaning can reduce mental health disparities (Smid et al., 2018). People exposed to ongoing, violent structural oppression will likely have different perceptions of and responses to disasters (Brown, 2008). Not surprisingly, the lived experiences of Indigenous people will often affect their willingness to engage with social welfare services or engage directly with a social worker, particularly when the individual is from outside the tribal community.

According to the reference guide, *Cross-Cultural Skills in Indian Child Welfare: A Guide for the Non-Indian*, when working with Indigenous communities, it is important to remember that each has its own norms or unwritten rules of etiquette that are unique to that tribe. Some tribal members, by choice or by necessity, are more assimilated to mainstream U.S. culture than are others. Remember that the Indigenous person's readiness to share and build rapport will depend largely on how comfortable they feel with you as a social worker. It is not uncommon for different communication norms than you may be used to—such as long pauses during conversation, eye contact when conversing, or even physical displays of their emotions. Keep the door open for discussion of cultural differences. Social workers can place the issue of differences early on the agenda, making it okay to deal openly with feelings of distrust or discomfort (Northwest Indian Child Welfare Institute, 1996).

ADEQUATELY PREPARING SOCIAL WORK PROFESSIONALS

There is a dearth of disaster content in social work curricula and training, resulting in many practitioners feeling unprepared to respond in the immediate aftermath of a disaster. Since many social workers may not have specific training in disaster preparedness or disaster recovery interventions, social work educators should consider how to prepare social work professionals to have the knowledge and skills to work with clients during a disaster (Torgusen & Kosberg, 2008). This is particularly relevant as many social work roles intersect with disaster preparedness, response, and recovery. Social work curricula should incorporate disaster assessments, examples of disaster-specific crisis interventions, and related research into class assignments and course discussion to expand students' understanding of the role of social work in disasters. Infusing case studies and policy examples in the classroom that highlight the experience of individuals and their communities during disasters could help prepare students for this work. Continuing educational trainings that address disaster planning and response could support seasoned social workers in this practice arena. Finally, when appropriate, social work programs should explore the incorporation of course electives and certificates that enhance future professionals' training on disasters.

Currently, most social work professionals who have learned about the role of social work in disasters have obtained this knowledge firsthand when their community was affected by a disaster event. For these professionals it would be worthwhile to share their experiences to inform the profession and increase practice knowledge with regard to disaster planning, response, and recovery.

FROM THE FIELD 9.2

U.S. GULF COAST TRIBAL LANDS

Recent hurricanes have devastated the U.S. Gulf Coast, an area that is particularly vulnerable to natural disasters. For one coastal tribe, despite repeated efforts to obtain federally recognized status, government entities have blocked them from gaining federal recognition through imposing excessively demanding procedures. This, in turn, has made it difficult for them to receive federal recovery assistance. Even more, tribal citizens rely on a rapidly changing coastal environment for their livelihood. Land losses have occurred due to hurricanes, flooding, and industry. As a result, hurricanes force many tribal citizens to relocate despite limited options for doing so. The tribal community is thus becoming increasingly dispersed, which disrupts their well-established family and community supports, both of which are vital to hurricane recovery, yet increasingly less available (Miller Scarnato et al., 2020).

COMMUNITY PLANNING

Most disaster preparedness takes place on the local level, because when disasters hit, it is the local community that initially responds, especially until outside support arrives. According to Elmore and Brown (2007), the planning process is particularly important for fostering relationships across stakeholder groups, ideally diverse groups, because these relationships can prove helpful were disaster to strike. When disasters happen, there are often a number of formal arrangements already in place between local government and disaster response entities such as the American Red Cross and the FEMA. Included at the planning table should be expert representatives from all involved parties including Native American government bodies, their administrators, emergency service providers, and local governments adjacent to the reservation (Chico-Jarillo et al., 2018).

Any planning should be accompanied by clarification about agency roles and local, state, and federal levels as well as drills to ensure responders are able to respond quickly to meet the needs of reservation residents (Pekovic et al., 2007). Social workers should be involved with local government and disaster preparedness entities in developing feasible disaster plans and drills to ensure settings are adequately prepared, working to avoid the "bureaucratic shuffle" of disaster planning (Gibson et al., 2019; Hyer & Dosa, 2018). A social service agency may be asked to help identify residents in need of evacuation assistance (i.e., due to challenges with mobility) or follow up with families they serve after a disaster event. Further, social workers should advocate with affected communities for enhanced recovery services, particularly in situations where a tribe is not federally recognized and may not be eligible for the U.S. Bureau of Indian Affairs' disaster assistance (Miller Scarnato et al., 2020).

CULTURALLY APPROPRIATE DISASTER BEHAVIORAL HEALTH INTERVENTIONS

Engaging in interventions that promote increased social connectedness and restoration of cultural meaning can reduce mental health disparities (Roh et al., 2017; Smid et al., 2018). This is particularly true among those who have already endured other traumas, especially those who were already oppressed prior to the disaster (Mostofi & Brown, 2020). Disaster-related mental and behavioral health services aim to protect and promote the mental well-being of all those who are affected by reduced access and use disparities. Just as people's understanding of and response to a disaster differs significantly based on their values, beliefs, and life experiences, so does their comfort level and willingness to use available disaster mental health services (Figley & Burnette, 2017). People who would potentially benefit from disaster mental health services might be reluctant to use available treatment, even when offered free of charge, because of personal or social stigma and their impressions concerning the value of behavioral health treatment in general.

Psychological First Aid (PFA) is the response intervention many organizations utilize following a disaster event, including social workers. PFA seeks to mitigate stress and provide support in order to enable coping skills. PFA can be performed in an initial contact and can address healthcare needs, locate those who are missing, identify shelter, and "obtain community and family support" (Gibson et al., 2018a, p. 367).

Engaging clients into services while building upon their existing community and family support can empower individuals to link with mental/behavioral health and support services. The screening and delivery of PFA are conducted in tandem and guide the disaster responder to select the appropriate assistance for the survivor. While the initial goal of PFA was to have a single intervention that meets the needs of all people regardless of individual differences, it soon became apparent that specific populations would benefit from tailored intervention. Organizations such as the American Red Cross train their volunteers with PFA. The National Child Traumatic Stress Network also provides an online training available to the public (learn.nctsn.org/course/index.php?categoryid=11).

To provide accessible and effective care, disaster mental and behavioral health providers must accurately assess the needs of the local communities and successfully engage them in services that are deemed as acceptable and culturally sensitive. The importance of having well-trained, competent professionals to provide culturally appropriate disaster behavioral health interventions simply cannot be overstated.

COMMUNITY LOSS

Often when we consider the loss to a community at large, we think about physical damage and the financial consequences of a disaster. However, when disaster affects entire communities, there is often a shared grief that is experienced community-wide. Immediately postdisaster, it is not uncommon for a community to become united in the aftermath. Following the September 11, 2001, terrorist attacks, the country began rallying around the popularized phrase "United We Stand." But despite shared grief and the resulting support and unity, when communities have to make decisions around utilization of funding for recovery, building and planning memorials, and the process for rebuilding, these political, bureaucratic discussions can become quite ardent (Shughart, 2006). Social workers may need to facilitate conflict resolution and mediation for these community conversations—especially when these conversations become divisive over political affiliations (Gibson et al., 2019; Kusmaul et al., 2018).

REBUILDING OF COMMUNITIES

Depending on the severity of damage in a community, there may be a need to rebuild or renovate structures that house social work clients. In early October 2015, South Carolina experienced a historic one in a thousand years flood. At the time, much of the southeastern region of the state experienced 20 to 24 inches of rain in 120 hours. The following February, one of the local regional hospitals in Kingstree, South Carolina, had to close due to mold that developed from the extensive water damage (Gibson et al., 2019). For many residents, until a permanent structure would be rebuilt or a temporary structure was established, they had to travel 25 miles, a 31-minute drive, to access emergency medical services. Such a distance could be life or death for households, especially those with a person diagnosed with a chronic or terminal illness. Further, those with transportation limitations and/or financial burdens simply may be unable to access these services. In addition to providing emotional support to the community when affected by transitions, social workers can assist by providing case management to individuals and families on how to counter these temporary changes to accessing services.

COMMUNITY ASSESSMENTS

Just as assessments need to be readily conducted at the pre-disaster and immediate-recovery stage of disaster, assessments should also be conducted postdisaster to determine the needs of individuals and the community at large (Burnette & Sanders, 2014; Burnette et al., 2011, 2014; Gibson et al., 2019). With particular consideration to community assessment, social workers should be working alongside other professionals to conduct ongoing evaluations of residents within their community and determine if the impact of disaster has resulted in service limitations or other restrictions negatively impacting the community (Gibson et al., 2019; Kusmaul et al., 2018).

BUILDING COMMUNITY RESILIENCE

As previously introduced, developing community resilience, or enhancing communities to reduce the negative impacts of disasters, greatly supports our clients' well-being. Community resilience expands the traditional preparedness approach by encouraging actions that build preparedness while also promoting strong community systems and addressing the many factors that contribute to health. While communities tend to assess and implement community resilience elements

> ### SOCIAL WORKER PERSPECTIVE 9.1
>
> Taking care of one's self can be challenging for social workers when assisting with disasters, especially in the response and recovery phases. It is quite common for persons helping with disaster response to experience secondary traumatic stress (STS). STS is a stress response that can occur as a result of knowing or helping a person(s) experiencing trauma. Helping professionals can be traumatized as a result of their client's trauma. Symptoms often associated with STS include multiple factors such as avoidance of clients, exhaustion, physical and behavioral health responses, emotional impacts such as anger, pessimism, or hopelessness among others (The National Child Traumatic Stress Network, 2017).
>
> STS is well documented among helping professionals, especially in mental health professionals, social workers, clergy members, disaster responders, and counselors of victims of sexual assault (Beck & Gabe, 2011; Hyman, 2004). For those with sustained exposure in the helping role, long-term outcome effects are possible (Shah et al., 2007). In the general population, the lifetime prevalence of traumatic exposure ranges from 10% to 40%, with men experiencing slightly more trauma than women (Bride, 2007; Sareen, 2014).
>
> Strategies to help individuals cope with STS during a disaster include:
> - being able to take breaks and disconnect from the disaster event,
> - feeling prepared and informed in facilitating their disaster response role,
> - being aware of local resources and services to which one can refer clients for additional disaster recovery assistance,
> - having adequate supervision and peer support while facilitating disaster response as well as postdisaster recovery (Gibson, 2017).

following the experience of a disaster, there is a need for social workers to facilitate conversations on considering community resilience in the prestages of disaster and also at the long-term postrecovery of disasters (Chico-Jarillo et al., 2018; Gibson et al., 2019).

CONCLUSION

The health and well-being consequences of climate change disproportionately affect oppressed members of our communities. Particularly, persons who are income-challenged, persons of minority status, and older adults experience environmental injustice as a result of disaster events. Social work is suited to partner with our communities in developing and implementing innovative strategies to anticipate, mitigate, and respond to environmental injustice. Further, as stated in the NASW Code of Ethics (2017b, preamble), environmental justice is a foundational social work premise to acknowledge and address those environmental aspects that serve to contribute to and maintain challenges associated with living. Additionally, the current engagement of the social work profession in disaster response, environmental justice, and community development efforts positions social workers for research and intervention leadership in these domains (Kemp & Palinkas, 2015).

Recognition of the physical environment's critical role in social and economic sustainability and human health and well-being is rapidly growing within the social work profession (International Federation of Social Workers, 2012; Kemp & Palinkas, 2015). Social workers can learn from the experiences of those affected by past disasters as well as other social workers who have worked with clients affected by disaster. Disasters often result in physical and mental suffering due to their profound and enduring effects on the quality of life of those who are affected. Consequently, disaster-affected individuals and communities are at higher risk for developing financial stress, mental and behavioral health disorders, and the breakup of community and social supports that can be debilitating and disruptive to an individual's ability to adaptively recover postdisaster. Social work's professional background situates us to advocate for the unique needs of those disparately affected by the environment. Justice-informed social work practice requires that we accept this important mission and ensure we address environmental justice.

DISCUSSION QUESTIONS

1. Explain how the intersection of poverty, communities of color, and industrial waste sites reflect a lack of political power.
2. What are some reasons why someone may not seek assistance after a disaster?
3. Identify three ways in which the economic recovery differs for those who are impoverished.
4. The Red Cross is seeking social workers to aid in their disaster recovery efforts. Does this interest you? What might be challenges that would compromise your ability to serve in this way? What assets would you bring to this role in disaster recovery?

REFERENCES

Only key references appear in the print edition. The full reference list appears in the digital product on Springer Publishing Connect: connect.springerpub.com/content/book/978-0-8261-3539-1/chapter/ch09

Al-Rousan, T. M., Rubenstein, L. M., & Wallace, R. B. (2014). Preparedness for natural disasters among older US adults: A nationwide survey. *American Journal of Public Health*, *104*(3), 506–511. https://doi.org/10.2105/AJPH.2013.301559

Bethel, J. W., Burke, S. C., & Britt, A. F. (2013). Disparity in disaster preparedness between racial/ethnic groups. *Disaster Health*, *1*(2), 110–116. https://doi.org/10.4161/dish.27085

Chao, S. (2017). Social support, coping strategies and their correlations with older adults' relocation adjustments after natural disaster. *Geriatrics & Gerontology International*, *17*, 1006–1014. https://doi.org/10.1111/ggi.12807

Chico-Jarillo, T. M., Burgess, J., & Granillo, B. (2018). Strategies from American Indian and Alaska Native community partners on effective emergency response collaboration. *American Journal of Public Health*, *108*(S5), S336–S338. https://doi.org/10.2105/AJPH.2018.304842

Figley, C. R., & Burnette, C. E. (2017). Building bridges: Connecting systemic trauma and family resilience in the study and treatment of diverse traumatized families. *Traumatology*, *23*(1), 95–101. https://doi.org/10.1037/trm0000089

Gibson, A. (2019). Climate change for individuals experiencing homelessness: Recommendations for improving policy, research, and services. *Environmental Justice*, *12*(4). https://www.liebertpub.com/doi/full/10.1089/env.2018.0032

Gibson, A., Walsh, J. L., & Brown, L. M. (2018a). Disaster mental health services review of care for older persons following disasters. *Disaster Medicine and Public Health Preparedness*, *12*(3), 366–372. https://doi.org/10.1017/dmp.2017.60

Kusmaul, N., Gibson, A., & Leedahl, S. (2018). Gerontological social work roles in disaster preparedness and response. *Journal of Gerontological Social Work*, *61*(7), 692–696. https://doi.org/10.1080/01634372.2018.1510455

Levy, B. S., & Patz, J. A. (2015). Climate change, human rights, and social justice. *Annals of Global Health*, *81*(3), 310–322. https://doi.org/10.1016/j.aogh.2015.08.008

Naturale, A. (2018, March). *New evidence informed intervention approaches for social workers responding to natural disasters and other mass casualty events*. Paper presented at the Social Work Hospice & Palliative Care Network Annual Meeting, Boston, MA.

Smid, G. E., Drogendijk, A. N., Knipscheer, J., Boelen, P. A., & Kleber, R. J. (2018). Loss of loved ones or home due to a disaster: Effects over time on distress in immigrant ethnic minorities. *Transcultural Psychiatry*, *55*(5), 648–668. https://doi.org/10.1177/1363461518784355

10

FOOD JUSTICE

Michelle L. Kaiser | Erica K. Pence | Kathryn Burleson | Michelle D. Hand | Whitney Gherman | Nicholas A. Stanich | Mara Sydnor | Jennifer K. Weeber

Having enough to eat is the most basic of human rights.
The fight against hunger is not an issue of charity; it is an issue of justice.
—General Jacques Diouf, former director of the United Nations Food and Agriculture Organization

LEARNING OBJECTIVES

Students will be able to:

- Critically examine the multifaceted effects of food insecurity that can have a lifelong impact.
- Define food justice.
- Ascertain the differing aspects of food security (social, economic, and environmental justice) and articulate the role of social work in each of these types of justice work.
- Articulate the strengths and criticism of strategies related to reducing or ameliorating food insecurity.

INTRODUCTION

Every human across the world has a common connection through food. Before you begin reading this chapter, take a moment to think about your earliest memory of food. What image do you see? What sounds do you hear? Are there certain smells wafting into your memories? Go ahead and pause—close your eyes for a moment to let yourself see a memory of food, unique to you.

Perhaps your earliest vision was a meal specific to your cultural or ethnic background. Maybe it was tasting your grandmother's home-cooking, knowing that recipe had been passed down for generations. Perhaps it was not having enough food, feeling hungry, or standing in line at a food pantry. Maybe it was digging in the dirt in your backyard garden or climbing your neighbor's apple tree. It is likely that people were part of your memory. The feelings surrounding those images may have brought you feelings of warmth, celebration, and joy. Or perhaps they brought you painful memories of feeling empty, alone, or anxious.

It is possible some of those memories are connected to your values, motivations, and even your decision to become a social worker.

Food connects us all and is a basic human right. Yet food, and especially the lack thereof, is representative of grave inequalities across the world and in the United States. Strategies to address hunger are rooted in our moral obligations to ensure food for all people. Centuries of historical, religious, moral, and ethical debates exist about who is deserving of food aid, how much is appropriate to provide, and who is responsible for providing the aid (i.e., individuals, families, private sector, government, nonprofit organizations).

The food we eat is also rooted in economic, social, and environmental systems of oppression. Indigenous people have had their lands taken from them and their food sources killed off, resulting in isolation, poverty, and hunger. Enslaved individuals from the continent of Africa were responsible for feeding people through backbreaking work in harsh conditions, and yet to this day, African American communities face some of the highest rates of food insecurity and environmental racism. Our modern food system and its fields of monocrops and chemicals are possible because of migrant farmworkers and immigrants coming to the United States, yet Latinx households face dire public health concerns, high rates of food insecurity, and exploitative social, economic, and environmental conditions every day. The tomatoes we eat are connected to low wages, sexual assault, and poor working conditions. Food is used as a weapon of war across the world. Food has existed in these interacting systems, and social workers have a responsibility to address these issues because of our roots in social justice and belief in the dignity and value of every human in this world and of our natural environment. As you read this chapter, consider ways that our profession can lead efforts to address food insecurity and sustain life.

FOOD SECURITY

In the United States, "food security" is the term used to describe access by all people at all times to enough food for a healthy lifestyle. Achieving food security for all people and communities is a laudable and an achievable goal—yet food security is still out of reach for many households and communities. Policy makers and antihunger organizational leaders have often stated that there are enough resources to ensure food security, and that it is a matter of basic human rights; however, the lack of political will to achieve and maintain food security across all communities has been a recurring challenge.

Strategies to increase food security include short-term and long-term local, state, and federal programs and policies that are intended to address and/or alleviate the underlying factors contributing to food insecurity and the consequences of food insecurity for individuals, households, and communities. This chapter offers you an opportunity to gain a greater understanding of various strategies to address social, economic, and environmental injustices as they relate to food security in the United States. We want you to think critically about how these issues and strategies have been informed by U.S. social welfare values, the U.S. political system, historical systemic racism, and competing perspectives about who bears responsibility for addressing food insecurity and how to intervene.

Food insecurity threatens the stability and well-being of individuals, families, and communities. The causes and consequences of food insecurity intersect with social, economic, and ecological systems that have historically produced, and continue to sustain, inequalities and injustices. Social work professionals are well-suited to influence food insecurity by working across multiple systems in a variety of practice settings, and throughout this chapter, you will read about the diverse ways social workers are addressing interconnected issues related to food insecurity. We frame this work in terms of the National Association of Social Workers (NASW) professional values, the Council on Social Work Education (CSWE) competencies, and the 1948 Universal Declaration of Human Rights (Article 25).

We invite you to think critically about several thematic threads throughout this chapter that underscore the complexity of U.S. food insecurity. This includes tensions among practitioners about *how* to address food insecurity. For example, some strategies to address food insecurity are intended to be short-term emergency solutions to alleviate the immediate need and direct consequences of food insecurity (e.g., food pantries, Supplemental Nutrition Assistance Program [SNAP]). Others may be considered more long-term and multipronged approaches intended to focus on coalition-building and policy-setting (e.g., food policy councils, local food action plans) or changing underlying oppressive conditions leading to food insecurity (e.g., community organizing around racist laws or low wages). In addition, you will see that some strategies focus more on individuals, families, and households, while others focus on communities, while still others focus on policy-level changes at local, state, and federal levels. Some interventions relate more to consequences of food insecurity, like chronic diet-related health problems, while others relate more to underlying issues of poverty, food access, and social justice. In Social Worker Perspective 10.1, you will read about an experience that led one college student to a social work career that connects issues of social, economic, and environmental justice.

SOCIAL WORKER PERSPECTIVE 10.1

HOW A CUP OF COFFEE CHANGED MY LIFE

by Michelle L. Kaiser, MSW, MPH, PhD, Ohio State University College of Social Work

When people ask me how I became interested in social work, and specifically a career in which I have focused on poverty, housing issues, public health, community food security, and ecological–social connections, I honestly say that it boils down to one cup of coffee.

During summers in college, I worked for a nonprofit relational ministry called the Appalachia Service Project (ASP) that provided free home repair in Central Appalachia. Our mission was to make homes warmer, safer, and drier. During my first summer working for ASP, following my freshman year, I got to know one of the families on whose single-wide mobile home we worked for 8 weeks. Mr. Jay Hill was referred to our organization by a home healthcare agency. He lived in a remote area of East Tennessee, back in the hollows of the Appalachian Mountains. His home was, quite literally, on top of a hill, reachable only by a steep, gravel driveway. Tucked away from view of the interstate, Jay lived a quiet life. His connection to the outside world was his CB radio.

Jay had numerous health problems, including diabetes, high blood pressure, high cholesterol, and heart disease. His home healthcare workers visited once each month, bringing him food staples (often canned fruits, vegetables, and protein) and sometimes fresh produce. Every day we visited Jay, he would have a cup of coffee waiting for us. It tasted like mud to me. I wanted to spit it out or politely decline and let him know that, at the time, Mountain Dew was more to my liking. But I did not. Why? Because I understood what that cup of coffee represented to Jay.

That cup of coffee was a generous expression of care from a man who toiled daily in deep Appalachian poverty. What he invested to offer that cup of coffee was a humbling gift that reflected the great inequalities in our food system.

Jay lived at least 20 miles from a grocery store, and *if* his car was running, he would go there once each month. With a limited fixed income, he stocked up on canned goods and nonperishable food items. In the interim, he might hitch a ride with a neighbor or drive the 10 miles

(continued)

SOCIAL WORKER PERSPECTIVE 10.1 (continued)

to a convenience store for his food. But that was just part of the story. Jay Hill did not have running water. He would drive weekly to a spring several miles away and fill large Rubbermaid containers of water. At 65 years of age, he lifted those heavy containers into the trunk of his car, hoping the car would make it back up the hill. When it did not, he trudged up the hill carrying the water, sometimes spilling it along the way. Jay did not have a working stove or oven. To boil the water, he used a hot plate.

When I think back on that cup of coffee, and the effort he made to share something he loved as a way to connect with us each day, that cup of coffee no longer tasted like mud. In fact, I think that the cup of coffee tasted pretty amazing.

For me, that cup of coffee led to a deeper sense of valuing the dignity and worth of every human being, the recognition of deeply rooted health disparities, and a profound respect for the interconnectedness of people and the natural environment. My time with Jay Hill helped me understand the interplay between food, poverty, and health. I saw the earth provide clean water; I also opened my eyes to the impact of soil erosion, pollution, and extractive industries in the mountains surrounding Jay Hill. I saw the consequences of Jay's challenges accessing food, water, and healthcare. I recognized the impact of poor housing conditions and subsequent environmental health issues in Jay's life.

I witnessed both vulnerability and resiliency in one cup of coffee.

That summer planted many more questions than answers for me. It helped me recognize that I no longer wanted to be a physician in a healthcare system wrought with injustices. Instead, I wanted to work on addressing underlying conditions related to poverty and work toward social, economic, and environmental justice for all people. Since then, my understanding of how a cup of coffee can represent any number of human and environmental injustices has deepened. From production to distribution to consumption, we can identify inequalities in which social workers can, and should, intervene. As social workers, we might think about how climate change impacts weather patterns and soil conditions, putting people at risk of drought and famine in coffee-producing countries. Social workers should be working to change poor working and living conditions, and address associated issues of low wages, child labor, human trafficking, and high rates of sexual assault for farmworkers. Food insecurity intersects with immigration issues, child welfare issues, educational disparities, health issues, rising housing costs, mental health, and racist laws.

My experiences as a social worker and community-engaged researcher have framed my vision for the food system and continue to guide my work. Food security is just one lens through which social workers can impact a variety of issues and work toward justice. You never know what one cup of coffee will mean in your life.

FOOD SECURITY MEASUREMENT AT THE INDIVIDUAL, HOUSEHOLD, AND COMMUNITY LEVELS

The establishment of a uniform measurement for food insecurity is an integral part of defining the problem, and the multifaceted nature of food insecurity has led to a variety of methods for its quantification. Experts in economics, nutrition, and medicine were part of the earliest documented efforts to create a nutritional status–monitoring system for the United States through a proposal in the 1977 Food and Agricultural Act (i.e., the Farm Bill). Following the 1990 National Nutrition Monitoring and Related Research Act and the 1994 National Conference on Food Security Measurement and Research, household and individual food security have been measured nationally through a variety of methods that include the federal government's Household Food Security Survey Module (HFSSM), Feeding America's Map the Meal Gap, and the interdisciplinary Community Food Security (CFS) framework.

The HFSSM is a valid and reliable survey conducted annually with a representative sample of U.S. households as part of the U.S. Current Population Survey Food Security Supplement. The HFSSM originated in consumer and behavioral economics, biomedical sciences, nutrition sciences (Kaiser, 2017), and is free and available online on the United States Department of Agriculture (USDA) website. Researchers, federal and state agencies, evaluators, policy analysts, and nonprofit or local program administrators use the HFSSM to assess food security from the household to national level. This measurement tool indicates four levels of food security (high, marginal, low, and very low); low and very low levels are referred to as "food insecurity." In these cases, there are reported dietary changes, indications of missed meals, reduced food intake, and/or reduced quality of food consumed over the course of 12 months. In addition, there is often a stated concern about running out of food before there is money or opportunities to obtain more. The USDA releases an annual national report noting statewide rates of food insecurity, very low food insecurity, and prevalence of food insecurity.

Since 2011, Feeding America, the largest domestic hunger relief organization in the United States, has published its estimates of household and individual food insecurity for all U.S. counties and congressional districts. Their map reports, the Meal Gap, help policy makers, county agencies, and community-based organizations identify the greatest need for their work at a more localized level and communicate this research to different constituents. Feeding America's research is free, user-friendly, and accessible, allowing social workers to utilize the data to inform their own community needs and develop resources. In addition to food insecurity, their reports highlight differences in food costs. They estimate weekly food budget shortfalls that create food hardships for households, which allows for comparison of experiences across different-sized communities in different geographic regions across the United States. Feeding America also provides insight into the need for communities to fill the gap in services for over 25% of food-insecure individuals who do not qualify for federal assistance programs. According to their reports, those gaps show the need for increased charitable response in communities, alongside efforts by policy makers to strengthen public food programs with creative partnerships in the public, private, and nonprofit sectors (Gundersen et al., 2018).

CFS is a framework that was developed in the late 1990s and early 2000s and has roots in community development, sustainable agriculture, and antihunger movements. This framework shifted the emphasis from households and individual economic conditions (i.e., having enough food) and nutrition (i.e., enough nutrient-dense foods for use as fuel for the body) to community-level conditions of the food environment (e.g., availability of stores, price differences between stores, accessibility of food stores). CFS is a useful frame for social workers because of its focus on how the environment can influence individual and household behaviors. In addition, the interdisciplinary CFS framework focuses on food that is "safe, culturally acceptable," and emphasizes a broader goal of sustainable access to food so that "community-self-reliance and social justice" are developed and maintained (Hamm & Bellows, 2003, p. 37), which aligns with social work professional values. Later in the chapter, you will read about how different framings of food security have impacted the strategies designed to respond to, prevent, and/or intervene to improve food security for individuals, households, and communities.

WHAT'S IN A LABEL? HUNGER VERSUS FOOD INSECURITY

Have you ever said in an exacerbated sigh, "I am sooooo hungry"? What does hunger feel like? What physical sensations would you equate to the feeling of "being hungry"? Have you ever heard the term "hangry," a colloquial phrase describing the anger or grumpiness associated with being hungry? The difference between temporary hunger and chronic hunger, and the differences across the types of chronic hunger often resulting from systemic inequalities, deserve detailed discussion. The way hunger is defined and used as a term to influence government policy can greatly affect global political stability and the overall health of a nation.

While the previous examples are temporary and/or rare experiences people may have felt at some point in their lives, hunger as a chronic and/or severe condition can be life-threatening. The World Health Organization (WHO) describes hunger in terms of undernourishment; in 2018, the WHO estimated that nearly 822 million people were hungry in the world, the majority of whom live in the Global South; this includes Asia (513.9 million), Africa (256.1 million), and Latin America and the Caribbean (42.5 million; WHO, 2019). So, does the same undernourishment we frequently hear about in the Global South exist in the United States? The answer is convoluted as the definition of hunger in America has morphed since the 1980s as high-calorie foods became widely available in the United States, and it has been in the country's interest as a stable global superpower to disassociate hunger from its identity.

Several reports from the 1980s document hunger in the United States, distinguishing between the "scientific, clinical" definition of hunger as "actual physiological effects of extended nutritional deficiencies" and hunger as a "social problem" that is related more to poverty and the "inability, even occasionally, to obtain adequate food and nourishment" (U.S. Department of Health and Human Services & USDA, 1986, p. 22). People who had to obtain food at soup kitchens, steal food, or move around because of their circumstances, were considered hungry, even if they did not suffer from any nutritional inadequacies. The concept of hunger as a social problem was generally accepted, but the concept of nutritional hunger was gradually redefined in our country by the later part of the 20th century.

The shift from "hunger" to the use of the term "food insecurity" occurred in the 1990s when experts working to develop national monitoring systems to better document these issues in the United States developed definitions of "food security," "food insecurity," and "hunger." These terms were used in order to operationalize language for standardized measurement. In the reports, *hunger* was defined as a potential consequence of food insecurity. It was defined in terms of the physical symptoms caused by "a lack of food," while *food insecurity* was defined as "limited or uncertain availability" of adequate or nutritionally appropriate food or having to obtain foods through less "socially acceptable ways" (e.g., stealing, emergency food resources; Anderson, 1990, 1575–1576, 1598). Globally, the term food insecurity has long been used to describe a country or region's food supply to meet population needs to avoid malnutrition, though this definition has been expanded to include household-level and individual-level food access.

Versions of the U.S. HFSSM identified the most severe form of food insecurity as "food insecure with hunger," though *with hunger* was removed in 2006 and is now referred to as "very low food secure." Around 5% of U.S. households are very low food secure, which is about 34% of all food insecure households (approximately 43 million). This shift away from using the term "hunger" resulted from the recommendation of a Committee on National Statistics that determined that "hunger" was not a household-level condition, but an individual-level condition that was physiological. Since the HFSSM was measuring household-level food security due to household economic and social conditions rather than individual-level physiological conditions, "hunger" was eliminated from categories.

Does any of this matter? Is discussing this issue at length just semantics? Were these decisions around terminology based purely on measurement, operationalization of variables, and statistics? It is hard to definitively answer these questions, though there are political, historical, and ideological considerations you should think about as social workers engaging in critical thinking around complex social, economic, and environmental justice issues.

Several dates punctuate the measurement discussion. These dates correspond with reports from task forces and committees appointed to serve as advisors to government agencies. These reports and recommendations about hunger and food security measurement occurred during three Republican-led presidential administrations (Ronald Reagan, George H. W. Bush, and George W. Bush). During the Reagan administration, there was bipartisan leadership across Congress; Republicans were the Senate majority, while Democrats led the House of Representatives. During the 1990s when George H. W. Bush was in office, the Senate and House majority were Democrats, while George W. Bush's executive branch worked with an all-Republican majority legislative branch of government.

We know there are vast social and economic ideological differences between the two major political parties in the United States. These differences can influence what gets discussed in the Senate or House, what issues are prioritized, who serves on committees that have decision-making power, and what strategies traditionally would be supported to address an economic or social issue. For example, traditional Republican perspectives would generally favor less federal government intervention and putting power into the hands of states, and believe in the private sector to address social and economic issues.

Federal investment in hunger and food insecurity is strongly impacted by the political majority, and partisan trends around hunger are evident. The 1984 task force recommendations focus on allowing states to choose whether they will participate in food assistance programs (e.g., Food Stamp Program, now referred to as SNAP) and develop their own programs with their own eligibility standards and distribution method (i.e., cash vs. in-kind). The task force also recommended the government should support and encourage the private sector to play an important role in addressing food needs because they are "often models of compassion and efficiency" (pp. 45–46), but limit any amount of "undue government interference" (p. 46). This advice explicitly supported corporations receiving "enhanced deductions for donations of food," providing incentives for gleaning efforts on farms, and increasing the donations to food banks by military suppliers. Two of the task force's recommendations were more representative of utilitarian perspectives as they relate to measurement, program efficiencies, procedures, and maximizing benefits for the greatest number of people. Their final recommendation is rooted in conservative economic perspectives that focus largely on the free market capitalistic system and individual-level behavioral change programs to participate in federal food assistance programs (e.g., work incentives).

As a social worker, it is important to be cognizant of legislation around issues that impact your clients. These reports have shaped decades of dialogue around hunger and food insecurity. Beyond considering the influence of the executive and legislative branches of government, we know that power exists for those who "have a seat at the table." The 1984 task force included: a Republican mayor, two law and economics experts, a director of a neoconservative anti-Communist think tank, a child malnutrition expert, a director of a Christian ministry serving people in poverty, a director of a community center serving an African American/Black community, a director of a community kitchen, a CEO of a company that was an industry leader in fertilizers, restaurants, petroleum, and mining minerals for a nuclear program, a president of an association serving U.S. counties, a bank executive, a Democrat governor who endorsed Reagan (and later joined the Republican party), and a government relations director for a sealant company. The task force included seven men and five women, and few people of color. While three task force members led ministries and/or agencies addressing issues of poverty and hunger in their communities, consider what a professionally educated and trained social worker could bring to the table. What about our profession's values might benefit this space and conversation? This is an excellent example of ways in which social workers can advocate with, and on behalf of, our individual clients and communities. Serving on committees, task forces, and providing legislative testimony could offer new insights to this work.

The last consideration that is important in this discussion relates to ideologies—more specifically, hunger as it relates to the Cold War and the U.S. status as a superpower. If you conduct an online search of hunger in the 1960s, you will likely see black and white photos of Black children in Mississippi and White children in Rural Appalachia on their porches. President Johnson's 1964 War on Poverty and subsequent legislation was intended to eliminate U.S. poverty. During this time, the United States and the Soviet Union were competing to be dominant world leaders in military might, sports, technology, and space exploration. There was an assumption that being a superpower meant there should be no people who are poor or hungry, with the underlying sentiment that people living in the greatest, richest country in the world should not have distended bellies, be malnourished, or display outward appearances of poverty and desperation.

As the social safety net expanded during this time (e.g., introduction of Medicare, Medicaid, federal housing programs, food stamps), the poverty rate fell from 19% in 1964 to 11.2% in the mid-1970s. The highest it has been since 1964 has been during recessions, but never more than 15.1%. During the mid-1970s, income for low- and middle-income households slowed, while it increased greatly for higher income households. The Reagan Administration (1981–1989) wanted to reduce the role of the government and win the Cold War. Images of Americans who were experiencing poverty, homelessness, or standing in government cheese lines were common in the early 1980s, which is not an impression a superpower wants to have broadcast across the world. Think about the number of times you have heard how there should not be poverty or food insecurity in the richest country in the world. Those sentiments are rooted in the U.S. desire to be a superpower.

Headlines from the 1984 Report of the President's Task Force on Food Assistance are somewhat misleading as they report that there is no evidence of hunger in the United States. However, headlines did not include that this is because of the way hunger was being defined and measured. Ask yourself what impact this could have on you as a consumer of the news. What images come to mind when you read or hear the word "hunger" versus "food insecurity"? None of us reading this chapter were in public or private task force and committee meetings during this time, therefore we have no way of knowing the intentions of people involved or what discussions about compromises occurred. However, words and language matter, and knowing that government-appointed committees and task forces do not exist in a vacuum or have a specific charge, and are led by people with different expertise, values, and experiences, it is essential to ask critical questions.

So, now you decide. Does *hunger* exist in the United States?

- If it does, why does our government not call it "hunger"?
- If it does not, why does Feeding America, the largest network of food banks, food pantries, and meal programs in the United States, discuss the issue as "hunger"?

The following section describes current U.S. food insecurity trends. As you read through the data, consider how you associate the examples with your preconceptions of hunger in the United States.

PREVALENCE OF FOOD INSECURITY IN THE UNITED STATES

In 2018, 11.1% of U.S. households were food insecure, which is comparable to prerecession levels. Around 5.6 million households (4.3%) were very low food secure. Seven percent of children experienced food insecurity, while 220,000 U.S. households reported children having to not eat for a day, skip a meal, or experience hunger due to limited financial resources.

Using national data sets, trends of the prevalence of household food insecurity and estimates of county-level food insecurity can be described in terms of sociodemographic and geographic characteristics. Given the way food insecurity is measured, it is not surprising that food insecurity rates align with poverty rates and income inequalities in the United States. The USDA food security reports routinely indicate that food insecurity is highest among people living below 185% of the federal poverty threshold ($25,465 for a family of four in 2018). Food insecurity rates are also highest among single female–headed households with children at 27.8% in 2018, but keep in mind, the U.S. Census currently defines families in three different ways: single female–headed, male and female headed, and married couple families. Additionally, people of color have increased rates of food insecurity with Black households at 21.2% and Hispanic households at 16.2% in 2018 (Coleman-Jensen et al., 2019). Around 13.2% of households in cities and 12.7% of households in rural communities were food insecure. An extremely vulnerable and overlooked group are adults with disabilities. In 2013, over one-third of households that had an adult who was unable to work because of a disability were food insecure, and nearly one-fourth of households that had a working adult with a disability were food insecure (Coleman-Jensen et al., 2019).

Very low food security was highest among single female–headed households with children (9.4%), single women and single men living alone (6.5%, 6.6%), households with incomes below 185% of the poverty line, and households in the South (4.8%). Very low food security was also highest in households that had an adult with a disability and who was unable to work due to the disability (17.3%) and with households who had an adult with a reported disability, but who was still able to be in the workforce (11.8%; Coleman-Jensen et al., 2019).

In 2018, 12 states had food insecurity rates that were higher than the national average. Feeding America's county-level estimates indicate that food insecurity ranged from 4% (Loudon County, VA) to 36% (Jefferson County, MS; Gundersen et al., 2018). The top 10% of food insecure U.S. counties had lower rates of homeownership and higher rates of unemployment, poverty, and median income. Rural counties had the highest percentage of food insecurity. Counties in the densely populated New England region had some of the highest food security rates (Gundersen et al., 2018).

In the United States, American Indians and Alaskan Natives (AI/AN) experience the highest rates of poverty and food insecurity. According to the U.S. Census, around 2.9 million people in the United States identify as AI/AN (0.9% of the U.S. population), though that number increases to 5.2 million (1.7% of the U.S. population) as people identify AI/AN in addition to other racial identities. Nearly one in four AI/AN households is food insecure, and poverty rates are generally around twice the national average. High unemployment and low education levels also contribute to poverty in AI/AN households. AI/AN children, in particular, are at a greater risk for chronic diet-related diseases like type 2 diabetes, compared to the general public. Around 22% of AI/AN households live on reservations or trust lands, and 60% live in metropolitan areas. Not all AI/AN communities face hunger in the same way. Reservations themselves are as diverse as their cultures, landscapes, people, and histories. Read more about food insecurity on the Pine Ridge Reservation from a practitioner who has been working with the community there since 2009. As you read, think about the complex history of the Oglala Lakota tribe and the impacts of various social, economic, and environmental challenges in their lives. Also pay attention to the creative partnerships described and consider what strategies are used to address food insecurity on the Pine Ridge Reservation (From the Field 10.1).

FROM THE FIELD 10.1

FOOD INSECURITY ON THE PINE RIDGE RESERVATION

by Kathryn Burleson, PhD, Program Director, Conscious Alliance

I am a non-native who has been working with the hunger relief nonprofit, Conscious Alliance, in some capacity since 2009. Conscious Alliance supports gardening and distributes meals and snacks through schools and our food pantry on Pine Ridge Reservation in South Dakota.

The Pine Ridge Reservation is home to the Oglala Lakota tribe and spans 3,469 square miles. Pine Ridge (PR) is geographically isolated, and with 80%–90% unemployment, it is one of the most financially impoverished areas in the United States. Poverty, food insecurity, and low food access on PR are rooted in a history of systemic racism. The Lakota have survived a U.S. Army-led attempted genocide and 200 years of ongoing oppression. PR is where the 1890 Massacre of Wounded Knee happened in which 300 people (200 of whom were women and children) were killed by the U.S. Army. The American bison (also called "buffalo") was a primary source of food for the Lakota and was hunted to extinction by European settlers in order to create hunger and angry chaos among the Indigenous people.

Inadequate infrastructure and the U.S.-led assignment of families on the Reservation to reside on scattered lots have combined to leave people isolated and contribute to hunger and health consequences. Access to the only full-service grocery store is limited. While one dozen gas stations with convenience stores also sell food, it is not enough and there are dire repercussions from inadequate access to healthy food. Chronic diet-related disease continues to be a challenge, with 40% of the population struggling with diabetes. The life expectancy for men is 48 years, and for women it is 52 (compared to U.S. life expectancy rates of 76 for men and 81 for women).

In spite of the atrocities and human rights violations that have occurred, PR is also a place of many strengths and much resilience. Though jobs, banks, and stores are scarce, social relations are paramount in keeping relatives fed; many Lakota families participate in extensive trading networks that include food, housing, and transportation.

To be clear, there is not enough food to meet everyone's nutritional needs; people go without, but the food that exists typically comes from a few common sources. Some tribal members receive monthly commodity boxes from the government that contain shelf-stable foods and a notorious big block of cheese. If there is produce in the box, it is the type that will transport well—potatoes or apples for example. Some tribal members have access to a vehicle and will go to the grocery store on many people's behalf when SNAP funds are available or when there is money for food and gas. Many households live entirely on sharing what is obtained via the SNAP food program. Hunting opportunities exist nearby, including tribal-owned buffalo herds that are maintained for controlled harvesting, though this is not simple as hunting requires gear,

(continued)

FROM THE FIELD 10.1 (continued)

a license, and a safe way to butcher and preserve the meat. There is increased attention on the importance of wild foods as Indigenous diets are understood to be healthy, and traditional knowledge is valued and shared. However, not everyone has access to lands with wild food. Although family gardens have gone in and out of favor, they are currently having a resurgence. Gardening provides desperately needed fresh produce, but the short and intense growing season on PR is difficult because of the soil quality, climate, temperature fluctuations, and intense snow, wind, rain, and hailstorms. Finally, for children attending school, lunch is provided Monday through Friday during the school year.

These sources of food are each imperfect and do not provide the solution to the hunger that residents face. Until the 1900s, the Lakota diet was high-protein that consisted mostly of lean meats, but now the offerings are high in processed meats, sugared drinks, convenient snacks that are high in sugar and fat, and a lack of fresh produce and fresh meat. While food sovereignty (i.e., sole reliance on local foods) is a goal of many, families living on the Reservation would suffer greatly without support from the outside, at least for now. It is not that people do not want to help themselves, but that the local and national food systems are not sufficiently working on the Reservation at this time.

Conscious Alliance was born on the Reservation to help address the scarcity of food. The idea was sparked around Floyd and Natalie Hand's kitchen table with a college student from Boulder in 2002. Floyd, an appointed buffalo chief of the Oglala Lakota, was committed to feeding people in his community, but needed greater quantities of food. Justin Baker, the college student, had an innovative idea for how to bring food to the people who needed it; he leveraged his internship in the music industry to initiate "Art That Feeds" Food Drives at concerts and then he trucked the food up to PR from the Front Range of Colorado. Within a few years, a pantry was opened and began to regularly distribute food—all supported by the music industry and live music fans.

Today, Conscious Alliance continues to build creative partnerships. In addition to connecting with the music and art industries to host 100 "Art That Feeds" Food Drives each year, we formed partnerships within the food industry to rescue surplus pallets of food that would otherwise head to the landfill. We distribute to our food pantry on the Reservation as well as all K–12 schools so that students can go home with additional nourishment. We also maintain a school and family garden program that teaches gardening and has produced fresh food for over a hundred families.

While some people wish we would approach only "long-term solutions" to hunger, at least for me and my work on Pine Ridge, I believe we must nourish first. I have never seen anyone do better when they are constantly wrestling with hunger. I believe long-term solutions will come from within the community, but it is unrealistic to expect so much when a base level of nourishment is not met. Floyd Hand taught us the significance of *mitakuye oyasin*, the idea that we are all related and it is from this philosophy that we will continue to nourish as many people as we can until we are no longer needed.

FACTORS CONTRIBUTING TO HOUSEHOLD AND COMMUNITY FOOD INSECURITY

Food insecurity is connected to a number of other social, economic, and environmental justice issues. This can make it hard to specify exact causes of food insecurity. However, poverty is the main predictor of food insecurity. Food-insecure households have financial limitations and instability connected to low-paying jobs or unemployment, childcare expenses, health crises and costs, housing costs, transportation, and high amounts of debt. Food-insecure households are more likely to be cost-burdened by their housing costs, meaning they are paying more than one-third of their incomes on rent. Food-insecure households also spend 21% more on food compared to food-secure households (Coleman-Jensen et al., 2019).

CASE STUDY 10.1—PERSPECTIVES ON FOOD INSECURITY

So much of the good stuff we're talking about here ends up costing more than your Twinkies … That's just wrong … and I think there are some creative ways that we can get around that. But when you think about the amount of money it's causing for people who have health issues and things, you know. It's cheaper to get processed food.

—Focus Group Participant in Columbus, Ohio

It is important to acknowledge the overlapping factors that result in increased rates of poverty. Structural discrimination, racism, and racial inequality contribute to the high rates of poverty for Black, Indigenous, and People of Color (BIPOC) communities. Racial segregation, racist laws that systematically excluded communities of color from fair wages, and racial pay gaps have all impacted who is in poverty. Women in the United States face gender discrimination, earn less than male counterparts, work in the lowest paid occupations, experience financial consequences of violence, and have challenges accessing affordable childcare, healthcare, and adequate benefits. Black individuals have been systematically left out of an important asset-building opportunity of home ownership through racist laws that prevented Black individuals from obtaining home loans. Communities of color were considered too risky for lenders, which resulted in increased racial segregation and reduction in quality of life and services in Black communities.

CASE STUDY 10.2—PERSPECTIVES ON FOOD INSECURITY

We don't have a lot of grocery stores close by. That would cut down a lot having to travel to the grocery stores, trying to catch the bargains and get our produce. We could grow our own, and that would save me a lot every month.

—Focus Group Participant in Columbus, Ohio

Affordability, availability, and accessibility are also functions of the local food environment. This includes the types of stores available (e.g., corner stores, convenience stores, supermarkets, dollar stores), the food items available at those stores (e.g., fresh produce, meat, dairy), and price differences between types of stores and between stores in different locations. In the United States, supermarkets tend to be perceived as the best type of food store because of their prices, variety, complementary services (e.g., banking, bakery, butcher shop), ability to use coupons and loyalty cards, and availability of fresh and/or nutrient-dense foods. While most people are able to get to a supermarket, variation exists around frequency, time involved for transportation (e.g., taking public transportation, driving in own car, getting a ride from friends or relatives), and distance traveled. In low food-access communities, formerly referred to as "food deserts," there tend to be concentrations of poverty, poor transportation (e.g., unreliable transportation, no personal vehicle), and low-quality food stores with higher prices and limited options. Many of these low food-access areas, especially in urban areas, exist because of red-lining, racist zoning laws, and disinvestment in communities of color.

CASE STUDY 10.3—PERSPECTIVES ON FOOD INSECURITY

Sometimes it's challenging ... because a typical grocery store or corner store doesn't always have the quality that I'm looking for, so it requires a trip to another whole quadrant of town for me on a monthly basis, but the gas, this, that, and the other, to balance that out to get higher quality ... food by looking at the ingredients at a better price ... it's weighing out the price of gas to do that ... I end up sometimes spending more money because it might cost less in gas ... that's real critical for me and my family.

—Focus Group Participant in Columbus, Ohio

It is a common misnomer that food grown in rural areas of the United States primarily feeds people, and therefore that individuals living in rural areas do not lack food. In actuality, the majority of crops are used to feed livestock and produce ethanol. Nearly half of all corn, the primary feed grain crop in the United States (it constitutes 96% of grain crops), is used for livestock feed, and 40% is used for ethanol production. The remainder is used for cereals, sweeteners, and high-fructose corn syrup. Rural food insecurity stems from a combination of higher rates of poverty in rural areas (15.8% compared to 12.2% in urban areas), limited availability of grocery stores, and transportation distance and costs.

Unlike household food security, there is not a single CFS measurement tool that is currently used since there is so much variability across U.S. communities. Common indicators used in research and community food program evaluations focus on accessibility, affordability, social justice, healthy community economic development, sustainability, and community self-reliance (Kaiser, 2017). Grant-funded programs are often asked to identify the availability of alternative food network activities and participation in those activities specifically for low-income households (e.g., Community Supported Agriculture [CSA] programs, farmers markets, gardens). Other CFS indicators concentrate on measures related to fair wages, safe working conditions, and civic participation by historically marginalized communities. CFS indicators are focused on environmental issues, and sustainability values measure exposure to toxins and pollution from the industrial agricultural food system, water and energy consumption patterns, and food waste (Kaiser, 2017).

> **CASE STUDY 10.4—PERSPECTIVES ON FOOD INSECURITY**
>
> My problem is finding it and getting it at a reasonable price. Like she was saying about canning and doing the freezing thing, this is the—last year and this year is the first two years that I've not been able to stockpile like I used to, and it's really—it's just me, and my income's gone down, and it makes it harder when I can't put up for later on, you know what I mean. And I feel like I'm—you know—I know how to do all the cost cutting, I know how to stretch stuff, and I'm not getting it done, and that's getting a little scary for me. I've got the background to do it. I know how to garden, I know how to cook, freeze it, can it, everything. I know how to turn one piece of meat into three meals, but lately I can't get two meals out of one piece of meat.
> —Focus Group Participant in Columbus, Ohio

CONSEQUENCES OF FOOD INSECURITY

Food insecurity can result in a multitude of health-related and academic consequences. Food-insecure households and people living in low food-access communities often face barriers of price and availability of food options defined as healthy by the U.S. Department of Health and Human Services and USDA (e.g., fresh produce, whole grains, lean meat, low-fat/fat-free dairy products, low sodium). This often results in lower consumption of nutrient-dense foods, and higher consumption of foods that cost less, are often easier to access, and tend to be higher in calories, sugar, salt, and fat.

Food insecurity in childhood can have lifelong consequences. Nutrition is necessary to support the development of children's brains and bodies. Poor nutrition and food insecurity have been linked to poor cognitive and emotional development. In severe cases, children may be born with birth defects and be at increased risk for illnesses. This can result in increased hospitalizations, which can be financially straining for families and cause children to fall behind their peers in school when days are missed. Children who are experiencing hunger in school may also have a harder time concentrating which can make learning difficult. Food-insecure children are more prone to anxiety, behavioral issues, and aggression, even when we account for poverty. When students are struggling in school, they may be categorized as troublemakers, and their full academic and social potential may be unrealized because of the consequences of food insecurity.

Diets of food-insecure adults are linked to increased risk for obesity, type 2 diabetes, heart disease, high blood pressure, cancer, and high cholesterol. Similar to children, adults may have to miss work due to illness or may have mobility limitations. Common co-occurring conditions may result in expensive healthcare and medication costs. Low-quality diets lack nutritional supports that can reduce the risk for strokes and Alzheimer's disease. Moreover, food-insecure households that are located in high poverty, low food-access areas are less likely to be near parks, recreation facilities, green spaces, and safe sidewalks.

Food insecurity can also have dire mental health consequences. When parents are struggling to feed their children, they may experience shame, social isolation, poor self-esteem, anxiety, and depression. Eating a low-nutrient diet can contribute to these issues as well. Food-insecure households may be situated in neighborhoods with high rates of crime, which can add another dimension of stress. Households experiencing these issues face the devastating consequences of toxic stress on the brain and in the body's defense mechanism system. These mental health issues may also contribute to missed days of work and high healthcare costs. The compounding effects of food insecurity, poverty, poor physical and mental health, and toxic stress can be devastating to neighborhoods and larger communities.

CASE STUDY 10.5—PERSPECTIVES ON FOOD INSECURITY

> Some people have to decide whether to get ... medication and eat ... most of the people have to skimp on the food in order to get the medication.
> —Focus Group Participant in Cleveland, Ohio

STRATEGIES TO ADDRESS FOOD INSECURITY FOR HOUSEHOLDS AND COMMUNITIES

In the United States, food insecurity has largely been addressed at the individual and/or household level, with an emphasis on nutrition and household economics. Of course, this is not surprising, given the way in which food insecurity is measured in the United States. The strategies used to address food insecurity are reflective of the historical, political, and social climate. The following section provides an overview of federal and private food assistance programs in the United States that have traditionally been used to address food insecurity. We have included more recent strategies that are reflective of social work values and arose out of the interdisciplinary academic and activist CFS and sustainable agriculture movements in the late 1990s and early 2000s. This is a fairly comprehensive list of larger food assistance programs, but a number of other programs exist through local governments, grassroots efforts, faith-based initiatives, charitable programs, and social supports. Policies and changes in government administration priorities, ideologies, and strategies to address poverty and food insecurity also routinely change.

We would be remiss not to mention that individuals, households, and families have a number of other strategies to manage poverty and food insecurity. These include making budgetary trade-offs (e.g., paying less for food to make sure there is money to pay rent, not buying medications that are too expensive), hunting and/or fishing for food (as opposed to these activities as sport), gardening for food, scavenging, stealing, limiting dietary intake, skipping meals so children in the household can eat, purchasing food using credit or savings, pawning household items, moving frequently, having multiple jobs, and sharing food with friends, neighbors, and coworkers.

Government Food Program Agency Structure

Strategies to address food insecurity generally have some connection to federal government funding and/or federal food and farming policies. The USDA currently houses 29 agencies related to food, nutrition, agriculture, and natural resources. The federal agencies that most relate to food security are the Food and Nutrition Service (FNS), Economic Research Service (ERS), and National Institution of Food and Agriculture (NIFA). FNS is a key administrator of the U.S. nutrition assistance programs that focus on health and hunger. ERS provides in-depth analyses and reports that have been crucial to shaping public conversations and research about food insecurity, food access, food prices, and food and farm policies. NIFA has been in existence since the Food, Conservation, and Energy Act of 2008. It administers funding for research, education, and extension related to food, agriculture, and the environment. Its current priorities are food security, climate change, water issues, bioenergy, childhood obesity, and food safety. In addition to the USDA and associated federal agencies, each state has state-level agencies and local partners to administer federal food assistance programs and address food insecurity. Table 10.1 provides an overview of federal food programs. The right column briefly describes the delivery mechanism for each federal program.

TABLE 10.1 U.S. Federal Food Assistance Programs

PROGRAM NAME	PROGRAM PURPOSE	TARGET POPULATION	PROGRAM ORIGINATION DATE	PROGRAM MECHANISM OF DELIVERY
Child and Adult Care Food Program (CACFP)	CACFP provides healthy meals and snacks.	Children Adults	1968, became permanent in 1978	• State agencies receive funding from USDA FNS. • State agencies administer this program that reimburses public and private nonprofit childcare centers, adult day-care centers, emergency shelters, and after-school centers meeting eligibility requirements.
Commodity Supplemental Food Program (CSFP)	Each month, participants receive a selection of fruit, juice, vegetables, milk, cheese, grains, and protein (including plant-based protein).	Low-income individuals 60 years of age and older	Originated in 1969, but Agricultural Act of 2014 limited program to seniors	• State agencies receive food and funding from the USDA FNS. • State agencies provide CSFP food to local agencies. • Local agencies distribute food, determine eligibility, and provide education.
Expanded Food and Nutrition Education Program (EFNEP)	EFNEP offers nutrition education program and hands-on meal preparation.	Low-income individuals and families	1969	• This federal extension program is implemented through land grant universities. • EFNEP is funded by the USDA NIFA.
Food Distribution Program on Indian Reservations (FDPIR)	FDPIR provides food to supplement household diets including traditional foods like bison and wild rice.	Low-income households living on Indian reservations All households living in approved areas near reservations or in Oklahoma	1973, authorized through 2023	• USDA FNS distributes funds to participating Indian Tribal Organizations (ITO) and state agencies. • ITO and state agencies store and distribute food.
Fresh Fruit and Vegetable Program (FFVP)	FFVP provides free fruits and vegetables and encourages kids to try new foods.	Elementary-age children in low-income areas	Introduced in 2002 Farm Bill (Farm Security and Rural Investment Act)	• This is a federal program administered through the USDA FNS. • State agencies develop partnerships with elementary schools that have a high percentage of students who participate in the free and reduced meal program. • Schools distribute the fruits and vegetables during the school day.

National School Lunch Program (NSLP)	NSLP provides nutritionally balanced free or reduced-cost lunch.	Students at participating public schools, nonprofit private schools, and residential childcare facilities.	Established as part of the Richard B. Russell National School Lunch Act of 1946	• USDA FNS administers NSLP at the federal level. • State agencies develop partnerships with school authorities. • School districts and public schools, nonprofit private schools, and residential child care facilities are provided cash subsidies and USDA foods for reimbursable meals served. • Schools providing after-school snacks with programming can be reimbursed.
School Breakfast Program (SBP)	SBP provides nutritionally balanced free or reduced-cost breakfast.	Students at participating public schools, nonprofit private schools, and residential childcare facilities	Began in 1966, became permanent in 1975	• USDA FNS administers SBP at the federal level. • State agencies develop official agreements with school authorities. • School districts and public schools, nonprofit private schools, and residential childcare facilities are provided cash subsidies for providing breakfast that meets nutritional requirements and is available for eligible children to have for free or at a reduced price.
Senior Farmers' Market Nutrition Program (SFMNP)	SFMNP increases access to locally grown fruits, vegetables, honey, and herbs. SFMNP benefits can be used to purchase these items at participating vendors.	Low-income seniors 60 years and older	Permanent in 2002 Farm Bill and funded through the Farm Bill, which is updated ~5 years	• USDA FNS provides cash grants to state agencies (e.g., Area Agency on Aging). • Agencies administer the program by providing coupons to eligible participants. • SFMNP participants purchase food from authorized vendors (e.g., farmers markets, CSA programs, roadside stands). • Authorized vendors redeem coupons for reimbursement by the state agency.
Summer Food Service Program (SFSP)	SFSP ensures children receive healthy meals and snacks during the summer when school is not in session.	Children and teenagers at participating sites	1968	• Funded by USDA FNS • States administer program by working with sponsors (e.g., schools, camps, community organizations) that manage feeding sites (e.g., schools, parks, health clinics, faith centers, housing projects, migrant centers). • Sponsors are reimbursed by the program for healthy meals served.

(continued)

TABLE 10.1 U.S. Federal Food Assistance Programs (continued)

PROGRAM NAME	PROGRAM PURPOSE	TARGET POPULATION	PROGRAM ORIGINATION DATE	PROGRAM MECHANISM OF DELIVERY
Supplemental Nutrition Assistance Program (SNAP)	SNAP provides a monthly allotment of money through an Electronic Benefits Transfer (EBT) card to purchase food.	Means-tested program in which eligible recipients meet income requirements and asset limits with rules varying by state	First Food Stamp Program was in 1939, made permanent with 1965 Food Stamp Act	• SNAP is administered by USDA FNS. • State Child and Family Services agencies distribute benefits directly to individuals. • Individuals use their EBT to make food purchases from authorized retailers.
Supplemental Nutrition Program for Women, Infants and Children (WIC)	WIC provides nutritious foods to supplement diets, nutrition education, and referrals for healthcare services.	Low-income pregnant, postpartum, and breastfeeding women and children 5 years and younger	1974	• Congress authorizes annual funding to provide federal grants from USDA FNS to state agencies. • State agencies work with retailers and local clinics, health departments, mobile clinics, public housing programs, migrant camps, and Indian Health Service facilities. • Most WIC participants receive checks or vouchers for specific food items each month (e.g., milk, eggs, iron-fortified cereal), which can be redeemed at authorized WIC retailers.
Emergency Food Assistance Program (EFAP)	EFAP provides emergency food assistance to low-income households at no cost.	Low-income individuals who receive services from local food organizations	1983	• USDA FNS distributes food to state distributing agencies (i.e., food banks). • Food banks distribute food to food pantries, soup kitchens, and other organizations. • Organizations distribute food to low-income households.
WIC Farmers' Market Nutrition Program (FMNP)	FMNP provides coupons to buy fresh fruits and vegetables from participating farmers markets, farmers, and roadside farm stands.	WIC participants or people on waiting list	1992	• Congress appropriates annual funding for FMNP. • USDA FNS provides cash grants to state agencies (e.g., health departments). • Agencies administer the program by providing coupons to eligible participants. • FMNP participants purchase food from authorized vendors (e.g., farmers markets, roadside stands). • Authorized vendors redeem coupons for reimbursement by the state agency.

CSA, Community Supported Agriculture; EBT, Electronic Benefits Transfer; FNS, USDA Food and Nutrition Service; ITO, Indian Tribal Organizations; NIFA, National Institute of Food and Agriculture; USDA, U.S. Department of Agriculture.

Government Food Program Funding Sources

In other social work policy courses, you learn about the U.S. budgeting process at the federal and state levels. For federal programs, recall that there is funding for mandatory and discretionary programs. Mandatory programs are those that are required by federal law and not funded through annual appropriations, while discretionary programs are those that are funded through an annual appropriations process. In 2019 the USDA budget was $140 billion, with $23 billion in discretionary spending. The majority of the USDA budget (71%) is for nutrition-assistance programs. Their website provides an annual budget summary describing how different programs align with their strategic goals. The 2019 budget included $73.2 billion for the SNAP, $23.1 billion for Child Nutrition Programs, and $5.8 billion for the Special Supplemental Nutrition Program for Women, Infants, and Children (WIC; USDA, 2019). Table 10.1 denotes the agency's funding mechanism.

Government Program Strategies

Government food programs have been developed largely to improve the purchasing power for low-income households and the ability for households to consume healthier food. Table 10.1 includes the targeted population for the program (e.g., children, adults). Under the Program Mechanisms for Delivery, you will find the different groups involved that implement the program and the partnering locations where the programs exist (e.g., schools, community centers, homeless shelters).

Several programs are specific to addressing childhood food insecurity and nutrition and are generally carried out in schools, community centers, and childcare centers. These programs provide free or reduced-price food for low-income children and/or students living in high-poverty school districts. These programs are delivered at a local level and involve school administrators, school social workers, and school nutrition services. Imagine the variables involved with coordinating breakfast, lunch, and summer meals. Schools must adhere to local, state, and federal policies related to public health, food safety, and USDA-specified foods. They need to also follow federal dietary guidelines, keep equipment maintained, and feed students efficiently. Many of these programs are based on reimbursements, so the budgeting process and schedule for administrative work are very important.

Programs like SNAP and WIC are intended to provide supplemental food for households, though many households rely on these benefits to meet the majority of their food needs. People with SNAP receive an Electronic Benefits Transfer (EBT) card that is similar to a debit card. Each state has different regulations about eligibility, and when EBT cards are reloaded with money, that is used at SNAP-authorized stores for food. SNAP cannot be used for nonfood items like toiletries, alcohol, or cigarettes. Certain rules also apply to prepared foods. WIC works similarly, but there is an educational component and vouchers are for specific items intended to improve nutrition (e.g., fresh produce, milk, cereal, protein). WIC can be used at authorized stores, and WIC Farmers Market Nutrition Program (FMNP) can be used at authorized farmers markets and produce stands. SNAP is a program that is often a target of political debates. As a large part of the USDA budget, the debates are generally related to reducing the number of people who are eligible for SNAP, limiting what people can purchase with SNAP (e.g., cheapest brand, no soda or junk food, nonorganic), and requiring work, service, or education for SNAP users.

The USDA also provides important emergency food assistance programs to food banks, food pantries, soup kitchens, community agencies, and American Indian reservations. This includes monthly commodity food boxes for seniors that include specific foods like dry beans, cereal, juice, rice, pasta, canned meat, and canned fruits/vegetables. The Emergency Food Assistance Program provides USDA foods to states based on market conditions and state preferences. This includes over 120 food items. It is intended to feed hungry families and support agricultural markets.

Public–Private Program Strategies

Few purely private programs exist to address food insecurity. Federal grants, state funding, local investments, and in-kind contributions are all used to support programs to address food security. Charitable organizations have been crucial, especially during times when government funding is scarce. In addition, public and private partnerships have been created to address food insecurity through leveraging federal food assistance programs in private sector markets. This section highlights some of these strategies.

Feeding America is the largest network of approximately 200 food banks across the United States. Food banks have expanded greatly since the early 1980s during the Reagan administration. This was, in part, related to the large percentage of Americans who were struggling financially and the Reagan administration's ideological perspectives on decreased federal government interventions for social issues. Food banks generally distribute food they purchase, glean, or have donated to their network of food pantries, soup kitchens, and community agencies. Food banks and food pantries provide emergency food assistance to families in order to prevent hunger, though research has shown that very low food-secure and low-income households may be persistent users (using the food pantry regularly for more than 2 years) or prolonged users (periodically using the pantry for more than 2 years).

Critics of food banks suggest that they have become part of the nonprofit industrial complex, giving corporations power on their board of directors and massive tax advantages for donations (Poppendieck, 1999). Those critics would like food banks to use their power and relationships with corporations to work toward long-term solutions to address hunger. This includes being involved in the development of policies that could reduce hunger (e.g., living wage jobs) for individuals who are working for their network of corporate supporters (Fisher, 2017).

Until this point, the food programs discussed in this chapter address the issue of food insecurity through interventions that provide food, vouchers for food, or cash assistance to be used directly for food. Other programs have broader goals that are intended to reach low-income individuals, producers, and markets. These interventions are designed to improve the purchasing power for low-income individuals, expand access to healthy food options, increase the affordability of healthy foods, improve health and nutrition, and improve economic development. These are generally referred to as "supply-side strategies" that are focused on providing opportunities for diversified points-of-sale for business owners and producers. Programs like the FMNP and Senior Farmers Market Nutrition Program (SFNMP) simultaneously offer incentives for low-income WIC users and older adults to purchase local and healthy food options from producers, but also provide producers with access to consumers who may not have been able to purchase their items without those incentives. Producers can also keep their food prices at a level that will be profitable for them. In communities where there are no supermarkets, corner store initiatives have been implemented. While corner stores offer a limited number of food items, they are often the most convenient and accessible option in low-income urban areas, especially in areas with poor transportation. These initiatives include stocking healthy and affordable food items, improving store fronts, and working with store owners on marketing healthy food items to increase consumer purchases.

Another example of a supply-side strategy is the Gus Schumacher Nutrition Incentive Program (GusNIP). This program was first authorized as part of the 2014 Farm Bill under the program's original name, the Food Insecurity Nutrition Incentive Program (FINI). GusNIP is operated by NIFA and supports increased fruit and vegetable consumption by SNAP recipients through point-of-purchase incentives and produce prescriptions. When SNAP recipients purchase fruits and vegetables at participating locations, they receive incentives (e.g., for every $1 spent on fruits and vegetables they receive $1 in incentives) that allow them to purchase additional fruits and vegetables. NIFA disburses GusNIP in the form of monetary grants to government agencies and nonprofit organizations that implement these points of purchase and produce prescription programs. The goal of GusNIP produce prescription programs is to increase accessibility of fruits and vegetables and reduce diet-related health disparities among low-income individuals and households by providing "prescriptions" that are redeemed to obtain free fruits and vegetables. Nonprofits and government organizations collaborate with local healthcare partners to implement produce prescription programs. From the Field 10.2 describes how the Kentucky Double Dollars program addresses food insecurity, economic development, and healthy nutrition through federal, state, and local private and public partnerships.

FROM THE FIELD 10.2

ADDRESSING FOOD INSECURITY, ECONOMIC DEVELOPMENT, AND HEALTH

by Jennifer Weeber, MSW, Northfork Local Food Coordinator, Community Farm Alliance

Kentucky Double Dollars is an innovative program that addresses food insecurity, economic development, and health. It is a partnership between Community Farm Alliance, a statewide organization devoted to supporting family-scale agriculture, and Bluegrass Farm to Table, an initiative of the City of Lexington, devoted to the development of a vibrant local food economy. The program is financially supported by the U.S. Department of Agriculture, the Kentucky Governor's Office of Agricultural Policy/Kentucky Agriculture Development Fund, and a variety of private financial and health-related business partners.

Kentucky Double Dollars incentivizes the purchase of Kentucky-grown agricultural products by households who are low-income by doubling the value of such purchases when they are made with one of three federal nutrition-assistance programs:

- The SFMNP provides nutrition assistance to people who are 60 years or older and are low-income to purchase Kentucky-raised fruits and vegetables at certified farmers markets. In 2019, eligible seniors received vouchers worth $28 which, when supplemented with Kentucky Double Dollars incentives, resulted in $56 of additional fresh produce for their households. Forty farmers markets across Kentucky offered this complement of incentives to their customers resulting in $57,498 worth of local produce purchased.
- The WIC Farmers Market Nutrition Program provides nutrition assistance to WIC-eligible households to purchase Kentucky-raised fruits and vegetables at certified farmers

(continued)

FROM THE FIELD 10.2 (*continued*)

markets. In 2019, eligible households received vouchers worth $16 which, when supplemented with Kentucky Double Dollars incentives, resulted in $32 of additional fresh produce for their households. Thirty-four farmers markets across Kentucky offered this complement of incentives to their customers resulting in $19,071 worth of local produce purchased.

- Within Kentucky Double Dollars, there are two SNAP incentives. The first is for Kentucky-grown fruits and vegetables. These incentives can be redeemed at participating farmers markets, Fresh Stop Markets (community-driven, sliding-scale farmers markets), or retail locations. Customers can double up to $12 ($10 at retail locations) of SNAP benefits per market day. In 2019, 28 farmers markets, 10 Fresh Stop Market sites, and one retail grocery store offered this program resulting in $32,241 worth of local produce purchased. The second incentive is for Kentucky-raised meat, eggs, and dairy. Customers can double up to $8 of SNAP benefits per market day. In 2019, 18 farmers markets offered this incentive to their customers resulting in $6,652 worth of local agricultural products purchased.

Increasing access to fresh, local food for low-income households benefits the entire community. The increased purchasing power provides greater food security and better nutrition for participating households. Katie D., a Hazard, Kentucky participant, noted: "The program brought color and taste to my dinner table that I would not have been able to afford had Double Dollars not been available to my family."

Kentucky Double Dollars has a significant impact on local economies, particularly in rural areas. While Kentucky's overall poverty rate is slightly above the national rate, many of its rural areas experience widespread poverty. In rural Magoffin County, just over one-quarter of its residents have incomes under the federal poverty line. The acceptance of nutrition assistance programs coupled with Kentucky Double Dollars at the Magoffin County Farmers Market composed nearly 20% of their 2019 market sales, enabling the farmers at the market to increase their customer base and overall income as a result. Maggie Bowling of Old Homeplace Farm in Oneida sells regularly to the Fresh Stop Market in Hazard and notes "participating in Fresh Stop and Double Dollars allows me to sell more food to my home community of Eastern Kentucky and facilitates the difficult balance between the farm business demands of creating a living wage for myself, while also trying to make sure food is affordable for consumers" (personal communication, September 30, 2019).

Community Food Security Strategies

CFS strategies developed by grassroots leaders and researchers work in tandem with antihunger interventions that are intended to be short term and focused largely on providing ways for individuals and households to improve their purchasing power, especially for healthy food items (Kaiser, 2017). While public and private programs have been a crucial part of improving the social welfare of low-income households, CFS strategies are more prevention-oriented practices that focus on individual and community empowerment and long-term community planning. These multipronged approaches link together values and ideals that can be difficult to measure. These include social justice and fairness, sustainability or sustainable ecosystems, and community self-reliance. CFS strategies work to improve affordability and accessibility for entire communities through economic development, community development, public health, and social justice–oriented practices.

CFS strategies target various aspects of community-based food systems to address social, economic, and environmental injustices throughout the food system. These include food production, processing, distribution, preparation, consumption, retail, and food waste. CFS strategies tend to connect different sectors to address underlying issues of household food insecurity and community economic development, such as providing safe job opportunities at appropriate wages in new food businesses.

Some CFS strategies may focus more on conservation, farm preservation, and environmental stewardship, while others may work to improve the health and viability of small-scale or non-commodity crop producers. Common CFS strategies include CSA programs, community gardens, institutional gardens, and farmers markets that accept SNAP, FMNP, and SFMNP. To more overtly target social injustice, CFS strategies may include initiating living wage campaigns, advocating for improved working conditions, and increasing leadership opportunities for food-policy councils. Social workers have a clear role to support underrepresented groups (e.g., women, immigrants, persons of color) that have faced innumerable challenges (e.g., sexual assault, low wages, pesticide exposure, abuse, and withholding backpay) and have limited power and voice at the decision-making table.

The USDA NIFA Community Food Projects (CFP) program has been one grant-funding mechanism intended to link different parts of the food system together to work toward community food security. Since 2007, the USDA CFP program has funded over 260 projects to improve food access, expand opportunities for food production, increase leadership opportunities for minority populations, strengthen creative economic and community development initiatives, strengthen cross-sector partnerships, and enrich culturally diverse production operations. In From the Field 10.3, you will read about a 2016 CFP recipient, Franklinton Farms (FF). A soil scientist who served as director of FF through January 2020 and a social work professor who has served as a volunteer since 2012 describe how they have been implementing CFS strategies to address social, economic, and environmental injustices.

FROM THE FIELD 10.3

FROM FOOD DESERTS TO FOOD OASES! TRANSFORMING A COMMUNITY THROUGH URBAN FARMING

by Nicholas A. Stanich, MS, Executive Director of Franklinton Farms (2013–2020), and Michelle L. Kaiser, MSW, MPH, PhD, Ohio State University

"Food deserts" and "food swamps" are common labels affixed to many poverty-stricken inner-city and rural communities that struggle with healthy food access. Food swamps are areas in which the number of unhealthy food options (e.g., fast food, junk food, convenience stores, and liquor stores) outnumbers places where healthier food can be accessed. The story that follows details efforts by one community organization in Columbus, Ohio to transform its stigmatic label as a food desert, into an abundant reality of healthy food access made possible through urban farming. Franklinton is a neighborhood on Columbus, Ohio's West Side. For years, it has been referred to as "The Bottoms," originally because of its location at the confluence of rivers and subsequent flooding that led to widespread homelessness and disinvestment until a flood wall was built. The Bottoms became a derogatory term as it suffered through 20 years of neglect, urban decay, population decline, human trafficking, and limited economic development.

(continued)

FROM THE FIELD 10.3 (continued)

Franklinton Farms (FF) originated in 2007 as an informally organized community garden led by neighbors in the Franklinton neighborhood. Grassroots activists were driven to action over concern about the neighborhood's preponderance of unhealthy processed food and lack of access to fresh and healthy produce. The neighborhood's health situation was and still is dire—over 30% of neighbors are very low food secure, more than 70% are overweight or obese (a significant portion of whom are severely obese), 44% of households earn less than $15,000 per year, and high rates of high blood pressure, high cholesterol, prediabetes, and diabetes exist. The life expectancy is the lowest in the state of Ohio at just 60 years. Poverty, food insecurity, chronic diet-related disease, crime, substance use and misuse, mental health issues, and poor access to fresh fruits and vegetables all contribute to the life expectancy rate.

In 2007 FF set out to change this dismal health reality by creating a number of food gardens that grew an abundance of fresh, nutrient-dense produce that was distributed throughout the neighborhood. Over the next 12 years FF formalized into a 501(c)3 designated nonprofit organization that grew to become the largest urban fruit and vegetable farm in the entire city, organically growing over $100,000 per year worth of produce on just 1.5 acres that spanned 12 distinct gardens in 2020. The organization's expansion as a farm was explosive and unparalleled in the region, quite impressive for a nonprofit farm located in one of the most impoverished neighborhoods in the U.S.'s 14th largest city. Much of the farm's growth can be attributed to inspiration by the urban farming renaissance that has been rapidly developing across North America since 2014, and by the hard work of thousands of volunteers who showed up year-over-year to build and sustain the farm. Distribution of the produce grown on this farm within the Franklinton community remains a top priority for FF, and the organization has developed multiple strategies for ensuring individuals struggling with poverty have affordable access to the farm's food while also ensuring the produce generates adequate revenue to support a living wage for farm workers. Support from federal, state, and local governments, and support from private philanthropy, enables subsidized produce distribution through the following programs:

Funded in large part by a USDA Community Food Projects grant, FF was able to create a neighborhood food distribution program modeled on the spirit of CSA. The CSA concept offers customers the opportunity to commit to a full season of weekly farm produce, which helps the farmer ensure stable sales, while providing the customer with the diversity of produce across the season. FF's CSA program works with upwards of 60 households in Franklinton each season, and offers a 50% subsidy to half of those households that self-identify as low-income and in need of a subsidy. Produce is delivered to each household to ensure opportunity for participation by those who do not have the capacity to pick up the produce themselves. The CSA is also about building relationships with neighbors through outreach and engagement. Each season we collect extensive data through surveys and regularly host potlucks and community events. We invite neighbors to share food, exchange recipes, meet one another, and participate in free cooking classes hosted by community partners. FF provides a weekly newsletter with recipes, food storage tips, and information about farm operations and community events.

People have been participating in the CSA for many reasons. Many neighbors are looking for healthy options since most of the food store options are convenience stores, corner stores, dollar

(continued)

FROM THE FIELD 10.3 (*continued*)

stores, and discount stores. Participants appreciate the delivery because of its accessibility, while others take part to set an example for their kids and grandkids. Participants have said that they look forward to their Thursday food bag so they can try new vegetables and recipes with their families. One participant stated they participate "because finding a ride to the store to buy fresh fruits and vegetables is a pain 'cause I have no car, no job, no money, and they deliver." Another expressed: "We like the idea of knowing exactly where our produce is coming from." Still others are interested in supporting FF because of their values around sustainability and environmental justice, choosing to participate because the "produce is free from harmful pesticides or chemicals."

FF also hosts a weekly Produce Stand in the neighborhood and vends produce at a local farmers market. We participate in the SFMNP and WIC programs and allow participants in our programs to pay with SNAP/EBT. In our community, we also use Produce Perks for the CSA and markets. These incentives double the value of EBT for customers, up to $20 per day. It allows FF to meet the needs of our neighbors, while also considering the economic sustainability of our organization and fair wages for our workers. FF reduces the cost of its produce by 50% for anyone who uses these programs, and for anyone who self-identifies that they need a subsidy. FF donates produce throughout the year to specific individuals in need, and to organizations that distribute to individuals in need. These organizations include after-school youth programs that serve homeless families, food pantries, and free community meals.

Affordable access to fresh produce is only part of the solution to achieving CFS. Other strategies used by FF include installing solar arrays on its buildings to help run operations, using environmentally friendly agriculture management practices, composting materials, and striving for conservation efforts where possible. We are moving towards inviting neighbors to share their knowledge about canning, preservation, and gardening with others.

FF also refers neighbors to programs within walking distance that provide free stress management classes, cooking classes, civic engagement opportunities, and social support programs. Our Patrick Kaufman Memorial Learning Garden hosts children's education, as it is located across from a settlement house and elementary school. In addition, the space hosts neighborhood festivals and holds community wellness events. We continue to work with agencies that are supporting persons in poverty, persons in recovery, and persons who have been trafficked. They have volunteered on the farm, participated in festivals, and become CSA members. Through these efforts, we are working towards building and sustaining a self-reliant community that does not need to be dependent on help from "outsiders." The past 12 years of FF's efforts have created an oasis of fresh food abundance within a food desert saturated in nutritionally detrimental processed foods, and the organization's work is a testament to the transformative power of community-driven grassroots organizing.

Social workers trained in community organizing, community planning, community development, program development, policy work, and advocacy are well-suited to lead CFS efforts. Since hunger has long been defined as a social problem, it is necessary to address underlying historical, social, economic, and racial injustices. In Social Worker Perspective 10.2, social worker and Ohio State Extension educator Whitney Gherman reflects on some of her community's efforts around racial justice, community social work, and addressing past injustices by institutions in low-income communities of color.

SOCIAL WORKER PERSPECTIVE 10.2

COMMUNITY ORGANIZING AND COALITION-BUILDING TO REBUILD RELATIONSHIPS AND HISTORICALLY OPPRESSIVE FOOD SYSTEMS

by Whitney Gherman, MSW, Ohio State University Cooperative Extension Educator, Marion County

The smoke from incense swirled around the porch. Herbs and a lavender plant waned from the summer heat. The rocking chairs beneath us creaked as neighbors came and went, some stopping by only briefly to exchange meals and others staying longer to share stories from around Center Street. Throughout the summer of 2019 we talked about dilapidated properties and the city's disregard for Ward five. We discussed barriers to having the first African American getting seated on city council, the effects of climate change, the prison industrial complex, gender-based violence, and most notably, food apartheids and the devastating consequences of an unequal food system.

In Marion County, Ohio, the per capita income is approximately $40,000. Many neighborhoods that were once middle class are now run-down (14%). Black children are four times more likely to experience poverty compared to their White peers (71% and 22%, respectively). This, combined with high levels of adult obesity (36%) and food insecurity (15%), paints a picture of a struggling community. Given this, I knew one initiative could not easily address decades of community neglect and disinvestment. I understood that to some, I would be seen as an outsider, as a middle-class, White woman who lived 30 miles south of town, working for a system with a long history of discrimination, Cooperative Extension. Back in my office, where previous ways of doing things were sufficient, my peers were also skeptical. Nevertheless, I persisted.

I found solidarity on Ms. Harriet Davis's porch, generating plans with people directly affected by the outcomes of my work. To her and to others I was a welcome ally: "Whitney is giving us a chance to ask questions and providing opportunities to express concerns in our community." Consensus was built on how we were going to ethically share resources, knowledge, and relationships. We agreed on tenets for democratic organizing. We read books from queer Black feminists. We took trips. We talked about our growing relationships on radio shows, webinars, and via formal presentations. Alone we could do so little, but together we could affect change in this community.

The most prominent program was a 15-week series aimed at developing multicultural, leadership capacity at the grassroots level. *Community Voices's* central premise was that when voices are raised in unity, we can enact positive change. After only the first few meetings the cohort increased urgency around Marion's food ways. With a historically Black church, a city council representative, two farmers, and disability rights activists, we acquired land bank properties to transform them into accessible urban farms. As a community educator at Ohio State University Extension, my responsibility was to organize and link resources that could provide starter plants and seeds, water tanks and rain barrels, small tools and equipment, soil testing, and picnic tables. Together we sponsored community planting days, taste-testings at the garden, educational events, a farm tour, and at the end of the season, initiated the development of

(continued)

> **SOCIAL WORKER PERSPECTIVE 10.2 (*continued*)**
>
> a neighborhood association. A year later, we continue to assert land cultivation as a significant part in the fight for freedom.
>
> There are several lessons learned from my experience. I am outraged by inequality in our food system, yet in my efforts to mobilize others around anti-Black racism, I sometimes became too passionate and may have hurt people who were trying. At times, I forgot the long-time community members who have been fighting for decades. In other instances, I became suspicious of people who have been part of the movement with me and sincerely love me. But here is what I also know: Oppressive systems require isolation. Patriarchy, White supremacy, and capitalism want us to feel alone. Building with each other is one way we can fight against this lie. "Nurturing the slowness of community rather than the speed and isolation of convenience" is part of how we do this.
>
> For students who may be reading this, if a movement for radical social justice is not already in your community, recruit others and build one. Our profession calls social workers to advocate for truth and justice. Wherever you are, whatever workplace or neighborhood you are in, you can make a difference. When people feel belonging and when everyone is at the decision-making table, transformation becomes easier to access and there is enough support to yield healing for everyone. Be justice, be peace, be community.
>
> From our front porch to yours, we are rooting for you.

COLLEGE FOOD INSECURITY

College campuses are another space in which food insecurity exits. College food insecurity is a prevalent problem across the country, and college students have recently been identified as one population that experiences high rates of food insecurity. In fact, a 2019 study of 86,000 U.S. college students found that 45% of students were food insecure. The rising cost of higher education has contributed to college food insecurity because college students often do not have the financial resources to obtain enough nutritionally appropriate food because of high tuition bills and other costs (e.g., housing, transportation) associated with college attendance. Additionally, many college students are now nontraditional students who are older and raising families while attending college. Despite working and receiving financial aid, many students still are food insecure. Unlike the programs available to students enrolled in primary and secondary education that support food access (e.g., School Breakfast Program, National School Lunch Program), there are no universal programs to address the needs of college students facing food insecurity.

College campuses across the country have begun addressing student food insecurity in several ways. This includes on-campus food pantries, helping students apply for SNAP benefits, including questions about food insecurity on admissions paperwork, participating in food-waste recovery networks, creating food-buying cooperatives, and using college land to grow fresh fruits and vegetables for students in need. In From the Field 10.4, master's degree social work student Mara Sydnor describes her undergraduate honors research thesis that examined food insecurity on a college campus and the barriers students face in accessing food resources like the campus food pantry.

FROM THE FIELD 10.4

COLLEGE FOOD SECURITY

by Mara Sydnor, BSSW ('19), MSW ('20), alumna, Ohio State University

As an undergraduate honors student, I decided to complete my thesis about an issue that hit close to home for myself and some of my peers at the Ohio State University, where a 2015 Center for Student Life study found that 19.9% of students they surveyed were food insecure. The objective of my research was to identify factors related to food insecurity and housing vulnerability of undergraduate college students. Many students are not able to work full-time and/or earn enough money to afford tuition, rent, utilities, and food, resulting in the use of student loans to pay for living expenses. College students who face food insecurity and housing vulnerability are more likely to fail or withdraw from classes, and many students are unaware of resources that are available or fear stigma associated with using those resources.

The 2019 study examined institutional practices and perspectives that influenced student food insecurity through three 75-minute focus groups with on-campus and off-campus students to learn about their personal experiences and knowledge of budgetary challenges, food insecurity, housing issues, and campus resources. Participants completed a survey developed from the literature and standardized instruments that included questions about demographics, food-security level, housing challenges, and food access. A review of university resources was conducted to understand current programs that are addressing these issues.

The nine focus group participants provided rich, in-depth insights to help us explore these issues. The discussions resulted in five major themes: the rising costs of housing and food related to gentrification near campus; lack of resource awareness; relying on loans and outside help to pay expenses and afford living; transportation challenges to access grocery stores and fresh produce; and stigma related to shame, isolation, self-blame, and embarrassment about disclosing financial challenges. Of the nine students, 44% experienced some level of food insecurity, two-thirds of them relied on loans to cover regularly occurring living expenses, 50% identified their living expenses as unreasonable, and one-third shared that they did not pay for some necessities in order to afford rent. Despite the results of the survey, few students were able to identify that they were food insecure. This discrepancy can be attributed to the major theme of stigma that participants identified. Students did not want to be singled out or feel different among their peers. One student shared: "Everything for me has to come from loans because, like, that's my only option." Another said: "There have been times, like I said, where my meal plan hasn't been enough." Yet another student explained: "It's more of a struggle because [students] have to keep a job and go to classes and make sure that they can keep their apartment."

An additional review conducted by the researchers analyzed the resources currently available to support students who experience food insecurity. Students felt that more support and education about existing university resources should be made visible and accessible to the campus community. They suggested including resources in syllabi, orientations, and on high-traffic university applications and course websites. Since this study, a second campus food pantry has been established. The additional location features extended hours and days of operation. This is a significant step toward increasing the accessibility of the pantry.

(continued)

FROM THE FIELD 10.4 (*continued*)

A central finding of the study is that food and housing insecurity among college students remains an issue, particularly when resources fail to address the needs of vulnerable students. Improving education and accessibility about resources may counter existing financial stressors and improve the quality of education for at-risk students. From a social work perspective, it is crucial to be aware of existing resources and knowledgeable about how clients can access them. Of the students in the study who were food insecure, none of them were using campus resources. The reasons they gave included a lack of awareness, accessibility, and most importantly, the stigma that comes with being food insecure. Accessibility was a major concern addressed during focus group discussion and plays a large role in resource utilization. Clients who have classes and jobs may not have the opportunity to visit the food pantry's limited service hours. Clients without a car may find it more difficult to get fresh groceries. Having resources for clients is important, but if they are not using or accessing resources, are the institutional practices in place at all helpful? Social workers should consider any barriers to resources clients may experience and make recommendations accordingly. Understanding the risk factors clients may face associated with food insecurity is of great importance. Access to affordable and healthy food is essential in maintaining quality of life.

CONCLUSION

As you read this chapter, you may have noted a few central themes. While we know that hunger has been accepted as a social problem, without addressing poverty and racism, completely eliminating hunger will be a great challenge. We also know that existing measurement methods focused on household- and individual-level economics drives current strategies for addressing these issues. Social work, however, aligns more closely with the CFS frameworks that are value-driven and build upon community strengths to address ecological–social issues in long-term and sustained ways. The reality is there is not one solution to hunger. The current strategies must work together to address emergency food needs and plan for the likely impacts of climate change on food prices, weather patterns, and biodiversity. As social workers, we must ask ourselves: What is our individual and professional role in being part of transforming our food system and moving toward social, economic, and environmental justice? We must consider how our profession can be included in decision-making processes and use our social justice framework, social work values, ecological–social perspectives, strengths-based perspectives, and person-in-environment perspectives to lead efforts to improve the health and well-being of the people, land, water, and everything that lives on this planet. We cannot solve hunger and food insecurity through food alone. We must be willing to address the underlying, deep-rooted causes of these issues, challenge ourselves to make connections across political ideologies, racial lines, and sectors. In order to solve complex problems, we need to be part of the solution.

DISCUSSION QUESTIONS

1. Identify why we measure food security as opposed to hunger. Why was hunger removed as a measurement variable in determining food security?

2. Ethical Dilemma: A family is above the income guidelines to receive food from the emergency food pantry where you are a social work intern. You know donations are down at the pantry and the family just received the one emergency food allotment they are allowed every 4 months, just 3 weeks ago. You are in a rural area and are the only food pantry for 35 miles. Would you provide the family food? What are some of your considerations for making this decision?
3. Research student organizations and efforts at your college or university related to food security. Do you have food recovery programs? Food pantries? Do they address the consequences or underlying causes of college food insecurity?
4. What does a hunger-free world look like? What resources do we already have now to make this possible?

ACKNOWLEDGMENTS

I (MLK) honor the land, water, and air in which we exist. I am grateful for the land and water that foster living plants and beings that have supported generations of people. I honor the people who have stewarded the land in the past and endured oppressive forces. I vow to seek justice for those who continue to be enslaved by our food system.

REFERENCES

Only key references appear in the print edition. The full reference list appears in the digital product on Springer Publishing Connect: connect.springerpub.com/content/book/978-0-8261-3539-1/chapter/ch10

Anderson, S. A. (Ed.). (1990). Core indicators of nutritional state for difficult-to-sample populations. *Journal of Nutrition, 120*(11), 1555–1660. https://doi.org/10.1093/jn/120.suppl_11.1555

Coleman-Jensen, A., Rabbitt, M. P., Gregory, C. A., & Singh, A. (2019). *Household food security in the United States in 2018*. Advance online publication. https://www.ers.usda.gov/webdocs/publications/94849/err-270.pdf?v=963.1

Fisher, A. (2017). *Big hunger: The unholy alliance between corporate America and anti-hunger groups*. MIT Press.

Gundersen, C., Dewey, A., Crumbaugh, A. S., Kato, M., Engelhard, E., Odeen, B., Kriss, M., & Ratulangi, P. (2018). *Map the Meal Gap 2018: A report on county and congressional food insecurity and county food cost in the United States in 2016*. Advance online publication. https://www.feedingamerica.org/sites/default/files/research/map-the-meal-gap/2016/2016-map-the-meal-gap-all-modules.pdf

Hamm, M. W., & Bellows, A. C. (2003). Community food security and nutrition educators. *Journal of Nutrition Education and Behavior, 35*(1), 37–43. https://doi.org/10.1016/S1499-4046(06)60325-4

Kaiser, M. L. (2017). Redefining food security in a community context: An exploration of community food security indicators and social worker roles in community food strategies. *Journal of Community Practice, 25*(2), 213–234. https://doi.org/10.1080/10705422.2017.1308897

Poppendieck, J. (1999). *Sweet charity? Emergency food and the end of entitlement*. Penguin Books.

United States Department of Agriculture. (2019). *Fiscal year 2019 budget summary*. https://www.usda.gov/sites/default/files/documents/usda-fy19-budget-summary.pdf

United States Department of Health and Human Services & the United States Department of Agriculture. (1986). *Nutrition monitoring in the United States—A report from the Joint Nutrition Monitoring Evaluation Committee*. DHHS Publication No. 86-1255. Public Health Service. US Government Printing Office. https://www.cdc.gov/nchs/data/misc/nutri86acc.pdf

World Health Organization. (2019). *World hunger is still not going down after three years and obesity is still growing—UN report*. https://www.who.int/news-room/detail/15-07-2019-world-hunger-is-still-not-going-down-after-three-years-and-obesity-is-still-growing-un-report

11

UTILIZING POLICY TO ADDRESS UNAFFORDABLE AND UNAVAILABLE HOUSING

Terri Lewinson

LEARNING OBJECTIVES

Students will be able to:

- Articulate the varying reasons why housing is unaffordable for so many.
- Assess the impact on the individual who is seeking or lacks affordable housing.
- Describe the variety of federal programs to support housing availability, accessibility, and affordability.
- Identify resources to be developed or improved to protect people from unfair lending practices and exploitative eviction strategies.

INTRODUCTION

Secure, affordable housing is a basic human right. Housing provides not just a home but also the context of our lives; it is hard to function in a society without adequate housing. For many Americans, housing is inaccessible due to lack of affordability. Social workers should know the policies associated with the burdens and adverse outcomes of unaffordable housing for financially vulnerable people as housing, employment, and socioeconomic well-being are inextricably linked. Stable housing improves employment, mental and physical health, and school attendance; thus, housing is an integral part of justice-informed social work practice. But the policies in place fail to provide adequate affordable housing, leading to the fundamental question in the early to mid-20th century that continues to this day—what is the government's role in housing?

UNAFFORDABLE AND UNAVAILABLE HOUSING AS A CHALLENGE TO JUSTICE

Why is housing unaffordable? Simply put, there is not enough of the right kinds of housing available and accessible to the many people who need it. Housing is too expensive, too far from work, too long-term of a commitment, requires too much of a background check, is too unsafe, is too inaccessible, and the list goes on. On its face, these sound like easy issues to address, right? Just make more housing available—more rentals, more houses to buy, more accessible apartments, and so on. Unfortunately, it is a bit more complicated—actually a lot more complicated. As an active and informed social worker, it is imperative that you understand the complexity of housing affordability, even if your practice is not centered on housing. We all need a place to call home. Without a warm, safe, dry, affordable, and accessible place to live, it is difficult to function in society. Thus, let us explore housing, as it impacts, well, *everyone*.

Take a minute and think about your housing history. Where have you lived? How connected were you with your community? Who were your neighbors? What did you do for recreation? Which school did you attend? What was the best thing about where you lived? What was the worst? We all come from various situations, and your housing history is an essential aspect of your unique journey. I can guess, with some certainty, that where you have lived in the past has undoubtedly influenced how you live today.

UNDERSTANDING AFFORDABLE HOUSING

A reasonable place to start is by describing what is meant by "affordable housing." However, the conceptualization of this construct is complex, depending on your perspective. The most publicly accepted definition of affordable housing is by the U.S. Department of Housing and Urban Development (HUD), which describes affordable housing as that in which the inhabitants' rent or mortgage payments do not exceed 30% of the household income (HUD, 2021). Do you think this is a reasonable definition? How would you define affordable housing? Would you consider a definition that included the number of people in the home, as housing advocates suggest? After all, a household of three people with fewer material needs should have less of a burden paying rent from 30% of their income than a household of six, right? Or, you might consider the ability of a household to sustain payments over a specific period, which is a central concern of the banking industry. Perhaps you might take a market perspective. Could a housing unit be considered affordable if there were many competitive buyers to purchase it? Or, is income all that matters when we consider housing affordability?

Over the last 20 years of my social work practice, through home assessments and community-based research, I have had access to many homes of people who have low income. My clients and participants lived in single-family houses, apartment complexes, assisted living facilities, senior housing units, high-rise public housing, mobile home parks, rural cabins, and even budget hotels. Despite the housing situation, I have witnessed spiraling losses of homes due to financial constraints and life circumstances, as well as decrepit environments in which people live as a result of unavailable and inaccessible affordable housing. I can easily recall my visit to a rural mother who was too sick to work, but tried her best to raise her teenage daughter in a trailer that had a hole near the kitchen sink so large that you could see straight through to the dirt below. In one case, a young mother of two children fled domestic abuse only to fall prey to eviction by a landlord because she refused to pay her late rent with sexual favors. Most humbling was an older husband who moved into a budget hotel with his wife because he could no longer afford his rent and the cost of medical treatment for his stage 4 prostate cancer. Unfortunately, these stories, and many others, are commonly reported from clients on social work caseloads. Therefore, students who prepare for a career in this helping profession should understand the burdens and adverse outcomes of unaffordable housing for financially vulnerable people.

In this chapter, you will learn about how housing affordability, availability, and access in our nation are seamlessly intertwined. We start by revisiting federal policy and considering multiple factors that influence housing affordability and availability. We also explore resident access and the basic right to housing. This chapter also highlights unfair and predatory lending practices that systematically deny vulnerable populations access to wealth accumulation. By the end of this chapter, you will be able to do the following:

- Understand the influence of American housing policy on housing affordability, availability, and access.
- Identify federal policies that regulate mortgage and rental housing markets.
- Explain the outcomes of unfair housing policies for disenfranchised residents.
- Describe exploitative strategies used against renters in the eviction process.
- Identify factors that lead to housing instability and homelessness.
- Explain how shrinking funds for federal assistance programs reduce the affordable housing stock.

Mostly, you will learn from this chapter why housing is out of reach for many American households. Before we can know what needs to be done as social work advocates to improve housing affordability, it is useful to know about previous strategies. Therefore, we begin by learning about housing policy since the 1930s to provide some context for the challenges we currently face.

OVERVIEW OF HOUSING POLICY

In the wake of the 1929 stock market crash and the Great Depression, the American housing market was fragile. However, it was made worse by an accumulation of mortgage foreclosures due to rising unemployment numbers. As a result, instead of receiving mortgage payments as a liquid asset, lending institutions had excess defaulted home loans and little capital to finance home builders. Short of cash, developers were unable to build homes, which contributed to reduced housing-related employment in the U.S. economy. It was a circular problem because middle-class families needed jobs to pay short-term mortgages. Banks needed mortgage payments to repopulate cash assets and advance developers the capital needed to pay workers who built housing and housing products. During the 1920s and 1930s, as it is today, housing, employment, and socioeconomic well-being proved to be inextricably linked.

For a country struggling with the Great Depression outcomes, several initiatives were brought forth by President Franklin D. Roosevelt's New Deal programs that focused on supporting banks and improving access to affordable and decent housing for U.S. citizens. In 1933, the Federal Emergency Administration for Public Works (PWA) expanded to accommodate socioeconomic recovery by creating jobs in low-cost home construction and reconstruction through its Housing Division. In addition to building new housing, a primary responsibility during these years was the clearance of inner-city poverty-stricken areas with the stated mission of improving neighborhood and community conditions. Postwar, families had few housing options. Many crammed into overcrowded shack-like tenements situated in unsafe and unsanitary urban conditions. Heating, toileting, bathing, or cooking amenities were missing or in disrepair. Such unlivable conditions contributed to public health risks for disease and death.

Some families were able to rent better quality apartments in the private rental market. However, the cost of rent in these units was too high for many low-income families. The federal government had both an obligation and an opportunity to bolster affordable housing supply and job creation through home construction and reconstruction. Since the demand for affordable housing exceeded the supply, the PWA, in its public regulatory capacity, would have a long tenure of employment opportunities for people constructing supplies and buildings in the housing industry.

Initially, the PWA attempted to outsource housing development by funding loans of up to 85% to low-profit private corporations that were state-regulated to build low-cost housing. PWA also offered 30% grants and 70% loans to local housing authorities for the same purpose. However, given the difficulty of private corporations to leverage loans with 15% equity and low construction yield from both measures, the PWA Housing Division created the Public Works Emergency Housing Corporation (PWEHC) and gave federal authority to this entity for direct housing development. This authority allowed them to purchase or acquire land and property for building low-cost housing. PWEHC enacted the urban renewal practice of "slum clearance," the process of reclaiming impoverished areas in the urban core and rebuilding. Additionally, the PWEHC built low-rent housing on cheap, vacant land on the periphery of towns. PWEHC was also explicitly authorized, through eminent domain, to take ownership of personal property considered in "slum" condition if the real estate could be used for a PWA housing project.

In 1934, the U.S. Congress passed the Federal Housing Act (FHA), which improved access to homes by making homeownership attainable for middle-class families. Before creating FHA, it was challenging for families to purchase housing due to prohibitive down payments and short mortgage repayment terms. Imagine having to put down 50% of the cost of a home as a down payment with an agreement to repay the balance within 5 years. For most people, especially during the Great Depression, this was simply not possible. Therefore, the FHA established a financing system that allowed more purchasers to borrow funds with lower interest rates and down payments for sizable home mortgages with extended repayment periods.

FHA legislation also created a secondary market, which insured mortgage loans and freed up cash reserves for banks by allowing investors to purchase interest in mortgages from lenders. However, for very low-income families, purchasing homes was still not a feasible option. Therefore, in 1937, Congress passed the Wagner-Steagall Act, which eliminated the PWA Housing Division and provided subsidies and loans to local public housing agencies through a newly created U.S. Housing Authority (USHA) to improve dilapidated conditions of state-regulated public housing units. This Act also included the provision that only one public housing unit could be built for every "slum" unit cleared. Immediately following the passage of this legislation, there were aggressive goals to build 50,000 units of public housing annually. However, due to shifts in political favor, by 1942, Congress cut funding for public housing programs.

After much acrimonious debate in Congress about the government's role in public housing development and fears about disruptions in the private housing market, public housing construction and "slum clearance" continued through the passage of the Housing Act of 1949. However, due to concerns about the continued middle-class flight from the urban core, which escalated impoverished housing development due to mass abandonment of dwellings, the strategy was repackaged as "urban development" to attract residents back into the urban core. Inner-city clearance during these times was significantly different from a decade before. New strategies included cities acquiring blighted urban neighborhoods from landlords unwilling to sell or improve properties and working with private developers to improve housing infrastructure and public facilities. This redevelopment was possible by using the power of eminent domain and federal loans and subsidies. However, a significant problem with this approach was that even if only 20% of homes were dilapidated, the land and properties would be acquired through eminent domain and the entire community cleared for redevelopment.

During this period of "slum clearance," ethnic communities were unfairly targeted and displaced. After redevelopment, doubled rents and explicitly racist policies prohibited these residents from moving back into the revitalized units. These outcomes were antithetical to the stated purpose of the 1949 legislation, which was President Truman's Fair Deal intention to provide an adequate and appropriate home and living environment for all families. In fact, since its beginning, public housing planning has been influenced by sociocultural conceptions of deservedness, based primarily on race. In practice, model village homes were built for White workers and their families, while shoddy barrack-styled homes or high-rise, densely packed buildings located at a distance were built for Black workers, even if employed by the same company. Racial segregation was codified in housing projects, officially excluding Black people from well-built communities to push them into overpopulated areas. The PWA's administrator implemented a "neighborhood composition rule," which segregated White public housing residents in designated units and Black residents in designated units. This policy was also enforced in neighborhoods that were already racially integrated.

Techwood Homes in Atlanta, Georgia was the first public housing unit built by the PWA and is an example of how the federal government destroyed racially integrated communities to build exclusively White public housing. In this project, 1,600 integrated low-income families, who lived close to where they worked, were removed from their homes. Their demolished units were rebuilt to accommodate 604 White-only families, displacing nearly 1,000 families into surrounding, overcrowded poor areas. Such segregated projects had a lingering effect, moving Black citizens away from jobs and critical resources and shifting them to, as noted by Rothstein (2017, p. 32), "high-rise ghettos," resulting in limited economic opportunities and making the sense of community "impossible."

In addition to these discriminatory practices repeated in most major cities across the United States, Black families were also systematically prohibited from moving out of public housing and into suburban communities, partially as a result of unequal economic standing but also due to exclusionary policies that restricted access to mortgage-assistance programs offered to White families. Although the G.I. Bill was created in 1944 to assist World War II veterans with low-interest mortgages to move into newly designed single-family home communities in the suburbs, Black veterans were denied access to G.I. Bill benefits and subsequently to the suburbs. Postwar, the housing market was booming, and Black families were left out of the wealth-building homeownership opportunities.

Another unfair tactic took the form of color-coded residential security maps in urban neighborhoods. For Black neighborhoods, a red marker was used by lending institutions to draw lines on maps to indicate which areas were unsuitable and too risky for loan approval, a process called "redlining." In this way, Black applicants were denied access to loans for purchasing homes in their neighborhoods or elsewhere.

In 1968, the Fair Housing Act was passed to address these violations of basic rights. The policy prohibits discrimination in housing sales, rentals, and financing based on race, religion, national origin, sex, and family status. Also, the Community Reinvestment Act of 1977 officially made redlining an illegal practice. This legislation also required lending institutions to invest credit resources in low- and moderate-income neighborhoods. However, many of these discriminatory practices are still evident today, using new tools, such as low-income market targeting and predatory lending for subpar loan products.

Social work practitioners must be aware of these discriminatory practices and advocate to mitigate the long-term effects of such policies. These early decisions have contributed to generational poverty and economic inequality for many families that struggle in present times. The temporal relationship between past housing discrimination and current poverty levels cannot be understated. According to a U.S. Census Bureau report, and as illustrated by Figure 11.1, the median household income from 1967 to 2018 has consistently demonstrated a gap between White and Black households.

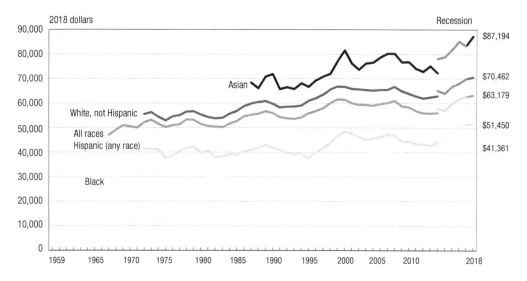

FIGURE 11.1 Real median household income by race and Hispanic origin: 1967 to 2018.
SOURCE: U.S. Census Bureau. Current Population Survey, 1968 to 2019, Annual Social and Economic Supplements. https://www.census.gov/content/dam/Census/library/visualizations/2019/demo/p60-266/figure2.pdf

As practitioners, we must think critically about the injustice of unfair housing practices on health disparities, educational and vocational inequities, and economic insecurity in affected communities. These lingering effects resulting from residential displacement, racial policies, and under delivered public housing resources continue to impact communities of color as well as public sentiments regarding housing.

PUBLIC HOUSING

Vale (2000) described public housing as a splinter, because it is "painful and difficult to dislodge." The federal government's initial intention was to build public housing in the context of a well-coordinated community, including high-quality primary schools, parks, and local shopping centers within walking distance. Developers and urban planners were counseled to build low-height, quality units with the purview of a long-term investment in resident well-being, rather than a quick sale of aggregated and monotonous housing units. Despite these intentions, much of the public housing stock turned out to be bleak and identifiable institutions, essentially stigmatizing inhabitants. One could point to these buildings and know that poor people lived there.

Early public housing projects were large buildings with courtyards added for communal space, ventilation, and improved lighting. Some architects built two-story apartments with courtyards and inexpensive single-family dwellings. During the New Deal intervention, housing reform goals were "model communities, rural assistance programs" (Davis, 1995, p. 11). Concerns with clearing slums began during the post-Depression period where intentional housing projects in New York were planned around a block complete with an interior courtyard with social service resources provided onsite. These post-Depression developments were undertaken to stimulate the economy, which reflected the intended goal of improving cities with high-quality housing (Davis, 1995).

By the 1940s and 1950s, the generous financial attention to public housing had changed. The general public believed that the high-quality amenities in public housing were too extravagant and that the people's responsibility was simply to provide the basics for those in need. As the government cut budgets for public housing design, large towers were erected to contain costs and more boldly approach public housing. High-rise buildings were supposed to be a visible testament to caring for the poor. However, these massive structures isolated yet simultaneously concentrated poverty as well.

One famous high-rise building, often the icon of public housing failure, was the Pruitt-Igoe project in St. Louis, Missouri. The poor design of this building included several stories of small apartments without "viewable, accessible play areas for children" (Davis, 1995, p. 6), as well as "alternate-floor elevations ... dark hallways" (Wright, 1981, pp. 236–237), and "unlivable" (Hayden, 2002, p. 168) conditions. By the 1960s, these high-rise buildings were in dilapidated condition and generally considered a government's failure to provide public housing. The deplorable and dangerous conditions of these buildings included broken windows and stinking waste, with plumbing and wiring pulled out of the walls. Gangs formed in these buildings, resulting in common physical and sexual assaults in stairwells, elevators, and abandoned floors (Bell et al., 2001).

In the early 1970s, many of these high-rise buildings were demolished and residents were relocated according to the Uniform Relocation Assistance and Real Property Acquisition Policies Act of 1970. This policy allowed the PWA to dispose of public housing property and use the proceeds to provide alternative low-income housing. Some families were dispersed into mixed-income communities considered less distressed than poverty-concentrated high-rise buildings. However, more units were destroyed than replaced and only a fraction of tenants were relocated. Some tenants were given housing vouchers that they could use to find housing in the private rental market, though, some property owners discriminately refused the vouchers. Among those landlords who would accept, many were located in distressed, segregated communities.

Being uprooted and displaced, tenants' social ties were broken and mutual aid was lost. Relationships that were built between residents for childcare, collective cooking, caregiving, emotional support, and transportation to the grocery store and doctors were ruptured by the forced relocation. Moreover, when residents were resettled into new communities, they were stigmatized, alienated, and left socially isolated and unsupported. These tenants were new to an unforgiving private rental market. They struggled with negotiating with landlords, paying utility bills, meeting work requirements, and being subject to eviction (Keene, 2016).

According to Keating (2000), four major problems diverged on public housing: (a) there was an increased number of families living in poverty and public housing due to federal legislation; (b) most of the public housing built before 1980 was physically deteriorating; (c) the crack cocaine epidemic of the 1980s left many families in public housing in devastating conditions; and (d) between 1980 and 1998, HUD's annual appropriation for housing issues was underfunded. To address the failures of public housing, mission-driven developers began investing in a mixed-income housing strategy.

MIXED-INCOME DEVELOPMENT

Mixed-income development is considered a better solution to address affordable housing needs since federal, state, and local subsidies can be used to sensibly share apartment complexes for low-and moderate-income families. Mixed-income housing combines market rate with affordable units. Private and nonprofit developers are incentivized to build this type of housing with preferential (reduced) financing costs and tax credits through the Low-Income Housing

Tax Credit (LIHTC) program. Mixed-income properties typically designate 80% of units as market rate and 20% as affordable. One advantage of this approach is deconcentration of poverty. Low-income families can also become situated in healthy communities with improved access to local and municipal resources, such as schools, hospitals, and employment opportunities.

Development of mixed-income housing also engages private, nonprofit, and public entities in a collaborative partnership to address the affordability crisis. This arrangement relieves the federal government of sole responsibility for housing low-income people. However, the success of this approach rests on the ability to secure desirable marketable locations for building. Also, these multifamily properties must be desirable to drive competition among renters with various housing options. If the mixed-income property is not in a suitable community or does not appeal to the higher-income renter, the outcome will be concentrated poverty since only people with the fewest housing options will want to live there. Restrictive zoning that excludes multifamily dwellings in attractive neighborhoods can also be a barrier to success.

FROM THE FIELD 11.1

CODIFYING HOUSING AFFORDABILITY

To qualify for public housing, residents had to earn less than four or, in some cases, five times the rent. Even still, many low-income families could not afford PWA-developed public housing units. Therefore, in the 1960s, the newly formed HUD began subsidized public housing rents, and residents were required to pay only 25% of their income. This capped rent requirement was codified in 1969 by Congress with the Brooke Amendment. In 1981, the percentage changed to a 30% threshold. Later, the federal government dramatically cut back funding for low-income housing assistance. Between 1981 and 1988, the Reagan administration cut funding for affordable housing from $4.2 billion to less than $600 million and housing units from 18,000 to just over 3,000 (Squires, 1994). Despite the ebb and flow of support and opposition to public housing, over the next 20 years, 810,000 units were designed to fit municipal interests.

Housing Market Affordability

At the time of the first U.S. housing census in 1940, there were already 37 million housing units located primarily in central urban and metropolitan cities. Following the steady growth of home purchases, the dampening effects of the Great Depression left many households in foreclosure and in deficient units that required significant repair; some 31% had no running water, 44% had no bathing facilities, and 35% had no flushing toilet. Home values declined severely, and unlike the times before the war, renters outnumbered homeowners (Devaney, 1994). Foreclosure rates quadrupled from pre- to postwar times from 3.6 foreclosures to 13.3 foreclosures per 1,000 dwellings from 1926 to 1933 (Ghent, 2011).

Even in an unsteady housing market, negotiations for more affordable mortgages were a matter between the mortgager and the lender. Sometimes, banks would decide to forgive a percentage of the loan rather than leave a family with no other options but to foreclose the property. Due to the economic downfall, it was in the bank's best interest to try to hold on to the loan relationship. This simple relationship between the banker and family defines the primary housing market. However, as the national crisis demonstrated, dramatic economic shifts that result in high unemployment could leave banking institutions and homeowners vulnerable to loan defaults. Still, many bankers would not adjust mortgages and instead required homeowners to continue making payments. Many of these loans were short term with large final payments, called "balloon" payments. Therefore, in 1933, the federal government established the Home Owners' Loan Corporation (HOLC), which allowed struggling families to apply for assistance. The HOLC would acquire the troubled loan from the bank using a secured bond arrangement, thereby effectively allowing the family to "refinance" payments over an extended period. This idea of issuing bonds to allow a borrower more time to pay for housing contributed to our current system of securing mortgages through a secondary housing market. After the FHA of 1934 solidified the mortgage securitization and made home purchases readily available to middle-class families, there was a sharp growth in homeownership that spread beyond the urban core into primarily suburban areas.

In 1938, Congress created the Federal National Mortgage Association (renamed "Fannie Mae") to secure the secondary market further. This institution purchased FHA-insured mortgages from banks and independent brokers to free up capital for new home loans to low- and middle-income borrowers. The goal was to support a new generation of homeowners to fit the predominantly prevailing idea of fulfilling the American Dream. If individuals could commit to mortgage payments for many years, they were seen as more likely to remain independent, employed, and good citizens.

By 1968, Fannie Mae was so successful in securing loans that institutional debt was converted into publicly traded commodities to be bought and sold by investors on the stock exchange. In practice, banks would originate loans to home purchasers (primary mortgage market), then bundle multiple mortgages into a security to be sold to investors (secondary mortgage market). Although investors were not directly involved in the loans' originations, they could be assured about their investments because of the bank's screening practices and the secondary market's importance to the American home finance system. In essence, the U.S. government "backed" the transactions. This mortgage-backed finance system shored up banks' and mortgage brokers' capacity to loan money and opened opportunities for homebuyers and investors in the stock market. Life insurance companies were the largest investors of FHA-insured mortgages through the 1940s (Schwartz, 2015). In 1970, the government created the Federal Home Loan Mortgage Corporation (Freddie Mac) to provide competition for Fannie Mae and prevent it from holding a monopoly.

According to the U.S. Census Bureau, home prices increased dramatically from the 1940s to the early 2000s. The median home price in 1940 was $30,600, and in 2000, the median rose to $119,600 (Devaney, 1994). Major drivers of this price change were inflation, increased interest rates, and federal deregulation of lending institutions. Savings accounts played a significant role in the lending industry. In a simplistic depiction, banks (initially called "Savings and Loans") would pay small interest payments to people who deposited money into their savings accounts. The deposited money would then be loaned to borrowers who used the money to purchase homes. To reap a profit, banks paid out smaller percentages of interest to depositors than they charged borrowers with 30-year fixed interest payments. However, as inflation caused increasing interest rates, banks were stressed by having to pay more in interest than they could yield in fixed interest from borrowers. The federal government began to regulate the maximum amount of interest paid to depositors to avoid mass bankruptcies. However, in the 1970s, a series of banking policies such as deregulation and newer options for depositors pushed banks into more crisis. To compensate, banks began offering adjustable rate mortgages (ARMs) to pass the risk of increasing interest rates to borrowers.

Although this pass-through strategy helped stabilize banks, in 1989, the federal government interceded again by passing the Financial Institutions, Reform, Recovery, and Enforcement Act. This legislation set new regulatory standards on banks that restricted their ability to originate loans, hold on to mortgages in a portfolio, or support the borrowing needs of multifamily property investors (Schwartz, 2015). As a result, banks were more likely to package multiple mortgages into a bundle and sell them into the secondary market, through nonbank mortgage lenders, to liquidate capital for making new loans. Investors in the secondary market would purchase these bundled mortgages as bonds to earn income on an aggregated stream of payments (Massey & Rugh, 2018). Bundled mortgage bonds are good sources of market income for investors unless some mortgages in the bundle are defaulted. Missed payments on mortgages affect the stream of income to investors and disrupt the secondary market's economic security. These policy shifts, along with predatory lending practices and defaulted loans, would later lead to a housing crisis in the early 2000s.

After an economic boom in the 1990s and a swell in home prices during the early 2000s, America experienced a definitive bust of the housing market bubble in 2007. In fact, in February of that year, a senior economist in Community Affairs at the Federal Reserve Bank of Kansas City published an article entitled "Rising foreclosures in the United States: A perfect storm" (Edmiston & Zalneraitis, 2007). The article detailed the significant events leading to record-high mortgage foreclosure filings: subprime lending, ARMs, high loan-to-value origination, and falling home prices. "Storm" was an appropriate characterization because a combination of poorly transacted mortgages, predatory practices, and economic challenges led to mortgage delinquencies that rose sharply from 4.49% in 2006 to 10.06% in 2010 (Schwartz, 2015).

Subprime lending is a process of issuing high-interest loans to borrowers who are considered at risk for mortgage default. Although they do not have the best interest rates (prime rates), these loans may be attractive for low-income families because they often do not require large down payments, if any upfront payment at all. Meaning, a person could secure a home mortgage without bringing any money to the table. Therefore, even if you were financially vulnerable with impaired credit, a subprime loan would likely be approved because the high interest rate charged absorbs the bank's risk of taking a chance with you, the borrower (Immergluck & Smith, 2005). However, because these loans are often of variable rate, repayment amounts could vary widely as interest rates fluctuate. An ARM would benefit a mortgagor when interest rates are low because the monthly payment would drop lower. However, when interest rates rise, payments can be unpredictable and unaffordable.

Subprime mortgage loans, just like prime loans, were bundled together and sold into the secondary market. Instead of bundling all high-quality prime loans, investment bankers would sprinkle in low-quality subprime loans, thereby spreading riskier loans among the stable investments and increasing the number of bundles. Over time, the number of subprime loans increased because they became profitable for loan originators who received high fees from borrowers and investment firms that wanted to sell them.

Predatory and Fraudulent Lending Practices for Communities of Color

Black home buyers were attractive consumers to target for subprime loans. Even when Black applicants met the criteria for high-quality prime loans, lenders deceptively steered them toward inferior lending products with high interest rates, prepayment penalties, and exorbitant fees. Many of the predatory practices were focused on Black families that already owned homes. Billboards and posters were placed in Black communities, while telemarketers called homeowners in these neighborhoods to encourage subprime refinancing to pull out accumulated home equity. These strategies are called "reverse redlining." Predators bought mailing lists from Black business owners and paid contributions to Black clergy to endorse lending products. As a result, Black home buyers were 50% more likely to be channeled into expensive, risky loans and 70% more likely to end up in foreclosure (Massey & Rugh, 2018).

Fraudulent lending practices also significantly impact Hispanic and Native American communities. Although Hispanic applicants did not tend to pay more on refinanced loans, they paid significantly more for mortgage loans than White borrowers (Barwick, 2010). Tribal leaders in Native American communities reported additional predatory processes, such as lenders adding unnecessary fees to loans, pushing for repeated loan refinancing without benefit to the borrower, requiring credit insurance to be paid upfront or in a single payment, practicing abusive collection practices, and failing to report accurate loan balances (Smith, 2003).

Exploitative lenders also originated loans that were more than home values. When a person purchased a home without a down payment, they secured a mortgage for the home's value plus the cost of originating the mortgage, brokers' fees, and other miscellaneous charges that were a part of the process. The total loan might amount to 107% of the home price (Edmiston & Zalneraitis, 2007). In some cases, the applicant had to take out a first and second mortgage to afford the purchase of the home. So, the borrower was immediately "underwater" in mortgages, meaning that they owed more than the home's value and had negative equity. Therefore, if the buyer experienced financial trouble, selling the home to stabilize was not an option because they would be unable to sell the house for enough to repay the loan(s). The more likely outcome after missing a few payments was defaulting on the loan(s), foreclosure of the property, and damaged credit. These exploitative practices highlight the need for financial literacy for social workers and our clients. Social workers must be aware of these unfair methods and other exploitative tactics associated with finances in order to support clients navigating these risky practices.

Another contribution to the perfect storm was the sharp decline of U.S. home prices, which began in 2007. During the collapse, home values declined nationally by 35%, and by 2013, over 7.6 million homes had negative equity (Schwartz, 2015; Zonta & Edelman, 2015). Loss of home equity translated conclusively to loss of family wealth. From 2006 to 2013, U.S. households lost over $7 trillion in home equity. Furthermore, low-income homeowners and people of color were particularly hard-hit by these losses since home prices at the lower end of the housing market spectrum experienced the sharpest declines in value (Ellen & Dastrup, 2012). Between 2005 and 2009, compared to the decrease in White household wealth (16%), declines in Black (53%) and Hispanic (66%) household wealth were greater (Aguirre & Martinez, 2014).

Further complicating matters during this time of increased subprime lending, market instability, and mounting foreclosures was an increase in job loss. The unemployment rate rose to a high of over 10% in 2009. Therefore, in 2009, newly elected President Barack Obama created several housing initiatives under his Making Home Affordable Program. The Home Affordable Modification Program (HAMP) was an incentive-based program that paid lenders for working directly with homeowners to avoid foreclosure. If a mortgagor was paying more than 31% of household income on housing costs, they could claim financial hardship and receive reductions in their monthly payment, mortgage principal, or interest rate. In some instances, loan payments could be temporarily postponed. A complementary program, established the same year, was the Home Affordable Refinance Program (HARP), which assisted homeowners who were underwater on loans and had high loan-to-value ratios by allowing them to refinance their mortgages. The Home Affordable Foreclosure Alternative (HAFA) program provided incentives for lenders to assist underwater homeowners in selling their houses with forgiveness of remaining balances, whereas the

Home Affordable Unemployment Program (UP) reduced or suspended mortgage payments up to 1 year for borrowers seeking a job. Although these programs were successful in helping some financially stressed families, overall, the Making Home Affordable Program fell short of its benchmarks (Bratt & Immergluck, 2016). However, the American Recovery and Reinvestment Act of 2009 (ARRA), also called the "Obama stimulus package of 2009," was a bolder investment of over $800 billion used to jumpstart the economy, reverse unemployment, and improve healthcare, education, and infrastructure.

FROM THE FIELD 11.2

HOUSING IN RURAL AMERICA

There is much to be done to help rural communities with affordable and decent housing. According to the National Rural Housing Coalition, 20% of the population in rural America is living in poverty. Although 30% of rural households have major housing problems, such as affordability, physical deficiencies, and overcrowding, more attention is paid to urban housing development. However, the U.S. Department of Agriculture Rural Development and Community Facilities (USDA RD) assists in several rental and homeownership programs in rural areas. For example, low-income owner-occupants can secure guaranteed financing to purchase modestly priced homes. Very low-income households may seek loans and grants for home improvement and modernization through the Section 504 program. The Section 515 program issues loans to developers to build housing for older adults. And, farmers in aquaculture and agriculture benefit from Section 514/516 programs, which provide loans (514) and grants (516) to farmwork associations, nonprofit agencies, Native American tribes, and public agencies to develop and rehab on-farm and off-farm housing. However, funding for these programs has nearly diminished over the last few decades, and housing contracts developed through USDA RD have only 30-year guarantees (National Low Income Housing Coalition [NLIHC], (2019). Housing Needs in Rural America. https://nlihc.org/sites/default/files/Housing-Needs-in-Rural-America.pdf). Once the development agreements for funded properties mature, these units can convert to market-rate rentals, thereby further reducing the stock of affordable housing in rural communities.

RENTAL MARKET AFFORDABILITY

Discontentment about unaffordable rent traces back to strikes in the early 1900s. During those times, secondary landlords in New York, called "listers," leased buildings, then rented individual apartments to families. After being exploited by continuous rent hikes, tenant leaders organized strikes and ceased payments to express opposition. Many families were evicted and their items were tossed out onto the street. Similar strikes recurred in the 1930s when women and children picketed and demanded rent reductions. These organizers also fought to preserve rent-control policies put in place during wartime. From these often brutal encounters, poor conditions of slum tenements and acrimonious tensions between landlords and tenants became well known.

Rent control has a long history internationally but was adopted in the United States in the 1920s, following the Ball Rent Act of 1919. This law established a three-person commission to review and assess whether rent fees were reasonable and fair. An assessment of unreasonable or oppressive rent costs was enough to provide tenants a defense against landlords seeking to evict. After World War I, the first generation of rent-control policies was implemented to manage the shortage of housing available to low- and moderate-income tenants. Often used to manage housing emergencies, tenant strikes, and riots from the 1930s to the early 1970s, these regulations either froze rent levels or rolled back rent to a previous level as a form of affordable adjustment. Rent control was meant to be a legislative tool to protect financially vulnerable tenants but was also considered the landlords' rights to due process and fair returns on their investments.

The second generation of rent control was pushed during the 1970s, but these newer policies focused more on rent stabilization than strict control. The shift to stabilization was a response to complaints about rent control decreasing the supply of rental housing in communities. Instead of releasing all control of units, stabilization allowed municipalities to maintain commitments to affordable units. These newer policies allowed periodic rent increases on some, but not all tenant buildings, to a capped rental price threshold. Second-generation policies have been implemented mostly in coastal municipalities like New York and California, rather than throughout most states. Most states preempt rent control. Today, only New York, New Jersey, California, Maryland, and the District of Columbia have active rent-control and rent-stabilization laws (Rajasekaran et al., 2019). However, existing rent-controlled units can be changed to rent stabilization if the unit becomes vacant or if the incremental increases in rental price reach the stabilization threshold. Furthermore, rent-stabilized units can become deregulated and changed to market-rate units once they reach an absolute rent cap. Therefore, availability of rent-controlled and rent-stabilized units is declining.

Tenant advocacy groups oppose restrictions and state preemptions of rent-control policies. Rent control regulates adherence to fair evictions, reduces demolition of affordable units, and restricts the conversion of controlled units to owner-occupied condominiums. Rent control also mitigates gentrification's harmful effects in areas where affordable housing is needed, maintains neighborhood stability, prevents resident displacement, and maximizes inclusivity (Glaeser, 2003).

Despite these benefits, some research has found that rent-controlled units may reduce the supply of rental property in a community, thereby driving up the cost of available market-rate apartments due to renter competition for insufficient stock (Diamond et al., 2019). However, decontrolling units may also trigger median price increases in rental markets. For example, the elimination of rent control in Cambridge, Massachusetts increased median rent prices 40% between 1994 and 1997 (Autor et al., 2014). Decontrolling units also sparked a sharp turnover of residents from lower income to more affluent renters.

In 1974, Congress authorized HUD to issue rental assistance through Section 8 of the Housing and Community Development Act to help low-income families find decent housing in the private rental market and outside of public housing. The intention of this Section 8 Housing Choice Voucher program was to deconcentrate poverty and allow residents to choose where they lived. Low-income families apply for the voucher through their local housing authorities. If approved for the program, tenants search for, select, then negotiate the lease conditions directly with the landlord. Upon accepting the lease, the resident pays 30% of the rent and utilities, or a minimum of $50. The local housing authority subsidizes the remainder through direct payments to the landlord.

To provide guidance for reasonable rental agreements in the Housing Choice Voucher Program, and other initiatives, HUD sets standards for rental fees through a Fair Market Rent (FMR) schedule based on location. The amount of rent that is fair and reasonable varies widely depending on where one lives. For example, in San Francisco, California, the 2020 FMR for a two-bedroom apartment is $3,339 per month, while in Columbus, Georgia, the 2020 FMR for the same type of dwelling is $790. Notably, rent affordability is relative to where you live. Although long waiting lists to obtain a voucher have been a significant barrier, the program assists over 5 million people, including 2.2 million low-income tenants. Assisted renters can then compete for housing in the private rental market (Center on Budget and Policy Priorities [CBPP], 2020). Vouchers can also be distributed for project-based purposes and be used to improve the quality of mortgaged properties to serve the needs of low-income families. In this case, the voucher stays with the property, not the renter, to ensure that the home remains affordable. Despite the success of this program, only one of four people who qualify for federal housing assistance receives it.

According to an executive summary report published by the HUD, Office of Policy Development and Research, on the Worst Case Housing Needs in 2015, there were 8.3 million unassisted renters who earn less than 50% of the local area median income (AMI). These individuals pay more than half of their income in housing costs and live in substandard housing conditions. This population represents nearly 5% of American families, which has been the trend since 1997. Of this population, 77% are extremely low income, earning less than 30% of the AMI. Over 30% of these households are families with children, and 22% are people over the age of 65 years. Families with nonelderly members make up 10% of the worst-case population. Even today, racial disparities persist and are evident in current statistics that report 20% of Black households, 17% of American Indian or Alaska Native households, 15% of Hispanic households, and 10% of Asian households are extremely low-income renters, compared to only 6% of White households (NLIHC, 2019).

The private rental market does not provide enough affordable housing for low-income families. In a report documenting the availability of affordable rental homes, the National Low-Income Housing Coalition (NLIHC, 2019) estimates that, in the United States, there is an absolute shortage of 7 million affordable rental units available to the 10.9 million extremely low-income households that need them. Although there are 7.3 million affordable rental units, extremely low-income households must compete with very low-income and low-income households for limited units. Therefore, extremely low-income renters occupy only 4 million available units, accounting for only 6 of 10 of the extremely low-income renters in need of housing who have it with an additional 4 of 10 low-income renters with access to housing, leaving the majority of those renters without access to affordable housing.

FROM THE FIELD 11.3

FAIR MARKET RENT

What is the FMR where you live? Go to www.huduser.gov/portal/datasets/fmr.html to learn more about rental standards in your community. How affordable is rent in your community for someone earning minimum wage?

CASE STUDY 11.1—DENISE'S LOTTERY

Recently, I had a conversation with one of my closest friends about her plans to move from her apartment into another affordable unit. I was astounded by the complexity of the application process. Denise and I grew up in New Jersey, graduated from the same high school, and were college roommates. After graduating with two degrees, Denise pursued her lifelong dream of becoming a licensed sports massage therapist. At age 50, she is currently employed part-time with a minor league soccer team, part-time with a country club, and manages clients in her private practice. Denise earns $46,000 annually and currently lives with her adult son in an urban two-bedroom apartment. Her rent is $900 per month, and despite paying on time, she must often make complaints to the building superintendent about poor property management.

Since Denise believes her home environment is no longer conducive to her health, she endeavors to move into a one-bedroom affordable housing apartment. Her son is also moving out on his own. Denise explained: "Finding affordable housing in a good and safe neighborhood is like finding a needle in a haystack. There are programs like HUD, and websites that will guide you to affordable housing, but most of those rental units are run-down and in unsafe neighborhoods." Denise completed a preliminary application for an affordable housing unit in a mixed-income property located in a suburban community. Optimistically, she followed directions to register for a newsletter that would keep her informed of the selection process. After waiting 3 weeks, Denise received a letter in the mail informing her that she "may be eligible for the program and that a random selection will determine the priority order of [her] application." Out of 1,300 applicants, her lottery number was 867. Deflated, but persistent, she still waited to find out if she would be chosen. She stated: "The shocking part of this process was finding out that out of 225 apartments, only 35 were allocated as affordable units." Several weeks later, she is still waiting.

STRATEGIES FOR ENSURING AFFORDABILITY

Denise is a good example of even when families, financially vulnerable or otherwise, can access available housing, for most of them units remain unaffordable due to the income-to-rent cost burden. When households pay more than 30% of income on housing, they are considered cost-burdened. They are unlikely to be as able to afford other necessities such as food, clothing, medical care, childcare, transportation, or leisure activities. Severely cost-burdened households pay 50% or more of their incomes on housing costs. As expected, extremely low-income renters are most likely to be severely cost-burdened. Over 70% of Hispanic, Black, and White extremely low-income families pay more than 50% of their incomes on rent (Aurand et al., 2020).

People working for minimum wage cannot afford housing at the HUD's FMR. Therefore, many housing advocates support the implementation of a housing wage, a different metric used to measure housing affordability. A housing wage is the amount of money a person needs to earn to afford rent in a modest home without being cost-burdened. In 2019, the national housing wage was $22.96 per hour to afford a two-bedroom rental, while the federal minimum wage is only $7.25 per hour. This low rate means that a person earning minimum wage would have to work three full-time jobs or 103 hours per week to afford a two-bedroom apartment (Aurand et al., 2019).

Think about the impact of this wage gap on young adults, people who are disabled, and older adults on fixed incomes seeking a stable home.

Racial disparities are also evident as we look at housing affordability. According to the U.S. Department of Labor, during the first quarter of 2020, the median weekly income for full-time workers was $957, or nearly $24 per hour in a 40-hour workweek. However, the median weekly income for full-time Black workers was $775 ($19.37/hour), Hispanic workers $722 ($18.05/hour), White workers $979 ($24.48/hour), and Asian workers $1,221 ($30.53/hour). Gender disparities further complicate the wage gap since women earn less than men at all income levels. The inability to afford even modest rentals due to insufficient income keeps financially vulnerable families out of reach of housing opportunities. Further, being severely cost-burdened in unaffordable housing puts already vulnerable families at a significant risk of being evicted or falling into homelessness.

Evictions. Harvard sociologist and Pulitzer Prize Awardee Matthew Desmond published a compelling account of the state and nature of evictions in the United States. In his book, *Evicted: Poverty and Profit in the American City* (2016), he followed the lives and tragedies of eight families in Milwaukee who struggled to remain housed but succumbed to eviction in an exploitative rental market system. Detailed stories depicted in this nonfiction book describe the desperate and cyclical circumstances that push and keep low-income families in precarious housing situations. The book also documents how tenants experience serial evictions and are subject to reside in squalor housing conditions at the expense of predatory landlords seeking to capitalize on poverty.

Desmond (2020) defines eviction as a landlord-initiated action that involuntarily removes renters from the property. He estimated that in 2016, over 2.6 million evictions were filed in the United States, equating to a rate of four evictions every 4 minutes. Evictions can occur when renters are at fault by not making rent payments, boarding other people, or violating a lease. Renters can also be evicted without reason. These "no-fault" evictions are relatively common in the rental market. A renter's lease may be terminated because the landlord claims the dwelling is being foreclosed, sold, or being recalled for personal use (Rodriguez-Dod, 2013). Unfair evictions are also disproportionately discriminatory, and affected tenants may be unaware of laws that protect them, be unable to afford legal representation, or fear situations considered far worse than eviction. Whereas 90% of landlords have attorneys represent their interests in eviction court, only 10% of tenants obtain legal counsel (Desmond, 2015). Rarely do these unrepresented tenants win their cases, even when they have strong cases. For example, landlords may try to exploit renters sexually, then carry out evictions when refused (Purser, 2016). They may also turn off utilities or lock renters out of their homes. In some cases, landlords may pay renters cash to evict the tenant unofficially, thereby saving on court costs and usurping the legal eviction process (Rodriguez-Dod, 2013). Still, these landlords are likely to be successful in court. However, when renters appear in court with legal counsel, they are more likely to avoid eviction.

In power-laden positions, landlords can file several evictions against renters as a rent collection method or threat. Serial filings for routine rent collection or to control tenants is an increasing problem nationally. Eviction filings have doubled from 1.2 million in 2000 to 2.4 million in 2016 (Desmond, 2020). However, only a small portion of evictions are carried through. The consequence of this unchecked eviction filing power is that financially vulnerable residents are subjugated by landlords and locked in housing precarity. A common outcome is damaged credit and psychological suffering (Garboden & Rosen, 2019).

Involuntary residential displacement destabilizes access to social connections, neighborhood institutions, economic opportunities, and community resources. Adverse outcomes associated with evictions are deteriorating mental and physical health, such as depression, anxiety, social isolation, and even suicide. In a vivid book about the lives of people barely surviving on $2 a day,

Edin and Shaefer (2015) wrote that families have often "doubled up with kin or friends" (p. 73) because their income simply is not sufficient to maintain stable housing.

People forced into stress-inducing housing situations are exposed to overcrowding, violence, abuse, and toxic environmental conditions, thereby negatively affecting their health (Zewde et al., 2019).

CASE STUDY 11.2—JANEEN'S EVICTION

In 2014, I studied the narratives of 21 women who rented rooms in budget hotels after leaving or being evicted from their homes. All of the women suffered through many housing-related traumas. However, I will never forget Janeen's story. After being late on her rent, the hotel manager evicted her into housing instability, even after paying on time for 4 years. In her narrative, she describes late fees, eviction fees, legal fees, court fees, accumulating and compounding interest on arrears, and application fees that kept her locked in precarious housing and unable to participate in the housing market financially. Here is an excerpt of her story from that study:

> Being evicted from the apartment and having to pay attorney fees ... they add up. If you don't pay anything on them, they're going to keep charging interest on it. The interest per day is about $4 or $5 a day ... for the attorney fees. When I had to go to court on [an] eviction, the attorney was there. He said, "Well ma'am, if you can pay this amount by Wednesday of that following week, then you'll be caught up. But if you're unable to, then you're going to also owe attorney fees." You have to pay them for filing something in court and the court cost. I owed $1,059 for rent and a dispossessory warrant because they charge you $250 for that. I paid it by that day, but more was added afterward because I couldn't pay [attorney's fees]. When she sent me the letter in the mail, it was over $2,000 after they added the additional amount. Yeah, it's like a rip-off, and I'm still evicted. Prior to that, I hadn't had any problem paying my rent throughout that whole 4 years that we'd been there. (Lewinson et al., 2014, p. 198)

Like Janeen, renters who are late with payments may be responsible for paying an additional 10%–15% more in fees in an eviction (Purser, 2016). The unfortunate reality is that once a tenant is ejected from housing, the forced dispossession is recorded on rental history, making it difficult to obtain housing elsewhere. For Janeen, she later spent hundreds of dollars filling out declined apartment applications before paying week to week in a budget hotel. The devastating impact of evictions is evident not only on tenants' mental and physical health but also on their financial well-being as fees and accumulating arrears keep people in poverty.

Evictions are not only the result of poverty but also a contribution to being further marginalized. A record of evictions restricts rehousing options. Families are left more financially depleted since they must reconcile additional costs, penalties, and debts associated with eviction filing, court bills, interest on arrears, and apartment application fees. These compounding expenses create debt cycles that are profitable for exploitive landlords with the ability to wield eviction threats at vulnerable tenants. For many low-income renters, tenant-landlord tension, eviction threat, forced displacement, and insufficient affordable alternatives are pathways into homelessness.

Aside from usual challenges associated with evictions, tenants experience high risk of involuntary dispossession during times of recession, when unemployment, home foreclosures, and rising rents increase. Similar to the mass evictions that occurred during the Great Recession when unemployment and foreclosures were high (Kochhar, 2020), the economic downturn from the coronavirus disease 2019 (COVID-19) pandemic threatens record numbers of foreclosures and evictions. To circumvent mass housing expulsions and possible homelessness during the pandemic, Congress passed the Coronavirus Aid, Relief, and Economic Security (CARES) Act of 2020. The CARES Act provides federal funding for housing assistance and places a temporary moratorium on evictions and foreclosures of mortgages and housing projects backed and subsidized by federal programs. However, little is known about the extent of housing displacement that will occur when these protections expire.

SOCIAL WORKER PERSPECTIVE 11.1

JEANELLE JENKINS, LCSW, ACM-SW, SOCIAL SERVICES MANAGER, CARE COORDINATION, EMORY UNIVERSITY HEALTHCARE, ATLANTA, GA

As a social worker in a major metropolitan hospital, I often witness how a lack of fair and affordable housing negatively impacts medical care and convalescence. It is not uncommon to see patients who live in poor housing conditions face respiratory issues and inadequate space for appropriate medical equipment and postacute care services. Housing that does not address the needs of those with disabilities, even if temporary, is also a challenge. For patients who have become incapacitated due to a temporary or permanent medical condition, inadequate access to upper floors prevents them from returning home promptly as safety is a concern. Those with no housing have their care compromised upon discharge by an inability to manage the medications they require upon discharge, which often leads to multiple readmissions. Also, arranging for postacute care services is not even possible for those without housing, often leading to complications that adversely impact patients. Even the best medical care has no lasting effect if safe, affordable, and fair housing does not exist for those who desperately need it.

HOMELESSNESS

In 2019, an estimated 568,000 individuals were reported to be homeless on a single night (Henry et al., 2020). According to the National Law Center on Homelessness and Poverty (2015), the top five reasons for homelessness are (a) lack of affordable housing, (b) unemployment, (c) poverty, (d) mental illness and the lack of needed services, and (e) substance abuse and the lack of needed services. A shortage of affordable housing impedes individuals who are experiencing homelessness from improving or achieving an optimal health status. Housing is the primary form of intervention for homeless people with healthcare challenges.

The history of homelessness in the United States is expansive and quite beyond the scope of this chapter. However, as a social worker, you will likely work with people who are displaced from housing. It is helpful to understand how attitudes about homelessness have shifted over time, as populations in this situation have changed.

Ever since the American Revolution, homeless people were called the "itinerant poor," "hoboes," or "tramps." Middle-class America characterized these migrant people as radical, counter-cultured White men who traveled indiscriminately and asserted their independence from industrialism by working only temporarily (DePastino, 2003). However, in the 1920s, civil unrest and migrant labor disputes were associated with hoboes, which reduced these temporary and seasonal workers to an inferior and unequal class, especially for men from non-White racial groups. Since vagrancy was considered a migrant work matter, local and state solutions at the time centered on improving wages and expanding long-term employment opportunities.

By the 1980s, modern homelessness emerged as a chronic condition that affected not only men but also women, children, and families. Several factors explained the sharp increase in homeless numbers, including gentrification, unemployment, conservative budget cuts, and even the HIV/AIDS epidemic. Deinstitutionalizing several thousands of mental health patients into the community without appropriate resources also contributed to the problem. Many of these patients moved into single-room-occupancy residential hotels (SROs) for cheap housing. However, not unlike the decline of public housing units in the 1970s, the SROs were converted to expensive apartments at the same time, forcing many people into homelessness. These conversions continued well into the 1990s until they were ceded during a moratorium. Still, the loss of SRO units further reduced available affordable housing.

In the 1970s, disenfranchised, homeless people were unemployed and financially destitute (DePastino, 2003). Many ate at mission kitchens and then slept in abandoned buildings or overcrowded, impoverished alleyways. Skid Row in Los Angeles is an extreme example of people experiencing chronic homelessness, where they reside in a 50-block downtown perimeter. However, the majority of homeless people live in sheltered locations, such as emergency shelters and transitional homes (63%), and do not live on the streets. Still, there have been modest increases in street homeless among individuals since 2016. Moreover, although there have been slight decreases in homelessness among families with children and veterans, the number of unsheltered individuals with patterns of chronic homelessness has increased since 2018 (HUD, 2020a). Among the chronically homeless, nearly half of the 35,000 unaccompanied homeless youth between the ages of 18 and 24 years are unsheltered.

One of the first federal responses to the homeless crisis was the Homeless Persons' Survival Act of 1986, which after many iterations eventually became the McKinney-Vento Homeless Assistance Act in 1987 posthumously in honor of two supporting politicians. This legislation set in motion emergency relief measures and homeless resources, such as emergency shelter, education, job training, healthcare, and transitional and permanent housing. In 1997, the McKinney-Vento Act also created the U.S. Interagency Council on Homelessness (USICH). This independent council evaluates the effectiveness of federal homeless programs and publicizes funding opportunities for community organizations. McKinney-Vento was amended and renamed several times throughout the 1990s before being absorbed into the Homeless Emergency Assistance and Rapid Transition Housing Act of 2009 (HEARTH). Published in the Federal Registry in December of 2011, the HEARTH Act consolidated three separate housing assistance programs, established a final rule on the definition of homelessness, and codified in law HUD's commitment to Continuum of Care (CoC) planning. HUD's definition of "homeless" includes both families and individuals who lack a regular, stable, and adequate nighttime residence.

To address the needs of people threatened by or defined as homeless, HUD's CoC commits funds to rehouse individuals and families quickly, minimize the trauma associated with displacement, maximize access and utilization of programs, and optimize self-sufficiency among people experiencing homelessness. State and local governments, nonprofit organizations, and public housing agencies can apply for HUD grants through this program to develop permanent housing, transitional housing, supportive services, homeless management information systems (HMIS), homelessness prevention, safe haven plans, and existing SRO rehabilitation projects.

SO, WHY IS HOUSING STILL UNAFFORDABLE?

Given the progressive history of public housing development, mortgage financing, rental policy, eviction moratorium, and homelessness programming in this country, why is housing still unaffordable? Some of the many factors include: low income-to-rent/mortgage ratios, reduced supply to meet demand, increased transportation costs, increased gentrification, housing unsuitability for U.S. households, increased housing costs, slow-growth regulations, and exclusionary zoning and land use regulation. Let us take a look at each one in turn.

- **Wages/Housing Cost Ratios.** Many low-income families spend over 30% of their income on housing costs. Since 30% has been set as a benchmark for housing affordability standards, it is clear that many families are cost-burdened and must struggle to make rent and mortgage payments with insufficient income. Worse still, there are 11 million extremely low-income renters who have incomes at or below the poverty line (NLIHC, 2021). Nearly 73% of these renters pay more than half of their incomes on rent and utilities. Low-income wages have not allowed some renters to compete fairly in the rental market. As the cost of rent increases, real income (accounting for inflation) has decreased, causing an ever-growing disparity between what one earns and what one can afford to pay for housing (Edin & Shaefer, 2015). This mismatch between income and housing costs is a problem for the chronically poor, senior households, and people with disabilities and also for laborers earning 120% of the median income, such as teachers, salespeople, and construction workers.

- **Reduced Supply/High Demand.** Despite the high demand for affordable housing, the market has not kept up with the demand. As a reaction to the failed high-rise, high-density public housing programs of the past, HUD has demolished 61,000 of these older public housing units but replaced them with only 42,000 new mixed-income units. Even in these new units, developers were encouraged but not required to include subsidized units. The shortage of these units has caused the displacement of many families. There are 1.1 million public housing units serving 2.1 million low-income Americans. However, there are only 4.3 million available and affordable rental units for the 11 million extremely low-income people who need them (Blankinship & Winkler, 2019). Since the 1990s, the number of public housing units has been underfunded or lost to deterioration (Center on Budget and Policy Priorities, 2017).

- **Transportation Expenses.** How long does it take for you to get to work or school? And, how much does this travel cost you each week? Many employees commute long distances from their own homes and cannot afford to live where they work. Although transportation is often not considered when thinking about housing affordability, it is a key factor. It is estimated that for every dollar spent on housing, 77 cents is spent on transportation, further eroding household budgets (Jewkes & Delgadillo, 2010). This inability to reside where one works is a result of high housing prices in those employment centers. These expensive areas typically have fewer affordable housing units. Therefore, as families move out to suburban areas to find less expensive housing, the ratio of transportation costs increases and can account for up to 3% of a household's annual income.

- **Gentrification.** Imagine living in your community for generations with family and friends, but being forced to move out because you are evicted or the local government puts pressure on you to move out for redevelopment. How would you feel? What social bonds might you lose when you have to seek housing elsewhere? A community you call home is drastically shifting, and now you feel like you are no longer welcome. Gentrification is a process that displaces families and contributes to the lack of affordable homes available for vulnerable families. Neighborhood investment, although a positive strategy for neighborhood improvement, often leads to the displacement of lower-income residents when higher-income consumers buy up the new stock of revitalized housing. Such activity reduces the number of affordable units in the neighborhood, increases land value, and incites exclusionary displacement of previous inhabitants. Irresponsible purchase and consumption behavior by wealthy investors and homebuyers, without affordable housing development, decrease the number of homes available to low- and fixed-income residents.

- **Housing/Household Unsuitability.** Along with land consumption, designs of homes are becoming much larger than in the past. Americans today are requesting floor plans that exceed their need. This increase in housing size also increases housing prices, effectively reducing the availability of starter homes for young couples. More generally, the current housing stock has not kept up with the changing demographics of the U.S. population. Although only 20% of the U.S. families are nuclear families, 80% of the existing housing stock caters to this family type. Housing design should be developed to suit the evolving spatial and financial needs of a population consisting of 28% singles, 25% couples without children, 20% cohousing adults, and 7% single-parent households. The current housing stock and regulatory building policies also do not align well for the increasing number of aging Americans who live in homes that are too big, geographically isolated, and functionally incompatible for aging in place. Housing design should also fit the needs of a growing millennial population who struggle with limited income, but seek to move into modest homes.

- **Rising Housing Costs.** Economic prosperity at the end of the 1990s and beginning of the 2000s caused a rise in housing prices. Vigorous housing activity, sparked by risky lending practices, led to a housing bubble, then a bust in 2009. The Great Recession that followed was evidence of a devastated housing market with foreclosures and evictions that seemed to echo the adverse outcomes of the Great Depression era. Since this time, the market has rebounded and had tremendous growth. Housing prices have steadily increased. Housing prices are also inflated when speculators and investors systematically purchase affordable homes in low-income neighborhoods, remodel the homes, then sell or "flip" them for a quick profit. Since these investors have much capital, they can consistently outbid low-income and first-time buyers in the housing market. This flipping behavior inflates the cost of modest homes and encourages gentrification.

- **Slow-Growth Regulations.** As many states and municipalities are trying to control sprawl, they have advocated slow growth in some areas. Although the aim is positive, this reduces development and provides a disincentive or restriction for high-density apartments and structures. This slowing down, therefore, decreases the number of units available for affordable housing in remote locations. However, urban sprawl (expanding development from cities into remote geographic areas) increases transportation costs for families, so the benefits of reducing slow-growth regulations to promote affordable housing construction have been challenged (Hamidi & Ewing, 2015).

- **Exclusionary Zoning/Land Use Restrictions.** Similar to slow-growth regulations, exclusionary zoning and land use restrictions determine how the land can be used and where developers can build housing. These regulations also determine the type, density, and height of buildings in an area. Although zoning is meant to protect residents from development encroachment, the complexity of these requirements reduces the supply of affordable housing units to meet the demand. Exclusionary zoning and land use restrictions create barriers to the construction of apartment complexes in areas zoned for single-family housing (Calder, 2017). The socioeconomic impact of such policies is costly. Such exclusions and restrictions disallow denser housing units that could serve as multifamily units, older adult housing, student housing, or mixed-income housing. In effect, lower-income families are systematically locked out of the majority of desirable residential land and locked into segregated and overcrowded communities of poverty. For families that can afford to rent in sparsely available congregate housing units, they pay higher rents, which erodes their purchasing power in a competitive housing market (Blankinship & Winkler, 2019). Regulatory barriers also restrict workers' access to dynamic labor markets in productive cities, thereby effectively limiting income opportunities for low-income, and mostly, families of color.

AFFORDABLE HOUSING INTERVENTIONS

Funding for affordable housing has long been a subject of debate due to misperceptions that poor people are draining the federal budget. However, a cruel irony identified by housing historian Lawrence Vale is that subsidized housing "receives the least amount of … subsidy" (2000, p. 7). In reality, most federal subsidies, nearly two-thirds of funding, actually support middle- and upper-class families' housing costs in the form of tax deductions on mortgage interest payments (Dreier, 2006). In 2014, of the $130 billion the federal government spent on housing support, $51 billion was spent on low-income housing, mostly in the form of housing choice vouchers ($18 billion), project-based rental assistance ($12 billion), LIHTC ($7 billion), and public housing ($7 billion). The rest was spent on homeowner tax deductions for mortgage interest, mostly to people in the highest income quintile (Congressional Budget Office, 2015).

Governmental responses to the affordability problem have been addressed through HUD via shelter programs, rental subsidy programs, and local community-building projects. Although these programs have had some successes, the magnitude of the problem undercuts the effectiveness of these solutions (Anderson et al., 2003). The following are approaches for housing stability:

- **Shelters.** Reformed shelter programs of the 1980s have increased capacity but still struggle with questions about the role of shelters in purpose and utility (Bogard et al., 1999; Weinreb & Rossi, 1995). For example, should shelters provide specialized treatment for the health concerns (e.g., depression, substance addiction) of residents or focus solely on reintegrating individuals into the community? How long should homeless residents be allowed to stay? Should they pay for the use of the shelter?
- **Housing Choice Vouchers.** Housing choice vouchers, called "Section 8 vouchers," provide tenant-based subsidies that allow recipients to choose rental housing and pay only 30% of their income while federal monies finance the remainder of the rent. This program has been very successful overall (Kennedy & Finkel, 1994), but is criticized for geographic clustering and a concentration of poverty in particular communities where rental properties participating in the program are prevalent (Anderson et al., 2003; Popkin & Cunningham, 1999; Turner, 1998; Turner et al., 2000). Ironically, this is the problem it was created to remedy. Also, the voucher programs are limited in their ability to help because many families in homelessness or at risk of homelessness are turned away or put on extensive waiting lists. Although the federal government provides rental assistance to about 4.6 million extremely low and low-income renters, more than twice as many (9.7 million) such households receive no federal funding (Anderson et al., 2003, p. 49).
- **Hope VI Development Projects.** This affordable housing project supported mixed-income housing communities to improve families' living standards in distressed housing by relocating them to communities that are not concentrated with poverty (Cunningham et al., 2005). Typically, projects in this program sought to transform existing rundown public housing projects into functional housing communities where

low-income residents live among middle-income residents to restore a socioeconomic balance. Although this program considers the social and economic needs of low-income residents, often high-capacity public housing units are torn down, and only a small portion of those low-income families can remain in the revitalized community. Therefore, a massive number of families have been displaced from their communities without available resources or adequate income to pick up and secure housing in another location. Further, some of the relocated families are "hard-to-house" residents who may be older or disabled, previously incarcerated, recovering from substance abuse, or large families. This program has been discontinued in favor of other projects.

- **Low-Income Housing Tax Credits.** LIHTC delegates annual budget authority to states to issue federal income tax credits to private investors for the production and preservation of affordable rental units for low-income families. From 1987 to 2018, this program has supported nearly 50,000 projects and over 3 million housing units (HUD, 2020b). Despite this program's broad political support and success in continued affordable housing development, a drawback is that the properties funded through this program have to be affordable for only 30 years. Over 115,000 will expire soon. Another concern is that the LIHTC properties remain unaffordable for extremely low-income renters. Lastly, since this program is tied to private investors needing tax cuts, tax reform policy changes could lead to reduced interest in this resource. For example, in 2017, the Tax Cuts and Job Act reduced corporate income taxes, and this reduction may translate into lessened financial incentives for participation in LIHTC (Scally et al., 2018).

- **Community Development Block Grant (CDBG).** This grant program provides federal funding in the form of a block grant that can be used at the discretion of states for comprehensive community and economic development. States can choose to use this annual federal assistance for public housing, public facilities, disaster recovery, employment training, job creation, homeownership counseling, energy bill assistance, and other projects considered necessary to support the needs of low-income families and communities. A strength of the program is that decision-making about CDBG planning includes citizens who can review proposals and provide input. Despite this program's contributions to housing and community development, funding has declined and is threatened. For example, in 2018, President Trump's budget proposed to eliminate CDBG funding (Theodos et al., 2017).

SOCIAL WORKER PERSPECTIVE 11.2

CAROL COLLARD, PHD, LMSW, EXECUTIVE DIRECTOR, CARINGWORKS, ATLANTA, GA

Housing, like food and clothing, is a fundamental human need. Having a place that one can claim as a home is deeply connected to an individual's sense of security. Its value extends beyond just the provision of shelter, impacting the quality of life and well-being. Although safe, permanent housing is essential, not everyone can claim a roof overhead. Since fewer households are transitioning to homeownership, vacancy rates for rental properties have shrunk, creating more demand and thus ever higher rental rates. Households that are using more and more of their income on rent are more vulnerable to evictions, have more extensive use of social safety net programs, and are more financially fragile. They are less likely to have health insurance and more likely to postpone needed treatment.

(continued)

SOCIAL WORKER PERSPECTIVE 11.2 (continued)

In Georgia, dozens of nonprofit organizations and quasi-governmental agencies help households identify and secure affordable housing. Our agency, CaringWorks, Inc. (caringworksinc.org), was founded by me, a social worker. This nonprofit organization identifies decent, affordable housing for individuals and families experiencing homelessness. For households that are determined to have additional needs, CaringWorks provides case management, job readiness supports, as well as individual and group counseling to address behavioral health needs. Many of these households are led by individuals coping with mental illness or substance use disorders. With the help of a social worker, these households can live successfully and independently. Affordable housing, combined with social and behavioral health services, is called "supportive housing." According to the Corporation for Supportive Housing (2020), supportive housing improves housing stability, employment, mental and physical health, school attendance, and reduces active substance use.

CaringWorks is one of the largest, private, supportive housing providers in the metropolitan Atlanta area. Its mission is to "reduce homelessness and empower the marginalized by providing access to housing and services that foster dignity, self-sufficiency, and well-being." I believe the agency's ultimate mission is to increase access to social justice for our clients. Agency values align with social work values of integrity, competence, and respecting the dignity and worth of the person. Access to decent housing and healthcare is not a privilege, but should be the right of all citizens. In this setting, social workers are involved in leadership, management, advocacy, and direct practice. Since 2019, we have served over 1,000 clients.

Many of our clients experience positive outcomes. For example, Yusuf was born to a single mother, suffered from epilepsy, and had a lack of adequate medical care. By his teens, he was involved in drugs. Further complicating life was his undiagnosed bipolar disorder. Out of jail and homeless, Yusuf sought treatment in several programs but was repeatedly kicked out for his temper and aggressive behavior. In 2010, he was referred to CaringWorks. With support from his case manager, life skills classes, and the security of safe, decent housing, Yusuf blossomed. He was able to reestablish his social security benefits, find employment, and learn to manage his health issues. He explains: "Now I have a toolbox to deal with my emotions." Yusuf is 3 years sober and in good physical and mental health. Newlywed, he holds down a job and supports his family. He proudly reports that he takes time to give back some of the support he received as a CaringWorks client.

Since the days of Hull House, social workers have been advocates for individuals in need of decent, affordable housing. Be it a rural or an urban setting, social workers are engaged in advocacy, as well as direct practice to assist individuals whose daily functioning and well-being are hindered by the lack of affordable housing. I encourage social workers to consider roles in direct service or policy as the need is great to help clients optimize their well-being through housing stability. Housing is a form of healthcare. It is also vital for social workers to recognize the role that we can and should have in policy development and advocacy. Cuts to federal housing budgets are frequent. The lack of affordable housing nationwide manifests in higher eviction rates, homelessness, and community decay, which negatively impacts all people. So, what will be your contribution?

Social workers in a variety of work settings are involved in housing advocacy. Consider getting involved in advocacy for housing issues important to you by exploring Table 11.1 to identify organizations that support affordable and available housing through education, policy priorities, and social action.

TABLE 11.1 **List of Organizations That Support Affordable and Available Housing**

ORGANIZATION	MISSION	WEBSITE
Department of Housing and Urban Development (HUD)	HUD's mission is to create strong, sustainable, inclusive communities and quality affordable homes for all. HUD is working to strengthen the housing market to bolster the economy and protect consumers; meet the need for quality and affordable rental homes; utilize housing as a platform for improving quality of life; build inclusive and sustainable communities free from discrimination; and transform the way HUD does business.	www.hud.gov
Eviction Lab	We're unpacking America's eviction crisis. The Eviction Lab at Princeton University has built the first nationwide database of evictions. Find out how many evictions happen in your community. Create custom maps, charts, and reports. Share facts with your neighbors and elected officials.	evictionlab.org
Joint Center for Housing Studies of Harvard University	The Harvard Joint Center for Housing Studies advances understanding of housing issues and informs policy. Through its research, education, and public outreach programs, the Center helps leaders in government, business, and the civic sectors make decisions that effectively address the needs of cities and communities. Through graduate and executive courses, as well as fellowships and internship opportunities, the Center also trains and inspires the next generation of housing leaders.	jchs.harvard.edu
National Alliance to End Homelessness	The National Alliance to End Homelessness is a nonpartisan, nonprofit organization whose sole purpose is to end homelessness in the United States. We use research and data to find solutions to homelessness; we work with federal and local partners to create a solid base of policy and resources that support those solutions; and then we help communities implement them.	endhomelessness.org
National Coalition for the Homeless	The National Coalition for the Homeless is a national network of people who are currently experiencing or who have experienced homelessness, activists and advocates, community-based and faith-based service providers, and others committed to a single mission: to end and prevent homelessness while ensuring the immediate needs of those experiencing homelessness are met and their civil rights are respected and protected. We envision a world where everyone has a safe, decent, accessible and affordable home.	nationalhomeless.org
National Law Center on Homelessness and Poverty	The National Law Center on Homelessness and Poverty is the only national advocacy organization dedicated solely to using the power of the law to end and prevent homelessness in America. With the support of a large network of pro bono lawyers, we use our legal expertise to help pass, implement, and enforce laws addressing the immediate and long-term needs of those who are homeless or at risk. In partnership with state and local advocates, we work toward strengthening the social safety net through advocacy and advocacy training, public education, and impact litigation.	nlchp.org

(continued)

TABLE 11.1 List of Organizations That Support Affordable and Available Housing (*continued*)

ORGANIZATION	MISSION	WEBSITE
National Low-Income Housing Coalition	The National Low-Income Housing Coalition is dedicated solely to achieving socially just public policy that ensures people with the lowest incomes in the United States have affordable and decent homes.	nlihc.org
Urban Institute	When it comes to advancing the well-being of people and places across the United States, the Urban Institute holds a unique advantage: our capacity to produce new knowledge about social and economic issues and to rigorously mine the evidence for insight.	www.urban.org/experts/housing-and-housing-finance

CONCLUSION

Housing costs remain a critical concern for many families and have implications for individual and family well-being and stability. Social workers can effectively advocate for more affordable housing options at various levels of practice. At the micro level, clients need support identifying housing resources within the constraints of available income. At the mezzo level, social workers can explore unfair practices that keep people in substandard housing conditions. At the macro level, many state and federal policies affect the affordability, availability, and access to housing. There are many ways to implement justice-informed practice as a social worker, through varying roles as a clinician, community organizer, or administrator. All are needed to truly effect change.

DISCUSSION QUESTIONS

1. What impact does the fact that many communities built affordable housing on cheap, vacant land on the periphery of towns have on our clients?
2. Explain how "slum clearance" took advantage of the people living in those dismal conditions?
3. Why is it important for social workers to understand housing policy and the discriminatory policies employed by the banking industry?
4. Calculate the percentage of your income that you pay on rent. Based on your calculations, provide a short argument for—or against—the idea of 30% of income as an appropriate indicator of housing affordability.

REFERENCES

Only key references appear in the print edition. The full reference list appears in the digital product on Springer Publishing Connect: connect.springerpub.com/content/book/978-0-8261-3539-1/chapter/ch11

Aguirre, A., & Martinez, R. (2014). The foreclosure crisis, the American dream, and minority households in the United States: A descriptive profile. *Social Justice, 40*(3), 6–15. https://www.jstor.org/stable/24361645

Bell, P. A., Greene, T. C., Fisher, J. D., & Baum, A. (2001). *Environmental psychology*. Harcourt College Publishers.

Bratt, R., & Immergluck, D. (2016). Housing policy and the mortgage foreclosure crisis during the Obama administration. In C. Johnson & J. Defilippis (Eds.), *Urban policy in the time of Obama* (pp. 79–98). University of Minnesota Press.

Davis, S. (1995). *The architecture of affordable housing*. University of California Press.

Desmond, M. (2016). *Evicted: Poverty and profit in the American city*. Crown.

Lewinson, T., Thomas, M. L., & White, S. (2014). Traumatic transitions: Homeless women's narratives of abuse, loss, and fear. *Affilia: Journal of Women & Social Work*, *29*(2), 192–205. https://doi.org/10.1177/0886109913516449

Massey, D. S., & Rugh, J. S. (2018). The great recession and the destruction of minority wealth. *Current History*, *117*(802), 298–303. https://doi.org/10.1525/curh.2018.117.802.298

Rothstein, R. (2017). *The color of law: A forgotten history of how our government segregated America* (1st ed.). Liveright Publishing Corporation.

Schwartz, A. (2015). *Housing policy in the United States* (3rd ed.). Routledge.

Vale, L. J. (2000). *From the puritans to the projects: Public housing and public neighbors*. Harvard University Press.

12

FINANCIAL JUSTICE AND SOCIAL WORK PRACTICE

Diane N. Loeffler | Jennifer K. Weeber | Chloe McKenzie | Mae Humiston | R. Scott McReynolds

LEARNING OBJECTIVES

Students will be able to:

- Frame financial justice as a component of justice-oriented social work practice.
- Define key terms related to financial justice including financial literacy, financial capability, unbanked, underbanked, and credit invisibility.
- Understand and describe the privileged assumptions inherent in most financial literacy educational programs.
- Articulate the connection between the history of land and homeownership in the United States and financial inequities that exist in the present day.
- Identify the role of credit and debt in the systematic marginalization of certain groups.

INTRODUCTION

Financial justice, broadly discussed, encompasses aspects of social, economic, and environmental justice. The concept itself is not well defined—as evidenced by a quick Google search or a review of recent scholarly literature. Both yield few results and those resources that are found are centered in European Union policies/proposals that seek more equitable ways to balance inequity in wealth distribution or focus on efforts within the United States that look specifically at aspects of fees and fines that disproportionately impact lower wealth and lower income households.

Within social work education and practice, it is important to position financial literacy, capability, and justice in discussion and action. In order to do so, it is incumbent upon the social worker to better understand systems that have created advantage and disadvantage for clients and client groups as well as to examine the complex interplay between financial justice and other topics covered in this volume. Certainly, financial justice is related to—inextricably linked to—poverty, housing, food security, education, criminal justice, economic disparity, health, and more. Certainly, financial justice must be placed on the agenda of social work practitioners, activists, and researchers alike. What does financial justice mean to you?

- Could it mean having access to a traditional banking institution where you could deposit your paycheck?
- Could it mean having access to capital to start a small business?

- Could it mean having the opportunity to learn about finances and financial management in a meaningful and culturally relevant way as a part of K–12 education?
- Could it mean having access to fair loans for college? To buy a house?
- Could it mean having bail systems that do not disproportionately impact low-income individuals who do not have financial liquidity necessary for a lump-sum bail payment?
- Could it mean that students graduate from high school with basic financial acumen that allows them to make good choices, regardless of their income or wealth?
- Could it mean rethinking social policies and tax systems that advantage the wealthy?
- Could it mean redressing the wide racial and gender wealth and equity gaps that exist today?
- Could it mean radical redistribution of wealth within societies?
- What else might it mean?

Achieving financial justice could include all of these—and more.

For social work practitioners, a robust understanding of financial justice must include an understanding of financial literacy and financial capability. True financial justice requires us to be aware of the myriad ways in which financial institutions, social welfare policies, and even social work practice have systematically excluded some people from actualizing financial well-being. Within the context of just practice in the United States in the 21st century, financial justice cannot be realized when so many households are struggling to manage multiple facets of their financial life and when financial policies, programs, and practices are not inclusive.

In this chapter, we start by introducing the concept of financial literacy—how it is typically defined and understood in society and how it relates to financial justice. We suggest how and why this concept needs to be reexamined in order to create true financial literacy that protects and supports all people in their financial decision-making. Next, we discuss financial capability and offer an in-depth look at three aspects of financial life that are intrinsically tied to social work practice but often viewed as separate from our work: access to and utilization of banking, acquisition of land/homeownership, and debt. Within each area we highlight historical and current systemic inequity and discuss how policies and programs have negatively impacted marginalized groups. Each section provides strategies for change and the chapter concludes with a call for actualizing social work's role in bringing financial justice to fruition.

FINANCIAL LITERACY

"Literacy" simply refers to competence or knowledge. Thus, financial literacy is the competence or knowledge needed to make decisions related to personal finances/financial well-being. However, in research and practice there is not a universally accepted definition of what makes someone financially literate. Because financial literacy is often learned experientially or through observations of others' interactions, how and what we learn about the financial world differs greatly based on our own life experiences and those of the people with whom we live and work.

Financial literacy is something often talked about in the media in terms of the *deficits* in knowledge and abilities. Consumer news outlets seem to agree that we are not financially literate as an American society, yet there are conflicting ideas about what financial literacy is, where it should be taught/learned, and for whom it is necessary. The media, however, has reason to be worried.

Different measures are used to assess financial literacy of adults and teens in the United States, yet we do not perform well across these metrics. A global assessment of financial literacy, conducted by Standard and Poor's Rating Services (2014), examined financial literacy around the globe using the financial fundamentals of "risk diversification, inflation, numeracy," and reinvesting interest (Klapper et al., 2016, p. 4). Not surprisingly, while the United States ranks ahead of some emerging economies, our overall financial literacy rate as assessed with this instrument is just 57%. The data also confirm that experience and opportunity impact financial literacy; people who are engaged with formal banking and financial services are more financially literate than those who are not. Notably, across the globe, those with some experience with financial institutions have more knowledge, for example, someone with limited income who has a bank account is more financially literate than someone without.

The National Federation of Credit Counseling also regularly assesses financial literacy in the United States. Since 2007 they have surveyed and tracked financial literacy and financial literacy trends in the United States. While more nuanced, the 2019 data revealed noteworthy numbers: one-quarter of those surveyed indicated they are not paying bills on time, two-fifths of households indicate they carry credit card balances month to month, and 50% of those who attempted to purchase a home in 2019 faced some sort of barriers in that process (National Federation of Credit Counseling, 2019).

Additional studies of general financial literacy in the United States largely find the same thing: people tend to think they are more financially literate than the data suggest. This lack of awareness and limited literacy create danger for anyone, but that danger creates more exposure and has deeper consequences for a lower income/lower wealth household. Each of these reports confirms that our society does not understand the facets of money management and debt.

Financial Literacy Education

Typically, components of financial literacy education include aspects of budgeting, understanding and managing debt, and how to save money. However, as currently conceived of, financial literacy education assumes a lot—that households have enough to create a savings plan, that households have access to traditional banking institutions, that debt is carried through traditional and legitimate institutions (e.g., a bank or a credit union vs. an IOU to a family member), and so forth. The very way that financial literacy is taught—when it *is* taught—makes assumptions about income, expenses, and financial goals that are not always congruent with the lived experiences of the people engaged in the education and so are not culturally relevant for many.

Further, activist and writer Chloe McKenzie reminds us that "financial literacy education is born from an inherently racist and exclusionary financial system" that perpetuates generational and systemic financial stress and trauma for many (McKenzie, 2020). Traditional definitions/conceptions just described do not speak to the fact that financial literacy is not just about having the knowledge to manage money and understand debt. It is incumbent upon our profession to demand financial literacy more broadly include an understanding of and competence in navigating the oppressive financial systems we must engage to accrue and manage wealth and assets. Practice Perspective 12.1 elaborates on this shift in how we can think—and teach—about financial literacy.

PRACTICE PERSPECTIVE 12.1

TRANSFORMING FINANCIAL LITERACY EDUCATION AND OPPORTUNITY

by Chloe McKenzie

I decided to begin my work and research in wealth justice because in America, wealth disparity is a burden particularly felt by Black womxn and girls. So, I started a nonprofit called BlackFem,

(continued)

PRACTICE PERSPECTIVE 12.1 (continued)

which has the mission to transform school-based learning so that Black girls and girls of color have the skills, understandings, and resources to build and sustain wealth.

If we are to succeed in achieving wealth justice and close the wealth gap, then we must root our practice in these realities: (a) financial literacy education is born from an inherently racist and exclusionary financial system and currently serves only to perpetuate financial trauma stemming from chronic financial stress and abuse; (b) providing knowledge and standardized tools as a way to build wealth is not enough; and (c) Black womxn and girls are more susceptible to the deleterious effects of financial trauma, financial shame, and financial abuse because wealth inequality is so pervasive that it facilitates a cycle of economic hardship that is intergenerationally reinforcing.

Systemic racism pervades our financial system just as it pervades all other aspects of society. It champions the false narrative of individual responsibility, success, and personal agency to dismiss the crippling ways our country has oppressed and harmed communities of color. Messages that students should save weekly allowances, mow neighbors' lawns to raise money, or find extracurricular work to build cash for themselves, alienate Black girls from low-income communities who stand to benefit most from financial education rooted in wealth justice. Even before being given an appropriate financial education, tools and resources need to be provided to build a foundation for success. This includes ensuring we provide strategies to this demographic to build a healthier relationship with money and wealth.

Society likes to think of money, wealth, and the financial system as a numbers game, but our country's enormous wealth and unchecked (even criminal) financial system were built from Black slave labor and stolen Indigenous land. It has created a toxic value system that prioritizes money, wealth, and the "pursuit of more" above all, and subsequently assigns personal worth based on financial quantity and value. The existence of these systems prevents Black communities from benefiting, moving forward, or receiving reparations for their suffering. At BlackFem I felt it was necessary to never shy away from or deny these realities, but I had been focusing on financial literacy education as a way to change our circumstances until I began my research. I realized later that we cannot move forward without acknowledging and dismantling what got us here.

Today, financial literacy education oversimplifies wealth so much that it tricks us into thinking it is possible to "take control" of our finances. Quippy tips, tricks, and tools touted by experts, blogs, financial institutions, and organizations under the guise of financial literacy education have created a disconnect from the historical and emotional implications of wealth and money. By purposefully requiring us to ignore and dismiss our own experiences (and trauma), money becomes one-dimensional. The very thing that dictates how we live in and interact with the world is now "objective," leaving no room for nuance or systemic change.

We cannot budget or save our way out of multigenerational poverty when the same system we are working in has continuously exploited and harmed our community. We cannot continue to legitimize a system that has not seen us as legitimate. Without also taking into account the cognitive, behavioral, and psychological effects of money, we perpetuate the addictive, harmful notion that we should be in the pursuit of more at any cost (or we fail). We will never achieve true financial equity and security for Black girls and Black communities without a fundamental shift in the larger system and our curriculum. That is what it means to work for and fight for wealth justice—to lead in our work through a new lens, focusing less on linear instruction of financial literacy and more on the multidimensionality of value, money, and wealth. My commitment to wealth justice is rooted in my desire to help Black womxn, girls, and their communities heal from and name financial trauma and create an enriching relationship with their finances.

Most of our socialization around finances and financial literacy *is* experiential. Consider this: Do you own a home? If you do, you are likely (hopefully) familiar with the terms of your mortgage and you might be conversant when it comes to talking about the components of your monthly mortgage payment. If you have never owned a home, you are likely less conversant in the language of mortgage finance because you have not been through the process. Similarly, if you have never had a job in the formal economy where taxes are paid at the local, state, and federal levels, you are likely not aware of or familiar with what percentage of your paycheck goes to support the local school board, state, and federal taxes. If you have never had a credit card—or applied for one—you may not be knowledgeable about credit scores and compounding interest. If you have never had a bank account, you may not be aware of the services that can be provided within/by your bank. You may never have had the opportunity to gain this knowledge. Yet, there are implicit expectations in our society around this type of knowledge. Not knowing is disempowering and can ultimately lead to shame and fear around interfacing with financial systems.

In the absence of knowledge about how financial systems work, decisions can be made that encumber a family or individual in unanticipated ways (e.g., not using financial institutions and relying upon alternative means for accessing and saving cash, using a credit card and not understanding compounding interest and even signing a mortgage and not understanding the terms of the loan and how the payment might change over time) and can create financial stress and turmoil. Those who engage in consumer finance but do not understand how it works often end up with more debt and less savings (Stango & Zinman, 2009). On the flip side, for those who are adept in interacting with financial systems, there are many benefits—including planning and saving for retirement and engaging in/with investments. However, in many ways this becomes a "chicken and egg" quandary as a person who does not have the luxury of saving a percentage of their paycheck may simply not be in a position to even consider investments and stock portfolios.

Implementing Financial Literacy Education

When financial literacy is taught within our school systems, it is often done so in a Life Skills course and typically is not considered requisite knowledge for graduation. Both the federal government and the nonprofit sector have developed recommendations and strategies to increase financial literacy in the United States. The Jump$tart Coalition, a national nonprofit organization, has developed K–12 financial literacy standards and has worked to incorporate financial literacy components into education across the United States. However, given the competing demands for student time, while the importance of financial literacy has grown, there is still much room for improvement in financial literacy education.

At the federal level, the Department of the Treasury established a Financial Literacy and Education Commission (FLEC) in 2003. Yet this commission lacked a clear and identifiable mission and the many different programs (within different government agencies) that emphasized financial literacy do not always coordinate with one another. Because there are not uniform curricula for financial literacy—and because curricula that do exist are built on flawed assumptions and narratives around what it means to be financially "successful"—we are not, as a whole, equipped to make good financial choices for ourselves and for our communities. Activists like McKenzie (Practice Perspective 12.1) who have dedicated their careers and research to advocating for new and *better* financial literacy cannot do this work on their own. As social workers, it is time for us to become engaged in this work and service.

FINANCIAL LITERACY AND SOCIAL WORK PRACTICE

Financial literacy—as a topic or area of practice—is scantly named within social work literature. Kindle (2010) points out that it was not until 2004 that this term was found within social work academic literature. Contemporary social work practice related to financial literacy is, in part, grounded in the asset accumulation tradition as introduced and powerfully articulated by Sherraden (1991) whose groundbreaking work *Assets and the Poor: A New American Welfare Policy* demonstrated how social work and social welfare practitioners could radically change the way we think about social welfare policy and income assistance by shifting from policies that focus on minimal income and maintenance, to policies that create opportunities for low-income and low-wealth households to accumulate wealth and/or asset holdings. This work introduced asset building to social work and social welfare practice and was the beginning of a groundswell of research and policy work that demanded change.

Still, as a profession and certainly within our educational programs, social work does not widely include financial literacy content in curricula and practice. It is clear that social work students—and practitioners and researchers—need to become more knowledgeable about how to best serve clients and client groups. Social work students seem to have an awareness of the relevance of financial literacy to common practice areas, for example, health, criminal justice, mental health, child welfare (Kindle, 2010) yet are only moderately "literate" themselves when it comes to understanding personal finance and the application therein to work with clients (Gillen & Loeffler, 2012; Kindle, 2013). While there have been recommendations (e.g., Anderson et al., 2007; Gillen & Loeffler, 2012; Kindle, 2010, 2013; Sherraden et al., 2007) for inclusion of financial literacy curricular components in social work education, the specifics of what should be included are not clear.

In part, this is due to the overwhelmingly "middle-class" lens to approaching financial literacy that is utilized widely inside and outside of the profession. These traditional approaches to budgeting and financial management may not have wide application to our clients' reality and, in many ways, are built upon normative culturally and socially bound expectations around what financial success is and how it is operationalized. Further, it bears repeating that personal financial literacy is tied to one's own lived experience and is inherently experiential in nature (Kindle, 2013). Thus, there is much more work to be done.

Social work practitioners routinely work with vulnerable households and communities. While giving financial advice or council is not within the profession's purview, social workers are often engaged in work around household finances, budgeting, and planning as well as educating regarding financial implications of varying strategies. Certainly, for households managing at the margins, social workers may be charged with helping them to apply for safety net benefits such as TANF (Temporary Assistance for Needy Families), SNAP (Supplemental Nutrition Assistance Program), or housing assistance through subsidized housing or Section 8 vouchers. In these processes, budgeting and revealing financial information and decision-making become the norm. Social workers, then, need to be competent and *truly* financially literate so that they can be advocates, brokers, educators, and strength builders with clients and client groups. In turn, social workers need to advocate for access to relevant financial literacy education and resources for clients and client groups. As social workers deepening acumen and literacy in these areas, we become better allies in the fight for financial justice. One cannot, for example, fight for equitable tax reform without a modicum of understanding the U.S. tax code itself. One cannot advocate for consumer finance protection without understanding facets of compounding interest and loan terms. Additionally, social workers need to bravely call out the status quo, question what is commonly taught in financial literacy workshops and classes, and be advocates for reform to financial literacy education and financial counseling and services. We cannot be content to work within systems that are broken and that do not justly serve our clients' needs.

Further, as practitioners who engage in financial literacy-related work with clients, we must understand the biases and assumptions we bring to our own work. Talking about money is hard. Conversations about money are often intensely private and fraught with emotion. Clients may have a myriad of emotions such as fear of being judged, shame, embarrassment, and anxiety which makes it difficult to broach the subject of finances much less establish an effective working relationship. Being able to approach discussions of finances requires a nonjudgmental and compassionate disposition that does not further contribute to a client's own emotional stressors. In order to do this, a social worker must examine their own thoughts, patterns, learned behaviors and rules, and biases around money. Think briefly about the lessons about money you learned growing up—not formal lessons per se, but the informal messages you received by watching adults in your life interact with money and financial institutions and by observing those interactions. Think about language too. Now, consider a series of questions:

- What assumptions do you have about financial literacy and money management?

Digging deeper, consider how you would answer the following questions:

- What does someone who is financially literate look like?
- What should a household budget look like?
- How should people prioritize their spending?
- What does financial success look like?
- What financial resources are available to people to help them manage their money and build their wealth?

Now, consider your own experiences and observations and how they have shaped your assumptions. What did you learn about money as a child or young adult?

- What did you learn as you were growing up about what people "should" or "should not" do when it comes to money?
- From whom did you learn about managing money?
- What have been your own experiences in managing money?
- What have been your own experiences with banks, other mainstream financial institutions, and alternative financial institutions?

How do your responses to these questions impact the way in which you might approach financial knowledge and money management with clients? How might clients' experiences differ from your own? How do your race and gender shape what you learned and how you view financial literacy and money management? Further, how does your own privilege—or lack thereof—shape your thinking about what is right/wrong/good/bad about money management? Many assumptions about what is "right" and "wrong" in managing personal finance are codified by the banking industry and are tied to behaviors, opportunities, and resource allocation that is not always accessible to those who have been oppressed and marginalized from access to meaningful, culturally and socially appropriate financial education and financial institutions.

Strengths-Based Approach to Financial Literacy

Utilizing a strengths-based approach to financial literacy is imperative. As a practitioner, it provides a foundation from which you can identify your clients' financial skills, their existing resources, and their priorities. It enables you to determine their *actual* needs and not just their needs as perceived by their circumstances or a cursory look at their budget. For your clients, a strengths-based perspective is a powerful tool to help clients build their confidence and recognize the skills and resources they bring to the table. Further, it is important to consider frameworks that empower and engage in just practice. Viewing financial literacy through a critical or intersectional feminist lens may also shift one's ideas and tools for creating just practice around financial literacy.

Moving forward, within social work practice, financial literacy cannot be wholly separated from financial capability.

FINANCIAL CAPABILITY

To understand financial capability, one must first return to the moral framework Sen introduced in his capabilities approach as discussed in his essential work *Development as Freedom* (1999). Here, Sen posits that quality of life/well-being is constructed of both functioning and capability. Here, functioning is the active state of *doing* something or *being* something and capabilities are the *opportunities to do* something. Capabilities reflect choices/opportunities to choose between functions. This is inherently related to justice. Nussbaum (2000, 2003) takes the capabilities approach a step further and articulates 10 basic capabilities required for a just society. In this, Nussbaum includes "control over one's material environment" as an essential capability. Certainly, in the current context, access to and utilization of financial resources, programs, policies, and products are essential in creating that control. Thus, extending this concept of capabilities to the financial realm is intuitive and can help social workers to thoughtfully engage in the pursuit of financial justice.

Sherraden (2013) extends this concept to social work practice and specifically to practice related to financial justice, constructing the concept of financial capability. "Financial capability" can be defined as having *both* opportunity and ability to execute functions that are within one's own best interest, financially speaking. For this to happen, financial literacy and inclusion are required (Sherraden, 2013). As financial literacy has already been discussed, we turn now to an examination of financial capability and aspects of inclusion, or opportunities.

FINANCIAL CAPABILITY AND SOCIAL WORK PRACTICE

Justice-informed social work will require financial capability practice. Not only do social workers need to have financial literacy skills to best serve clients (and arguably to also best access and utilize scarce resources at the organizational level), but we need the ability to address financial injustices at more macro levels of practice. One may have the ability to execute functions but in the absence of opportunities, justice is not viable.

Financial justice cannot be actualized until we, as practitioners—and as a society—are financially literate and until financial capabilities are extended to all persons. To that end, it is imperative that social workers examine and understand the structures—institutions, policies, and programs—that represent barriers to financial capability and to financial literacy. Here we must amplify the voices of those marginalized from discussions on financial matters—tax policy, mortgage lending and equity, fair wage labor—and ensure that our voices and actions are in solidarity with those who are impacted by but excluded from decision-making processes. The example of Finding a Way, Even with Little provides an excellent opportunity to consider functioning and capabilities and to see clients through a strengths-based and capabilities-oriented perspective.

CASE STUDY 12.1—FINDING A WAY, EVEN WITH LITTLE

Maggie, a 36-year-old single mother of two school-aged children, has come to you in need of assistance. She is living in a homeless shelter and tells you that she is struggling to make ends meet. Maggie works at a minimum-wage retail job with fluctuating hours. As she reaches into her purse to pull out paycheck stubs and bills, you tell her you would rather first focus on understanding her and her situation before looking at any numbers. She gives you a strange look but seems to relax a bit. You ask Maggie about her priorities for her family, how she is currently managing her money, where she feels like she is doing a good job, and where she feels like she could improve her skills.

As you explore Maggie's situation, you not only learn enough about her income and expenses that, when you actually look through her paycheck stubs and bills, you find no surprises, but you gain a deeper understanding of her stressful relationship with money. You find that she brings home an average of $170 a week, receives about $400 a month in SNAP benefits, and is uninsured though both her children are covered through Medicaid. Through an intricate system of juggling payments in a manner that maintains a trickle of cash flow, periodic odd jobs, bartering (e.g., babysitting for a friend in exchange for haircuts for her children and herself), and perseverance, she manages to meet her family's basic needs and even some of their wants. She (mostly) keeps up with her bills, keeps her car running and insured so she can get herself to work and her kids to school and activities, and has money for her kids' field trips, book fairs, and daily school snacks. You learn that Maggie's priorities for her family are at odds with how she actually spends her money, but that she is often forced into a decision that pits her long-term priorities against her short-term survival, which is how she ended up with a monthly payment to a rent-to-own business and one to a payday loan business.

As Maggie shares some of her strategies for staying "in the black," she also shares some of her frustrations with her bank itself. While Maggie routinely checks her account balance and ensures that she does not overdraw her account, she is sometimes surprised when her bookkeeping and the bank's statements do not add up, leaving her with overdraft fees. This is not due to Maggie's accounting errors and, when you point this out to Maggie, she is both frustrated and bolstered by the knowledge that she was not making a mistake in her accounting. By using a bank account, she *does* lose control of *when* her account fluctuates because of a practice called "debit resequencing." In short, it is legal for banks to reorder transactions in our accounts to have account balances fall faster, increasing the likelihood of overdraft and the subsequent collection of overdraft fees by the bank.

During this conversation, you come to understand that Maggie is highly skilled at financial management—she has a wide array of functionings. She can maintain cash flow with less income than she has expenses, understands the costs of delaying payments, and how to put off a creditor. She is creative, has a clear sense of priorities, but is also grounded in day-to-day survival. What she lacks are the actual resources—the capabilities—to make ends meet. Her use of a payday lender or her preference for funding school snacks versus a "rainy day cushion" would put her at odds with many of our socially accepted "rules" around what good financial management looks like. Yet, Maggie's ability to manage her family finances is, by all accounts, savvy and thoughtful.

This situation provides the opportunity for practitioners to flex both their micro and macro social work muscles. There are a variety of programs to which Maggie could be connected to

(continued)

> **CASE STUDY 12.1—FINDING A WAY, EVEN WITH LITTLE** *(continued)*
>
> meet her day-to-day needs—financial assistance to repair her car, rental assistance to obtain housing, educational opportunities that may help her attain higher paying employment, credit counseling and repair that could help her pay off her high-interest loans. For Maggie and others like her, to go beyond the houses of cards they have created for day-to-day survival, advocacy is needed to change the systems that fundamentally do not work. Employment that pays a living wage, fair access to credit and financial services at a reasonable cost, and healthcare for all are three systemic changes that could directly increase Maggie's ability to meet her family's needs.
>
> What else strikes you about Maggie's situation? What else could you do on a micro, mezzo, and/or macro level to improve Maggie's situation? How might you think differently about Maggie now that you have read and thought about financial literacy and capability?

FINANCIAL INCLUSION AND ACCESS

Access to Banking and Banking Services

At the beginning of this chapter, if you thought that the ability to deposit your paycheck into your bank account should be considered an element of financial justice, you were correct. In 2020, for many, banking is a fully automated and remote process. Checks are deposited by smartphone, paychecks are received by direct deposit, and access to a physical bank is rarely needed. However, this is not the reality for many individuals and households. Being unbanked—and underbanked—is a barrier to financial justice that cannot be overlooked within our profession.

We are conversant in and understand the justice implications and negative ramifications of food deserts and lack of access to affordable fresh foods. However, have you considered the lack of access to a bank as a critical issue of justice? If not the lack of access to a bank, what about access to an *affordable* bank? What about a bank where you do not face language or cultural barriers? Or a bank where you are able to safely engage in transactions without fears of racial profiling and/or violence? Access to the internet so that you can engage in electronic banking? These barriers to bank access are a reality for many.

UNBANKED AND UNDERBANKED

Since 2009, the Federal Deposit Insurance Corporation (FDIC) has taken stock of underbanked and unbanked households in the United States. An "unbanked" household refers to a household wherein no member of the household reports having a bank account with an FDIC institution. An "underbanked" household has at least one account but still uses financial products or services outside of the banking industry. Use of these alternative financial services (AFSs) can come with high transactional costs and less oversight than a traditional bank, though the high cost of banking (carrying a minimum account balance, overdraft fees, etc.) may discourage many from using traditional banking services. Looking back to Case Study 12.1, Maggie is underbanked. She is reliant upon a payday lender and although she has a bank account, that account is costly because of the recurrence of overdraft fees due to debit resequencing. While banks may seem expensive due to these types of fees, utilization of AFSs can come with high transactional costs and less oversight than a traditional bank. AFSs include practices such as using pawn shops and money orders, payday loans, auto title loans, rent-to-own options, and international remittances (FDIC, 2017).

WHO IS UNBANKED? UNDERBANKED?

In 2017, 6.5% of households in the United States were unbanked. While this number has decreased over time, 6.5% still represents over 8.4 million households without any access to banking. An additional 24 million households identify as underbanked (FDIC, 2017). While it may seem that the proliferation of large national banks would increase access to banking, the changing landscape of the banking industry has actually decreased access for some households. Consolidation of banks and the decrease in smaller banks has been associated with increased banking fees for some households (Xu, 2019). Being unbanked or underbanked is more likely to occur in households that are lower income, typically younger and less educated and are Black or Latinx, households with a disabled earner and/or "households with volatile income" (FDIC, 2017, p. 2). This is consistent with Xu's findings related to underbanked households and AFS users. Further, Xu (2019) confirms that AFSs are more likely to be found in communities with lower incomes and higher percentages of consumers of color.

Financial Disparities

It is important to acknowledge—and to interrupt—the racial disparity that shows up in access to banking. The banking industry is not exempt from this country's history of institutional racism and exclusion. When examining why households remain underbanked, FDIC data show that not having enough money to maintain an account is the most prevalent reason, followed by some groups' lack of trust in banks themselves. Certainly, mistrust can be connected to systemic oppression. Thus, the underlying reason why minority households—specifically why Black households—remain the most likely to be unbanked must no longer be ignored and concealed. The history of banking in the United States is deeply rooted in racism—from the fraud perpetuated by the Freedman's Saving Bank (1865–1874) to redlining that systematically segregated communities through mortgage lending practices. History shapes present-day realities. Ongoing exclusion from financial institutions and financial products has long-term consequences.

Historically, women have also been excluded from banking due to heteronormative sexist policies and practices. Prior to 1974, decisions around a woman's credit worthiness could be based on her marital status and on whether or not she had—or planned to have—children. Banks often required a single, divorced, or widowed woman to have a man cosign for her on a loan, as it was assumed she could not make payments on her own. In 1974 the Equal Credit Opportunity Act (ECOA) made it illegal for creditors to make credit decisions based on many facets of identity—including race, religion, marital status, and sex. The passage of legislation alone did not eradicate these biases in banking policies. Credit and banking policies, procedures, and products are still biased based on historic White heteronormative assumptions about how people should make choices about their families, work, and finances.

When marginalized aspects of identity intersect, the oppression experienced by people becomes even more pronounced. If access to banks and to consumer banking products is mired in racist history and practices, then a lack of access to and trust in banks and consumer banking products are even more nuanced when gender and race intersect; when race, gender, and income status intersect, or when gender identity, ability, and race intersect—and even when income and geography intersect. It is vital to remember that access to banks and banking are not available to all people even when these services are vital to daily life in our society. Further, even when banks are physically present in communities, they are not always accessible. Language barriers, limited hours of operation, or a person's own fear of safely entering a banking establishment may limit one's ability to utilize services therein. Practice Perspective 12.2 highlights the specific challenges of banking for rural households in the United States.

PRACTICE PERSPECTIVE 12.2

RURAL BANKING

Becoming or being banked has challenges across urban, suburban, and rural spaces. However, these challenges can differ in substance and severity depending on where someone lives. Think about how you use your bank. How do you use it? Do you go in person, or use an internet app? Do you feel connected to your bank? Do you know the tellers or bank personnel? How might you use your bank differently if you could not access the internet? What if you did not have a car? What if the bank was farther away, or had more limited hours? These are some of the challenges that rural households face daily in terms of how they engage with banking.

Hazard is the county seat of Perry County, Kentucky, a rural county in eastern Kentucky of 340 square miles and a population of approximately 26,000. The majority of bank branches present in Perry County are located within Hazard, which, for residents of the outlying communities of Buckhorn or Cornettsville, is almost an hour's drive away. Like other errands, visits to the bank must be planned as part of trips to town, and scheduled to make it to the bank during their business hours. For some, this means leaving work early to get to the bank before it closes. For others, this means not going to the bank at all.

For those with low and/or limited income, travel time is not the only factor. Simply accessing reliable transportation can be a major barrier. In urban areas this might look like using a bank along a public transit route, but in rural places there is very little or no public transit and without a personal vehicle, individuals may be largely dependent on family and friends. With no vehicle and long travel distances, keeping money in an institution that is not consistently accessible because of personal transportation reasons can easily negate the intended sense of security offered by that institution.

Online banking has made remote banking much more accessible for many people, eliminating the need to go to the bank for basic banking tasks such as depositing a check or transferring funds. However, access to these services is contingent on access to the internet. In February 2020, BroadbandNow Research calculated that over 42 million Americans still did not have access to broadband internet, and most of these individuals reside in rural areas (Busby et al., 2020). In part because of an increase in the usage of online banking services, many banks are closing or reducing the hours of physical branches, which makes banking for those with limited transportation and limited internet access an even greater challenge.

In addition to the shuttering of branches, the Federal Reserve reports a decline in the number of community banks in rural areas, most notably due to mergers and consolidations (Board of Governors of the Federal Reserve System, 2019). Such mergers often move the headquarters of a community bank to an urban region. A local bank with community members on the board of directors may inspire a greater sense of trust among bank users and that same local connection may create more knowledge of the needs within the community. When community banks are lost to larger national chains, this is all but lost.

What is our role, as social workers, in helping create bank access for those who are unbanked and underbanked? Solutions can be found at the individual level and certainly at the macro level as well. Let us return to Maggie's case (Case Study 12.1) one more time—and let us extend our knowledge of her situation by placing her geographically in Hazard, Kentucky—as described in Practice Perspective 12.2. Structurally, there are changes that could lead to improved banking access that could also have many other benefits. Having affordable broadband internet might give Maggie additional bank choices, allowing her to find a bank with a slate of account and service offerings that best met her needs. Social workers can work collectively with others who are pursuing broadband access and affordability. Social workers can also help to amplify the voices of those impacted by poor regulation of AFSs and can be advocates for oversight and consumer protection. As a profession, the more we know about banking access, consumer protection, and regulation, the more we can advocate for changes that benefit all people.

Social workers can also engage in individual-level work with clients and community members to help create positive change. Maggie's finances were negatively impacted by the overdraft protection fees on her account. Most consumers are not aware of their choices in how their bank accounts deal with insufficient funds. Legally, consumers have the choice to opt into—or out of—overdraft protection for debit and ATM transactions on their account(s). Educating ourselves about banking policy may seem *outside* of our practice area, but imagine if helping a client to set up or change their bank account preferences could save them from excessive overdraft fees. The Consumer Finance Protection Bureau (2013) found that, on average, consumers who had overdraft protection paid close to $200 in banking fees each year whereas those who had opted out paid just under $40. So, while banking preferences feel outside of social workers' typical areas of expertise, advocating for clients and helping them save over $150 seems perfectly aligned with our work.

ACCESS TO THE "AMERICAN DREAM"

Landownership is a primary pathway to economic and political power. Further, it has been codified in our society as a hallmark of success and worthiness. Still, it is inaccessible to many.

Think back to the early days of the United States when only male landowners had the right to vote and thus take part in the formal political system. Land provides an asset to its owner which can be employed to produce income, leveraged to grow wealth, and used to gain societal and political access. Landownership, whether in the form of vast acreage worth millions of dollars or a small city lot on which a single-family house sits, provides an economic advantage to those who have it and an economic disadvantage to those who do not. It can be inherited by one's descendants and, in doing so, provides them with an existing foundation on which they can build their own wealth. Over time, even a relatively small asset, such as a few thousand dollars in home equity, a value that compounds over time and continues to provide advantages to the original owner's descendants, can create a vast gap between a person who has access to this wealth and a person who does not.

Why is it important to consider landownership? Many of the issues we address in this chapter have their roots in financial inequities that stem from past policies related to land—from the outright taking of land from people of color by White people to barriers put in place to prevent people of color from owning land. Today, even though only 60% of people living in the United States identify as White, non-Hispanic (U.S. Census Bureau, n.d.-a), they own nearly 93% of farmland (U.S. Department of Agriculture, n.d.) and 84% of owner-occupied housing units (U.S. Census Bureau, n.d.-b). While land policies over the centuries which have brought us to our current point in time could fill volumes, we highlight a few significant policies here. You are encouraged to seek a deeper understanding of these practices and policies and their continued impact on our society and the clients you are serving. Consider the following:

- Settler expansion, first along the Atlantic coast and then westward to the Pacific coast, stole a country's worth of land from Native Americans via conquest, forced removal, and consisted of treaties which were often subsequently broken (Geisler, 2014).
- After the Mexican American War of 1846, former Mexican citizens living in the newly acquired U.S. territory were supposed to be able to maintain their property rights according to end-of-war treaties. However, the United States required the landowners to petition for title confirmation, which was an arduous and expensive process and, even for successful petitioners, often resulted in the loss of some portion of land (Raish, 2000).
- A number of Pacific coast states enacted "Alien Land Laws" in the early 20th century that were explicitly intended to bar access to landownership by Asian Americans (Wilson, 2011).
- A generation after slavery was abolished, Black ownership of farmland reached its height of approximately 19 million acres in 1910 (Hinson, 2018) and a number of Black communities across the country were thriving with successful businesses (Brown, 2020). However, during the course of the 20th century, much of this hard-earned wealth would evaporate. Taking of Black farmland via heirs and partition sales, taxation, and other methods, as well as U.S. Department of Agriculture policies which systematically denied Black people access to programs, resulted in massive losses of land. By 1978, 57% of Black-owned farmland was gone as compared to 22% of White-owned farmland (Hinson, 2018). In urban areas and small towns such as Tulsa, OK, Rosewood, FL, East St. Louis, IL, and Elaine, AR, the destruction of Black communities by White people resulted not only in the loss of lives, but also in loss of property and other wealth, much of which has never been returned to those communities or their descendants (Brown, 2020).
- The stock market crash of 1929 and the ensuing Great Depression resulted in the failure of thousands of banks across the country. In response to this, Congress passed the Home Owners Loan Act which both helped people maintain their homes and created new entities that would support and oversee the banking industry. One of these entities, the Home Owners' Loan Corporation, created appraisal techniques which were subsequently adopted as appraisal standards by most of the banking industry. These standards, which helped banks determine the risk level of potential loans and therefore their willingness to provide a loan, determined the presence of any people who were racial or ethnic minorities or low income in a neighborhood, and made the entire neighborhood high risk. Literally, red lines were drawn around these neighborhoods on maps to show where banks should not provide loans or other types of investments. Thus, the practice of redlining was born (Woods, 2012). Despite laws passed over the years prohibiting discrimination in access to loans and credit, such practices still exist, yet now often take subtler forms such as lower investment rates in low income and communities of color than in White and higher income communities, or "reverse redlining" where subprime or predatory loan products are targeted at racial and ethnic minority and low-income communities (Burniston & Boccia, 2017).
- The economic boom following World War II laid the foundation for the development of suburbs. William Levitt, often considered the father of modern suburbia, envisioned his developments of affordable family housing for working people to be White only

communities. This was often enforced through restrictive covenants and pressure applied to banks to not approve loans for these developments for people of color. The Federal Housing Administration enabled this discrimination by claiming they had no role in challenging racial discrimination and by declining to provide mortgage insurance to mixed-race neighborhoods alleging the mixed-race characteristic could lead to instability and declining property values (Wolfinger, 2012).

In Case Study 12.2, we take a closer look at this last bullet point as an example of how homeownership—or lack thereof—compounds inequities and privileges from generation to generation. We then examine some of the nuances of homeownership itself as it relates to access and justice.

CASE STUDY 12.2—INTERGENERATIONAL IMPACTS OF HOMEOWNERSHIP

Returning from war, both John and Robert find good jobs at the same factory, get married, and decide to settle down and seek to buy homes in which they can raise their families. John finds a good deal on a beautiful new home in a new subdivision, easily obtains a loan, and moves in. Robert looks into buying a home in the same neighborhood as John but is barred from doing so because he is Black. He also is unable to obtain a loan that he can afford for a home in a neighborhood in which he wants to live, so Robert continues to rent. Through various tax advantages afforded him through homeownership, John is able to save money which he then uses to send two of his children to college. He also borrows against the equity in his home to help one of his children start a business. When he dies, he is able to pass both accumulated savings and a land asset onto his children. His children start their lives out wealthier than John did and are able to build on that wealth.

Robert, however, loses his good-paying job when the factory moves from the city out to the suburbs and he can no longer commute. He does obtain a new job, but it pays much less and never affords him the opportunity to own a home. He is unable to send his children to college and when he dies is able to pass on only a small cash savings. His children start out their lives no wealthier than their father and also struggle to find good-paying jobs and decent housing. Four generations later, John's great granddaughter Tanya is in college. Her family is able to help her through college. So, when she charges her books on her credit card, they are able to help her pay it off without incurring any charges or damage to her credit score. Robert's great grandson, Blaine, is also in college and is the first one in his family to do so. His family is supportive of his efforts but has very little money they can put toward his education, so he works to put himself through college and uses credit cards to make ends meet. (See Case Study 12.3 for the rest of the story.)

HOMEOWNERSHIP TODAY

Homeownership is often associated with "making it" and with financial security or independence. Further, we ascribe many social and economic benefits to homeownership in the United States. While it is true that, for many households, homeownership is an excellent economic and social decision that has benefits for the household for years to come, this is not the case for all who purchase a home. Further, many households are excluded from the opportunity to purchase a home because of policies and practices that are unjust. This is indeed tied to the previous discussion of banking access and utilization and to the history of oppression and injustice related to landownership.

Today, lower income households that do want to purchase homes are often penalized in the lending process because they are viewed as "high risk" by mortgage lenders. While not all minority households are low income, many are—and these borrowers then face intersectional oppression when accessing financial services such as mortgage loans. This is indeed reflective of our financial capabilities discussion, where consumers are not given options that reflect equitable opportunities.

While some banking policy has incentivized working with lower income borrowers, there are still many ways in which low-income borrowers are treated differently than their higher income counterparts. Mortgage finance is complex and involves many different parties. When lower income borrowers apply for mortgage financing, they are often encumbered by lower credit scores (which flag them as high risk) and have less liquidity or cash available for their purchase. Additionally, they may have limited opportunities for mortgage financing. Thus, lower income borrowers often end up with loans that have higher interest rates, high fee structures, and low introductory rates that escalate over time. So, while society tells borrowers to "buy a home to get ahead," the very act of buying a home may inhibit the ability to "get ahead" because of these institutional practices.

This discussion of housing finance is brief and incomplete, yet it is sufficient to raise awareness among social workers of the many inconsistencies and injustices that exist in this process. While many of us will work far outside of the housing industry, housing is a basic, essential human right for all. A working knowledge of how banking and lending practices perpetuate injustice is an important piece of our overall financial justice education. So too is understanding debt and credit.

ACCESSING CREDIT AND DEBT

It is difficult to finance the necessities in life without debt. One could argue that our society encourages us to take on debt. Automotive dealers want us to "buy here, pay here" and offer helpful "no credit, no problem!" banners waving in their lots. Big box stores tell us that we can shop for big ticket items with "no payments for 90 days!" and credit card companies regularly send solicitations offering balance transfer and introductory offers that seem enticing. Necessities of daily life (transportation, housing, furniture, phones, and other technology) are impossible to purchase without the extension of credit for all but the wealthiest among us.

Consumer debt comes in many forms and, as discussed previously, may be connected to traditional banking institutions or may be tied to AFSs. Whether a household can access "traditional" avenues for consumer debt and how much they can access is tied inherently to one's track record with repaying debt as measured by a consumer credit score. For many, though, building a credit score is very difficult. This credit invisibility is a growing issue of financial justice in the United States.

Credit Invisibility

Typically, loans made by financial institutions rely on a consumer credit score to determine if you can borrow money, how much you can borrow, and what the terms of your loan will be. Your credit score stands in as a proxy for how much of a risk you are to a lender.

What Is a Credit Score?

Credit-reporting agencies have created credit scores to estimate your risk to lenders—this risk comes in the form of a score. This credit score has become the default data point for credit worthiness. Three major credit bureaus in the United States produce credit scores (called a

"FICO score") and there may be variance in your score across the three credit bureaus. Complex algorithms based on a variety of factors compute credit scores utilizing data about the amount of debt you currently have, payments you owe, your payment history, your recent credit, the length of your credit history, and the different types of credit you have utilized.

What then happens to people who have never borrowed money or have a very limited borrowing history? Simply put, if you have not borrowed and paid back debt or your history of doing so is too old, your credit will be unscorable. The Consumer Finance Protection Bureau (2016) identified 26 million people as credit invisible (having no credit history) and another 19 million as unscorable. Together, it means that 45 million adults in the United States do not have a credit score. Paradoxically, some of these people have no credit score because they have followed financial advice and have not borrowed money or bought things they could not afford. Many, however, have utilized alternatives to regulated consumer credit to meet their financial obligations. The lack of a credit score can lead to profound challenges. Without a credit score borrowers cannot access mortgage financing, consumer loans from banks, and more. When these borrowers are approved, their loans are encumbered by higher servicing costs and interest rates (often referred to as "predatory loans"). Often, these consumers either do without credit or use alternative services where they remain credit invisible because pawn shops, payday loan providers, and businesses that might allow one to "carry a tab" do not interact with credit bureaus. Not surprisingly, being credit invisible or unscorable is more likely for those who live in low-income neighborhoods (rural and urban) for Black and Latinx individuals.

The impact of a credit score—or lack thereof—goes beyond approval for consumer loans. Credit scores are routinely used by landlords when deciding to whom to rent, insurance companies when deciding whom to insure and what rate to charge for their product, and even employers when making hiring decisions.

Being credit invisible or credit unscorable is a Catch-22. The way to become credit visible and credit scorable is to use credit. But without a credit score, consumers typically cannot get credit (or at least *affordable* credit). Since credit invisible and credit unscorable consumers cannot access credit, they cannot build the credit history needed to become credit visible and credit scorable.

One thing that can be especially frustrating for credit-invisible and credit-unscorable consumers is that they are making regular and timely monthly payments that are not counted toward their credit score. Businesses are not required by law to report to credit bureaus. Reporting to credit bureaus can be complicated and expensive so many smaller businesses choose not to report. In fact, even some small banks do not report mortgage and car loan payments to credit bureaus. Furthermore, many monthly payments consumers make do not typically count toward credit scores including rent, cell phones, internet, utilities, and insurances. Thus a consumer can pay numerous bills on time every month, and still be told that they are not credit worthy.

Strategies to become credit visible often include utilization of credit builder loans or taking on retail store credit cards. Credit builder loans originate within banks, so those who are underbanked or unbanked will not have access. Further, these loans come with constraints and do not extend an immediate line of credit to the borrower. Retail store credit cards are sometimes recommended as a form of credit building. These cards often have limited utility (limited to just one store) and have high interest rates and fees. Many retail businesses such as gas stations, department stores, and retail chains offer store credit cards. Since the retailer gets the benefit of making a sale to the consumer, these cards are often easier to access for credit-invisible and credit-unscorable people. Since one aspect of a person's credit score is the amount of credit used as compared to their allowable limit, even making modest purchases on a low-limit credit card can sometimes result in a low credit score. Having a store credit card also typically means a consumer will receive lots of high-pressure marketing from the store which can result in unplanned spending. Finally, consumers may be hit with high fees if they go over their credit limit or are late on a payment. Thus, neither of these are true solutions.

This discussion of credit scores, credit invisibility, and debt may feel outside of your area of expertise as a social worker. However, consider how much value and knowledge this information has and can have as you enter into your professional career. Think back to the case of Maggie (Case Study 12.1) and consider your depth of knowledge to help in her budgeting and planning now that you are more equipped to understand the complexities of credit, debt, and credit invisibility. Practice Perspective 12.3 provides insight into how one rural Community Development Financial Institution (CDFI) is working to address gaps in banking and credit access in their region.

PRACTICE PERSPECTIVE 12.3

REDBUD FINANCIAL ALTERNATIVES, INC.

Redbud Financial Alternatives, Inc. is an organization in Hazard, KY that uses small loans and financial education to make fair credit accessible to more people in rural Appalachia.

Redbud is a Community Development Financial Institution (CDFI), which is a designation of a nonprofit financial institution that is dedicated to filling credit access gaps in the market. There are CDFIs all over the nation serving those communities that banks cannot or do not serve. The U.S. Treasury supports these organizations through a dedicated fund to ensure all communities have access to credit. Many CDFIs focus on lending to small businesses or mortgage lending for low-income and first-time homebuyers.

Redbud focuses on "transforming credit from an obstacle to an opportunity" in eastern Kentucky where long travel times, high poverty rates, and limited access to information and options limit many communities' use of credit.

Redbud works closely with Housing Development Alliance, a Community Housing Development Organization that helps low-income families in eastern Kentucky become homeowners. As mentioned elsewhere in this text, homeownership is commonly thought to be one of the best ways to grow personal wealth. However, to be qualified for a home mortgage, borrowers need to have a certain credit score and a certain debt-to-income ratio (the amount of their income that goes out to their debt payments every month), depending on the lender. Redbud works with clients who have low credit scores or high debt-to-income ratios to help them become eligible for homeownership through small loans and financial education.

For example, Bonnie wants to own her own home, but several years ago the interest and fees on a credit card became unmanageable for her while she was in between jobs. She let the credit card bills pile up until the card was closed by the company and sent to a collection agency. While her credit report shows that she has made regular payments on her car loan, the credit card collections brought her score down to below the minimum score that the mortgage lender will accept.

(continued)

PRACTICE PERSPECTIVE 12.3 (continued)

Redbud can help Bonnie in two ways:

1. Redbud will show Bonnie how to monitor her credit and avoid situations that will make it worse again in the future. If Bonnie knows that the collections account was hurting her score, she can make a plan to address it, such as setting up a payment plan or settlement agreement with the collection agency. Credit scores take time to improve, and so a low score can significantly delay homeownership plans. A major action item that Redbud emphasizes is that everyone should check their credit report at least once a year. That way, bills that slipped through the cracks and ended up in collections do not continuously hurt a borrower's credit scores without their knowledge. Redbud also makes sure that clients understand how their credit score is composed and what behaviors contribute to a good credit score.

2. Redbud may give a small loan to Bonnie. This loan helps Bonnie in two ways, if she makes her payments on time. First, Bonnie can use the loan to pay off the collections account. Paying off this account will close the account and it will cease to negatively impact her credit score month to month. Second, as long as Bonnie can maintain good payments on her Redbud loan, she will have two good accounts—her Redbud loan and her car payments—working to improve her score over time.

Relevant financial education and access to fair credit products are important strategies to increase the ability of low- and moderate-income families to build their assets and gain financial independence. CDFIs like Redbud enact these strategies where they can, but credit has such a wide-reaching impact on our lives that in order to enact widespread change in how families understand and use credit, conversations about credit must become much more commonplace among helping professionals, like social workers, who have the skills and knowledge to help create change for individuals and within institutions.

Credit Cards

Consumer credit cards (MasterCard, Visa, American Express, and Discover) may feel ubiquitous, yet they are relatively new to the consumer finance world. It was not until the 1950s that credit cards began to play a role in consumer finance. While regulation has changed over time, the premise remains the same. A borrower is issued a line of credit and is given an opportunity to carry a balance from month to month, making minimum payments and paying compounding interest on any unpaid balance. Many who use credit cards do not understand the premise of interest that compounds monthly, or daily (as is typical with most consumer credit cards). In the United States, debt.org reports that almost 200 million adults have credit cards and that, on average, if someone has one card, they are likely to have at least four. Further, average credit card debt is about $9,000 per household (Debt.org, 2019). While those who are credit invisible or unscorable are less likely to access credit cards, for borrowers who do access credit cards, how they are used is important to understand. Case Study 12.3 provides an overview of two different credit card users and their experiences with consumer debt.

CASE STUDY 12.3—A TALE OF TWO CREDIT CARD USERS

Consider two college students with different financial situations, both of whom use a credit card. For one student, we will call her Tanya, the credit card provides a quick and easy way for her to buy her books. Tanya buys her fall semester textbooks from an online retailer and uses her credit card. The total purchase is $498.76. By buying online she saves money. Typically, she would pay cash for her books, but the online transaction makes that impossible. Thinking little of it, Tanya stuffs the receipt in her pocket.

Tanya is able to call her parents, tell them how much she spent, and get some help paying the bill. Because her mom is able to direct deposit into her bank account, Tanya has $500.00 in her account the next day and is able to go online to pay her credit card bill. She pays the bill in its entirety and thinks nothing of it. Her credit card balance returns to $0.00 and she is encumbered by no additional debt. She tends to use her credit card this way, never carrying a balance month to month.

For a second student, Blaine, the same decision is made. Online textbook outlet—easier, cheaper, no hassle with campus bookstore lines! Blaine uses his credit card to pay for his texts, totaling $377.33.

Blaine relies on his tips and hourly wages to pay his bills, credit card bill included. In addition to the textbooks, he charges a commuter/evening parking pass and a few housing essentials. Blaine budgets $40.00 per month to pay back his credit card bill, which now has a balance of right around $1,000. If Blaine were to stop using his credit card and just make payments, it would take him 29 months to pay off his credit card and he would pay $141 in interest (assuming an interest rate of 10.9%). However, as the semester moves forward, Blaine reduces his hours at work and therefore reduces his credit card payments (to $20.00 per month). He made a few payments, but charged a few groceries and in October is back at a $1,000 balance. Now, paying $20.00 per month, it would take Blaine 67 months to pay back the debt, accruing $349 in interest paid. This cycle repeats for Blaine over the course of the semester as he pays down the debt, but spends a little more, becoming comfortable carrying a $1,000.00 balance on the credit card. Without savings or a safety net, when Blaine ultimately quits his job to focus on school he misses a payment and the late fee ($65) is added to his balance. In order to try to make the payments more manageable, Blaine transfers half of his credit card balance to his other credit card—spacing out his payment due dates on the two cards.

Tanya and Blaine both use credit cards, but in very different ways. Blaine is more characteristic of consumers in the United States in 2020—carrying a balance, shifting debt, and making ends meet any way he can—economists might caution that his consumer behaviors are not rational, yet Blaine is doing what he has learned to do all of his life—to make ends meet. Because of their widespread availability and convenience, credit cards often allow consumers to spend beyond current means—and even encourage us to do so. Without an in-depth understanding of how interest compounds, many consumers find themselves paying exorbitant amounts of interest over time. Consider an average credit card debt of almost $9,000. If Blaine's $1,000 debt was going to cost him $349 in interest if he made payments that were manageable for his budget, imagine how much he would pay in interest on $9,000 of debt.

Linking the narratives from Tanya and Blaine's experiences with credit card debt (Case Study 12.3) back to John and Robert and their experiences with homeownership (Case Study 12.2) demonstrates the intergenerational nature of exclusion from financial systems.

WHERE DO WE GO FROM HERE?

Equipped now with an understanding of some of the ways in which financial systems are inherently unjust and with case studies that help to illuminate these injustices, what is our next step? With justice centered in our practice, we must disrupt the status quo and demand changes that enable financial capability and begin to redress the long-standing inequities in banking and finance.

The social work profession does have a history of engaging in change to help overcome financial injustice. Individual development accounts (IDAs) are an excellent example of how social work's voice and understanding of financial justice can be used to create change at the macro level. Introduced in the early 1990s, IDAs are savings accounts designed specifically to help low-income households save for education, homeownership, and small business start-up. In IDAs, savings are incentivized by matching funds from partners (e.g., CDFIs, credit unions, and nonprofits). The use of IDAs was legislated into policy in the 1996 Personal Responsibility and Work Opportunity Reconciliation Act and again in the 1998 Assets for Independence Act. Research bears out the success of IDAs as tools to increase savings (assets) among low-income households (Sherraden et al., 2003). Building on this tradition, social work can do more.

As we consider how to include financial justice in our practice, it is important to ask questions about programs and policies we envision as a part of the change needed. At the programmatic level, we must consider:

- How does this program function for different client groups (e.g., a situationally poor White man versus an intergenerationally impoverished Black woman)?
- How does this program enhance capabilities?
- Who really benefits from the success of the program?
- Is this program premised on traditional views of financial literacy or does it take into account systemic racism and sexism? Does it challenge the status quo?
- Who among your clients could benefit from this program?
- For your clients who are not benefited by this program, why? What does the program need in order to benefit this group of clients?

Another critical piece of this work is building one's network—having people who can help analyze existing policy or develop new policy, colleagues who can do legislative advocacy, groups who can launch campaigns in addition to all the micro and mezzo work being done with clients and in communities. It is overwhelming to think of having to help meet Maggie's immediate needs while developing and launching a campaign to address the systemic issues which impact her situation. It is incumbent on social workers to use their skills to best serve their clients and client groups. This does not mean we pigeonhole ourselves and opt out of developing skills in other areas. We need well-developed networks so we can all use our unique skills to better client outcomes. If I am a frontline social worker, I need to be able to clearly communicate with policy advocates about what is happening with my clients on a day-to-day basis. The policy advocates can use this information to shape policy and then lobby for its passage. The policy advocates can also help me to understand how a particular piece of policy is supposed to work that helps me to better serve my clients and advocate for them at the SNAP office, for example.

CONCLUSION

In this chapter, we have introduced the idea of reframing financial literacy and focussed on financial capability and access to financial institutions and resources as components of financial justice. What has been discussed herein does not do justice to the myriad other ways in which financial injustice shows up in the world around us. However, it is our hope that the chapter lays the foundation for further education and that it sets the stage for your own just practice.

DISCUSSION QUESTIONS

1. Why must financial justice encompass both literacy and capability?
2. Explain the intergenerational aspects of financial injustice.
3. Describe the systematic influence of lacking financial capability—what consequences occur?
4. Check your biases toward those experiencing financial injustice—for instance, what would you say to someone who smokes a pack of cigarettes each day but states they cannot afford the fee for the school field trip?

REFERENCES

Only key references appear in the print edition. The full reference list appears in the digital product on Springer Publishing Connect: connect.springerpub.com/content/book/978-0-8261-3539-1/chapter/ch12

Board of Governors of the Federal Reserve System. (2019, November). *Perspectives from Main Street: Bank branch access in rural communities.* https://www.federalreserve.gov/publications/files/bank-branch-access-in-rural-communities.pdf

Consumer Finance Protection Bureau. (2016, December). *Who are the credit invisibles? How to help people with limited credit histories.* https://files.consumerfinance.gov/f/documents/201612_cfpb_credit_invisible_policy_report.pdf

Debt.org. (2019). *Key figures behind America's consumer debt.* Retrieved July 15, 2020, from https://www.debt.org/faqs/americans-in-debt

Federal Deposit Insurance Corporation. (2017). *2017 FDIC National Survey of unbanked and underbanked households.* https://www.fdic.gov/householdsurvey/2017/2017execsumm.pdf

Kindle, P. (2013). The financial literacy of social work students. *Journal of Social Work Education, 49*(3), 397–407. https://doi.org/10.1080/10437797.2013.796853

National Federation of Credit Counseling. (2019). *2019 Consumer Financial Literacy Survey.* https://www.nfcc.org/resources/client-impact-and-research/2019-consumer-financial-literacy-survey

Nussbaum, M. (2003). Capabilities as fundamental entitlements: Sen and social justice. *Feminist Economics, 9*(2–3), 33–59. https://doi.org/10.1080/1354570022000077926

Sen, A. (1999). *Development as freedom.* Alfred A. Knopf.

Sherraden, M. S. (2013). Building blocks of financial capability. In J. M. Birkenmaier, J. Curley, & M. S. Sherraden (Eds.), *Financial capability and asset building: Research, education, policy, and practice* (pp. 3–43). Oxford University Press.

Sherraden, M. S., Laux, S., & Kauffman, C. (2007). Financial education for social workers. *Journal of Community Practice, 15*(3), 9–36. https://doi.org/10.1300/J125v15n03_02

Xu, X. (2019). The underbanked phenomena. *Journal of Financial Economic Policy, 11*(3), 385–404. https://doi.org/10.1108/JFEP-09-2018-0125

13

THE PERVASIVE INFLUENCE OF ECONOMIC INEQUALITY AND INCOME DISPARITY

Keith M. Kilty

LEARNING OBJECTIVES

Students will be able to:

- Understand how economic inequality has reached an extreme point now, since it started increasing in the 1980s.
- Articulate economic inequality from a social justice perspective.
- Explain the difference between income inequality and wealth inequality.
- Understand minimum wage, low wage, and living wage.
- Express the impact of economic inequality on people's lives.
- Identify steps toward social change and the reduction of economic inequality.

INTRODUCTION

In his second inaugural address in 1937, President Franklin D. Roosevelt stated that we should not measure prosperity by those who have so much; rather our prosperity as a nation is directly tied to the "abundance" of what we provide for those who do not have enough. What was Roosevelt trying to tell us? What exactly is abundance? How much is too much? How much is too little? How much is adequate? How much is reasonable? Should those who have share what they have with those who have not? If so, how much should they share? Why? Do we as a society have a moral obligation to take care of those who are vulnerable? How do we know who is privileged and who is vulnerable? Are some people more deserving of help than others? These are the kinds of questions that lie at the heart of economic inequality. Our values and sense of social justice—both on a personal and social level—guide us in trying to answer them. But are there clear answers to any of them—or to the concept of inequality itself?

Understanding the wealth gap—income inequality—is essential to justice-informed social work practice as so many of our clients experience adverse conditions as a result of disparate economic opportunities. We work within societal constraints, including negative sentiments toward the poor, or those who misuse substances, or have health or mental health diagnoses, and so forth, but that work is grounded within the core values of our profession, especially social justice and how economic inequality impacts on our work from an economic justice perspective. Ensuring sustainable, adequate, and appropriate income is a basic human right and is an essential aspect of justice-informed social work practice.

ECONOMIC INEQUALITY

We see the issue of economic inequality raised frequently in the media, on television news programs, in newspaper and magazine articles, on social media, and web sites. Some long-standing members of Congress and former candidates for president—particularly Bernie Sanders and Elizabeth Warren—have made economic inequality a major part of their national campaigns. However, there is no consensus on how to address income inequality and whether it even should be addressed in a capitalistic economy.

In order to highlight wealth disparities, the Occupy Wall Street movement brought income inequality into the national and media spotlight, giving rise to the conception of the 1% vs. the 99%—or the billionaires versus the rest of us. To some extent, the Occupy Wall Street movement grew out of the recession of 2007 to 2009—sometimes referred to as the "Great Recession"—when the housing bubble burst and markets throughout the world collapsed (Stiglitz, 2012). We saw images of people losing their homes and their life savings. Now it was not just the traditional poor, but many previously middle-income families that found themselves in dire straits. No longer was it just the urban homeless who were living on the streets or in tents. Many who lost their jobs found themselves unemployed for long periods and struggling to find new ones that paid as well. Some older people who had "followed the rules" by working hard and saving for their retirement found themselves destitute when the stock market collapsed. However, as we emerged from the recession and the economy recovered, we as a society seem to have lost much of our sympathy that was generated by the Great Recession of the early 2000s (Collins, 2018).

Yet why *should* economic inequality be seen as a social justice problem? Has there not always been inequality? Is that not simply an inevitable aspect of capitalism? Do those who work hard not deserve what they earn? Should the rewards society offers not go to those who worked hard to earn them? After all, the notion of "pulling oneself up by one's bootstraps" is one of the most significant values in American society, embodying the so-called "American Dream" (Kilty, 2015). Even when resources are provided for those who are struggling, there is a common belief that aid should go only to the "deserving poor." This idea goes back to the English poor laws which shaped the philosophical underpinnings of our country's values and laws when the British brought these ideas to the Americas. This philosophy still serves as the foundation for our current social safety net programs, such as Temporary Assistance for Needy Families (TANF), the Supplemental Nutrition Assistance Program (SNAP), and Medicaid, which have work requirements that individuals must meet in order to qualify and maintain benefits (Kilty & Segal, 2006).

DEFINING ECONOMIC INEQUALITY

Economic inequality fails to fairly distribute income across the population leaving some with excessive amounts of wealth, and some with no real wealth at all. We know that there are extremes of economic inequality, from the very poor to the very rich. In fact, a good way to think about inequality is to look at it as a continuum ranging from virtually nothing on one end to vast wealth on the other:

absolute poverty --- **absolute wealth**

According to the Knight Frank *Wealth Report* (Shirley, 2020), there are 240,575 individuals in the United States who are worth over $30 million, known as "ultra high net worth individuals" (UHNWI). That is a very heavy concentration of economic resources in the hands of only a handful of people, since the U.S. population is currently over 328 million people. Of those UHNWIs, 614 of them are billionaires. That is what, in fact, has given rise to much of the current concern with economic inequality. While a great deal of wealth is concentrated with a startlingly small number of people, the aforementioned "1%," a growing number of people are clustered toward the bottom of the continuum (where they possess little income or wealth) and a shrinking group represent what we consider the "middle class." In fact, in 2020, we note that while income has grown for all income categories since the recession of the early 2000s (see Figure 13.1), the richest households have actually *added* to their wealth while the other categories have not (Schaeffer, 2020).

LESS EXTREME INEQUALITY

Inequality has not always been so extreme. There have been times when the wealthy were still quite wealthy, but the continuum shrank (Wolff, 2017).

The Gilded Age of the late 19th century and the Roaring Twenties of the 20th century are other examples of extreme inequality. But economic collapses ended those periods, especially the Great Depression, which led to more progressive income tax policies that redistributed a significant amount of wealth.

Unfortunately, according to *Washington Post* writer Greg Sargent (2019), there has been a "massive triumph of the rich" during the first two decades of this century. He cites two major reasons for his statement: first, there has been a huge increase in incomes at the top of the income distribution; and, second, the tax code has changed dramatically so that the highest earners are taxed at a much lower rate than they were 50 years ago. That underscores what emerged from the Occupy Wall Street movement—there are two Americas: the 1% and the 99%. As we will see later, there are also large differences among those at the top. Indeed, it is the richest of the rich—the 0.1%—who have benefited most in recent decades.

The Stanford Center on Poverty and Inequality (2011) published "20 Facts About U.S. Inequality that Everyone Should Know" that helps to illustrate the depth of inequality. The fact sheet demonstrates how wage inequality has grown, how the gap between the pay of CEOs and the workers in their organizations has widened, and how gender wage gaps, education wage premiums, and child poverty, among other issues, have continued to rise. These gaps still remain today with racial segregation, incarceration rates, homelessness and the lack of affordable housing, and other critical factors also contributing to the current level of economic inequality in our country.

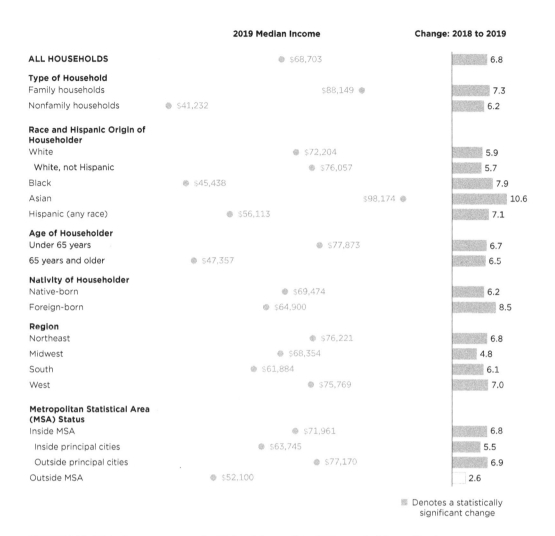

FIGURE 13.1 Median Income in the United States for All Households and by Race, Age, Navitity, Region, and MSA Status.

SOURCE: United States Census Bureau. (2020). *Income and poverty in the United States: 2019-current population reports.* www.census.gov/library/visualizations/2020/demo/p60-270.html

While income inequality is the main focus of this chapter, there is another type of economic inequality we need to appreciate: wealth inequality. It is an easy mistake to think of income inequality and wealth inequality as the same thing, but one is based on earnings from employment while the other is based on assets—all the things that are owned. Many wealthy people make a lot of money off their assets, but those earnings may not be treated as income because it is not employment related. Let us get a better understanding of the difference between these two types of economic inequality.

SOCIAL WORK IN ACTION 13.1

The Clintonville-Beechwold Community Resources Center (CRC) is one of six settlement houses in Columbus, Ohio. These institutions originated in the late 19th century, in an effort to bring educational, recreational, and social services to local neighborhoods. The founders, such as Jane Addams, typically wanted to bridge the gap between rich and poor, to unite neighborhoods in order for them to work together in alleviating the problems of poverty. Over a century later, many like CRC are still active in the effort to help those who are poor or low income and struggling to maintain adequate and safe homes and neighborhoods.

One of the programs offered by CRC is the Family Services and Choice Food Pantry. Food pantries like this are instrumental in reducing food insecurity, and this one is open 5 days a week (Monday through Friday). The setting is similar to a grocery store, where consumers can walk through the aisles with a shopping cart, free to choose the items they need. On Wednesdays fresh produce is available. Meals are available, including a sack lunch at noon Monday through Friday. There is also a community dinner on Tuesdays, after which diners are asked to help unload the fresh produce that is delivered every Tuesday evening. The goal here is to blur the line between service provider and client by having people interact with each other and helping CRC to provide services.

Other services are also available in the food pantry building, such as the Ohio Benefit Bank (OBB), which links clients to a variety of social service programs including SNAP, Home Energy Assistance Program (HEAP), and Medicare. Other programs available there are the assistance closet for clothing and household items, employment support, and a community garden. Again, many of these programs encourage participants to interact with other people in their neighborhood, encourage them to come to CRC for help with their particular needs, as well as encourage interaction with each other. That includes more affluent individuals in the area who may be interested in volunteer opportunities and in making in-kind or monetary donations.

In large urban areas, many people may feel isolated and have difficulty in developing social connections, especially the elderly. The programs offered by the Family Assistance Program are designed to bring people together for positive support. Discussions typically take place at the lunches and community meals, where people can find others with whom they can connect, crossing age, racial and ethnic, and class boundaries. By engaging together, members of the local community can find not only material assistance but also personal connections.

Recently, a crisis desk was added to the food pantry. The crisis desk is staffed by a social worker who can make referrals to case managers in CRC, in order to resolve a wide variety of problems. One of the most common is dealing with an eviction notice. According to the executive director, Bill Owens, the Franklin County area has one of the highest eviction rates in the state of Ohio. When people receive a notice, they will need to go to eviction court, and many, especially older people, can become very anxious and unsure of what they can do to keep from losing their homes. Nonpayment of rent often leads to these situations, where the crisis desk or a case manager can help individuals to look at their options and try to resolve their situations in a positive way. According to the Census Bureau, the poverty rate in 2017 in Franklin County, Ohio was 16.7% and the child poverty rate was 24.2%—affecting nearly one out of every four children in the county (data.census.gov).

The social workers and other social service providers working for CRC are on the frontline every day in helping those who are most vulnerable to the impact of economic inequality. The Family Assistance and Food Pantry Program at CRC has helped many clients over the years, and in turn many of those clients have helped others in the community as well, as a result of their experience at CRC.

INCOME INEQUALITY

Every year, the U.S. Census Bureau releases a report on household income and poverty which is typically available in September and includes information for the previous year. The information is drawn from the Current Population Survey Annual Social and Economic Supplements. Sources of income are compiled for each person in a household who is age 15 years or older.

It is important to note that a number of income sources are excluded, one of the most significant of which is capital gains that individuals receive from the sale of property, including stocks, bonds, houses, or cars, as well as lump-sum inheritances or insurance payments. Capital gains are especially important for wealthy individuals, who often receive large amounts of income from them. Additionally, not reporting this additional money has implications for how taxes are reported and paid.

Actual income of the wealthy, then, is likely underestimated in the Census Bureau reports on household income, as we will see when we turn to wealth inequality. At the same time, while there may be some limitations in the way that income is defined, the information provided by the Census Bureau's annual report is the most reliable that we have for gaining a picture of income inequality in the United States, especially since the Census Bureau has been compiling information on household income and poverty rates for over 60 years. That allows for long-term comparisons of income inequality.

One way to get a picture of the extent of income inequality for any given year is to look at the quintile distribution for household income. That is, we take the distribution of income and break it into five equal parts (or quintiles). Table 13.1 shows household income by quintile for 2019. As we can see, those at the top have much greater incomes than those at the bottom. The top quintile actually controls over half of the total earned income in 2019 (51.9%), more than all of the other 80% of Americans combined, while those in the bottom quintile took home just 3.1%. That is a ratio of 16.8 to 1—or $16.80 for someone at the top for every $1.00 for a person at the bottom—in terms of share of income.

The median household income for the country in 2019 was $68,703 (Semega et al., 2019), while the mean household income was $90,021. The median is the point at which a distribution is divided into two equal parts, while the mean takes every value into account (i.e., we add up all the values in a distribution and then divide by the total number of values). The mean is much more affected by skewness, where a distribution has more scores in one direction than in another. For

TABLE 13.1 **Household Income by Quintile: 2019**

QUINTILE	MEAN INCOME	SHARE OF AGGREGATE INCOME
Lowest fifth	$22,880	3.1
Second fifth	$53,823	8.3
Middle fifth	$86,261	14.1
Fourth fifth	$131,610	22.7
Highest fifth	$289,141	51.9
Top 5%	$511,287	23.0

SOURCE: United States Census Bureau. (2020). *Historical income tables.* www.census.gov/data/tables/time-series/demo/income-poverty/historical-income-families.html

income, there are more people with values at the bottom, but the fewer values at the top pull the entire distribution up.

It should be noted that the poverty threshold in 2019 for a household of four was $25,750 (U.S. Department of Health and Human Services, 2020) with the overall poverty rate at 10.5% (U.S. Census Bureau, 2020) meaning that half of the lowest quintile are in poverty but the remainder is very close as well, depending upon household size. The poverty rate provides another way of seeing the gap between rich and poor. The poverty rate is based on thresholds set by the Department of Health and Human Services. The Federal Poverty Line (FPL) for a family of four at $25,750 means that a family with an income at or below that point was considered to be in poverty.

We may well have an undercount when it comes to the level of poverty in the United States. Many current poverty experts have argued for years that the poverty thresholds we use are set too low (Kilty, 2015), and these numbers on household income and poverty suggest they may well be correct. Many poverty researchers (Kilty, 2015) now identify low-income families as those that are below 200% of the poverty line—or double the poverty line. If correct, that includes most of the bottom two quintiles or, *40% of all American households as low income.*

Income inequality has varied over time, but we are currently in a period where there has been dramatic growth in income at the top with a lesser percentage of growth going to those at the lower quintiles. According to Bannerjee and Duflo (2019), the Roaring Twenties saw extreme wealth with the wealthiest 1% accounting for 24% of the overall income; "that ratio was almost back to where it was in 1929" (p. 238). We can see how compelling this issue is when we look at what those at the top earn in a very short period of time compared to the typical wage-earner, with the top 1% of the wealthiest receiving more in a week of income than the bottom 40%, or bottom two quintiles, of annual income (Stiglitz, 2012).

WEALTH INEQUALITY

Understanding and measuring wealth can be complicated, just as we saw with income where there are many potential sources. Wealth, though, is usually treated as "net worth" at the household level: the difference between the assets that are owned and the debts that are owed (Eggleton & Munk, 2019). What is important to note here is that net worth (or wealth) can be negative, since some households may owe more than they have assets. In 2016, the value of household net worth varied dramatically depending on where a household fell on the distribution of net worth, with households at the bottom quintile owing more than they owned, while those at the top had significant net worth.

If we focus more specifically on the top, we can easily see the depth of wealth inequality. According to Collins (2012, p. 3), "The 1 percent has 35.6 percent of all private wealth, more than the bottom 95 percent combined. The 1 percent has 42.4 percent of all financial wealth, more than the bottom 97 percent combined." Those are truly staggering facts.

The typical middle-class household's wealth is largely reflected in home equity, not in the ownership of stocks, bonds, businesses, or rental properties. Housing value is not static and can change during an economic crisis, such as the housing bust that occurred in the first decade of this century, when some homeowners found the value of their home falling below what they owed on their mortgage—a phenomenon known as being "underwater" (McArthur & Edelman, 2017; Stiglizt, 2012). Furthermore, while owning a home may provide a degree of net worth, home equity is not always readily available as a liquid asset. Further, not all home owners experience growth in equity since whether or not a home's value increases can be proximal not only to the market itself but to neighborhood and location. For most homeowners, the house that is owned is where the household lives and is likely heavily mortgaged. Some may be able to draw on a home equity line of credit, but that is a loan that needs to be repaid with interest, just like a mortgage; in fact, home equity loans are second mortgages in banking terms. Further complicating this picture, most U.S. households have significant debt. As Eggleton and Munk (2019) show, the median debt in 2017 for credit card and store bills was $7,500, while it was $20,000 for student loan– and education-related expenses. Keep in mind that the median is the midpoint in a distribution, so half of all households had debt above those values.

That brings us back to the wealth gap between the 1% and the rest of Americans. We have probably all heard of the Forbes 400, an annual list of the wealthiest Americans that is published annually by the Forbes corporation. Everyone on that list is a billionaire, with Jeff Bezos (founder of Amazon) as the richest person in 2019, with a net worth of $116 billion, while the bottom of the list was a 13-way tie, where each was worth a "mere" $2.1 billion. The Bloomberg company publishes a daily index of the 500 richest people in the world. Jeff Bezos also led that list on December 27, 2019, with a net worth of $116 billion. The next two richest were Bill Gates and Bernard Arnault, both worth over $100 billion. Just the top ten billionaires on this list had a total value of $831.5 billion. Of those 500 on the Bloomberg list, 171 are from the United States alone, some 34.2% (or over one out of every three). That is a staggering amount of wealth in the hands of such a small number of people.

Just as with income inequality, wealth inequality has grown at times and shrunk at other times. We saw great increases in inequality during the Gilded Age at the end of the 19th century, then during the Roaring Twenties, and now in the 21st century (Wolff, 2017). Following the Gilded Age and the Roaring Twenties, the U.S. economy collapsed, with very large unemployment and declining opportunities for many. Now we are in another era where the wealthiest are seeing vast increases in their incomes and wealth. Income inequality reflects a certain point in time while wealth inequality is a more continuous measure reflecting "differences in access to resources" (Stiglitz, 2012, p. 2). Economic inequality ebbs and flows, but it has been part of our history since our country was colonized (Lindert & Williamson, 2016).

Wealth and income inequality cannot be discussed without acknowledging and calling out the disparities that exist, in particular with communities of color. The United States has a history of institutional and structural barriers to wealth and income accumulation that disproportionately impact people of color. Wealth and assets are, often, handed down from one generation to the next. If a family was denied the right to own property just two generations ago, their ability to generate wealth has been substantively impacted. Further, institutionalized racism that has limited access to banks, home ownership, and equitable pay—to name just a few—has furthered the wealth chasm between White and non-White households in the United States.

INEQUALITY, SOCIAL JUSTICE, AND SOCIAL WORK

What does inequality mean from a social justice perspective? Social justice focuses our attention on fairness and equity as they exist throughout society. Yet how can we achieve fair and equitable access to the resources of a society when those resources are distributed in a staggeringly disparate way? How do we ensure fair and equitable access to education, to housing, to medical care, to employment opportunities, to safety, and so forth, when the resources for those at the bottom are shrinking and being appropriated by those at the top?

An example is housing—who can afford not only adequate but comfortable housing in our major urban areas? Just look at the San Francisco Bay Area, where the median cost of a house is $1.3 million and the average rent is over $3,600 a month. And education—how do we ensure fair access to higher education? Just look at recent scandals involving the wealthy buying their children's admission into elite universities. The gap between rich and poor leads to a serious level of corruption that may threaten democratic institutions. There is indeed a price to pay for inequality (Stiglitz, 2012).

All societies have a set of values underlying what is considered to be just. In the United States, our social welfare policies reflect a belief in the need to be industrious, for people to earn what they have. As a result, our social safety net—that is, those services that are provided to protect those who are most vulnerable—is based on the idea of providing for the deserving poor, those who have fallen on hard times because of social circumstances rather than personal failings. Widows and people who lose their jobs because of economic crisis are believed to be more deserving than those who misuse substances or individuals who are viewed as not willing to work. Our social safety net is based on providing services in a means-tested manner, where those seeking assistance have to prove that they are poor and available for whatever menial work may be available. Not only do people have to prove that they have incomes below the poverty line, but they must also accept work requirements. That is not the case in many other societies, especially modern industrialized societies. In Western Europe, for example, most countries provide a mother's or children's allowance. All women and children are eligible, not just those who are poor or low income. These benefits are universal, and there is no need for means-testing. That contrasts sharply with the TANF public assistance and the Medicaid programs in the United States (Kilty, 2015).

In 1948, the United Nations General Assembly adopted the Universal Declaration of Human Rights, a set of human rights seen as necessary in order to ensure a safe and peaceful world. The 30 articles include protections from discrimination, protection from arbitrary arrest, just and fair criminal proceedings, protection from torture—essentially, basic human rights as envisioned in the founding of the United States. As stated in the Declaration of Independence: "We hold these truths to be self-evident, that all men are created equal, that they are endowed by their Creator with certain unalienable Rights, that among these are Life, Liberty and the pursuit of Happiness." Embedded in the U. N. Universal Declaration of Human Rights are also economic human rights, including the right to work and receive fair pay, the right to rest and leisure, the right to an adequate standard of living, and the right to education, including free public education at the primary and secondary levels.

The values expressed in the Declaration of Independence and the U. N. Universal Declaration of Human Rights reflect the core values of the Social Work profession. Social justice is integral to our profession, as well as our commitment to the dignity and worth of the person and the importance of human relationships. Much of social work practice is focused on the most vulnerable of our citizens, including children, low-income families, those with serious health and mental health conditions, the elderly, and those who are institutionalized including the 2.1 million American citizens in prisons and jails. We work within societal constraints, including negative sentiments toward the poor, those who misuse substances or have health or mental health diagnoses, sex workers, and so forth, but that work is grounded within the core values of our profession, especially social justice, and how economic inequality impacts on our work from an economic justice perspective We need to give careful thought to the core professional values identified by the National Association of Social Workers, as well as their Code of Ethics. I especially encourage you to look carefully at the Code of Ethics and to bring what the Code means to you to discussions in your social work classes, particularly practice classes. After all, you will be living with these values and codes as professionals.

EARNING A LIVING IN AMERICA

Most adults in the United States are part of the labor force and employed at least part-time. In many cases, individuals may work more than one job at a time. The problem that most working people face is whether their jobs pay them enough to support their families. As we saw earlier in Table 13.1, one out of every five households in this country had a household income of $22,880 or less, and the mean for this quintile was $13,775—about $1,148 a month. Think about where you live. If you were living in a household with that income, would you and your family be able to pay the rent every month, as well as food, transportation, clothing, and so forth? The next 20% of households had a mean of $37,293—about $3,108 a month. Those households are certainly better off, but, if living in most large cities, many would struggle to pay all the usual household expenses. According to Rentcafe.com (2020), the average rent cost for a one-bedroom apartment in the United States at the end of 2019 was $1,474—over one-third of the total income of the second quintile and beyond the average income for the first quintile. Yet we know that rent prices vary substantially around the country. The Northeast region was the highest, followed by the West. The Midwest and South were lower, but in no region was the average for a one-bedroom apartment below $1,100. Two-bedroom apartments ranged from over $3,000 in the Northeast to nearly $1,500 in the Midwest and South. According to the Pew Center (Fry, 2019), the average household size in the United States is 2.6 persons, meaning that most one-bedroom apartments would be very cramped. Paying the rent is obviously a serious problem for many households.

The Federal Poverty Line (FPL) for a two-person family in 2019 was $16,910, while it was $21,330 for a three-person family. The FPL was created in 1962 and based on the assumption that a typical family spent one-third of its income on food. Six decades later, that is still how the poverty line is determined (Kilty, 2015). Yet we have already seen that rent costs have become very high, and the typical family can no longer afford to spend a third of its after-tax income on food and still pay the rent. In fact, nearly the whole bottom quintile of the household income distribution falls near, if not below, the poverty line, especially when we take into account average household size. The official poverty rate in 2019, though, was 10.5%, much less than the 20% of Americans who fall into the bottom quintile of income. That means that far too many working families are struggling to make ends meet and may not be eligible to receive public resources because their incomes are above the poverty guidelines.

Minimum Wage Workers

The Federal minimum wage is $7.25. Twenty-one states also accept that as their minimum wage, but others have higher minimums. My home state is Ohio, where the minimum wage is now $8.70. In California, it is $13.00 for employers with 26 or more employees and $12.00 for employers with fewer employees. The state of Washington has the highest state rate, at $13.50. The District of Columbia has the highest overall at $15.00. The lowest is the territory of Puerto Rico at $6.55. There are also some cities and counties that have set higher rates. These minimums, though, apply to non-tipped workers; those who may get tips generally have a lower minimum that employers can pay.

Let us look at what the minimum wage means for someone who works full-time. They would earn a gross (before tax) income of $15,080 a year if working 40 hours per week and would be above the poverty line for a one-person household. However, every family size from that point on falls further and further below the poverty line, if there is only a single working family member earning minimum wage in that household. For the typical four-person household, with two adults and two children, that income puts them at 59% of the poverty line. It is widely recognized that minimum wage will not meet minimum needs. The U.S. social safety net potentially provides healthcare, housing assistance, childcare, food, and so forth—resources that in effect subsidize the minimum wage. That alleviates the need for employers to pay a better wage, even a living wage, and which increases business owners' profits at the expense of American tax payers.

According to the Bureau of Labor Statistics (2019), there were a total of 1.7 million working people whose wages were at or below the federal minimum wage for 2018, only about 2.1% of all workers. That seems to suggest that most people are earning higher wages. The question, then, is how much higher than the minimum are many people receiving. We know that the average household income for the first quintile is $13,775, which is 65% of the FPL for a family of three. Many households, then, may include workers earning above minimum wage but still receiving relatively low wages.

Low-Wage Workers

Before we turn specifically to low-wage workers, we need to look more generally at the term "worker." We have already seen that there is an official government definition that establishes the poverty line and adjusts it for family size, an absolute point at which a family of given size can be categorized as in poverty or not. The same is true for what it means to be a worker. Workers are members of the labor force, but what is the labor force? We might think that all adults are part of the labor force, but that is not actually the case. The labor force is defined as those who are 16 years old or older and who have been working or looking for work during the past 4 weeks. It excludes a number of groups, including homemakers, full-time students, retirees, military, and those who are institutionalized (including in jail or prison). Someone who is not working and has not looked for work in the past 4 weeks will be excluded. The labor force, then, consists of those who are working (regardless of how many hours per week) plus the unemployed (those who have been looking for work during the past 4 weeks). The unemployment rate is the ratio of the unemployed to the labor force.

According to the Bureau of Labor Statistics (2019), there were over 118 million full-time, year-round wage and salary workers during the third quarter of 2019; their median weekly earnings were $919, an annual income of $47,788. That is about $15,000 below the mean for the third quintile of household income, although these are individual earnings; many households have more than one earner present. As Table 13.2 shows, there were significant gender and race and ethnicity gaps. Men had higher median wages than women, in all race and ethnicity categories. Overall, women earned 82.3% of the median for men. Among some race and ethnicity categories, women's earnings as a percentage of men's was lower; the lowest is among Latinx women (73.9%). While there appears to be a substantial income benefit for Asian Americans (both male and female), the Asian American population is typically concentrated in large urban areas where salaries are higher, while the White, Black, and Latinx populations are more broadly spread around the country.

Ross and Bateman (2019) made modifications to some of the categories used by the Bureau of Labor Statistics, primarily around student status and self-employment. They also took into account the cost of living in various parts of the country and adjusted for the gender gap in wages. Their final count of workers was a total of 122 million, similar to that of the Bureau of Labor Statistics. To ascertain how many of these workers were low wage, they used a common standard where those falling below two-thirds of the median wage for full-time, year-round workers

TABLE 13.2 Median Weekly Earnings by Gender and Race and Ethnicity, in Dollars, for Third Quarter 2019

RACE/ETHNICITY	GENDER		
	MALE	FEMALE	OVERALL
White	1,025	843	943
Black	768	683	727
Hispanic	757	661	718
Asian	1,360	1,138	1,247
Overall	1,002	825	

SOURCE: Bureau of Labor Statistics. (2019, October 16). *Usual weekly earnings of wage and salary workers third quarter 2019* (USDL-18-1818) [News Release]. Bureau of Labor Statistics, U.S. Department of Labor. https://www.bls.gov/news.release/wkyeng.htm

are considered low-wage earners. Ross and Bateman found that 53 million workers (43.4%) met their definition of low wage, while 69 million were mid- to high-wage workers (56.6%). The fact that over 40% of workers are low wage reflects what we saw regarding household income, where the first quintile mean falls below the poverty line for a three-person family, while the second quintile mean falls below 200%—a common measure of low-income status. Economic inequality in America has become a zero-sum game in this era of increasing inequality, where trickle-up economics characterizes our country; that is, those at the top are gaining at the expense of those at the bottom.

CONSEQUENCES OF ECONOMIC INEQUALITY

As social workers, we work with some of the most vulnerable individuals, families, and groups in our society. These are people who find themselves struggling even in the best of times. In 2007, I began a documentary project which was intended to show the reality of those living in poverty and to challenge the myths and stereotypes about poverty and the poor that are still prevalent in our society. We titled the film, "Ain't I a Person" (borrowing from Sojourner Truth). The Great Recession had not yet started, but the people we interviewed had struggled throughout their lives. All had work histories and many had 2-year and 4-year degrees. Contrary to the stigmatized image that many have of the poor as lazy and unwilling to work, they were working or looking for work in an economy that provided them limited opportunities to climb out of poverty. The social safety net—those public services intended to help the poor and near poor—provided little then and less now (Kilty, 2015). A large number of working Americans receive low wages. Unemployment and "official" poverty numbers may be down, but wages during the past decade have remained stagnant for many. Low and stagnant wages, coupled with rapidly growing inequality, illustrate what Stiglitz (2012, p. 275) refers to as "certain stark and uncomfortable facts about the U.S. economy," including the fact that most recent economic growth in our country has benefited mainly the top 1%; that those at both the bottom and in the middle are more disadvantaged than they were at the beginning of this century; that the middle class has declined sharply; that the bottom is sinking deeper into hardship; and that economic mobility in the United States is increasingly limited at the same time that the social safety net continues to be cut deeper and deeper.

Stiglitz and others (e.g., Collins, 2012; Graeber, 2018) raise alarms about where we as a society are going. Greed permeates those at the top, who seem interested only in acquiring more and more. The flow of income and wealth from the bottom to the top is a clear indication of the insatiability of the already privileged. We see an increasing mean-spiritedness in our society, a coarsening of all of us—a fear that what little we have will be taken from us by others. Blaming the victim is back in vogue, where those at the bottom are blamed for their plight rather than blaming the social conditions that are actually responsible for their circumstances (Kilty, 2009). I am not trying to paint a picture of a dystopian future for America, but many people are indeed living lives of despair and helplessness.

We as social workers need to keep in mind that there are certain stereotypes and myths about the poor and near poor that are part of our culture and that affect us as well. We must challenge our own personal conceptions regarding some of our clients. Regardless of intentions, each of us experience implicit bias, perceptions regarding others that are influenced by experiences, culture, and social context. Implicit bias is not a phenomenon connected only to race; it refers to any sentiments or stereotypes we may have about various categories of people, whether on the basis of race and ethnicity, gender, economic class, religion, nationality, and so forth. As members of this society, we are all subject to these common elements of our culture, and we need to learn to identify and reflect on them in order to deal effectively and fairly with many of our clients who come from vulnerable social groups. Not only are we susceptible to implicit bias but so are our clients as well; many share social constructs of expectations related to specific identities, even when those relate to their own group. Implicit bias can yield inequality with consequences that can be seen in virtually any aspect of everyday life. Examples that specifically relate to economic injustice and income inequality include housing and homelessness, health and mortality, and food security.

CASE STUDY 13.1—SOCIAL WORKER PERSPECTIVE

Social work developed as a profession in the late 19th century, when the industrial revolution was fueling large-scale economic changes in the United States. Between 1880 and 1920, immigrants from southern and eastern Europe were coming in large numbers to fill the labor needs of the Industrial Revolution. Those immigrants were concentrated in the large cities in the Northeast. The poverty and harsh living conditions overwhelmed many of these new Americans, and a variety of social service organizations emerged that came to be known as the Charity Organization Societies (COS). These were typically private philanthropic associations, with the goal of providing for self-sufficiency of the poor under a set of proposed "scientific principles." There were two important approaches that developed in the fledgling profession of social work: one a focus on the individual and the other on the community. The first was exemplified in the writings of Mary Richmond, particularly her classic book *Social Diagnosis* which was published in 1917. She believed in making social work a profession by requiring educational credentials. The second was embodied in the work of Jane Addams, one of the leaders of the settlement house movement and one of the founders of Hull House in Chicago. She was a social activist and reformer.

Most of us cannot imagine living in the poverty-stricken areas of Boston, New York, or Philadelphia at the turn of the 20th century. Tenements were overcrowded and rampant with hunger and disease. Both infant and maternal mortality were very high. These conditions grew out of the extreme gap between rich and poor during the Gilded Age, conditions similar

(continued)

CASE STUDY 13.1—SOCIAL WORKER PERSPECTIVE (*continued*)

to what we are experiencing again. Unfortunately, a tension grew between the two approaches advocated by Addams and Richmond, a strain that is still part of the social work profession. Should we focus on individuals and families living in poverty, or should we focus on the social conditions underlying that poverty? Perhaps an alternative approach is to focus on both.

Social workers find themselves dealing with the impact of economic inequality every day. Many of the agencies in which we work provide important services for the most vulnerable in our society, especially mothers and children and those who are members of racial and ethnic minorities or recent immigrants or marginalized because of sexual orientation or disability or homelessness, and so forth. Settlement houses, such as CRC, provide critical resources in their neighborhoods. Social service workers determine eligibility for many public resources, such as WIC, SNAP, TANF, Medicaid. The resources clients receive are essential for their well-being as well as the well-being of their families. Helping someone to find job training or a job can lead them toward self-sufficiency. In sum, many people come to us overwhelmed by their problems and in need of the assistance we can provide.

At the same time, there are those who would argue that those services—public or private— are a band-aid and will not lead to resolving the more fundamental problem of why there is extreme economic inequality in the first place. That is a valid point, but it does not negate the assistance that many social workers provide in direct practice. We need to help those who are in need in the here and now. But we must not stop there. We also need to be advocates for change. Our profession has a great history of change agents: Bertha Capen Reynolds who believed in unionizing low-income workers; Frances Perkins who was the first woman to hold a presidential cabinet position as Secretary of Labor from 1933 to 1945; Harry Hopkins who was Franklin Delano Roosevelt's closest advisor and a key mover in creating the New Deal and the relief programs of the Works Progress Administration. In order for us to help our clients achieve self-sufficiency, we need to work at both the micro level in direct service and at the macro level of policy and reform. We must deal with the here and now while we try to create a better future for our clients and ourselves.

Housing and Homelessness

We have already noted that housing costs have risen substantially in recent years, but there are areas of the country that are more extreme than others, notably the Northeast and the West. Metcalf (2018) shows the impact of current housing policies which provide very limited public subsidies in the United States (what he refers to as "social housing"), in contrast with many western European societies. In those cities where the economy is strong, typical rents and housing prices are very high. Many people cannot afford these costs on their own. We see regular stories in the media of working people who are living in their cars or tents or sharing housing with others. A lot of new construction is for so-called "luxury" apartments, condominiums, and homes. That construction—as well as much existing housing stock—is well beyond the means of those in the bottom half of the household income distribution. While there are large numbers of homeless people, the real issue in housing is the extent of affordable housing. Many people are not considered homeless because they are living with other family members or nonfamily members.

All the same, homelessness continues to be a serious and growing problem in this country. The National Alliance to End Homelessness (2019) estimates that there were 552,830 homeless on any given night in 2018. However, the National Coalition for the Homeless (2018) argues that that estimate is far too low and that the actual number is over 1 million, because of the large numbers of recently homeless people who are staying in supportive housing. Whether half a million or a million, it is shocking that in a country as wealthy as the United States, so many of our citizens are homeless. Many cities and counties have homeless shelters, but too many people still find themselves spending nights on the streets, often in cold and hostile locations. Tsai (2018) calculated a lifetime prevalence rate of 4.2%—meaning that about one out of every 25 Americans is homeless at some point in their lives. According to Rahman et al. (2015), increasing numbers of homeless families have led to an increase in the number of homeless youth, with estimates from 22,700 to 100,000 at any given time. The next time you are in class, look around; there is likely at least one person in that class who would be considered homeless.

Health and Mortality

Health and well-being are affected by economic inequality. In fact, how long one lives is related to economic status. Egen et al. (2017) found that high-income women lived 7 years longer than low-income women, while for men the disparity was 9 years. Others have shown that health disparities are not simply a matter of differences in economic status and income, but rather inequalities related to the lower income status. Indeed, Vega and Sribney (2017) identify risk of disease as a byproduct of the environmental hazards associated with impoverished neighborhoods and communities as well as the "learned behavior in specific social contexts" (p. 1606) that places people at risk of poor health and well-being.

Inequality puts many people at long-term risk. As inequality sustains, those toward the bottom are living in more precarious situations for longer periods. In fact, they may live most, if not all, of their lives in increasingly lower economic circumstances, leading to concern that the stress associated with pervasive and chronic income inequality for adults may "spill over and affect their children" (Williams & Rosenstock, 2015, p. 618).

Further, Williams and Rosenstock (2015) note how long work hours and job insecurity—common in many contemporary minimum and low-wage jobs—are factors in mental health. Even suicide rates are affected by income inequality and can be reduced by increases in the minimum wage (Kaufman et al., 2019). It is astounding to realize that how long we live can be so dramatically affected by inequality.

Access to health care is another continuing problem. Although the Patient Protection and Affordable Care Act (ACA)—commonly known as "Obamacare"—increased access for many, not all states adopted all of its provisions, especially Medicaid expansion (Garfield et al., 2020). Currently, the ACA is under legal challenge and may well be struck down, which could put healthcare coverage for millions of people at risk, especially those who are low and middle income.

Hunger and Food Insecurity

Our economic situation has a direct and profound effect on the availability and nutritional value of the food we eat and subsequently on our health. Obesity rates are typically higher among low-income individuals, but that is not simply a function of eating high calorie foods. What kinds of foods are available to people are a function of their income. We saw that the poverty measure itself is based on the cost of a subsistence basket of food, not a highly nutritional one. The better one's diet is, the better one's health is, whether among adults (Egen et al., 2017) or children (Schmeer & Piperata, 2016). When we are standing in line at the supermarket and watching what others are buying, especially when they are using public benefits like SNAP, we have probably heard others making judgments about what beneficiaries are buying, without understanding their needs or requirements. For the most part, though, households including large numbers of people will choose inexpensive foods that fill a lot of stomachs, regardless of actual nutritional value.

Food insecurity is a common problem in this country. Roughly one out of every nine households was food insecure in 2018 (Coleman-Jensen et al., 2019). The largest public program for food insecurity is SNAP, formerly known and still often referred to as "Food Stamps." SNAP is managed by the Food and Nutrition Service of the U.S. Department of Agriculture which states a total of 36,406,681 individuals received benefits in October, 2019. The average monthly benefit was $122.57—or a daily benefit of $4.08. A household must be under 130% of the poverty line in order to qualify for benefits. Some 44% of recipients are children, while another 21% are adults living with those children. For most adults, there are now work requirements that must be met in order to be eligible. Since nutrition is so significantly related to health, food insecurity is an important consideration for social workers who are providing services for low-income families.

These are important benefits that help many people. Yet eligibility rules can be changed by any president. A current administration, whoever it is, can propose and enforce changes in eligibility, potentially increasing or decreasing the numbers of people receiving benefits. Note again that the daily benefit for SNAP recipients is about $4.00. That is $28.00 a week; to understand just how little that is, try living on that budget for a week. This exercise is especially meaningful for current college students, since increasing numbers of students are food insecure. According to Freudenberg et al. (2019), recent research has found food-insecure rates of 20% to 50% among students, well above the 11.1% rate in the general population. Being able to afford a college education is a growing problem for many young people, with tuition, fees, and room and board becoming more and more expensive (Rahman et al., 2015).

CASE STUDY 13.2—CLIENT PERSPECTIVE

The Special Supplemental Nutrition Program for Women, Infants and Children (WIC) is important for the health and well-being of pregnant, postpartum, and breastfeeding women, infants, and children up to age 5. We need to keep in mind, though, that WIC is a means-tested public assistance program. That means that recipients must be able to document that they are low income. While there is some discretion about eligibility at the state level, typically women and children in families with incomes below 185% of the FPL may be eligible. The program offers more than just food, including health screenings, nutrition and breastfeeding counseling, and immunization screening and referral, among other services. Encouraging new mothers to breastfeed their infants is an integral part of the program. In 2019, there were 6,400,000 total recipients, and the average monthly benefit for each was $45.00. Often more than one individual in a household will be a participant.

In addition to meeting an income standard of 185% of the FPL for their family size, a mother and her infants or young children may be eligible for other programs after WIC eligibility has been established, including SNAP, Medicaid, and TANF. Recipients also need to meet residency requirements for where they live, as well as being considered at nutritional risk by a healthcare provider. While WIC is a public assistance program, it is administered by the

(continued)

CASE STUDY 13.2—CLIENT PERSPECTIVE (*continued*)

U.S. Department of Agriculture through the Food and Nutrition Service, not the Department of Health and Human Services as are most other social service programs.

These are valuable services, and, according to the Food and Nutrition Service, over half of all infants in the country are WIC participants. That fact illustrates once again how many households in America are low income. At the same time, the level of benefits is quite low. Just how far will $45.00 a month go? Even if both mother and infant in a household qualify, that gives them a total of $90.00 a month.

The next time that you are in a grocery store, take a look at what qualifies for WIC. Not all foods do. Fresh foods are emphasized, although some packaged goods (e.g., infant cereals and cereals for older children that have limited added sugars) and canned goods (fruits and vegetables without added sugars, sodium, and other materials) qualify. Certain types of breads may not be eligible. Most grocery stores that accept WIC—and most do, just as they accept SNAP electronic benefit transfers (EBT) cards—will identify which items are WIC eligible. For example, you need to be careful since there are exclusions, such as fruit drinks, fruit-flavored -ades, sodas, or other non-juice beverages. Soups are excluded, as are yogurts with mixed-in ingredients or drinkable yogurts, or peanut spreads, or fruits and vegetables sold on salad bars, or peanuts or other nuts. Clearly there are many exclusions, much more than for SNAP benefits.

Imagine for a moment that you are a new mother with an infant, and you are walking through the aisles in a grocery store. You plan to use your WIC benefits and are looking at fresh produce—vegetables as well as fruits. How much is a pound of grapes? A pound of bananas? A pound of apples? Or celery, lettuce, green beans, tomatoes? Or eggs? Or cheese? Again, keep in mind that what is WIC-eligible will be identified, and that may limit your choices. Even if both mother and infant are eligible and receive benefits, that amounts to $3.00 a day. How far will that $90.00 go for a mother and infant who are eligible together? Will your benefits last a whole month or even 2 or 3 weeks? If you are also receiving SNAP benefits, you and your family may be able to make it through the month. But maybe not. You may also need to visit your local food pantry before the end of the month, although not all local food pantries have fresh produce available.

SOLUTIONS TO ECONOMIC INEQUALITY

What can be done about economic inequality? Has the gap between top and bottom become too great? Is this a threat to our future as a nation, as Stiglitz (2012) claims? We know that the gap between the rich (the 1%) and everyone else (the 99%) has been growing sharply for some four decades now, accelerating after Ronald Reagan became president. That is true of both income and wealth inequality. Yet, as we noted before, we have seen extreme inequality at other times in our history as well. The Gilded Age and the Roaring Twenties were both periods of economic inequality where those at the top got more and more of the national income and wealth. Both periods ended in economic crises, leading to movements for change. The Gilded Age led to the reforms of the Progressive Era, while the Roaring Twenties led to the Great Depression and Franklin Delano Roosevelt's New Deal. Both changes represented efforts to reclaim a common good, to bring about a redistribution of income and wealth that benefited society as a whole (Karger & Stoesz, 2018). Since the Occupy Wall Street movement and the past presidential campaigns of Bernie Sanders and Elizabeth Warren, we seem to be at a turning point once again.

As in the past, there are a variety of ways in which economic inequality can be reversed—perhaps even eliminated. Redistribution of wealth and resources is the key (Collins, 2018). Since the Great Depression, redistribution has come about largely through public efforts at the national level. The Social Security Act of 1935 created a variety of successful programs, especially old age pensions but also disability and public assistance programs. Lyndon B. Johnson's War on Poverty programs were significant policy extensions during the 1960s, including improving the level of Social Security benefits, public assistance benefits (monthly welfare checks and food programs), expansion of resources for K–12 and higher education, and Medicare (healthcare for older people) and Medicaid (healthcare for the poor). The War on Poverty reduced poverty rates in the United States from 19.0% in 1964 to 12.1% in 1969, a 36.3% reduction in the first 5 years of an underfunded program (Kilty, 2014).

There are fundamental questions that need to be addressed in understanding how economic inequality became as great as it is and in deciding what we should do about it (Kilty, 2015). Do we want to live in a society where it is everyone for themselves, or do we want to live in a society where there is a common good and a willingness to share the vast wealth that is available? Are we inherently driven only by greed and self-interest? Or are we compassionate and caring and willing to share? I am one of those who believe that humanity is capable of compassion and empathy and a commitment to the common good, that the vast wealth of America should be shared in a fair, equitable, and socially just way. Let us look at some ways in which those values might be given life.

Affordable Housing

One aspect of the so-called "American Dream" is to own one's own home. That may have been possible at one time but is becoming increasingly difficult in many parts of the country. That is particularly the case for low-wage workers. In 2016, median home values in the San Francisco Bay area were $813,108, followed by Los Angeles at $576,200 and San Diego at $515,325. In Seattle, the median is $396,717. In the Northeast, Boston led the way at $399,100, followed by New York City at $390,275, Washington, DC at $372,375, and Philadelphia at $209,900. In the Southeast, Miami was $236,867 (Metcalf, 2018). For families in the first two quintiles of the household income distribution, these are insurmountable barriers to living the American Dream. Those home prices will affect local rents as well. Finding affordable housing in most large urban areas in this country is clearly going to be a challenge for many.

Unfortunately, that means that many families may find themselves essentially homeless at one time or another. They may not be identified as homeless due to sharing living space with other family or nonfamily members. Housing policy in the United States tends to focus primarily on single-family housing or increasingly on "luxury" apartment complexes (i.e., apartments with amenities such as pools, workout centers, party rooms). What is needed is what Metcalf (2018) refers to as "social housing," housing that is public or subsidized or rent regulated. Public housing and rent subsidies are very uncommon, and rent-regulated or controlled housing is uncommon outside of the New York, San Francisco, and Los Angeles areas. Much of housing policy focuses on developers and builders, not on owners or renters, and that has been true since the Great Depression era housing policy (Karger & Stoesz, 2018). The tax law changes of 2017 have reduced certain ways that homeowners could benefit from income-tax deductions. According to Steuerle (2018), because interest is higher for more expensive homes, the tax subsidy for home mortgage interest deductions will go increasingly to those earning at least $100,000 a year (over 90%) while those earning under $50,000 will see only about 1% of the subsidy—less than $400 million dollars out of a total of $40 billion.

The numbers of people struggling to maintain a quality home are staggering. Nearly a million people are subject to eviction proceedings in any given year. Losing a job or having hours cut puts many families at risk, and as many as one out of two families among the 43 million who rent face high costs with their rents consuming 30% to 50% of their income (Tobias, 2018). Just as with the efforts to bring about a living wage, there are growing numbers of grassroots activists and community organizers working to create more social housing, from rent control to public housing and vouchers, around the country. In some cases, local social service organizations, such as settlement houses, are involved in trying to organize residents in their neighborhoods. In Richmond, California, new ordinances for rent control and just-cause eviction procedures were enacted in 2016. Another example is in Chicago, where activists are trying to overcome a longtime ban on rent control.

Living Wage

Earlier, we discussed the concepts of minimum wage and low-wage work. As we saw, a large proportion—over two out of every five workers—are doing low-wage work. Yet the federal poverty line is still based on the assumption that one-third of disposable income goes to food. Spending that much on food is obviously unfeasible for many families, who are spending as much as half their income on rent. That has led to a focus on a living wage which allows variation due to actual costs associated with the local community, including not just a single commodity such as food but also housing, health, childcare, clothing, transportation, and so forth: A living wage is intended to provide a "basic standard of living" (Sosnaud, 2016, p. 4) specific to the community, not the average in the United States. A basic standard of living varies from one proponent to another but generally is considered one that puts a family above the FPL, even the low-income standard of 200% of the FPL. As Sosnaud (2016) describes, a large number of social activists, including community organizers, labor unions, and grassroots activists have led living-wage campaigns around the country, such as those advocating the minimum wage to be $15 an hour.

The Massachusetts Institute of Technology provides a means for estimating a living wage for various cities and states around the country (livingwage.mit.edu). This site provides valuations for how much a person needs to be paid on an hourly basis in order to make a living wage, depending on the number of adults who are working and the number of children in a family. The site also provides a comparison between this living wage and the poverty wage (enough to bring a family of a given size to the FPL) and the minimum wage. Further, the site provides information on typical annual expenses, such as rent, food, transportation, medical expenses, and so forth. Think about your own family: how many adults and how many children? What would be a living wage in your hometown? What are typical expenses?

Another option is a universal basic income (UBI). We have heard recent calls for a UBI, including from recent political candidates (e.g., Andrew Yang). This is similar in many respects to the mother's or children's allowances, which are common in many Western European countries, where all children are provided a monthly benefit typically through the mother. In terms of a UBI, the benefit applies to every member of a society. Providing one to every person means that this is a universal benefit, at a level that would sustain a comfortable life. There would be no more means-testing, and the benefit would be paid out on an ongoing basis—weekly or monthly (Scialabba, 2017).

Tax Policy

Tax policy may not often be thought of as social welfare policy, but tax policy has been a major factor in the escalation of economic inequality since the Reagan years (Saez & Zucman, 2019) and can subsequently be a tool in the reduction of economic inequality. During the middle of the 20th century, the income tax was progressive, where one paid increasing levels of tax as income went up. That is hardly the case now. While there are seven brackets currently, the highest rate is 37% and applies to income above about $500,000 or more depending on marital status and how one files (single or joint). The current brackets are about what the rich were paying in the 1920s. The brackets were much higher during World War II, which helped to finance the war. That all started to change in the 1980s. Keep in mind, as we noted earlier, not all sources of income are subject to income tax. Some are taxed under capital gains, which are much, much lower. Current tax law allows the wealthy to hide much of their income as assets so that capital gains tax applies rather than income. We also need to be aware that corporations—especially large ones—pay very little in the way of taxes on corporate incomes. Most taxes are paid by individuals, and those at the bottom pay much more in terms of what their incomes are versus those at the top, especially when we take into account sales taxes, excise taxes, property taxes, and so forth.

In addition to the income tax is the payroll tax (or Social Security taxes), which is a flat tax. Everyone pays the same percentage—except that there is a cap. For 2019, the cap was $132,900. Once a person reaches the cap, they pay no more no matter how much they earn. That is, all earnings above the cap are exempt. This is a regressive tax, in that it affects those at the bottom much more than higher earners. Someone who earns $500,000 pays the same amount as someone at the cap. As a result the effective tax rate declines steadily after going past the cap (Kilty, 2015).

Income tax cuts have benefited the 1% to the disadvantage of most Americans during the last 40 years. Obviously, those who earn enough to put themselves into the top 1% have a lot of money at their disposal. They can use those resources to contribute to political campaigns, which has had a great deal to do with why and how these tax cuts came about (Saez & Zucman, 2019). It will likely take action at the grassroots level to make a socially just change in tax policy, as happened after the Great Depression. Hopefully, the rhetoric coming from some national political leaders will facilitate this effort. Actually, a good way to think about this issue is the idea of a maximum wage. If we can have a minimum wage, why not a maximum wage? When a person reaches the maximum bracket point, their effective tax rate becomes 100% for all income at that point or higher. Here again is where our beliefs about social justice are critical. Do we need the incentive of money to make us work hard? Or will we work for the satisfaction of doing what we do? If we accept that we are motivated to do what we do because of inherent satisfaction or pleasure or a commitment to the common good, then income beyond a certain point should not matter to us personally or to anyone else. We can set the maximum very high, perhaps $1,000,000 a month. That should be sufficient to live well and comfortably. All that income taken by taxes then contributes to the common good.

CONCLUSION

While we are at a crisis point once again in our society, we need to understand that this is nothing new. We have experienced many crises, from abolition and antislavery to the Civil War, to the women's suffrage movement, to the Great Depression, to World War II, to the civil rights movement of the 1950s and 1960s, to the housing crash of the 1980s, to the Great Inequality of the 21st century, through the pandemic of 2020, and beyond.

As national and state leaders had to react to the serious public health problem caused by coronavirus disease 2019 (COVID-19), stay-at-home orders were issued in most states, and much of the economy was shut down. By late May 2020, over 36 million Americans had filed for unemployment compensation with fears of unemployment rates rivaling that of the Great Depression. We saw images of overwhelmed public hospitals, lines miles-long at food banks, renters fearful that they will be evicted from their apartments, while the rich just get richer. Congress passed legislation to help people who have lost their jobs and the owners of small businesses. Yet we heard that the stimulus checks did not reach the unemployed and that large corporations received loans and grants ostensibly intended for small, so-called "mom-and-pop" businesses. According to Collins et al. (2020), Jeff Bezos's personal fortune jumped by $25 billion between January 1 and April 15, 2020. He is not the only billionaire profiting from the pandemic. Mark Zuckerberg's wealth is up by $21 billion, Steve Ballmer by $11.6 billion, Elon Musk by $11.3 billion, and Michael Bloomberg by $10 billion. According to Payne et al. (2020), many members of the U.S. Congress took advantage of the stock markets to increase their own wealth. Are these the people who are being called "heroes" because they are on the frontlines of the pandemic? Are these the people who stock grocery shelves or clean hospital rooms or drive busses?

The 21st century has seen a dramatic escalation in economic inequality, both in terms of income and wealth. Those at the top not only earn more than their fair share, but they also own a great deal more than most of the American public. These inequities have led to an increasing focus on the very top—the 1%—versus the rest of us—the 99%. Yet as we have seen, there is more to inequality than just the division between the top and everyone else. There was a time when being part of the Forbes 400 meant having millions of dollars. Now the entire Forbes 400 are billionaires, but not all billionaires can make that list. Over 200 American billionaires now fall short (Collins et al., 2020).

Many social critics are concerned now about the state of our society and whether our democratic institutions can survive extreme inequality (e.g., Collins, 2012; Graeber, 2018; Stiglitz, 2012; Wolff, 2017). Vast wealth leads to more than just accumulation based on vast greed and corruption; it also leads to immense power and influence in the hands of a few. Over 30 years ago and long before the Citizens United versus Federal Election Commission Supreme Court decision in 2010, Philip Stern (1988) published a book titled *The Best Congress Money Can Buy*, raising the alarm about how big money was taking over American politics. A decade later, Kevin Phillips (2002), in *Wealth and Democracy*, began to question whether democracy could survive the rich. Later, in *Dark Money*, the journalist Jane Mayer (2016) detailed the machinations of the billionaire class in furthering their control over national politics, including having to face the ire of the extremely wealthy Koch brothers.

Inequality has always been present in American life, manifesting itself in the everyday lives of ordinary citizens. Yet now more than ever, it impacts on quality of life: on who can live where, on the quality not only of our homes but of the neighborhoods in which we find ourselves able to afford to live, on access to adequate and equitable healthcare, on the value and worth of our education, on the employment needed to sustain a quality life, on an adequate and nutritious diet, and on and on. We saw that at least two out of every five Americans are low-wage earners. These are people who work long, hard hours struggling to care for their families. These are people who were being left behind by the American Dream, even before the 2020 COVID-19 pandemic.

According to Quart and Serkez (2020), the rich need only 2 months to save enough to get them through 4 weeks of expenses, while it takes middle income Americans more than 2 years to save for that same 4 weeks of expenses. Imagine what it would take for the typical low-wage worker, many of whom are on the frontlines in meat-packing plants and doing personal care in a hospital. Similarly, as devastating and long lasting as the health impact of the COVID-19 pandemic is, the economic consequences will be with us for years.

How will we emerge from this latest crisis? We have seen great change in the past. We have seen struggles for freedom and justice succeed. We have also seen periods of great inequality where our core values and principles shrank away. Throughout these times of tumult and change, social workers have often been in the forefront advocating for social, economic, and political justice, making efforts to redistribute the vast wealth and resources of our society in a more fair and equitable way. In the first half of the 20th century, it was social workers such as Jane Addams, Frances Perkins, Harry Hopkins, Bertha Capen Reyonlds, and Whitney Young. Later it was Frances Fox Piven and Mimi Abramovitz. But our voices too have always been important in the struggle for a just and humane society. If we want a more just and humane society, then it is up to each and every one of us to stand up and demand—as individual citizens and as professionals—the life that we really want, not just for ourselves, but for all.

DISCUSSION QUESTIONS

1. Explain the connection between economic inequality and mental health, including the association of suicide and income.
2. What benefit is there to not having capital gains count as income?
3. How do Americans justify that those in the upper quintile of income have more wealth than all of the other quintiles combined?
4. Explore your own biases with those who are impoverished. What automatic thoughts are generated when you think of someone who is poor? What message can you use to combat those automatic thoughts?

REFERENCES

Only key references appear in the print edition. The full reference list appears in the digital product on Springer Publishing Connect: connect.springerpub.com/content/book/978-0-8261-3539-1/chapter/ch13

Bannerjee, A. V., & Duflo, E. (2019). *Good economics for hard times*. Public Affairs.
Collins, C. (2018). *Is inequality in America irreversible?* Polity.
Karger, H. J., & Stoesz, D. (2018). *American social welfare policy: A pluralist approach* (8th ed.). Pearson.
Kilty, K. M., & Segal, E. A. (2006). Welfare reform: What's poverty got to do with it? In K. M. Kilty & E. A. Segal (Eds.), *The promise of welfare reform* (pp. 109–120). Haworth.
Metcalf, G. (2018). Sand castles before the tide? Affordable housing in expensive cities. *Journal of Economic Perspectives, 32*(1), 59–80. https://doi.org/10.1257/jep.32.1.59
Ross, M., & Bateman, (2019). *Meet the low-wage labor force*. Brookings Institution. https://www.brookings.edu/wp-content/uploads/2019/11/201911_Brookings-Metro_low-wage-workforce_Ross-Bateman.pdf
Sargent, G. (2019, December 9). The massive triumph of the rich, illustrated by stunning new data (The Plum Line). *The Washington Post*. https://www.washingtonpost.com/opinions/2019/12/09/massive-triumph-rich-illustrated-by-stunning-new-data
Schaeffer, K. (2020, February 7). *Six facts about economic inequality in the U.S.* Pew Research Center, Fact Tank. https://www.pewresearch.org/fact-tank/2020/02/07/6-facts-about-economic-inequality-in-the-u-s
Sosnaud, B. (2016). Living wage ordinances and wages, poverty, and unemployment in US cities. *Social Service Review, 90*(1), 3–34. https://doi.org/10.1086/686581
United States Census Bureau. (2020). Income, poverty and health insurance coverage in the United States: 2019. https://www.census.gov/newsroom/press-releases/2020/income-poverty.html
Wolff, E. N. (2017). *A century of wealth in America*. Belknap.

14

IMPLEMENTING JUSTICE-DRIVEN SOCIAL WORK PRACTICE

Kalea Benner | Natalie D. Pope | Diane N. Loeffler | Elaine C. Strawn

LEARNING OBJECTIVES

Students will be able to:

- Articulate the multifaceted and complex ways in which intersectionality and interconnectivity of injustices result in someone who is impacted by one aspect of injustice is likely to have that impact compounded by an effect from another.
- Assess ways in which intersectionality of identities compounds the injustices that one experiences.
- Define justice and articulate the importance of framing justice as a collective, and not individual, endeavor.
- Identify ways in which strategies essential to justice-driven social work practice are utilized and how those skills align with the mission and vision of the social work profession.

INTRODUCTION

Social work practice is dedicated to those who are the most vulnerable in our society, including those with physical and mental health conditions, those who are incarcerated or under supervision of the criminal justice system, children, the impoverished, the disenfranchised, the marginalized, and most of all, those who need a voice. While it is the individual who experiences the trauma of injustice, the solutions must be identified and achieved in larger structural systems. Many of our systems are broken, and increase the risk of poor outcomes once someone engages in them. This is the task, and the challenge, of justice-informed social work practice, working with individuals at the micro level but effecting change in the larger macro environment.

JUSTICE-INFORMED SOCIAL WORK PRACTICE

As social workers, justice-informed practice is a professional imperative. Social workers must proceed with clarity in fulfilling our role, yet do so within the context of a multitude of settings and systems that often fail to share a common purpose of yielding transparent, equitable opportunities for all. As the preceding chapters have highlighted, injustice(s) impacts individuals and communities but they are most frequently a result of structural and systematic problems. Allowing injustice to continue stands in the way of allowing individuals, families, groups, communities—and our entire society—from truly living into our capabilities. Changing unjust and inequitable systems is a compelling start to achieving justice and removing structural discrimination. Repeatedly, unjust systems produce unjust results that ultimately culminate in poor outcomes for individuals. Thus, our practice must be firmly planted on the multitude of systems in which our clients are engaged. Our work with these systems must be guided by knowledge that is culturally and contextually driven and that amplifies the voices of those who have been marginalized.

CASE STUDY 14.1—SEEKING INDIVIDUAL ANSWERS TO SYSTEMIC AND STRUCTURAL ISSUES FAILS OUR CLIENTS

Celia is a 6-year-old kindergartener whose teacher has just referred her for an evaluation by the social worker, stating she is sure Celia has attention deficit/hyperactivity disorder (ADHD). The teacher notes that Celia struggles to stay on task, often looks out the window, has few peer relationships, distracts easily, and frequently falls asleep at her desk. The last incident leading to the referral is that Celia slept through dismissal, a particularly noisy time when students are gathering their backpacks, and announcements are delivered over the loudspeaker. The teacher states that at this point in the school year, most of the students are used to the routine but as other children find the rhythm of the day, Celia seems to fall further behind, often appearing confused, inattentive, and struggling to focus.

During the assessment, the social worker notes that Celia does appear tired but is able to focus throughout their time together. Celia describes a family situation where her mother's ex-boyfriend is "mean" and sometimes "hurts" her mom who has filed an ex-parte against him, in an effort to have law enforcement ensure that he leaves them alone. Mom cannot afford to move so feels stuck in their housing. Celia's mom has been very clear that if and/or when he shows up at their house, Celia is to leave immediately, get to the neighbor's house, and call 911. This is an appropriate parental response, seeking to keep her child safe. The challenge is that it is usually late at night when he does show up, and typically after he has been drinking. Developmentally, Celia has internalized her mom's instructions as something for which she is responsible; she has not yet developed the cognitive means to understand conditional aspects (e.g., *if* he shows up rather than waiting for him to show up) of that responsibility for her own and her mom's safety. Ultimately, Celia tries to stay awake every night until her mom goes to bed, thinking he does not typically come after that.

The reduced sleep and sense of anxiety related to mom's ex-boyfriend possibly returning is taking a toll on her performance at school, and she is struggling to engage. While her teacher was right to refer Celia to the social worker, a thorough assessment reveals that Celia's behavior is a consequence of a lack of safety and security due to familial challenges. Repeatedly, individuals are identified as the problem but, as you can see, Celia's behavior is an understandable response to larger systemic and structural issues within her family. We must be careful to understand our clients' contexts and examine these larger issues or the result will be to unfairly blame the individual, ultimately compounding the injustices our clients experience.

OVERLAPPING JUSTICE NEEDS

Celia's example illustrates the influence of critical theory, reflecting there is never just one aspect to address with a client and that targeting a single point of change, especially individual behavior, fails to acknowledge the complexity of causes and subsequent needs. Each chapter of this text, whether related to housing, education, poverty, criminal justice, health, and so forth, discusses the overlapping and entangled work of systems that have disproportionately unjust impacts. While the social work profession conceptualizes justice as social, economic, and environmental, each of these are interrelated, forming an interconnected impact related to the lack of justice, meaning that individuals affected by one aspect of injustice are likely to be impacted by another. For instance, those living in poverty are more likely to experience environmental degradation which in turn leads to disparate health outcomes. This can be further compounded by intersectionality in which vulnerable identities place the individual at even greater risk of injustice. An example is if there are two women who are single mothers, and one is a person of color and one is not, the mother who is a person of color a has a higher risk of being poor, and is therefore more likely to experience the negative outcomes of poverty associated with single parenthood in addition to the oppression and racial trauma often associated with being a person of color.

As a justice-informed practitioner, it is important that you are aware of the collective impact of injustice. For social workers, we identify social, economic, and environmental justice as the context for our practice. Working with individuals to encompass social, economic, and environmental solutions provides a holistic perspective that allows social workers to view clients within the context of the situational and structural settings that create, as well as obstruct, access and availability to resources. This access and availability to resources are critical for understanding social, economic, and environmental justice.

Social Justice

Social justice is one of six core professional social work values designated by the National Association of Social Workers (2017a) and forms the bedrock foundation for all social work practice. Social justice is a virtue (Center for Economic and Social Justice, 2017), yet also an action, a mutual obligation to ensure fairness (Rawls, 1999). By emphasizing mutual obligation, this fairness approach takes the onus off those who are vulnerable, and places responsibility for achieving justice on all of society. Social justice is frequently thought of as equality, yet this is an unlikely outcome. Instead, social workers seek to facilitate equity, in resources, in opportunities, in access and in utilization, and in removing barriers such as stigma, discrimination, and ill-intentioned policies.

Historically, seeking social justice has often been left to the marginalized and oppressed populations who are denied equity, rather than being an expectation associated with those who have privilege, those with benefits ascribed simply due to dominant identities, particularly being White, heterosexual, and male. Privilege also serves to maintain the marginalization of other populations. Expecting social justice to be achieved by those without power is an oxymoron, tantamount to expecting that you as the student in a course will dictate to your instructor what grade to assign: it's unlikely to have the result you desire. Those who need justice are at the other end of the spectrum from those in power, are far from privileged, and typically experience marginalization through oppression.

Oppression is the opposite of privilege, a traumatizing form of injustice experienced through exploitation, marginalization, powerlessness, cultural imperialism, and violence (Young, 2004).

When clients face oppression with these all-encompassing effects, they face an absence of choice, of empowerment, of self-determination, all of which are the antithesis of what we seek. Social workers must identify these deleterious effects in order to address the lifelong, and generational, impacts that oppression can have.

Social workers must be attuned to this impact of oppression and ensure that all members are heard. Oppression silences. One aspect of consideration is to examine who the community informants are and ensure that all voices are shared. Effective change occurs only when a collective decision is made to work alongside others for a common goal. Critical theory would suggest that those voices that are most commonly heard do not always have the lived experiences to properly understand and address the needs. Yet those populations most vulnerable to social injustice typically have the least amount of social capital and should not bear the brunt of bringing about social change. Social workers, using the available (or developed) strengths and resources, must feel the responsibility to work with and on behalf of others to bring about change for the better.

Economic Justice

Economic justice interfaces with social justice as it relates to wealth and income. The United Nations (UN, 2006) refers to economic justice as a human right and describes efforts to close the wealth gap as distributive justice, whereby resources are allocated based upon need. We also see efforts to address income disparities as a form of distributive justice. Other considerations of economic justice include opportunities for meaningful, sustainable work and fair compensation (UN, 2006) in addition to addressing structural discrimination that unfairly targets the poor such as predatory lending practices and a criminal justice system whose fines and fees are excessively burdensome to the poor (Southern Poverty Law Center, n.d.). Pierson (2019) identifies economic justice as a basic human right, yet economic insecurity and income disparity remains inescapable for far too many.

Economic justice also encompasses financial justice, the ability to have financial literacy and capability. Many traditional approaches to budgeting and financial management are not culturally relevant and are not reflective of our clients' experiences because they are built upon normative culturally and socially bound expectations around what financial success is and how that is operationalized. For instance, the suggestion of saving 10% of a monthly income is simply not realistic for many of our clients and feels patronizing and dismissive to even discuss when food insecurity or housing instability exists.

Finally, economic justice encompasses the policies and practices that disproportionately impact the poor through income and availability of resources. These economic policies and practices are inextricably entwined with social justice as many are intended to offset the consequences of social injustice. Sometimes, policies are intended to restrict access to resources, such as time-limiting access to Temporary Assistance for Needy Families (TANF) resulting in families accessing support for only a maximum of 5 years, or the work requirements for obtaining Medicaid. Other times, there are unintended consequences of policies such as requiring recipients of Social Security Disability Insurance (SSDI) payments to not work or face a reduction of benefits, thus compromising the individual's autonomy in determining income.

It is important that we understand the impact of economic policies on our clients and realize that even good intentions can have poor outcomes. Indeed, social workers need to shift from policies and practices that focus solely on minimal income and maintenance, to policies and practices that create opportunities for low-income households to accumulate wealth and/or asset holdings (Sherraden, 1991). Social work practitioners implement economic justice by focusing on meeting immediate needs through access of existing resources, but also work toward meeting future needs through asset building.

Environmental Justice

Similar to social and economic justice, environmental justice is a human rights issue. The concept of fairness is again present as the Environmental Protection Agency (n.d.) describes environmental justice as fair treatment in the development and application of environmental policies and regulations. Despite recognition of the need for fairness, environmental injustice disproportionately impacts individuals, typically based upon wealth, income, and location. The environmental effects of industry most significantly impact our communities of color and those who are poor (Skelton & Miller, 2016) which then creates additional disparities in employment, food insecurity, and access to affordable housing. Additionally, environmental and natural disasters unduly affect those same communities whose vulnerability is deepened by the lack of sufficient resources to ensure a robust recovery.

Environmental waste, disasters, and destruction are not the only aspects of concern with people's physical environment. When we examine how people are impacted by their environment, by the place and the community in which they live, we know that impoverished settings are more likely to have schools and students with poorer educational outcomes (Taylor, 2017), reduced health outcomes, and higher mortality (Mode et al., 2016).

Environmental justice, therefore, aims to achieve an "equitable" distribution of environmental degradation so that one population is not impacted significantly more than any other in order to establish healthier and more equitable communities. Social work's experience in working with community strengths and needs, responding in crises, and mobilizing disparate groups all contribute to addressing environmental justice. Social work interventions must be holistic in nature, and address the health and behavioral health, social, cultural, and spiritual needs of individuals and impacted communities (National Association of Social Workers [NASW], 2017b).

Environmental justice reflects aspects of living most often seen as universal human rights that can be compromised in areas where there is limited access to adequate healthcare, affordable housing, or secure, safe environments. The impact of injustice has lingering effects, sometimes experienced over multiple generations. For instance, children who grow up impoverished, even if as adults they have higher socioeconomic status, are still at higher risk for poor health outcomes like diabetes and hypertension. This connection between environment and health is just one way in which justice interconnects, much as identities intersect. Interconnectivity as it relates to justice implies that someone who is impacted by one aspect of injustice is likely to have that impact compounded by an effect from another.

CASE STUDY 14.2—INTERSECTIONALITY OF MARGINALIZED IDENTITIES AND INJUSTICE

Zoe is a first generation, 19-year-old college student who has taken out $13,626 in student loans even though she works 30 hours a week and lives with her boyfriend, Robbie, who pays for most of the living expenses. Zoe had an excellent high school grade point average (GPA), but she did poorly on the American College Test (ACT) exam so is having to take college preparatory classes just to be able to then take college-level math and English courses. Zoe feels like the strategies that helped her succeed in high school are not helping her in college. She currently has a 2.3 GPA and this GPA puts her at risk of not being able to be accepted to

(continued)

CASE STUDY 14.2—INTERSECTIONALITY OF MARGINALIZED IDENTITIES AND INJUSTICE (continued)

the bachelor's degree social work (BSW) program which requires a 2.5. So far, she has taken (and paid for) 30 credit hours but has course credit for only 24 hours because of the college prep classes. She recently met with her advisor and was told that she is behind in credits, even though she has taken a full load every semester, and will either need to take summer classes or extend beyond her planned 4 years. Zoe's mom is questioning whether college is really what she should be doing, going significantly into debt when she may not even be able to graduate. She is suggesting to Zoe that she talk to her uncle about working for him instead of finishing college.

In meeting with her advisor, Zoe seems fairly stressed and became teary as she expressed uncertainty over her future. She stated that it has been "rough" with Robbie lately, but she is not sure how to get out of the relationship. She does not have her own bank account (her paycheck is added to a debit Visa) so she does not have a credit score to apply for housing, and realistically she cannot afford to live on her own. Zoe's father died of a heart attack at the age of 45 when she was in eighth grade, a time in which she describes being depressed. She is worried about becoming depressed again and not being able to afford her medication. While Zoe works hours that qualify as full time, her employer does not provide insurance. She can use the healthcare resources at her university but states she cannot afford the medication that worked for her in the past. Zoe describes a close family relationship but that her family is unable to help her financially and since her mom's response is to quit college, Zoe feels unable to talk to her about her concerns.

How are Zoe's intersecting identities compounding the injustices she is facing? Asking this question shifts the narrative from blaming Zoe for her "misfortune" and focuses on the many ways that she is experiencing complex and intersecting systems of oppression.

INTEGRATING JUSTICE STRATEGIES IN SOCIAL WORK PRACTICE

Social workers have multiple strategies to employ to implement justice-informed practice. These strategies are effective with clients across the micro and macro spectrum. A key aspect of justice-informed practice is culturally sensitive care or working from a culturally humble orientation. A second fundamental aspect of justice-informed practice is client empowerment which is operationalized as starting where the client is, manifesting the profession's commitment to meeting the client in the context of their life, their life as it is at the moment but also as the client desires it to be. Social workers must start with an understanding of empowerment as our desired outcome, must retain our value base, and develop skills in transitioning from a belief to an action. Client empowerment reflects our value of the inherent dignity and worth of the individual and associated right to self-determination, all of which are foundational premises of justice-informed social work practice. Finally, a primary justice-informed strategy for social workers must be communication, which encompasses effective listening, empathy, and advocacy.

Culturally Informed Care

Overwhelmingly, the literature tells us that culturally informed care is one of the best strategies to ensure justice-informed practice. Our culture reflects those pieces that are unique to us and includes people and places in our lives. Culture guides how we see ourselves as well as how we see others, and reflects our values, our beliefs and our orientation to the world. Culturally informed care is the purposeful inclusion of culture in our work, knowing that culture informs all that we do, and the recognition that culture can simultaneously exist, both as a strength and a source of stigma or even oppression.

As a strategy to implement justice-informed practice, social workers must understand the relevance and role of culture as it relates to all aspects of client engagement, assessment, and intervention. Here, the onus is on the social worker to be culturally sensitive, to have awareness of cultural expectations and nuances, and to ensure that a culturally humble approach is used. Culturally sensitive social work practice does not require knowledge of each culture but does imply that the social worker is aware of the influence of culture, not just the client's, but their own as well. The impact of culturally sensitive practice is well documented in improving client care as well as outcomes (Fisher-Borne et al., 2015).

Most commonly, cultural competence is historically used to describe culturally sensitive practice. However, competence implies being fully versed in someone's culture, something that is difficult and fails to acknowledge the client as the expert (Fisher-Borne et al., 2015). As a result, the concept of cultural humility was developed as a way to continuously engage culture in the change process. Cultural humility requires self-reflection, a continuous appraisal of the self to ensure that ethnocentrism, the practice of seeing other cultures from the perspective of your own, is in check and not impacting or influencing the client or the practitioner in any way (Chang et al., 2012). Cultural humility allows clients to be the expert in contrast to cultural competence in which the provider is the perceived expert (Ruud, 2018).

Part of being culturally humble is also to understand the role of implicit bias in our interactions with others. Implicit bias is the perceptions or feelings we have toward certain categories of people, based upon identities related to gender, socioeconomic class, religion, nationality, and so forth. This kind of bias is informed by experiences and culture and is not overt but does impact our relationships with others. This subtle form of bias is inherent in all of us and forms perceptions of which we might not be aware. For example, consider the mom who is sitting in her car in the parking lot waiting on her child to finish a breathing treatment on a portable nebulizer before they come in for their appointment. As you wave hello, she rolls down the window slightly to wave back and as she does, smoke escapes from the window and you can see she is smoking a cigarette as her child is completing his breathing treatment for asthma. While you will certainly have feelings about this situation, you should also consider the biases that may underlie your reaction. Typically, we respond to the more overt or noticeable reactions rather than the underlying assumptions that inform that reaction.

Notably, our clients are just as susceptible to implicit bias and may even share biased constructs relative to social identities, even within their own group. Cultural humility dictates that we must be aware of this form of biases as they are covert ways in which we establish expectations based upon social identities, not on individual features.

Cultural humility nurtures empowerment, facilitates respect, and maximizes client outcomes (Foronda et al., 2016). Despite the desired artifacts of empowerment, respect, and improving client outcomes, not all social workers are adequately equipped to understand how to engage in cultural humility (Julia, 2000). Thus, social workers must purposefully and continuously strive to engage in culturally responsive, respectful, and humble practice. Without that purpose or intention, we will over-rely upon our own cultural context to try to address our clients' needs which will ultimately fail our clients.

Merced et al. (2020) found that the social worker plays a significant role in determining utilization of services and that a perceived lack of inclusivity and biased messaging (unintentional or otherwise) are significant barriers to utilizing services. As we revisit Latonya's situation in Case Study 14.3, this becomes abundantly clear.

CASE STUDY 14.3—THE IMPACT OF JUSTICE IN PRACTICE

Remember Latonya, the 37-year-old mother of two who is employed on the assembly line at a local Toyota plant? In seeking an appointment with a social worker, she had had to wait 3 weeks to be able to have an appointment after her work hours. She uses public transportation and the bus took over an hour to get there and required two bus changes. Upon her arrival, right at the appointed time, the receptionist jokingly told her that she was lucky to get an evening appointment. The receptionist gave her paperwork to complete while stating that the appointment could not start until the paperwork was completed and that her appointment would not be extended for the time the paperwork took.

The social worker noted that Latonya was reserved and seemed hesitant to engage, which the social worker identified as reluctance. When the social worker sought to establish buy-in, and have Latonya agree to return, Latonya was cautious and asked if it would take another 3 weeks to get in. The social worker assured her that she had appointments available the following week and she could schedule one with the receptionist on the way out. When Latonya scheduled the appointment, the next one available outside of her working hours was 2 weeks away. The social worker was not surprised when Latonya failed to show for that appointment.

Latonya's example reminds us that access (or lack of) is a justice issue. In this case, there are many factors influencing the client's willingness and ability to engage in services, all of which contribute to her inability to engage in treatment and result in a lack of justice for Latonya. Many of the effects on Latonya's participation were not due specifically to the engagement with the social worker, but impacted more so by her social, economic, and environmental influences. Justice-informed social work practice must include not just the intervention with, and advocacy on behalf of, the client but also must ensure that the services are available in a manner that supports access and utilization. The time of the appointment and ensuing lack of immediate availability, the travel involved, the casual inference by the receptionist that Latonya was "lucky" to have spent the last 3 weeks waiting for an appointment, the last hour on a bus, and finally, the social worker's failure to recognize the social, economic, and environmental effects that ultimately culminated in what the social worker identified as hesitancy and reluctance. Social workers must cultivate awareness of these influencing factors as all can be addressed and subsequently result in better outcomes for the client by increasing access and utilization of services.

Latonya's example highlights many aspects in which culturally informed practice was not utilized. Had the social worker been more culturally aware, they would have recognized Latonya's concern regarding scheduling an appointment and ensured she was able to return in a timely manner. Given the transportation challenges, the social worker could also have offered alternative means for an appointment and considered technology as a way to address some of Latonya's concerns. Finally, the social worker should have followed up with Latonya rather than just assuming (and accepting) her failure to show was a form of reluctance. Latonya was not reluctant to engage in the work that needed to be done but she did encounter barriers to engaging. Make no mistake, failing to act in a culturally informed manner impacts client outcomes.

Client Empowerment

Client empowerment is always the intended outcome goal of social work. Zastrow (2014) describes empowerment in the role of social work as increasing "capacities for problem solving and coping," (p. 64), identifying, accessing and/or developing necessary resources, and making policy makers and organizations responsive to people who are impacted by their efforts. Empowerment is based upon the professional value of dignity and worth of the individual which allows the right to self-determination. Empowerment involves those skills, founded on mutual respect, that lead to a balance of power between the social worker and ultimately to decision-making that is based on a form of shared governance; an ability for the client to determine the best course of action based upon the identified, desired outcome. Akpotor and Johnson (2018) state that empowerment develops autonomy in our clients and "increased confidence, self-reliance, and self-management" (p. 743), all of which can contribute to future independence.

When the focus of social work practice is empowerment, this results in learning *with* the client, allowing the client to be the expert and director of their change process. Clients are not treated as victims, they are collaborators in identifying and implementing needed change. Ultimately, our clients are best served by having access and choice in terms of capitalizing on the opportunities that exist or are created. Social workers must facilitate that path to self-determination.

STARTING WHERE THE CLIENT IS

Social workers must employ justice-informed practice in a manner that recognizes the individual's situation is a result of larger structural influences. To achieve this, social workers must first start where the client is. While this is a commonly used phrase in social work practice, rarely is it acknowledged as the cornerstone of justice-informed practice. Starting where the client is remains the only starting point for any, and every, client. This starting orientation gives credence to the client's lived experience and authority to being the ultimate decision maker, thus empowering the client. Starting where the client is also acknowledges the inherent dignity of the individual and the right to self-determination, allowing each client to determine change efforts. Again, these guiding principles of the social work profession are fundamental to justice. Finally, starting where the client is provides an opportunity for the client's voice to be heard, leading to empathy and empowerment as well. Ultimately, starting where the client is reflects the social work commitment to see clients in the context of their lives, as they are, but also as they hope to be.

Depending on the client, and especially with larger client groups, a shared vision of whether or whatever change is needed is often rare. Whether working with an individual, family, or community, social workers often encounter multiple perspectives that must be articulated, understood, and integrated. This type of transparent communication emphasizes the value of differing perspectives in developing solutions.

Integrating multiple perspectives is an important task of social work practice; gaining consensus is integral to creating change, whether it occurs at the individual or community level. The iconic picture *Earthrise* was taken by Apollo 8 in 1968 and shows the earth rising over the moon (Figure 14.1). This is analogous to what social workers must do. On a daily basis we must negotiate multiple perspectives and be able to understand and articulate our own perspective while also being able to understand and articulate others' as well. This is the only way true change can occur, by having all perspectives articulated and common ground found that provides a path forward.

FIGURE 14.1 *Earthrise* as seen from Apollo 8.
SOURCE: National Aeronautics and Space Administration. (1968). *Apollo 8: Earthrise*. Updated December 23, 2020. https://www.nasa.gov/image-feature/apollo-8-earthrise

CLIENT RELUCTANCE

One of the biggest challenges to this commitment of empowerment, to start where the client is and see clients in the context of their lives, is when clients are reluctant to engage in the change process. Often, clients may have reasonable reservations about working to create change. Those reservations may manifest as resentment or indicating no need for services. Clients may express mistrust, which can make engaging challenging, or they may withhold information that reflects negatively on them, or that the social worker may not be trusted to understand. When clients experience oppression, especially due to intersectionality of multiple vulnerable identities such as race or ethnicity, sexuality, gender, and so forth, they may not believe the social worker will understand the impact of that oppression. Social workers must continuously assess for aspects of oppression and intersectionality and not rely exclusively upon the client to volunteer information.

There are multiple, complex reasons for client reluctance. Most commonly, some clients may not trust the process due to past negative experiences working with helping professionals. Other clients who are involuntary, or even court-mandated, might feel coerced to participate. These reservations manifest as reluctance, a hesitancy to engage in working toward change. Think about your own experience with making significant changes in your life (e.g., losing weight, maintaining an exercise program). Engaging in personal growth or self-improvement can bring about mixed emotions like uncertainty, hope, and fear of failure, among others. Likewise, our clients can experience ambivalence about change that can often manifest as reluctance to engage in the social work process.

CASE STUDY 14.4—UNDERSTANDING RELUCTANCE

Hank is a 24-year-old male who is meeting with a social worker because, when he was pulled over for speeding, the officer saw drug paraphernalia and found weed in his car. In order to avoid charges, Hank went through a Drug Court process that allowed him to seek drug treatment and if successful, avoid legal charges on his record. Hank is angry, however, about having to meet with the social worker and states that pot ought to be legalized in his state anyway. Hank feels threatened by this process and worries his job will be in jeopardy if his boss finds out about the weed. He states there are worse crimes out there than recreationally smoking pot and that he pays his taxes and his bills and the government needs to just leave him alone.

Reluctance may be overt, such as with Hank, or subtle and passive. Often clients are blamed for not wanting change. However, we should frame reluctance as a normal, situational response to social work intervention. Having a sense of reluctance *is* a normal response. For example, a client who is mandated to work with a social worker or risk having her children placed in foster care is likely to have some negative feelings toward that social worker based upon the ultimatum from the referral source, the court system. Right or wrong, the social worker is a representative of the system (i.e., child welfare, legal) that is forcing the parent to make changes to avoid losing custody of her children. Client reluctance is not abnormal and at times, is an expected part of social work practice.

Social workers must be able to assess and address this reluctance in order to work effectively with clients. Social workers must understand the pervasive nature of reluctance and accept it, rather than be intimidated or ignore it. Part of starting where the client is includes managing relationships with clients who are reluctant to engage in services. Social workers should acknowledge the emotions and experiences that result in the reluctance and validate client perceptions when possible. Most importantly, social workers should not take reluctance personally and should endeavor to maintain empathic awareness in understanding reasons behind the reluctance.

Communication as a Justice Strategy

Communication encompasses the tenets of values, knowledge, and skills. Social workers must be well equipped in each of the communication tenets to best understand and identify strategies to meet client needs. Communication is frequently challenging, which can be overt when a client speaks English as a second language or needs a translator or utilizes American Sign Language (ASL). But much of communication is culturally nuanced, whether it is expectations for eye contact, forthrightness of communication, or how family members express themselves; social workers must maintain cultural humility in the communication process so as to ensure effective communication in engagement.

Implementing values in communication ensures social workers hear all voices, an important component of starting where the client is. Ultimately, attending to all voices also reflects the social work commitment to see clients in the context of their lives, as they are at present, but also as they hope to be.

CASE STUDY 14.5—PRACTICE SKILL OF HEARING ALL VOICES

Jake is a 10-year-old fourth grader who lives with his mom and rarely sees his dad who lives in a different town. Because Jake repeated third grade, he is a year older than his classmates. His teacher is expressing concern with his ability to pass fourth grade, not due to lack of understanding the content but rather because of chronic tardiness and failure to submit homework. Jake's mom usually drops him off at school on her way to work which is typically just before 10 a.m. (school starts at 8.15 a.m.). Although Jake could ride the bus to school, he rarely wakes up in time to do so. Homework in his classroom is due when students first arrive; students are to place their work in a basket on the teacher's desk and the homework is collected when the tardy bell rings.

Jake's mom works from 10 a.m. to 3 p.m. so she is able to be home when he gets off the bus after school. She does not really understand why Jake's teacher is making such a fuss. Jake is a smart boy and is certainly doing better in school than she ever did. Mom insists that Jake can set an alarm and get himself up and ready to take the bus to school, stating that any 10-year-old should be able to do this. Jake does not like getting to school late because it means he misses art every week which is one of his favorite classes. He does not want to repeat a grade again either; he describes embarrassment and shame from having repeated third grade. But he also struggles to get up by himself in the morning which is understandable for a child his age and likely compounded by the lack of a set bedtime or rules set regarding how late Jake can play his XBox.

Jake's teacher and school administrators are concerned that Jake's mom is not invested in his education and worried that, as a result, Jake will adopt her attitude. Poor educational outcomes are associated with reduced economic opportunities and disparate health outcomes. Jake's situation clearly illustrates the need to work with multiple systems on his behalf, at the micro and macro levels. As a 10-year-old, he cannot determine his future by himself, so Jake, his mom, and the school must all be involved in order to change his educational path. In this situation, if either the micro or macro systems are not involved, then it is likely little will change for Jake.

This commitment to give equal attention to all voices and all perspectives should be present even when the social worker does not necessarily agree with others' perspectives or subjective understanding of the situation. Jake's situation is just one example of why this is important: if Jake cannot share his fear of repeating another grade, mom has little motivation to change. Likewise, if the school does not see an investment from Jake and his mom, the teacher has little incentive to adapt her homework acceptance policy.

Communication requires both knowledge and skills in social work and entails cultivating awareness of the impact of what is said while noting what remains unsaid. Most clients will not volunteer all relevant information so social workers must be skilled in identifying content and developing intentional questions to gain important information. Sometimes clients may not know what is relevant, or may prioritize what seems most pressing at the time. Some clients may also deliberately try to avoid topics that bring about strong feelings or may hold back particular details of their life because of worry about being judged. Justice-informed social work practice can occur only when social workers cultivate an ability to cognitively process what is being said while—at the same time—guide the discussion in a manner that ensures adequate information is gathered to develop appropriate intervention strategies.

Knowledge also includes implementing skills appropriately, through utilizing verbal and nonverbal behaviors to elicit information. Listening is an important skill in gathering information from clients and decreasing their anxiety. If clients do not feel heard, they will likely minimize their concerns or problems, or stop sharing altogether. Effective listening helps the social worker develop an accurate understanding of client needs, while also providing a context for effecting change. Essential keys to listening include the following:

- Manage your impulses. Sometimes when someone becomes uncomfortable or struggles for words, or silence extends too long, our impulse is to step in and speak on their behalf. Silence, or pregnant pauses, can feel awkward, but we must resist the impulse to interject too quickly; allow time for your client to process their thoughts and to share insights, reactions, and emotions at a pace that is comfortable for them.
- If you listen only for problems, you will hear only problems. All clients have strengths, capabilities, and resources and it is imperative that we recognize and celebrate these as they will yield solutions. While we need to understand the challenges that exist, social workers must listen to *all* of what is shared, not just the negatives, in order to recognize and appreciate the context of the client's life. Even when clients focus only on what is going wrong in their lives, we must ask purposeful questions to draw their attention to solutions and strengths.
- Social workers should hear not just the words but also the meaning and feelings behind the words. If we hear only the content of our clients' message but fail to understand their emotional state, then we have not demonstrated empathic communication. We have to go beyond a surface-level understanding of our clients. If we reflect only the facts of the message and not the feelings behind the words, this is not meeting our clients where they are. Utilize open-ended, neutral questions to elicit client conversation; practice empathy as you engage your own feelings to try to understand where your clients are coming from; and engage in active listening as you check your understanding both in terms of content and meaning.

Effective listening is a fundamental communication skill and grounds justice-informed social work practice in the client's understanding of their situation. Effective listening is necessary for accurate assessment that can then translate to effective, appropriate intervention strategies.

Social workers should also beware of common barriers to communication which negatively impact justice-informed social work. Some of the most common barriers include failing to acknowledge or consider cultural influences, and diminishing client autonomy through reassuring, advising, or suggesting solutions before fully understanding the situation. An example would be to imagine you are working with a Latinx client who has limited income and you suggest that your client find a better job or work more hours without understanding their limitations (e.g., whether jobs are available, if the client has skills or credentials for a better paying job) or understanding the justice context for that client.

A final common barrier to effective communication is judging, criticizing, or blaming the client. The justice lens of social work requires we see the client in their situation, not attribute the circumstances or situation to the client. Even without intentionally criticizing, social workers should beware of language that can still convey judgment. For instance, using the word "why" can often suggest a sense of blame but can easily be reframed, so that the question "Why did you do it that way?" (which seems to question judgment) can be modified to "Tell me what was most important about doing it that way." This reframe allows us to understand the thought process without ascribing blame.

Advocacy as a Culminating Justice-Informed Skill

Advocacy is the ultimate requisite skill for justice-informed social work practice. Advocacy entails the prior elements that we have discussed, including client empowerment, starting where the client is, and effective communication. Advocacy is associated with ensuring human rights are not ignored and that people have equitable opportunities. Hoefer (2019) describes advocacy practice as a way to promote social justice at individual, community, and society levels through the ability to "advance the cause" (p. 3), of the individual through seeking other constituents' support in creating change across all systemic levels. Thus, advocacy is seen as an important tool in seeking justice and one that each social worker must be competent in doing.

To truly make change, social workers must embrace advocacy, engage, listen to, and articulate all voices and find meaning in the change for all. While many social workers engage in advocacy at the micro, or individual, level, social workers must also have a presence at the macro level, where advocacy can create change for many. Macro-level advocacy typically involves addressing necessary policy change. Not all social workers will want to work at that macro level, creating policies, identifying funding solutions, making persuasive arguments to provide resources, or making policy changes to better support those in need. We do need social workers at both levels. However, practitioners must be aware of the multilevel approaches to addressing client needs. Macro practitioners must have compelling reasons for their advocacy so micro practitioners must ensure their clients' voices are heard at the macro level even if they are not directly working with legislators, local governments, or private entities.

Social workers are passionate but passion and good intentions are not sufficient to bring about real change; social workers must be articulate in convincing others to see the necessity in the change. The ultimate client empowerment in justice informed-social work practice would be to support our clients in becoming their own voice, their own advocate, in order to create justice-oriented change.

STRATEGIES TO SUPPORT CLIENTS

As has been evident from our prior chapters, injustice takes a toll. Social work practitioners support the most vulnerable people and communities in our society, those who are struggling financially, food insecure, and unable to find affordable housing even when our economy is strong, or experiencing poor health outcomes even when covered by health insurance. While there is certainly a societal cost of injustice, ultimately individuals and their communities are those most impacted by a lack of justice. Social, economic, and environmental injustice persistently impact health and mental health and lead to disparate outcomes for individuals.

One way in which we can support clients while working toward ameliorating change is through engaging in multiple strategies to develop social capital in the individuals and communities we serve.

Increasing Social Capital

Although a complex term, at its core "social capital" refers to networks of social relationships that may provide individuals and groups with access to resources and support (Policy Research Initiative Canada, 2005). Social capital is increased through building social supports, strengthening existing relationships, and maximizing mutuality in opportunities. Rinkel and Powers (2017) state that social resources are far more important than any governmental ones. Yet those relationships and resources are compromised when populations are marginalized. Building social capital has to occur with each of our clients in order to move clients toward the outcome goal of empowerment. Clients will be best positioned for empowerment and self-determination when their social capitalism is maximized.

CASE STUDY 14.6—BUILDING SOCIAL CAPITAL

Molly is a 21-year-old mother of two girls, ages 2 and 4. Molly is separated from her husband and reported him to the child abuse hotline because she thought he was sexually abusing her daughters. A sexual assault forensic exam (SAFE) was conducted and confirmed both girls were sexually abused, but of course could not determine the perpetrator. Because the perpetrator is unknown, and Molly is refusing to recognize the possibility of other perpetrators, remaining adamant it was her ex-husband, the girls were removed and placed in kinship care with her brother. Molly is experiencing considerable grief and regrets calling the hotline since it resulted in her daughters being removed, but feels her concerns were validated. Molly herself was sexually abused so she was emphatic that she would not let that happen to her daughters (yet it did).

Molly describes her mother as her best friend although she admits her mother knew about the sexual abuse from her childhood, and actually walked in on Molly being molested by her father, but then did nothing. Molly strongly believes her ex-husband is the culprit, and states that it could not be her father (the girls' grandfather) because he is never alone with the girls. Either she or her mother is present. Molly struggles to recognize that her mother might not protect the girls from her father, again repeating her mom is her best friend. Molly also struggles with being involved in a system that failed to protect her yet has removed her children from her home.

Molly's example exposes a significant gap in her support systems. Relying upon her family as her primary support has historically yielded trauma and harm, yet she has not broadened her network of supports despite being married and having children. In order to be successful in seeking the return of her children, and through her divorce, Molly will likely need to have additional supports in place, especially if she will be unable to have her girls around her father, a likely condition of their return.

Strengthening Intergenerational Aspects

Increasing social capital involves maximizing existing relationships as well as expanding mutuality to become better balanced in those relationships. Intergenerational aspects are an important aspect of social capital as families, regardless if positive, negative, or somewhere in between, are a social institution for most of us and serve to set expectations of how individuals function in society. Each family must be assessed from a perspective of cultural humility, where we engage the family to be the expert, and examine processes within the family's cultural context. Most of how we experience the world around us is informed by our experiences within our family.

CASE STUDY 14.7—INTERGENERATIONAL ASPECTS OF SUPPORT

by Elaine Strawn

Alicia is a 7-year-old living with her grandmother; her mother is incarcerated and her father died from a drug overdose. Alicia's grandmother finds herself in the precarious position of raising Alicia and her two older brothers. Not only does she bring her own history to their home environment, all three grandkids also come with one or more professional labels such as attention deficit hyperactivity disorder (ADHD), autism spectrum disorder (ASD), and oppositional defiance disorder (ODD). Their grandmother, always a single parent, is now a single grandparent, facing the challenge of working 40 hours a week while keeping up with doctors' appointments, school events, homework, and providing for her grandkids' basic needs. To maintain full custody and receive some financial assistance from the state, she also has mandatory visits from a social worker and court appointments. Although she loves her grandkids, she struggles daily and worries what will happen to them if she loses her job or if her health should fail.

As Alicia's situation demonstrates, another component of intergenerational dynamics is that of the economic domain. Economic justice requires a successful economy where profits go to people equitably with jobs that provide a sustainable living and education that produces measurable economic results. However, the current millennial generation of 20- and 30-something-year-olds entering the job market is less likely to be as economically secure as their parents were and less likely to own a home as their parents did (Lowrey, 2020). Economics drive health and well-being and thus impact multiple generations.

Social workers must recognize the intergenerational impact on social capital as clients cannot always rely upon systems, especially if wanting to minimize contact with unjust structures. Rather, most people rely upon families and communities first (Rinkel & Powers, 2017). Implementing justice-driven practice means social workers must recognize the intergenerational impact and help clients build sustainable social capital.

CONCLUSION

As social workers, we must understand that, though the impact of unjust practice is felt by individuals, the solutions must be identified and achieved at the macro level. Many of our systems are broken and increase the risk of poor outcomes once someone engages in them. Social workers must employ multiple, overarching strategies founded on associated values, knowledge, and skills in order to empower our clients to become change agents to better their lives. We must continuously assess for the impact of oppression and injustice in order to articulate our clients' voices in advocating for effective change. Structural discrimination within our multiple social welfare systems places those who engage in these systems in a position of relying upon an unfair system to achieve a just result.

We simply must do better.

DISCUSSION QUESTIONS

1. Why would cultural humility be considered more responsive to clients than cultural competence?
2. Consider how the systems that are designed to provide equity often fail to do so. How will you address this in your practice?
3. The role of advocacy in social work is integral to justice-informed practice. What assets do you bring to the advocacy role? What skills will you need to continue to develop?
4. As you consider what your clients will need, how will you know if you are not meeting those needs?

REFERENCES

Only key references appear in the print edition. The full reference list appears in the digital product on Springer Publishing Connect: connect.springerpub.com/content/book/978-0-8261-3539-1/chapter/ch14

Akpotor, M. E., & Johnson, E. A. (2018). Client empowerment: A concept analysis. *International Journal of Caring Sciences, 11*(2), 743–750. http://www.internationaljournalofcaringsciences.org/docs/14._akpotor_original_10_2.pdf

Foronda, C., Baptiste, D., Reinholdt, M., & Ousman, K. (2016). Cultural humility. *Journal of Transcultural Nursing, 27*(3), 210–217. https://doi.org/10.1177/1043659615592677

Hoefer, R. (2019). *Advocacy practice for social justice*. Oxford.

Merced, K., Imel, Z. E., Baldwin, S. A., Fischer, H., Yoon, T., Stewart, C., Simon, G., Ahmedani, B., Beck, A., Daida, Y., Hubley, S., Rossom, R., Waitzfelder, B., Zeber, J. E., & Coleman, K. J. (2020). Provider contributions to disparities in mental health care. *Psychiatric Services (Washington, D.C.), 71*(8), 765–771. https://doi.org/10.1176/appi.ps.201800500

Mode, N. A., Evans, M. K., & Zonderman, A. B. (2016). Race, neighborhood economic status, income inequality and mortality. *PLoS One, 11*(5), 1–14. https://doi.org/10.1371/journal.pone.0154535

National Association of Social Workers. (2017a). *Code of ethics of the National Association of Social Workers*. Author.

Pierson, J. J. (2019). Addressing economic justice in the face of inequality. *American Bar Association's Human Rights, 44*(3). https://www.americanbar.org/groups/crsj/publications/human_rights_magazine_home/economic-justice/addressing-economic-justice-in-the-face-of-inequality

Ruud, M. (2018). Cultural humility in the care of individuals who are lesbian, gay, bisexual, transgender, or queer. *Nursing for Women's Health, 22*(3), 255–263. https://doi.org/10.1016/j.nwh.2018.03.009

Taylor, K. (2017, May 30). Poverty's long-lasting effects on students' education and success. *Insight into Diversity*. https://www.insightintodiversity.com/povertys-long-lasting-effects-on-students-education-and-success

Young, I. M. (2004). Five faces of oppression. In L. Heldke & P. O'Connor (Eds.), *Oppression, privilege, & resistance*. McGraw-Hill.

15

A CALL TO ACTION: JUSTICE-INFORMED SOCIAL WORK PRACTICE

Laura E. Escobar-Ratliff

LEARNING OBJECTIVES

Students will be able to:

- Articulate the meaning and benefits of practicing from an expansive framework versus an inclusive framework.
- Explicate and apply cultural humility in practice.
- Delineate the role of resilience in empowering clients.
- Articulate the use of the Kaizen method in practice.
- Apply key concepts of celebration and self-care in developing a sustainable practice.

INTRODUCTION

Throughout history, social workers have been at the forefront of leading social change, challenging unjust systems, and working to create an equitable society. From the 19th century through today we see social work leaders fighting for justice: the Child Saving Movement, the Children's Bureau, Women in Industry Service, the National Consumers League, Consumer Reports, the Social Security Act of 1935, the Fair Labor Standards Act, Public Works and Public Employment Programs, Neighborhood Youth Corps and College Work Study Programs, Women's Suffrage Movement, the Civil Rights Movement, the National Association for the Advancement of Colored People (NAACP), the Urban League, the Bureau of Indian Affairs, the Great Society, the New Deal, Community Support Programs, Assertive Community Treatment, Critical Times Intervention, the Housing Act, HOPE VI, Housing First, Child Welfare Services, Communities That Care, and many, many more interventions and policies were developed and implemented with the support of social work across micro, mezzo, and macro levels of practice.

NEED FOR SOCIAL WORKERS

The need for social workers is arguably greater today than it was in the origins of the profession in the 19th century. Multiple examples exist: the wage gap between the wealthy and the poor continues to widen. As Oxfam (2013) reports, over the last 30 years the share of national income in the United States going to the top 1% had doubled from 10% to 20% since 1980 and quadrupled for the top 0.01%. The U.S. Census Bureau reports that in 2019, 38.1 million people were living in poverty (Pierson, 2019). Delineating poverty by race for this same year, one finds that 8.1% of people living in poverty were non-Hispanic White, 20.8% were Black or African American, 17.6% Hispanic or Latinx, and 10.1% were Asian. Of those living in poverty, 17.3 million met the definition of deep poverty (Pierson, 2019). In 2017, 11.8% of the U.S. population experienced food insecurity (Center for Sustainable Systems, n.d.).

Rates of food insecurity were higher in rural areas compared to urban areas while food insecurity rates for Black and Latinx/Hispanic families were higher than the national average (Center for Sustainable Systems, n.d.). Diversification of the population in the United States continues to grow and, according to the Economic Policy Institute, people of color will be the majority of the American working class in 2032 (Wilson, 2016).

We know that one in five people are impacted by mental health issues (National Institute of Mental Health, 2019) and 19.7 million adults struggle with substance use (Substance Abuse and Mental Health Services Administration, 2018). The United States leads the world for incarceration rates with 2.2 million people in jail or prison (The Sentencing Project, n.d.). In 2017, the United States withdrew from the Paris accord on climate change while remaining the second largest producer of carbon dioxide (Industry Today, 2020; Schoen, 2017; Union of Concerned Scientists, 2020). Toxic Release Inventory tracks emissions of facilities that release toxic chemicals that are a threat to human health and the environment (U.S. Environmental Protection Agency, n.d.). On average, over half of the population in the neighborhoods that house these facilities are people of color (Center for Sustainable Systems, n.d.). All of these factors culminate in the need for justice-informed social work practice.

The complexity of needs impacting society today continues to grow—social issues like poverty, the rising wealth gap, food insecurity, mental health and substance use needs, and environmental hazards. Increased diversity and disparities have, and can, continue to yield fear, assumptions, generalizations, scapegoating, discrimination, and oppression among communities, enhancing the risk of further codifying unjust systems that perpetuate harm, disenfranchisement, and oppression. However, with increased diversity comes increased opportunities for expanding our learning, creativity, knowledge, understanding, growth, and cohesion as a society toward supporting one another and creating systemic change.

As social workers, we are uniquely trained in understanding human dynamics from a holistic lens which humbly honors the uniqueness of the individual and builds on one's strengths and resilience to target systemic change across all arenas of practice. Our commitment to social justice, human rights (economic, social, cultural, civil, and political), and sustainable growth for *all* people readies us to lead strategic, systemic, and sustainable change. The need for social workers is now.

SOCIAL WORKERS ARE (NOT) SUPERHEROES

In the preceding chapters you have explored models of social justice, environmental justice, and economic justice, and the application of these models to practice. Our understanding of these models, our training across the spectrum of practice (i.e., micro-mezzo-macro-meta practice), and our theoretical understanding of the complexities of human dynamics poise us to best respond to the call for social justice, human rights, and sustainable social change. We are social workers—we've got this! Social workers are superheroes! (Insert sound of tires screeching to a halt).

That is *a lot* of pressure. How do we rise to the call for action without freezing in the complexities and vastness of the call?

We lean into our training and education. We lean into the realities that *we* do not have the answers, but *together* with the people we serve and one another, we will find a path forward. Social workers are not superheroes, we are super-listeners, -empathizers, -strategizers, -explorers, -empowerers, -advocates, and -agents of change. Superheroes create change *for* people. Social workers nurture, foster, and create change *with* people; we accompany people as they find their own inner superhero.

EXPERTISE IN CHANGE, NOT INDIVIDUALS

One of the wonderfully challenging aspects of working with people is the ever-present diversity of lived experiences. As of July 1, 2019, the U.S. population was estimated at 328,239,523 (U.S. Census Bureau, n.d.). The demographic breakdown of the population by sex and age is 50.8% female, 22.3% 18 years of age and under, and 16.5% 65 years and over. Of the people reporting identification with only one race: 76.3% are White, 13.4% Black, 1.3% American Indian and Alaska Native, 5.9% Asian, and 0.2% Native Hawaiian and Other Pacific Islander. While 2.8% of the population reported two or more races, 18.5% were Hispanic or Latinx, and 60.1% were White, not Hispanic or Latinx (U.S. Census Bureau, n.d.). Notably, information about who identifies as lesbian, gay, bisexual, transgender, and/or nonbinary is not gathered by the Census Bureau. According to Gallup Daily Tracking, 4.5% of U.S. adults identified as lesbian, gay, bisexual, or transgender in 2017 (Newport, 2018).

With varying social identities come varying cultures, subcultures, norms, history, positionality, and power. These demographics alone create complexities. Add in intersectionality, socio-political climate, geography, environment, physical and behavioral health issues, and so forth and the complexities can become overwhelming. How can we possibly be culturally competent and aware of all the intricacies?!

The simple answer is: we cannot. To think we can know *everything* about *everyone* in their varying individual, communal, and socio-political contexts is impossible, and, dare I say, arrogant. Do not misunderstand, we have an ethical responsibility to grow and stretch our knowledge, awareness, and understanding, but there is no expectation of being *all knowing* about *all people*. Furthermore, to focus only on people misses the mark of justice. Injustice is a result of systems and structures that unfairly advantage, or disadvantage, some people based largely upon social identities. Justice-informed social work targets those systems rather than simply focusing on people.

To value the dignity and human worth of *everyone* we serve is an ethical imperative in social work practice. To be a just social worker we must recognize the complexities of one's social identities *and* the intersecting discrimination and oppression that occur across personal, institutional, and cultural levels of our communities (Bundy-Fazioli et al., 2013; Lee et al., 2009). Doing so requires that social workers practice in an expansive and culturally humble manner to keep our focus on the perspectives and needs of our clients. The use of the terms "expansive" and "culturally humble" is intentional.

Rather than practicing from an *inclusive* lens, social workers must practice from an expansive lens. To "expand" means to increase in scope, to spread, to develop, to express in fuller form (Dictionary.com, n.d.-a). Whereas to "include" means to contain, to place in a class or category, "to contain as a subordinate element" (Dictionary.com n.d.-b). Practicing from an inclusive manner means that we are bringing our clients into our pre-established framework and making them fit. Fitting clients into our existing framework does not honor their uniqueness and the possibilities they bring. Finn (2016) delineates possibility as a key concept in social work practice, explicating that to expand our possibilities for thinking enables us to expand our perceptions for needs and change which in turn expands our ability to envision creative actions steps. Inclusivity limits our framework to a pre-existing lens which can restrain creative possibilities that may embrace one's holistic personhood and experiences. An expansive lens, on the other hand, enables us to enhance our own practice and effectiveness with people and communities and encourages clients to bring their uniqueness forward without hesitation.

CASE STUDY 15.1—TING-TING

Ting-Ting is a Karen immigrant who experiences symptoms of schizophrenia and trauma. She speaks no English, has been hospitalized multiple times, and has no biological family in the area. The local community mental health center has been working with Ting-Ting to manage her illness, establish housing, and develop connections to the Karen community in town. The social worker found a small neighborhood grocery operated by a Karen family. Upon entering the grocery store and meeting the family, Ting-Ting began to cry uncontrollably while flailing her arms and dropping to the ground in despair. The social worker's initial thought was that Ting-Ting had been triggered and was having a breakdown. As she observed the interactions between Ting-Ting and the grocer, she noted his ease with what was unfolding and how he and his wife were comforting Ting-Ting. From the social worker's initial lens, this behavior was a manifestation of trauma or psychosis. What the social worker learned from the grocer's family was that this display of grief and emotion was culturally normative. Ting-Ting was in a safe place with family and their role was to be supportive and help her.

Ting-Ting's situation is a good reminder that, as just social workers, we must be willing and ready to expand our framework and acknowledge our limits. We must be able to sit with the discomfort of not knowing or understanding and be willing to wade into the murkiness of the unknown. Practice from an expansive lens requires humility and reflective deference to those we serve. Our expertise as social workers is not in individuals. Our expertise is in understanding human behavior, the socio-political environment, and their interaction to create just change. Social workers' expertise is as change agents and we must clearly know the who, why, and what of our clients to ensure the how. That is, the change we seek must be the change our clients desire and must reflect their unique needs.

CULTURAL HUMILITY

Agents of change striving for a just society requires an expansive and culturally humble posture. Cultural humility requires practitioners to commit to life-long learning and critical self-reflection, to explore, recognize, and challenge power imbalances, and foster relationships with individuals and communities that are mutually respectful and dynamic (Murray-García and Tervalon, 2014).

If I am humble, then I am deferring to my client's expertise about their own personhood. A humble person releases arrogance and pride which opens oneself up to new learning and knowing. I have often referred to this approach as a "step-down" approach. If I step-down (and I visualize in bended knee) then I am honoring and respecting the person(s). I am deferring to their knowledge and recognizing their innate power within. I am actively listening and learning, acknowledging my ignorance and their expertise, and challenging myself to ask questions and explore their trust from their lens, while checking my own biases and norms.

Practicing in a culturally humble manner is challenging; sitting with ambiguity can be disconcerting; yet this commitment positions social work practitioners to better understand the transactional relationship between the individual and the environment from the lens of the client. Having a better understanding of this unique transactional relationship will highlight experiences of discrimination, oppression, *and* resilience.

BUILDING UPON RESILIENCE

Social work practice has a long history of looking holistically at social needs from an ecological perspective and building upon one's resilience from a strengths perspective. Creating sustainable change that honors the personhood of those we serve requires building upon resilience. Social workers are first responders to injustice. We work with individuals, communities, and systems in greatest need. We navigate, challenge, and attempt to change institutions that have historically codified, promoted, and protected injustice. The uphill climb toward justice is daunting to say the least. Recognizing the resilience of those we serve, who have survived and navigated these oppressive systems, enables us to establish foundational strengths from which to grow.

Resilience is the ability to "bounce back in the face of adversity" (Turner, 2001, p. 441) and be empowered to achieve well-being. Some would limit the concept of resiliency, the ability to bounce back, as dependent on one's individual attributes. Although individual attributes contribute to resilience, they are not the sole factors. Gitterman and Germain (2008) encourage us to consider the individual and the collective, the complex person: environment transactions. One must attend to biological, psychological, and environmental processes.

A resilient framework challenges social workers to explore, identify, and nurture strategies that individuals and communities utilize to cope with stress and hardship (Greene, 2008). This framework positions individuals and communities as survivors rather than victims. As social workers, we need to explore and tap into the drive and tenacity that enable survival. We should aim to identify and understand what strategies, talents, and initiatives were utilized as individuals and a community to protect what they have and find what they need. Doing so enables us to foster the power *within* individuals and *with* the community to partner and work toward systemic change.

Practicing from a resilient framework inherently positions social workers to empower individuals, communities, and systems. Survivors act, they are not passive. Fostering the energy and power within our clients positions them to mobilize for change. As social workers, it is our obligation to connect our clients to the mezzo and macro systems directly working on systemic change. Inherently this shift from client to change maker further legitimizes the innate worthiness of the individual, and reinforces that the injustice was not about one's personhood but rather about the socio-political system permeated by injustice.

CASE STUDY 15.2—JOSEPHINA

Josephina is an indigenous immigrant from Honduras. She has no formal education, is unable to read or write in English, Spanish, or her own indigenous language. She speaks no English and minimal Spanish. She and her three children are financially dependent upon her abusive spouse who has nearly killed her on multiple occasions. With the support of a local social service agency, Josephina and her children flee the abusive relationship. The agency social worker connects her with necessities of shelter, food, and clothing. Josephina expresses fear, sorrow, and despair for

(continued)

CASE STUDY 15.2—JOSEPHINA (*continued*)

what is to come with no income, no ability to communicate, and concerns about how to care for her children.

This agency has developed a support network of Latinx women surviving domestic violence who come together weekly to share a meal and be present with one another for support. If they are able, the women make a dish to bring with them to the meeting and children are welcome. Over a shared meal, the women begin to get to know one another, share their stories, and find strength within as a group. Josephina begins to share about her experiences, fears, and needs. With the support of the other women and the agency, Josephina begins to read and write in her own language and begins to learn English. She and the other women start making food for the agency, the basics of beans, rice, and tortillas so that other women and families seeking services can be greeted with a warm meal. Over time Josephina transitions from being a volunteer who helps make meals to the coordinator of the program which provides for the basic needs of women and families seeking services (a warm meal, clothes closet, food pantry, etc.). She also began sharing her story of survival and her recovery with other women and supporters of the agency. Josephina acknowledges that she gets nervous about speaking in public but also wants people to know that there is help and a path of support for women with experiences like her own.

KAIZEN METHOD

The Kaizen method is a Japanese management approach that focuses on gradual and continuous improvement (Mandel, 2005). The definition comes from two Japanese words *kai* and *zen*. Kai means change and zen means good (Rever Team, 2019). This method encourages gradual transformation from a grassroots approach to navigate incremental improvements that result in sustainable change. A key component of the Kaizen method is the grassroots method in which employees are empowered to identify problems and suggest ideas (Rever Team, 2019).

As social workers we are already trained to adopt a grassroots approach, to start where the client is. However, an area of growth for us is the recognition of gradual transformation. Working with those in greatest need means we are navigating complex human dynamics and systems. The change process, whether it be individual or systemic, is hard. Waiting for dramatic change will result in disillusionment for your client and burnout for you as a social worker. Adopting the Kaizen method shifts the focus to taking small steps toward change (Mandel, 2005). This balanced, pragmatic approach allows us to recognize small steps of progress. Being intentional about small steps allows us to redefine success and foster a sense of momentum for clients and practitioners.

CASE STUDY 15.3—JEFFERSON

Jefferson is an African American man who experiences symptoms of post-traumatic stress which has led to years of isolation and homelessness. Jefferson has spent most of his adult life, at least the last 15 years, living on the streets. Due to the history of community violence he has experienced, he refuses to stay in a shelter, asserting that he is safer on his own in the streets. A local homeless outreach program has been working with Jefferson for the last 5 or

(*continued*)

CASE STUDY 15.3—JEFFERSON (continued)

more years, working to develop trust and connectivity. During that time, they have been able to help provide Jefferson with supplies to live safely on the streets and address his physical and behavioral health needs. Throughout this time, the social worker has explored Jefferson's readiness to investigate housing options, Jefferson has continually refused. One day during a visit, the social worker again approaches the idea of exploring housing and shares with Jefferson that the agency now has transitional houses for people. The social worker explains that the transitional houses are an opportunity to practice living in a new environment and that their team would continue to work with him regularly if he wanted to try. On this day Jefferson agreed to try, acknowledging that it probably will not work out, but he would try.

The social worker and the team assisted Jefferson as he moved into the transitional house. The social worker and other team members visited Jefferson regularly to work on activities of daily living and home hygiene. Jefferson expressed happiness with being in his own home but continued to live as if he were homeless within the home. The team focused on small steps to help Jefferson acclimate to living indoors. During the initial weeks and months, the social worker received regular phone calls from the housing coordinator advising that Jefferson's transitional unit was a disaster and asking why the team was not working with him to do better. The housing coordinator was most frustrated with the fact that Jefferson repeatedly defecated in his room. One week the housing coordinator called the social worker in utter frustration exclaiming that she found a bucket full of feces in Jefferson's room during a housing inspection. The social worker yelled in celebration, began to jump up and down in excitement, and said *this is awesome!* Completely perplexed the housing coordinator asked: "*How* is this awesome? It's disgusting!" With continued excitement the social worker said: "He did it in a bucket and not on the floor! This is great! Now we just need to help him learn to dump the bucket in the toilet." The social worker explained to the housing coordinator that it was completely unrealistic to believe a person who has spent most of his adult life living on the streets will move into an apartment and have no challenges with the transition. Rather than constantly criticizing Jefferson for not meeting the standards set by the coordinator, the team explored small steps they could take with him to help him move toward the expectations. One of those small steps was to use a bucket instead of defecating on the floor.

SUSTAINABLE PRACTICE

Celebration is key to sustainable practice, the ability to achieve longevity in the field without experiencing burnout. To celebrate means to acknowledge a significant event (Lexico, n.d.). It should be noted that the definition does not state *major* event or *milestone*, it states *significant* event. Every small step toward one's goal should be celebrated. Whether it be Jefferson in our case study learning to defecate in a bucket or Josephina becoming a program coordinator, both are cause for jubilant celebration.

Finn (2016) delineates *celebration* as a core process in socially just social work practice. Celebrating all successes—big or small—in one's change process, honors one's work and accomplishments. Celebration fuels a sense of triumph and ignites energy in the change process for clients and social workers. There may be some who would argue that with all the discrimination, oppression, and injustice in our world, how can one think to celebrate. If that is your position, I would challenge you to reflect on your own sense of professional burnout, compassion fatigue, secondary trauma, and/or vicarious trauma. These are real risks in our profession. Just as we are committed to mitigating risks with our clients, likewise we must be committed to mitigating risks for ourselves as professionals. How one executes care for others as a social work practitioner is no more important than how one cares for self.

Caring for others, how we practice as social work practitioners must be sustainable. The work we do is rewarding but immensely difficult; without concerted effort to care for ourselves, we will not last or maintain in the profession. Noticing small, incremental change in our clients encourages us as their partners in change. Focusing on our role as culturally humble agents of change, who recognize and build upon existing resilience of people and communities, while delineating and executing small steps toward larger transactional change, allows us to find many opportunities for celebration in practice. Pragmatically, this approach to practice allows us to foster a celebratory spirit that honors the learning as part of the winning, thus reinvigorating our practice (Finn, 2016).

In addition to being intentional in how we care for others, we must also be intentional in how we care for ourselves. Social workers are *not* superheroes! We do not leap buildings in a single bound, we do not have super-speed or -strength, and we do not change the world with our individual actions. We do experience fatigue, exhaustion, stress, and pain—our own and often on behalf of those whom we serve. Social workers pushing through the emotional turmoil to navigate crises and challenges creates a sense of urgency and constant availability that can, and often does, lead to adrenaline addiction (Finn, 2016; Miller & Grise-Owens, n.d.; Owens, n.d.). Miller and Grise-Owens (n.d.) delineate foundational elements for self-care, which are that it is individualized, integrated, intentional, structured, and sustained. Taking time to understand self-care as a professional practice skill is just as important as learning a new modality of treatment, researching new program models, and/or evaluating upcoming social policies.

CONCLUSION

As the population of the United States continues to grow and diversify, so do the unique needs of our clients and communities and the challenges of injustice, privilege, and oppression. As stated earlier, the need for social workers is now! We are uniquely trained to work with individuals, families, communities, and organizations from a holistic lens. We are prepared to understand the complexity of need across the spectrum of practice (micro-mezzo-macro-meta practice). We are skilled to expand our lens of understanding, compassion, and strategy to honor *all* people. We are taught to honor ourselves and practice self-care as a professional practice skill and ethical imperative. Remaining steadfast to the tenants of cultural humility, expansive practice, resilience, the Kaizen method, celebration, and self-care, steady and ready us to lead the way toward a just and equitable society for all.

DISCUSSION QUESTIONS

1. How will you assess your own level of burnout? What physical, emotional, and relational signs will guide your assessment of self-burnout? How will you prevent this from happening?
2. Provide three different ways in which you provide self-care. Will those be productive as a social worker?
3. Discuss how self-care and burnout prevention is key to sustainable social work practice.

REFERENCES

Only key references appear in the print edition. The full reference list appears in the digital product on Springer Publishing Connect: connect.springerpub.com/content/book/978-0-8261-3539-1/chapter/ch15

Bundy-Fazioli, K., Quijuano, L. M., & Buber, R. (2013). Graduate students' perceptions of professional power in social work practice. *Journal of Social Work Education*, 49(1), 108–121. https://doi.org/10.1080/10437797.2013.755092

Center for Sustainable Systems. (n.d.). *Environmental justice factsheet*. http://css.umich.edu/factsheets/environmental-justice-factsheet

Finn, J. L. (2016). *Just practice: A social justice approach to social work* (3rd ed.). Oxford University Press.

Gitterman, A., & Germain, C. B. (2008). *The life model of social work practice: Advances in theory and practice*. Columbia University Press.

Industry Today. (2020, February 21). *Environmental issues faced by Americans*. https://industrytoday.com/environmental-issues-faced-by-americans

Mandel, D. (2005, November/December). Small steps, giant gains in self-care. *Social Work Today*. https://www.socialworktoday.com/archive/120105p44.shtml

Miller, J., & Grise-Owens, E. (n.d.). Self-care 'IS' an ethical imperative for social workers. *Social Work Today*. https://www.socialworktoday.com/archive/exc_020420.shtml#:~:text=Social%20workers%20are%20required%20to,structured%2C%20SMART%2C%20and%20sustained

Murray-García, J., & Tervalon, M. (2014). The concept of cultural humility. *Health Affairs (Project Hope)*, 33(7), 1303. https://doi.org/10.1377/hlthaff.2014.0564

National Association of Social Workers. (2017). *Code of ethics*. https://www.socialworkers.org/About/Ethics/Code-of-Ethics/Code-of-Ethics-English#:~:text=Preamble,oppressed%2C%20and%20living%20in%20poverty

Owens, L. W. (n.d.). Strategies during the coronavirus crisis: Three lessons from an administrator in crisis care. *The New Social Worker: The Social Work Careers Magazine*. https://www.socialworker.com/feature-articles/self-care/self-care-strategies-coronavirus-crisis-lessons-administrator/

Rever Team. (2019, January 29). *What is Kaizen and why continuous improvement drives results*. Rever. https://reverscore.com/what-is-kaizen-definition

INDEX

AAPF. *See* African American Policy Forum
AASWSW. *See* American Academy of Social Work and Social Welfare
absolute poverty, 49, 51, 237
absolute wealth, 237
ACA. *See* Patient Protection and Affordable Care Act
accreditation body, 2
ACEs. *See* adverse childhood events
ADHD. *See* attention deficit hyperactivity disorder
adjustable rate mortgages (ARMs), 193–194
adverse childhood events (ACEs), 125
advocacy, 3, 10, 270
AFDC. *See* Aid to Families with Dependent Children
affirmative action, 28
affordable housing, 252–253
   affordability strategy, 199–201
   codifying, 192
   community development block grant, 207
   description, 186
   Hope VI development projects, 206–207
   housing choice vouchers, 206
   housing market, 192–194
   interventions, 206–210
   list of organization, 209–210
   low-income housing tax credit program, 207
   mixed-income development, 191–192
   rental market, 196–198
   shelters, 206
   unfair lending practices, 187
African American Policy Forum (AAPF), 90
AFSs. *See* alternative financial services
Aid to Families with Dependent Children (AFDC), 58–59
alternative financial services (AFSs), 222–223, 228
American Academy of Social Work and Social Welfare (AASWSW), 63, 66, 93
American Dream, 225–227
American Indians and Alaskan Natives (AI/AN), 163–165. *See also* food insecurity; poverty

American Recovery and Reinvestment Act of 2009, 196
American Red Cross, 151
American Sign Language (ASL), 267
AMI. *See* area median income
anti-oppressive social work practice, 1, 30
anti-racist practices, 30
anti-racist, 18–19
area median income (AMI), 198
ARMs. *See* adjustable rate mortgages
ASD. *See* autism spectrum disorder
ASL. *See* American Sign Language
asset effects model, 62–63
assets, 5–7, 10
attention deficit hyperactivity disorder (ADHD), 79, 125, 272
authority as threat, 9
autism spectrum disorder (ASD), 272
autonomy, 9, 12

banking institutions
   credit and debt accessing, 228
   credit score, 228–230
behaviors, 19, 22–23, 29
biases, 18, 23–24, 28, 31
   explicit, 23
   implicit, 23
   role of, 31
biased messaging, 3
BIPOC communities. *See* Black, Indigenous, and People of Color communities
Black, Indigenous, and People of Color (BIPOC) communities
   food insecurity, 166, 167
   oppression, 20
   violence, 22
Black populations in the United States, 20, 23
   bias in the criminal justice system, 88, 92, 98
   crossover youth, 101–102
   education, 70–71, 74, 75, 78
   health disparities, 108, 111
   housing, 189

Black populations in the United States (*cont.*)
  marginalization, 21
  mental health disparities, 124–125, 128, 129
  mass incarceration, 89–90
  poverty, 28, 53–55, 180
  predatory and fraudulent lending practices, 194–196
  trauma, 24
  violence against, 90–91
Bureau of Indian Affairs, 143

CARES Act. *See* Coronavirus Aid, Relief, and Economic Security (CARES) Act of 2020
CBPR. *See* community-based participatory research
CDAs. *See* Child Development Accounts
Center for Economic and Social Justice (CESJ), 4
Center for Social Development (CSD), 61
CESJ. *See* Center for Economic and Social Justice
CFS. *See* Community Food Security
charitable organization society (COS) movement, 60, 247
CHCs. *See* community health centers (CHCs)
Child Development Accounts (CDAs), 61–62, 64, 66
Child Nutrition Programs, 173
Children's Health Insurance Program (CHIP), 48, 59, 67
CHIP. *See* Children's Health Insurance Program
chronic homelessness, 24–26
CIT. *See* crisis intervention team
client empowerment, 265
client experiences, 18, 23, 26
client reluctance, 266–267
client-centered therapy, 29
Clintonville-Beechwold Community Resources Center, 239
Cold War, and hunger, 162
Committee on Community-Based Solutions to Promote Health Equity in the United States, 115–117
communities of color
  environmental justice, 7, 261
  food insecurity, 166, 167
  health disparities, 108
  mental health disorders, 123
  mental health services, 127, 129, 130
  pollution and waste sites, 28,
  predatory and fraudulent lending practices, 194–196
  racism, effects of, 111
  social justice, 3–4
  trauma, 24, 123
  wealth and income inequality, 242
Community Food Security (CFS), 159, 167, 176–177
community health centers (CHCs), 121

Community Health Centers Act, 121
Community Supported Agriculture (CSA), 167
community-based participatory research (CBPR), 116
Convention on the Elimination of Discrimination Against Women, 43
Convention on the Rights of the Child, 43
Coronavirus Aid, Relief, and Economic Security (CARES) Act of 2020, 202
coronavirus disease 2019 (COVID-19) pandemic, 8, 17, 21, 254–255
COS movement. *See* charitable organization society movement
Council on Social Work Education (CSWE), 2, 44, 60, 95, 156
COVID-19 pandemic. *See* coronavirus disease 2019 pandemic
credit cards, 231–232
credit invisibility, 228
credit scores, 228–231
criminal justice system
  crime target vulnerable groups, 99
  criticisms of, 98–99
  crossover youth practice model, 102
  demographics of people, 92
  employment and education, social workers, 94–95
  juvenile justice, 95–96
  LGBTQ or transgender people 92
  mass incarceration, 89–90
  micro and macro levels of social work practice, 92–95
  person-in environment perspective, 100–101
  pervasive and structural barriers, 97
  public perceptions of crime, 88–89
  racial disparities, 97–98
  school-to-prison pipeline, 101–102
  social problems, 98
  structural discrimination, 87, 99
crisis intervention team (CIT), 93
critical race theory, 17, 27–29
critical theory, 27–28
crossover youth, 101–103
CSA. *See* Community Supported Agriculture
CSD. *See* Center for Social Development
CSWE. *See* Council on Social Work Education
cultural competency, 277–278
cultural humility, 278–279
cultural imperialism, 20, 22, 31, 33
culturally informed care, 262–265
culture, 19, 22, 27, 30

Declaration of Independence, 243
Department of Housing and Urban Development (HUD), 186, 191, 197–199, 203, 206–207, 209

depressive disorder, 2
distributive justice, 5

Earned Income Tax Credit (EITC), 66
EBT. *See* electronic benefits transfers
ECHO. *See* Extension for Community Healthcare Outcomes
ECOA. *See* Equal Credit Opportunity Act
economic inequality, 236
    consequences, 246–247
    definition, 236–237
    less extreme inequality, 237–239
    solutions, 251–254
economic justice, 5–6, 260
Economic Research Service (ERS), 169
Educational Policy and Accreditation Standards (EPAS), 6, 63
educational system
    achievement gap differences, 78
    children's experience, 72
    contemporary education, 71–72
    disparities and oppressive policies, 69–70, 77
    homeless and system-involved youth, 75–76
    immigrant youth, 74–75
    intersectionality in school settings, 78
    justice-informed social work practice, 81–84
    macro strategies, 83–84
    mezzo strategies, 83
    micro strategies, 81–83
    overview, 69
    preservice and in-service teacher professional development training, 82–83
    primary education, 70–71
    racial literacy, 81–82
    restorative practice, 82
    sexual minority and gender-expansive youth, 75
    social class, 72
    social worker's role, 78–79
    trauma-informed practice, 82
    youth of color, 73–74
EITC. *See* Earned Income Tax Credit
electronic benefit transfers (EBT), 173, 251
emergency shelters, 25
environmental justice, 6–7, 261
    challenges and pollution, 138–139
    climate change and disasters, 139
    disproportionate impact, 140
    dynamics of power, privilege, and oppression, 139–140
    impoverished families, 142
    indigenous tribal communities and nations, 143–144
    pervasive and structural barriers, 140
    social inequities, 137

social work practice, 145
    assessing and treating traumatic stress, 148–149
    assessing financial stress, 149
    assessing impact of displacement and relocation, 148
    community registry, 147
    cultural competence and assessment, 147
    disaster plans, 146–147
    education on preparedness and resources, 146
    linking families to shelters, 148
    role of evacuation orders and support, 147–148
    vulnerability of older adults, 140–141, 145–146
    unmet systemic needs, 145
environmental perspective, 26–29
Environmental Protection Agency (EPA), 138, 261
EPA. *See* Environmental Protection Agency
EPAS. *See* Educational Policy and Accreditation Standards
Equal Credit Opportunity Act (ECOA), 223
equality, 1, 4, 8–9
    versus equity, 8–9
equity, 1, 8–9, 17–19, 29
ERS. *See* Economic Research Service
ESSA. *See* Every Student Succeeds Act
Every Student Succeeds Act (ESSA), 83–84
evictions, 44, 200–202
expansive practice, 277–278
exploitation, 20–21, 27
Extension for Community Healthcare Outcomes (ECHO), 131

Fair Market Rent (FMR), 198
fairness, 2, 4, 9, 13
Farmers Market Nutrition Program (FMNP), 173–174, 177
FDIC. *See* Federal Deposit Insurance Corporation
Federal Deposit Insurance Corporation (FDIC), 222
Federal Emergency Administration for Public Works (PWA), 187
Federal Emergency Management Agency (FEMA), 146, 150
Federal Housing Act (FHA), 188, 193
federal poverty level (FPL), 48–49, 241, 244, 250, 253
FEMA. *See* Federal Emergency Management Agency
feminism, 29
    radical, 28

feminist theory, 17, 20, 27, 29–31, 33
   activism and, 29
FF. *See* Franklinton Farms
FHA. *See* Federal Housing Act
FICO score, 229. *See also* credit scores
financial disparities, 223, 225
financial capability, 63–66, 220
   social work practice, 220
financial inclusion and access
   banking and banking services, 222
   unbanked and underbanked, 222–223
financial justice
   programs and policies, 233
   social work education and practice, 213–214
financial literacy, 214–215
   education, 215, 217
   social work practice, 218–220
   strengths-based approach, 219–220
financial literacy education, 215, 217
   implementation, 217
Financial Literacy and Education Commission (FLEC), 217
FINI. *See* Food Insecurity Nutrition Incentive Program
FLEC. *See* Financial Literacy and Education Commission
FMNP. *See* Farmers Market Nutrition Program
FMR. *See* Fair Market Rent
FNS. *See* Food and Nutrition Service
Food and Agricultural Act, 159
food insecurity
   at college, 181
   consequences, 168
   household and community factors, 166–168
   hunger versus, 160–162, 248–250
   rural, 167
   strategies addressing, 169
   prevalence in United States, 163–164
food justice. *See also* food security
   overview, 155–156
food security, 156–157
   at college, 182–183
   central themes, 183
   community strategies, 176–177
   for individuals, households, and communities, 158–159
Food and Nutrition Service, 169
Food Insecurity Nutrition Incentive Program (FINI), 175
Food Stamp Program, 48, 161, 250. *See also* Supplemental Nutrition Assistance Program (SNAP)
Food, Conservation, and Energy Act of 2008, 169
FPL. *See* federal poverty level
Franklinton Farms (FF), 177–179

gender, 20–22
   justice, 29
   wage gaps, 21
government food programs
   agency structure, 169–172
   funding sources, 173
   strategies, 173–174
   public–private program strategies, 174–175
Gus Schumacher Nutrition Incentive Program (GusNIP), 175
GusNIP. *See* Gus Schumacher Nutrition Incentive Program

HAFA. *See* Home Affordable Foreclosure Alternative
HAMP. *See* Home Affordable Modification Program
HARP. *See* Home Affordable Refinance Program
health disparities
   and social work practice, 112–113
   disability status, 110
   gender-based, 108–109
   income inequality, 112
   manifestations of discrimination, 111
   and mortality, 249
   mitigation tips, 115–117
   overview, 105–106
   racial and ethnic groups, 108
   racism, 111
   sexual and gender minority, 109–110
   strategical solutions, 113
   structural factors, 110
   structural inequities, 110–111
   theoretical frameworks, 106–107
   unique populations, 108
health inequities, 106–107, 112, 114
healthcare, 26, 29
   COVID-19 impact, 35–36
Healthy People 2020, 106
HEAP. *See* Home Energy Assistance Program
HEARTH. *See* Homeless Emergency Assistance and Rapid Transition Housing Act of 2009
hierarchies, 29
   social, 30
helplessness, 24
heteronormativity, 28
heterosexism, 19
HFSSM. *See* Household Food Security Survey Module
High Obesity Program, 114
HIV/AIDS, 25–26, 108–109
HMIS. *See* homeless management information systems
HOLC. *See* Home Owners' Loan Corporation

Home Affordable Foreclosure Alternative (HAFA), 195
Home Affordable Modification Program (HAMP), 195
Home Affordable Refinance Program (HARP), 195
Home Affordable Unemployment Program, 196
Home Energy Assistance Program (HEAP), 239
Home Owners' Loan Corporation (HOLC), 193
Homeless Emergency Assistance and Rapid Transition Housing Act of 2009 (HEARTH), 203
homeless management information systems (HMIS), 204
homelessness, 202–204
homeownership, 227–228
HOPE VI Development Projects, 206–207
Household Food Security Survey Module (HFSSM), 159
household income, 240–241, 244–245
housing, 5–7, 10, 18, 25
   COVID-19 impact, 36
   and homelessness, 248–249
   discrimination, 189
   instability, 187
   interrelated areas, 17–18
   policy, 187–190
   public, 190–191
   quality, 40–41
   racial, 28
   securing, 25
   stable, 24, 29
HUD. *See* Department of Housing and Urban Development
human rights
   COVID-19 pandemic, 33–36
   environmental justice, 42–43
   history, 38–39
   as justice-informed social work practice, 44–45
   norms and social influences, 40
   overview, 33, 37
   in the United States, 43
   values and norms, 37–38
hunger, 160–162, 249–250
Hurricane Katrina, 7

IDAs. *See* individual development accounts
IDP. *See* internally displaced people
IEPs. *See* individual education plans
income, 5–6, 8, 10
   household income, 240–241
   inequality, 235
Indian Health Care Improvement Reauthorization Extension Act of 2009, 115

individual development accounts (IDAs), 233
individual education plans (IEPs), 81
injustice, 3–5, 7–10, 17–18, 20, 23, 26
   intersectionality of marginalized identities, 10–11
internally displaced people (IDP), 34
International Covenant on Economic, Social and Cultural Rights, 35
international poverty line (IPL), 51
intersectionality, 22–23, 26
IPL. *See* international poverty line

Joint Center for Housing Studies of Harvard University, 209
justice, integrating in social work practice, 11–13
justice-informed social work practice, 2–3, 8–9, 13, 18, 27, 30
   appropriate income, need for, 235–236
   bias, 23
   call for action, 275–282
   case study, 2–3
   contexts, case study, 18–19
   cultural imperialism, 22
   experience of disasters, 141–142, 144
   exploitation, 20–21
   implementation
      advocacy, 270
      client reluctance, 266–267
      collective impact of injustice, 258–259
      communication tenets, 267–270
      culturally informed care, 262–265
      economic justice, 260
      environmental justice, 261
      impacts on individuals and communities, 257–258
      integration of multiple strategies, 262
      intergenerational aspects of support, 272
      social capital, 271
      social justice, 259–260
      structural influences, 265
      supporting clients, 270–271
   intersectionality, 22–23
   marginalization, 21
   multiple threats, 9
   oppression, 20, 22
   Pine Ridge Reservation, 144, 149–152
   powerlessness, 21
   realities and failings, U.S. criminal justice system, 89
   school-level and structural barriers, 73, 76–77, 79–80
   secondary traumatic stress (STS), 152–153
   trauma-informed practice, 23–26
   violence, 22
Juvenile Court Committee, 96

Kaizen method, 280
Kennedy administration, 61
Ku Klux Klan, 97

LGBTQ populations, 75, 92, 109, 124
    sexual minority and gender-expansive youth, 75
LIHTC program. *See* low-income housing tax credit program
lived experiences, 18, 23, 29
living wage, 253
low-income housing tax credit (LIHTC) program, 191–192, 207
low-wage workers, 245–246

macro social work practice, 9
marginalization, 4, 10, 13, 20–21, 30–31, 33
    clear, 21
    race-based, 29
mass incarceration, 89–90
Medicaid, 48, 59, 67, 121, 236, 239, 252
mental health disorders
    impact of untreated mental illness, 123
    treatment, 123
Mental Health and Parity and Addiction Equity Act, 121
mental health services
    community health services, 132
    disparities
        access to service, 124
        community disadvantage, 125
        cost, 124
        lack of services for children, 124
        LGBTQ youth, 124
        need for navigators, 125
        neighborhood/community disadvantage, 124–125
        social justice concerns, 127–131
        social work practice, 132
        therapeutic alliance, 125–126
        treatments/intervention, 126
    history, 120–122
    mental health, meaning, 119–120
    prevalence in United States, 122
    service barriers, 119
    shared decision-making, 132–133
    social justice disparities, 122–124
    teaming/task sharing, 133–134
    trauma-informed care, 133
    use of technology, 133
minimum wage workers, 244–245

NASW. *See* National Association of Social Workers
National Alliance to End Homelessness, 209, 249
National Association of Social Workers (NASW), 2, 4, 17, 67, 91, 94, 156, 259, 261
    Code of Ethics, 60, 153, 243
National Child Traumatic Stress Network, 24
National Coalition for the Homeless, 209, 249
National Conference of Charities and Corrections, 95
National Conference on Food Security Measurement and Research, 159
National Institution of Food and Agriculture (NIFA), 169
National Law Center on Homelessness and Poverty, 202, 209
National Low-Income Housing Coalition, 198, 210
National Mental Health Act, 121
National Nutrition Monitoring and Related Research Act, 159
National School Lunch Program, 48, 171
NCLB Act. *See* No Child Left Behind
New Deal programs, 58
NIFA. *See* National Institution of Food and Agriculture
No Child Left Behind (NCLB) Act, 71
non-hierarchical work relations, 30

Obamacare, 114, 249. *See also* Patient Protection and Affordable Care Act.
OBB. *See* Ohio Benefit Bank
Occupy Wall Street movement, 251
ODD. *See* oppositional defiance disorder
OECD. *See* Organisation for Economic Co-operation and Development
Ohio Benefit Bank (OBB), 239
Omnibus Budget Reconciliation Act, 121
oppositional defiance disorder (ODD), 272
oppression, 17–18, 20–24, 26–27, 29–33
Organisation for Economic Co-operation and Development (OECD), 43, 51

paternalism, 9
Patient Protection and Affordable Care Act (ACA), 114–115, 121, 129, 249. *See also* Obamacare.
payroll tax, 254
people of color, 20, 28
Personal Responsibility and Work Opportunity Reconciliation Act (PRWORA), 59
person-centered theory, 27, 29–30
Pine Ridge Reservation
    environmental disaster, 144
    food insecurity, 164–165
PFA. *See* Psychological First Aid
posttraumatic stress disorder (PTSD), 24, 143, 148–149

Index

poverty, 18, 28
    asset effects model, 62–63
    consequences, 56–57
    definitions, 47–48
    financial literacy training/education, 64–65
    government welfare programs, 57–60
    as grand challenge for social work, 63–64
    macro strategies, 66–67
    measurement, 48–49
    mezzo strategies, 65
    micro strategies, 64–65
    overview, 47
    prevalence in United States, 51–55
    skills training and job readiness programs, 64–65
    social worker's role, 60–62
    structural inequality, 63
    theories of, 55–56
    types, 49–50
power, 19–22, 26–28, 30
    dynamics, 12
    as threat, 9
powerlessness, 20–21, 31, 33
PPPs. *See* purchasing power parities
privilege, 19–20, 22, 29, 32
progressive tax policy, 237, 254
PRWORA. *See* Personal Responsibility and Work Opportunity Reconciliation Act
Psychological First Aid (PFA), 151
PTSD. *See* posttraumatic stress disorder
Public Works Emergency Housing Corporation (PWEHC), 188
purchasing power parities (PPPs), 51
PWA. *See* Federal Emergency Administration for Public Works, 187
PWEHC. *See* Public Works Emergency Housing Corporation, 188

race, 3, 10, 12
racial justice, 3
racism, 23–24, 28, 33
    institutionalized, 29
    programmed, 19
Reagan Administration, 161, 162, 174
relative poverty, 49, 51
restorative justice, 100

SAFE. *See* sexual assault forensic exam, 271
safety plan, 9
secondary traumatic stress (STS), 152–153
self-determination, 19, 27, 30
Senior Farmers Market Nutrition Program (SFNMP), 174–175, 177, 179
sexist policies, 4

sexual assault, 14
sexual assault forensic exam (SAFE), 271
sexual orientation, 10, 12
SFNMP. *See* Senior Farmers Market Nutrition Program
SNAP. *See* Supplemental Nutrition Assistance Program
social capital, 271
social justice, 2–7, 259–260
social responsibility, 11–12
Social Security Act of 1935, 58, 61, 252
Social Security Disability Insurance (SSDI), 260
social work mission, 13
social workers, 1–5, 8–14
    culturally informed practice, 12
    justice integration of, 11
    opportunity, 12
    social responsibility, 12
    policy recommendations, 66
    working with societal constraints, 242–243
    challenges, call for action, 276–277
    cultural competency requirements, 277–278
    cultural humility, 278–279
    expansive practice, 277–278
    Kaizen method, 280
    need for, 275–276
    resilience from a strengths perspective, 279–280
    sustainable practice, 281–282
        celebration, 281–282
        self-care, 282
socio-ecological model, 112–115
socioeconomic status, 10
SSDI. *See* Social Security Disability Insurance (SSDI)
structural oppression, 24–26, 29
STS. *See* secondary traumatic stress
subliving wages, 21
Supplemental Nutrition Assistance Program (SNAP), 49, 57–58, 157, 161, 164, 173, 175–177, 181, 218, 236, 239, 250–251
sustainable practice, 281–282

TANF. *See* Temporary Assistance for Needy Families
tax policy, 253–254
Temporary Assistance for Needy Families (TANF), 53, 58–59, 218, 236, 243, 250, 260
trauma recidivism, 24
trauma, 23–24, 26, 33
trauma-informed practice, 23–24, 31

UBI. *See* universal basic income
UDHR. *See* United Nations Universal Declaration of Human Rights

UHC. *See* universal health coverage
ultra high net worth individuals, 237
unaffordable and unavailable housing
   exclusionary zoning/land use restrictions, 205–206
   gentrification, 204–205
   housing/household unsuitability, 205
   overview, 185–186
   reduced supply/high demand, 204
   rising housing costs, 205
   slow-growth regulations, 205
   transportation expenses, 204
   wages/housing cost ratios, 204
UNDP. *See* United Nations Development Program
UNICEF. *See* United Nations International Children's Emergency Fund
United Nations
   economic justice, definition, 260
   definitions of poverty, 47
United Nations Development Program (UNDP), 51
United Nations International Children's Emergency Fund (UNICEF), 51
United Nations Universal Declaration of Human Rights (UDHR), 35, 37–40, 42–45
United States Department of Agriculture (USDA), 159–160, 168, 173
United States Interagency Council on Homelessness (USICH), 203
universal basic income (UBI), 253
Universal Declaration of Human Rights, 156243

universal health coverage (UHC), 36
Urban Institute, 210
USDA. *See* United States Department of Agriculture
USICH. *See* United States Interagency Council on Homelessness, 203

violence, 20–23, 31, 33
Violent Crime Control and Law Enforcement Act, 97
violent relationship, 9
Voting Rights Act, 21

War on Poverty, 252
WCED. *See* World Commission on Environment and Development
wealth equality, 5
wealth gap, 216, 235–236, 242
wealth inequality, 241–242
welfare state, 5
WHO. *See* World Health Organization
WIC. *See* Women, Infants and Children
Women, Infants and Children (WIC), 48, 250–251
   Farmers Market Nutrition Program, 173
   Special Supplemental Nutrition Program, 250–251
World Commission on Environment and Development (WCED), 138
World Health Organization (WHO), 160
World War II, 226

Printed in the USA
CPSIA information can be obtained
at www.ICGtesting.com
CBHW082152280324
6039CB00009B/527